Everyman's
CONCISE ENCYCLOPAEDIA
OF ARCHITECTURE

A volume in
EVERYMAN'S REFERENCE LIBRARY

Everyman's Reference Library

DICTIONARY OF QUOTATIONS AND PROVERBS

THESAURUS OF
ENGLISH WORDS AND PHRASES

DICTIONARY OF SHAKESPEARE QUOTATIONS

DICTIONARY OF NON-CLASSICAL MYTHOLOGY

DICTIONARY OF DATES

DICTIONARY OF MUSIC

EVERYMAN'S ENGLISH DICTIONARY

ENGLISH PRONOUNCING DICTIONARY

DICTIONARY OF LITERARY BIOGRAPHY:
ENGLISH AND AMERICAN

DICTIONARY OF EUROPEAN WRITERS

CONCISE ENCYCLOPAEDIA OF ARCHITECTURE

CLASSICAL DICTIONARY

ATLAS OF ANCIENT AND CLASSICAL GEOGRAPHY

ENCYCLOPAEDIA OF GARDENING

FRENCH-ENGLISH—ENGLISH-FRENCH DICTIONARY

DICTIONARY OF ECONOMICS

DICTIONARY OF PICTORIAL ART (2 volumes)

EVERYMAN'S ENCYCLOPAEDIA (12 volumes)

Other volumes in preparation

Everyman's
CONCISE ENCYCLOPAEDIA
OF ARCHITECTURE

by

MARTIN S. BRIGGS
F.R.I.B.A.

*with line-drawings by the Author
and 32 pages of photographs*

LONDON: J. M. DENT & SONS LTD
NEW YORK: E. P. DUTTON & CO. INC.

© Letterpress and text illustrations,
J. M. Dent & Sons Ltd, 1959
All rights reserved
Made in Great Britain
at the
Aldine Press · Letchworth · Herts
for
J. M. DENT & SONS LTD
Aldine House · Bedford Street · London
First published in this edition 1959
Last reprinted 1969

SBN: 460 03002 7

FOREWORD

THE SCOPE of this book is limited to 'Architecture' as generally understood (*see* the article entitled 'Architecture, Definition of'). Any attempt to cover the whole field of building science, technology, and practice (including structural mechanics, the chemical properties of building materials, the physics of lighting, heating, and acoustics) would obviously be futile in so comparatively small a space.

The long article entitled 'Architecture, Periods of' is intended to explain the evolution of European architecture, from its beginnings in the Near East and the Mediterranean basin up to modern times. Thus it serves as an introduction and guide to the separate articles on the regional architecture of all the principal European countries, and of Australia, Canada, and the United States—which had a European origin. Other articles deal with countries outside the European orbit, e.g. China, India, and Japan.

The subjects of the photographic illustrations in this book have been selected as distinctively typical of traditional or modern architecture in the chief civilized countries; but are few in number and so cannot tell the whole story.

The line-drawings are all my own work. Those illustrating MAUSOLEUM, PAGODA, and SYNAGOGUE, are reproduced here by kind permission of the publishers of *Chambers's Encyclopaedia*, in which they originally appeared.

M. S. B.

1959

PLATES

Between pages 84 and 85

A

A.A., abbreviation for Architectural Association (q.v.).

Aalto, (Hugo) Alvar (*b.* Kuortane, 3 Feb. 1898), Finnish architect, town-planner, and furniture designer. Awarded R.I.B.A. Gold Medal for Architecture, 1957. Studied abroad, 1921–7. Principal buildings: Finnish Theatre, Turku; offices of the newspaper *Turun Sanomat*, Turku; Library, Viipuri (1927–35); Sanatorium, Paimio (1929–33); Finnish Pavilions at Paris Exhibition (1937), and at New York (1939); Students' Hostel at Cambridge, Massachusetts (1947); Pensions Office, Helsinki (1956); flats in Tiergarten, Berlin (1957).

See monographs published by Museum of Modern Art, New York, 1938, and by F. Gutheim, 1960.

Abacus, in architecture, the flat top of the capital of a column, supporting an entablature (q.v., *illustrated*) or other superstructure.

Abattoir, a public slaughter-house for cattle.

Abbey, a monastic community of monks under an abbot, or of nuns under an abbess: hence, the buildings occupied by them. (*Illustrated* MONASTERY.) An abbey is usually larger than a priory (q.v.), governed by a prior or prioress.

Abel, John (*b.* 1577; *d.* Barnesfield, 1674), carpenter-architect; reputed to have designed the timber-framed market halls at Church Stretton, Ledbury, Leominster, and Hereford (destroyed); also the House of the Butchers' Guild, Hereford, 1621.

Abercrombie, Sir (Leslie) Patrick (*b.* Ashton-upon-Mersey, 6 June 1879; *d.* Aston Tirrold, 23 Mar. 1957), English architect, town-planner and writer on town-planning. He was Professor of Civic Design, Liverpool University, 1915–35, and of Town Planning, London University, 1935–46. Royal Gold Medallist of R.I.B.A., 1946. He published an admirable handbook on *Town and Country Planning*, 1933. He was educated at Uppingham, then articled as a pupil in a Manchester architect's office. After three years as an assistant to Sir Arnold Thorneley (q.v.) in Liverpool, he became a lecturer at Liverpool University. In 1913 he won a competition for the replanning of Dublin. In collaboration with J. H. Forshaw, he prepared for the London County Council *The County of London Plan*, 1943, followed in 1944 by *The Greater London Plan*. The purpose of each report was to improve means of transport, distribution of population and industry, housing conditions, provision of open spaces, etc., with due regard for aesthetic considerations as well as for the welfare of the people. Both reports were very comprehensive and detailed, being illustrated and produced on a scale never attempted previously.

Other towns and areas for which Abercrombie prepared plans

included Edinburgh, Plymouth, Hull, the West Midlands, Clydeside, Bournemouth, Warwick, Sheffield, Doncaster, Bristol, Bath, Cumberland, and East Kent; also Hong Kong and Cyprus. He founded the *Town Planning Review*, served as a member of the Royal Fine Art Commission, as President of the Town Planning Institute, and as first President of the International Union of Architects. He was knighted in 1945, and received the Gold Medal of the American Institute of Architects in 1949.

Abutment, that portion of a pier or wall which sustains an arch (q.v., *illustrated*).

Academy (from Gk *akadēmeia*), originally the name of a garden near Athens where Plato taught his disciples. During the Renaissance the term came to be applied to various cultural institutions founded especially in Italy. In some of these instruction was given in the principles of architectural design. The French Academy of Architecture was founded by Colbert in 1671 under Louis XIV. In England the Royal Academy of Arts was founded in 1768. Among the thirty-four foundation-members were five architects: Thomas Sandby (q.v.), John Gwynn (q.v.), William Tyler, Sir William Chambers (q.v.), and G. Dance (q.v.). The following architects have served as presidents of the Royal Academy: James Wyatt, 1805-6; Sir A. Webb, 1919–24; Sir E. L. Lutyens, 1938–44; and Sir A. E. Richardson, 1954–6 (qq.v.). There has always been a Professor of Architecture since 1768 in charge of the Royal Academy School of Architecture; and the membership of the Royal Academy usually includes about six Academicians and four Associates who are architects.

The Royal Scottish Academy, founded 1826, has a somewhat similar constitution, with several architects among its membership.

ACANTHUS. A=*natural leaf;* B=*Greek type;* C=*Roman type*

Acanthus, a conventionalized leaf of the plant *A. spinosus*, used in the decoration of Greek, Roman, and Renaissance capitals. The Greek form of the ornament is more sharply pointed and more crisply carved than the Roman and Renaissance forms.

Acropolis (from Gk *akro*, top; *polis*, city), the highest part or citadel of a fortified Greek city. The most famous example is the Acropolis of Athens, on which stands the Parthenon (q.v.).

Acroterion (Gk), one of the pedestals for statues, placed at the feet and on the apex of a pediment of a Greek temple.

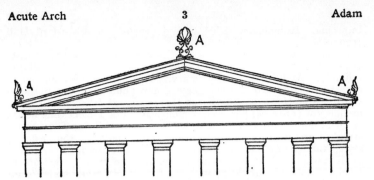

ACROTERION. *Acroteria* (A) *on the Parthenon, Athens (from a restoration)*

Acute Arch, *see* LANCET ARCH.

Adam, family of British architects in the eighteenth century.
(1) WILLIAM ADAM, SEN. (*b.* 1689; *d.* 24 June 1748), was trained by
Sir W. Bruce (q.v.) and completed Hopetoun House in Scotland,
which that architect had begun; then designed the Town House at
Dundee, Dumfries House in Ayrshire, and the Royal Infirmary at
Edinburgh.   He trained four of his sons as architects.   (2) ROBERT
ADAM (*b.* Kirkcaldy, 3 July 1728; *d.* London, 3 Mar. 1792), his
second son, was the most famous of the four.   He travelled extensively in Italy between 1750 and 1754 to study Roman antiquities,
especially the newly discovered ruins of Pompeii and Herculaneum.
A subsequent journey to the Emperor Diocletian's palace at Spalato
on the Adriatic resulted in a magnificent folio from his drawings and
restorations, published 1764, which made his reputation and benefited
the architectural practice which he had already established in
London with his three brothers.   He was the acknowledged head of
the four.   (3) JAMES ADAM (*b.* 1730; *d.* 20 Oct. 1794) acted as second
in command; but of (4) JOHN ADAM and (5) WILLIAM ADAM, JUN.,
not much is known.
   The four brothers having acquired an estate south of the Strand
in London, it was christened 'The Adelphi' (Gk *adelphoi,* the
brothers), and they proceeded to 'develop' it with new buildings,
but incurred some financial loss in this speculation, and again in a
venture concerned with a new type of stucco.   Among their other
buildings in London are the large town houses at 20 Portman Square
(1775–7); 20 St James's Square (1772–4); various houses in Mansfield
Street and Portland Place; the screen-wall of the Admiralty in
Whitehall (1760); the present headquarters of the Royal Society of
Arts in the Adelphi (1772–4); Lansdowne House and many other
mansions since demolished or altered.   Among several enormous
new country houses was Luton Hoo (1768–75).   A long list of others
remodelled or greatly extended included Kenwood (1767–9);
Osterley House (1761–80); Syon House (1762–9); Hatchlands (1758–
1761); Harewood House, Yorkshire (1759–61); Nostell Priory,
Yorkshire (1776–85); Kedleston Hall (*c.* 1765–70); Bowood (1761–4).
The list of Scottish mansions, new or remodelled, is hardly less

imposing. It includes Mellerstain (*c.* 1770–8) and Gosford Hall (1792–1803).

At Culzean Castle (1777–9) Robert Adam abandoned the delicate classical style that he favoured elsewhere, and created a castellated building. At Edinburgh University, where he had matriculated at a phenomenally early age, he designed new buildings (1781–91); also the Register House at Edinburgh (1774–92). His Royal Infirmary at Glasgow (1792–94) has been demolished. For a short time he sat as M.P. for Kinross-shire; and he became a F.R.S. The 'Adam style' of architecture and decoration (often miscalled the 'Adams' style,' though 'Adams'' is obviously permissible), seen to perfection at Kenwood and at 20 Portman Square, is extremely delicate in form and colour, contrasting with the robust 'Palladian style' (q.v.) favoured by Robert's chief professional rival, Sir William Chambers (q.v.). Much of the brothers' tremendous output of work was illustrated during their lifetime in three sumptuous folio volumes, published in 1773–9 as *The Works of Robert and James Adam.*

See also monographs by J. Swarbrick, 1903; A. T. Bolton, 1922; J. Lees-Milne, 1948.

Adobe (Sp.), walling of sun-dried clay or mud bricks, formerly much used in Latin America.

Adytum (Lat., from Gk *aduton*), the innermost part or sanctuary of a Greek temple, to which only priests were permitted entry.

Adzed Work, the treatment or smoothing of wood surfaces with an adze instead of a plane.

Aedicule (Lat. *aedicula*, dim. of *aedes*, a house), originally a small structure sheltering an altar or an image of a household god: hence, a small pedimented structure over a niche.

Aegean Architecture, *see* ARCHITECTURE, PERIODS OF, I(*c*).

Agnolo, Baccio D', properly BACCIO D'AGNOLO BAGLIONI (*b.* Florence, 1462; *d.* there, 1543), Italian carver and architect. He practised wood-carving for half his working life before turning to architecture. His wood-carving in Florence included the organ-case of S. Maria Novella, the high altar of SS. Annunziata, and the Salone dei Cinquecento at the Palazzo Vecchio. He acted as *capomaestro* of the cathedral from 1507 to 1515. Among his buildings were the Bartolini, Borgherini (later Roselli), Lanfredini (later Corboli), and (probably) Taddei palaces—all in Florence; the Villa Borgherini (later Castellani) at Bellosguardo, the Villa Bartolini at Rovezzano, the *campanili* of S. Spirito and of S. Miniato, also the façade of S. Lorenzo—all in Florence.

Agora (Gk), a space for public assembly in a Greek city (cf. the Roman *forum*, q.v.). It was usually surrounded with public buildings and colonnades, and was sometimes planted with trees. The famous Agora at Athens has recently been excavated and the Stoa of Attalos restored.

Aisle (from Lat. *ala*, a wing), an open space on one or both sides of a central space (or 'nave,' q.v.), in a secular Roman basilica (q.v.), or in a church or other building for public assembly. Very large churches may have double aisles on either side of the nave, and the choir and transepts may also be aisled. The division between nave and aisles is usually by piers and columns, often carrying arches. The width of aisles in modern public buildings is partly determined by regulations governing means of escape in case of fire. Such buildings also require aisles between the blocks of seating space.

Ala (Lat., a wing), in a Roman or Pompeian house, a small side apartment opening on to the atrium. *See also* AISLE.

Alabaster may be either (i) some variety of stalagmitic carbonate of lime used by the ancients and commonly called 'Oriental alabaster,' as seen, for example, in the famous Egyptian sarcophagus in the Soane Museum, London; or (ii) the so-called 'Modern alabaster,' a sulphate of lime or granular gypsum. It is found in certain midland counties of England, especially at Chellaston in Derbyshire; and was much used in the Middle Ages and for some time afterwards for carved tombs, etc. It is suitable for the purpose, as it wears well, and is of beautiful colour and texture, but must not be used externally.

Alan of Walsingham (*d.* 1364) is reputed to have designed the magnificent timber lantern of Ely Cathedral about 1322, while he was prior of the adjoining monastery; but it seems more probable that a lay architect was employed. (For a novel ingeniously centred round this theory *see* Charles Lowrie's *Castle Bedon*, 1948.)

Alberti, Leone Battista (*b.* Genoa, 18 Feb. 1404; *d.* Rome, April 1472), Italian architect, philosopher, and poet, was a pioneer of the Renaissance of Roman architecture. Originally trained as a lawyer, he obtained a doctorate in common law at Bologna; travelled in France, Germany, etc.; returned to Italy, 1432; and some years later he turned to the study and then the practice of architecture. His first and most important building was the church of S. Francesco (commonly called the 'Tempio Malatestiano'), at Rimini (begun 1446). It was followed by S. Sebastiano (1459) and S. Andrea (1472), both at Mantua; and by the Palazzo Rucellai at Florence. His book on architecture and building, *De Re Aedificatoria*, published 1485, became a classic and was translated into many languages. (Eng. trans. by G. Leoni, 1726.)

See biographies by G. Rettembacher, 1878; G. Mancini, 1882 (new ed., 1911); G. Semprini, 1927.

Alcove, originally a vaulted recess; now a recess opening out of a room, or occasionally a recess in a garden wall or in a garden hedge.

Aldrich, Dr Henry (*b.* London, 1647; *d.* Oxford, 14 Dec. 1710), English amateur architect, graduated at Oxford, 1669; took Holy Orders; D.D., 1682; dean of Christ Church, 1689 till his death; Vice-Chancellor of Oxford University, 1692–5. A most versatile man, he published translations from the classics and books on logic, music, and architecture. He certainly designed Peckwater Quadrangle at Christ Church (1706–14); probably All Saints Church (1706–10); possibly the Fellows' Building at Corpus Christi College

(1706–12); and has been credited with Trinity College Chapel (1691–4)—all in Oxford. *See* monograph by W. G. Hiscock, 1960.

Alessi, Galeazzo (*b.* Perugia, 1512; *d.* there, 30 Dec. 1572), Italian architect. He studied in Rome for six years, admired the work of Michelangelo (q.v.), and became the chief exponent of 'Mannerist' architecture (q.v.) in Genoa and Milan. In Genoa he certainly designed the Villa Cambiaso and the Porta del Molo; also probably the Cambiaso and Lercari-Parodi palaces in the Via Nuova (now Via Garibaldi), and the Villa Doria at Pegli near Genoa. In Milan he built the Palazzo Marino (1558) and the church of S. Vittore al Corpo (1570–6).

> *See* article by M. S. Briggs in the *Architectural Review*, xxxviii, pp. 26–32, 1915, and monograph by E. de Negri, 1957.

Alfieri, Benedetto Innocente (*b.* Rome, 1700; *d.* Turin, 9 Dec. 1767), Italian architect. After previously practising law in Piedmont, he turned to architecture. Having built a palace at Alessandria, he attracted the notice of King Carlo Emanuele III of Savoy, and became his court architect in 1739. Principal buildings: theatre and military tiding school at Turin; Seminario and façade of town hall at Asti; rower of S. Gaudenzio at Novara; Palazzo Ghilini at Alessandria.

Algardi, Alessandro (*b.* Bologna, 1602; *d.* Rome, 1654), Italian architect and sculptor. He studied under the painter L. Carracci and entered the service of the Duke of Mantua, 1622. Although a talented exponent of Baroque (q.v.), his only important building was the Villa Doria-Pamfili at Rome, begun *c.* 1650.

Almery, Ambry, or **Aumbry,** literally 'a place for alms.' Sometimes a detached alms-box standing at any appropriate place in church or cloister; occasionally, however, a cupboard in the wall of the sanctuary of a church, near the altar, where the sacred vessels could be locked up.

Almonry, in any medieval monastic or other church, a room or place where alms were distributed.

Altar, originally, in various pre-Christian religions, a stone table or slab upon which animals were sacrificed. Early Jewish altars are described in the Old Testament (Exodus xxvii. 1–8; xxx. 1–5; 1 Kings vi. 20; also in 1 Maccabees iv. 47, and in Josephus v. 5–6). Some of these were ornamented with precious woods and metals. Greek and Roman altars were square or circular in shape, and generally of stone. The first Christian altars were portable, and of wood, thus resembling a 'communion table' rather than a stone of sacrifice. Medieval churches in eastern Europe normally had stone altars; but the use of these in England was prohibited after the Reformation in the sixteenth century, when new regulations prescribed the substitution of a movable 'holy table' of wood, which was placed with its length east and west, this being the most convenient position for the sacrament. The canons of 1640 changed the position, in parish churches, to north–south, close to the east wall of the church, but the altar has since continued to be, in theory at least, a portable wooden table. The liturgical regulations of the Roman Catholic Church require that an altar, to qualify for consecration, must be of stone throughout, fixed permanently to the ground, and containing certified relics of martyrs. If it is of wood or other material, Mass may not be celebrated except upon an inserted stone slab enclosing or covering similar relics.

Altar-piece, *see* REREDOS.

Altar-rails, a railing or balustrade of wood or metal was prescribed for parish churches by direction of Archbishop Laud in 1640, partly to prevent animals from straying into the sanctuary and defiling it.

Alto-relievo (Ital.), sculpture in high relief.

Alure (from Fr. *aller*, to go), a place to walk in; an alley; more specifically a passage behind the parapet of a castle or of a church roof.

AMBO. One of the two ambos in the church of S. Clemente, Rome (9th century)

Ambo (Lat., plural *ambones*, or in Eng., ambos). Originally a small portable reading-desk or lectern (q.v.), used in early Christian churches, but subsequently developed into an elaborate 'three-decker' pulpit. This arrangement was then superseded by a pair of ambos: one on the south side for the gospel, the other on the north side for the epistle. There are several fine early Christian examples at Rome and Ravenna, and Romanesque examples at Ravello and Salerno—all these in Italy. The use of twin pulpits has recently been revived in some English churches, with a view to avoiding the unbalanced effect of a single pulpit beside the chancel arch.

Ambry, *see* ALMERY.

Ambulatory (Lat. *ambulare*, to walk), literally 'a place for walking in'; hence an open or covered arcade or cloister. More specifically, in large aisled churches, the processional aisle or walk round the east end, behind the high altar.

American Architecture, *see* BRAZILIAN, CANADIAN, MEXICAN, and UNITED STATES ARCHITECTURE.

American Institute of Architects, founded at New York in 1857. Since 1898 it has occupied as its headquarters 'The Octagon' at Washington, a building admirably designed by, strange to say, a medical practitioner, Dr Thornton (q.v.), who, like Perrault (q.v.) in France, forsook medicine for architecture in middle life without normal professional training.

Ammanati, Bartolomeo (*b.* Settignano, 18 June 1511; *d.* Florence, 22 April 1592), Italian architect and sculptor. At first he practised as a sculptor, but he turned to architecture about 1552, and worked with Vignola and Vasari in Rome for the Pope. In 1555 he moved to Florence, practising both arts simultaneously. Principal buildings in Florence: extension of the Pitti Palace (1560–77); the fine bridge of S. Trinita (1566–9, destroyed in the war, 1944, but since rebuilt); cloister of S. Spirito; several palaces. Outside Florence: extension of the Collegio Romano, Rome (1582–4); Palazzo Rucellai-Ruspoli, Rome (1586); buildings at Lucca and Volterra.

Amphiprostyle, in Greek architecture, a temple (q.v., *illustrated*) having a portico at either end.

Amphitheatre, an oval or elliptical building for displays, sports, or gladiatorial combats; having an arena (q.v.) surrounded on all sides by tiers of seats, usually protected by an awning (*velarium*, q.v.). Chief examples: the Flavian Amphitheatre (or Colosseum, q.v.) at Rome (*c.* A.D. 75–82), accommodating about 50,000 persons; others at Capua, Verona, and Pompeii, etc., in Italy; at Arles and Nîmes in France; at Seville and Tarragona in Spain; at Caerleon in Britain. There are modern examples, mostly bearing the name of stadium (q.v.), at Wembley near London, 1924 (100,000 persons), in Germany, the U.S.A., and elsewhere.

Anactoron (Gk), a sacred building or part thereof, used in connection with the Mysteries, e.g. at Eleusis.

Anaglyph (from Gk *anagluptikos*), an ornament carved in low relief.

'Ancient Lights,' existing windows constituting an 'easement' or obstruction to a person who may desire to erect an adjoining building in such a way as to interfere unreasonably with the amount of light hitherto enjoyed. The precedent usually followed in such cases is the House of Lords judgment of 1904 (*Colls* v. *Home and Colonial Stores Ltd*).

Ancient Monuments. From the Middle Ages onwards, in England, important buildings owned by the Crown were maintained by the royal Office of Works, Geoffrey Chaucer being one of the officials employed on this work, and Wren (q.v.) another. In 1873 a Bill was introduced into Parliament to extend this care to certain 'scheduled monuments,' numbering only sixty-eight in all and mainly prehistoric. After much wrangling this was approved as the Ancient Monuments Protection Act, 1882. In 1900 the first Amendment Act allowed commissioners to assume guardianship of any ancient monument which, in their opinion, 'is of public interest by reason of the historic, traditional, or artistic interest attaching thereto,' provided that it is unoccupied save by a caretaker. County councils were empowered to become guardians of, and to buy, such buildings; and public access to historical monuments was to be allowed under reasonable conditions. Further powers were granted under subsequent Acts of 1910, 1913, and 1931, and an elaborate programme of scheduling monuments has since been undertaken. All this work is controlled by the Ancient Monuments Branch of the Ministry of Works, advised by the Ancient Monuments Board.

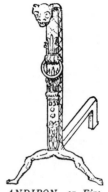

> *See* M. S. Briggs, *Goths and Vandals: a Study of the Destruction, Neglect, and Preservation of Historical Buildings in England,* 1952.

Ancon, *see* CONSOLE.

Andirons, iron firedogs, used for supporting logs on the hearth of an open fire-place.

Andron (Gk), in a Greek dwelling-house, the room (usually a dining-room) reserved for male use (*andros*, a man).

ANDIRON, or Firedog. (French, 15th century)

Anglo-Saxon Architecture, the name formerly given to English architecture of the period between the Roman evacuation of Britain in the fifth century A.D. and the Norman Conquest in 1066. The term now generally used by scholars is 'Pre-Conquest (or Early) Romanesque Architecture in England.' *See* ENGLISH ARCHITECTURE, **2.**

Annulet, literally 'a small ring.' In architecture a narrow stone ring or fillet around the shaft of a column.

Anta (Lat., plural *antae*), a flat pilaster projecting from the wall of a Greek temple, at either end of a range of columns.

Ante-chapel, a covered vestibule or transept forming a narthex (q.v.) to a collegiate chapel. Examples at Magdalen, New, and Wadham Colleges at Oxford; St John's College, Cambridge; and Eton College.

ANTEFIX. Use of antifixes (A) on the roof of a Greek Doric temple

Antefix, or **Antefixa** (Lat.). Ornaments made of marble or terracotta, used on Greek and Etruscan and Roman buildings to cover and protect the ends of the rafters. They were usually carved in the form of an anthemion (q.v.).

Anthemion (Gk *anthos*, a flower), in Greek architecture, an ornament resembling honeysuckle, based on the flower of the acanthus (q.v.) and carved on marble antifixae (q.v.) or on the cymatium of a cornice.

ANTHEMION. Two examples from the Erechtheum at Athens

Anthemius of Tralles (sixth century A.D.), Greek architect and mathematician, collaborated with Isodorus of Miletus (q.v.) in building S. Sophia and other great churches in Constantinople.

'Antique, The,' a somewhat vague term used to describe the art of the Greeks and Romans, especially sculpture.

Antoine, Jacques Denis (*b.* Paris, 1733; *d.* in the same place, 1801), French architect. One of the pioneers in France of the academic revival of orthodox classical architecture, though he did not visit Italy till 1777. Principal buildings (all in Paris): Hôtel Maillebois; Hôtel de la Monnaie (1768); alterations to the Palais de Justice. Outside Paris: Church of the Daughters of Mary, at Nancy; town house of the Duke of Berwick, at Madrid.

Apodyterium, a dressing-room in a Roman public bathing establishment. *See* THERMAE.

Apollodorus of Damascus (*b. c.* A.D. 60; *d. c.* A.D. 130), Greek architect. Apollodorus's design of a stone bridge over the Danube in A.D. 104–5 pleased the Emperor Trajan, who brought him to Rome where he planned the Forum of Trajan (112–13), the Gymnasium, and the Odeum; also triumphal arches at Ancona and Beneventum. Trajan died in 117, and Apollodorus succeeded in alienating the patronage of the next emperor, Hadrian (q.v.), who fancied himself as an amateur architect, with the result that Apollodorus was banished for imaginary crimes and put to death. *See also* HADRIAN.

Apophyge, the slight concave expansion at either end of an Ionic or Corinthian column, where the shaft joins the capital and the base.

Appentice (now obsolete), a lean-to structure or a penthouse (q.v.).

Apse (Gk *apsis*), a recess—usually semicircular on plan but occasionally polygonal—at the end of the presbytery or choir or aisle of a church; but also found in pre-Christian times in certain Roman secular buildings, e.g. *thermae* (q.v.). In the earliest Christian basilican churches of Rome the apse was usually on the west, e.g. at St Peter's, S. Paolo *fuori*, and S. Lorenzo; but, in Byzantine churches, the orientation (q.v.) was changed to the east, and this has since been normal practice. The roof of the apse was usually domed, and decorated with mosaics (q.v.) internally. The original Romanesque apses in many English churches were replaced by square east ends during Gothic times. (*Illustrated* CHURCH.)

Apteral (Gk, literally 'wingless'), a term applied to a Greek building, especially a temple, having no columns along its sides.

Aqueduct (Lat. *aquaeductus*), an artificial channel or conduit for the conveyance of water from a spring or other source to its place of distribution. The aqueducts supplying imperial Rome are particularly famous because for much of their length they traverse flat country on ranges of stone arches. At the height of Rome's ancient prosperity, *c.* A.D. 100, they numbered nine, with lengths up to sixty miles, from the Alban Hills to the city. Substantial portions of them still remain. (*See* the famous treatise by S. J. Frontinus, first century A.D., *De aquis urbis Romae*, which is available in a modern English translation in the Loeb Library.) Other famous aqueducts are the 'Pont du Gard' near Nîmes in France, 160 feet high; those at Segovia, 102 feet, and Tarragona, 83 feet, in Spain; and a huge example at Antioch in Syria, 200 feet.

AQUEDUCT (Roman) at Segovia in Spain (A.D. 109)

A.R.A., abbreviation for Associate of the Royal Academy. *See* ACADEMY.

Arab, or **Arabian Architecture,** *see* MUSLIM ARCHITECTURE.

Arabesque, in Hellenistic, Roman, and Renaissance architecture, a carved or painted ornamental panel, containing human, animal, grotesque, symbolical, or other elements in combination with delicate conventional foliage. The term Arabesque, though so used since the seventeenth century, is quite misleading as a description, because all representations of human and animal forms were forbidden in 'Arab' (i.e. Muslim) art. There are many examples of Arabesques in Rome and Pompeii; and also in English as well as Italian architecture of the early Renaissance. (*Illustrated overleaf.*)

Araeostyle, in classical columnar buildings, the spacing of columns at wide intervals: viz. more than three diameters apart. The term is used by Vitruvius (q.v.).

Arbour, a bower, shady retreat, or alley, usually covered with climbing plants (cf. PERGOLA).

ARABESQUE in marble: Church of S. Maria dei Miracoli, Venice (1480)

Arcade. (1) A range of arches carrying a roof, wall, entablature, or other superstructure. (2) A covered walk between two such ranges, or between an arcade on one side and a solid wall on the other (cf. CLOISTER). (3) In modern usage a covered walk between ranges of shops, e.g. the Burlington Arcade in London.

Arcading (especially in Romanesque architecture), rows of small arches forming arcades but used solely as decoration.

Arc Boutant (Fr.), *see* FLYING BUTTRESS.

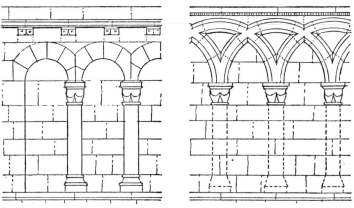

ARCADING. Left: St Peter, Northampton (c. 1140). Right: Bolton Priory (c. 1150), interlacing type

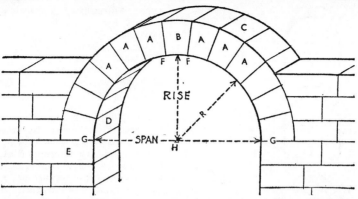

PARTS OF AN ARCH. A=*voussoirs;* B=*keystone;* C=*extrados;* D=*intrados or soffit;* E=*abutment;* F=*crown;* G=*springing line;* H=*centre;* R=*radius*

Arch, a self-supporting structure composed of bricks or of stone blocks (VOUSSOIRS, q.v.), and capable of carrying a superimposed load over an opening. Arches are usually curved in various forms, but may be cambered (*see* CAMBER), i.e. nearly flat, or may be actually flat. The component blocks are normally wedge-shaped to prevent slipping, but in rough work are occasionally rectangular, the joints between them increasing in width from the underside upwards.

The principle of the arch was known to the ancient Egyptians, Assyrians, and Greeks; but arches were seldom used until Roman times, when the semicircular type was universally adopted. This form continued through the phases of architecture known as Byzantine (q.v.) in eastern Europe and Romanesque (q.v.) in western Europe.

Pointed arches, first introduced in the Middle East about the seventh century A.D., were employed in Muslim architecture (q.v.) in Mesopotamia and Egypt from the ninth century onwards. They were introduced into England and France (probably as a result of the Crusades) at the end of the twelfth century (*see* ENGLISH and FRENCH ARCHITECTURE). Muslim arches, in Spain, North Africa, the Middle East, India, etc., often assumed the form of a horse-shoe, either round or pointed. In Renaissance architecture (*see* ARCHITECTURE, PERIODS OF) round arches were almost invariably used throughout western Europe.

The principal types of arch, listed according to their shape, are semicircular (or 'round'), segmental, stilted, round horse-shoe, pointed horse-shoe, lancet (pointed), equilateral (pointed), three-centred, four-centred, elliptical, cusped, and Venetian (*see* illustration). Separate entries describe most of these types. *See also* ACUTE, CAMBER, FLORENTINE, KEEL, MOORISH, OGEE, OGIVAL, RELIEVING, SKEW, SQUINCH, STRAIGHT ARCH. The following entries describe the principal parts of an arch, regardless of its

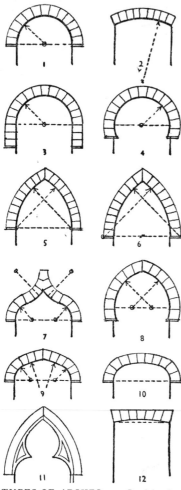

TYPES OF ARCHES. 1. *Semicircular.*
2. *Segmental.* 3. *Stilted.* 4. *Round
Horse-shoe.* 5. *Equilateral.* 6. *Lancet.*
7. *Ogee.* 8. *Pointed Horse-shoe.* 9. *Four-
centred.* 10. *Elliptical.* 11. *Cusped.* 12.
Flat (cambered)

type: ABUTMENT, ARCHIVOLT, CROWN, EXTRADOS, IMPOST, INTRADOS, KEYSTONE, RISE, SPAN, SPANDREL, SPRING, SPRINGER, VOUSSOIR. (*See also* illustration.)

During construction arches are temporarily supported by Centering (q.v.).

Arch, Triumphal, a form of monument favoured by the Roman emperors to commemorate a military triumph (Lat. *triumphus*) or some benefaction to the Empire; or, occasionally, as a monumental feature at the entrance to a Roman town. Those of the first type were generally enriched with bas-reliefs depicting incidents of the campaign or victory. They include the Arch of Titus, Rome (*c*. A.D. 82); of Trajan at Beneventum (114–17); of Septimius Severus at Rome (203); and of Constantine at Rome (*c*. 315). Outside Italy there are notable triumphal arches at St Remi and also at Orange (*c*. 30 B.C.), both in France; at Timgad (*c*.A.D. 165) and at Leptis Magna (*c*.A.D. 200), both in North Africa; on the bridge at Alcantara (A.D. 108), at Merida, and at Tarragona, all in Spain. There are memorial arches at Rimini, Aosta, and Ancona (A.D. 112), all in Italy; arches of Commodus and of Septimius Severus at Lambessa in North Africa; also several 'quadriportal' arches at the intersection of main streets or roads, e.g. at Tebessa in North Africa. The entrance gateways to late Roman and Hellenistic towns often took the form of an arch built into the city wall, e.g. at Susa and Perugia in Italy; at Autun and Nîmes in France; at Trier in Germany; at Spalato in Dalmatia. The Arch of Hadrian at Athens dates from the second century A.D.

Examples erected in Renaissance and modern times include the

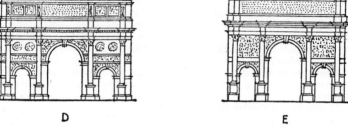

A   B   C

D   E

F

ARCH, TRIUMPHAL. Six examples drawn to approximately uniform scale.
(A) Arch of Titus, Rome (c. A.D. 82); (B) Marble Arch, London (1828); (C) Arc du
Carrousel, Paris (1806); (D) Arch of Constantine, Rome (c. A.D. 315); (E) Arch of
Septimius Severus, Rome (A.D. 203); (F) Arc de Triomphe, Paris (1806–36)

Arch of King Alfonso at Naples (1470); the Porte St Martin (1647), the Porte St Denis (1684), and the Arc de Triomphe (1806–36)—all in Paris; the Brandenburger Thor (1790) at Berlin; the Siegesthor (1843) and the Metzger Thor (1880) at Munich; the 'Marble Arch' (1828) and the 'Wellington' or 'Pimlico' Arch (1825)—both in London.

Archer, Thomas (*b*. Tanworth-in-Arden, ?1668; *d*. London, 23 May 1743), English architect, who was educated at Trinity College, Oxford. Leaving there in 1689, he travelled abroad till 1693. Presumably he made an intensive study of Baroque architecture in Rome, as his subsequent designs for buildings in England show more Baroque influence than those of any English architect except Vanbrugh (q.v.). As one of the commissioners appointed to build 'Fifty New Churches' in 1711, he designed those of St Philip, Birmingham, now the cathedral (1710–25); St John, Smith Square, Westminster (1714–28); St Paul, Deptford (1712–30). His other work included the north front of Chatsworth (1702–5); Heythrop House, Oxfordshire (*c*. 1705–10); Roehampton House (1710–12); and several other mansions since demolished or greatly altered. For many years he held lucrative but sinecure appointments under the Crown.

See biography by M. Whiffen, 1950.

Architect (from Gk *architektōn*, chief craftsman; hence Lat. *architectus*). In modern practice a person qualified to design buildings and to supervise their erection. In Greek and Roman times the architect's status was fully recognized, his duties being described in detail by Vitruvius (q.v.). During the Middle Ages the title was seldom used, the architect then being described as 'Master' in English (*magister* in Latin, *maestro* in Italian and Spanish, *maistre* in Old French, *baumeister* in German). The Victorian idea that large medieval buildings were designed by bishops and monks rather than by lay architects has since been disproved by many competent authorities, for contemporary documents have established the fact that the services of lay designers were utilized by ecclesiastical as well as by secular and royal employers, though obsequious scribes tended to record the name of the clerical employer rather than that of the lay employee.

The title of architect was revived during the sixteenth century (*see* SHUTE), and was used by Inigo Jones (q.v.) early in the seventeenth century. The status of the architect came to be more precisely defined during the seventeenth to eighteenth centuries; and in 1834 the foundation of the Royal Institute of British Architects established a recognized standard of qualification. This Institute has its headquarters at 66 Portland Place, London, W.1, and a membership (in 1958) of 18,170 qualified and practising members in Britain and the other countries of the Commonwealth, in addition to 612 retired members and 5,628 partially qualified 'students.' The Institute conducts examinations for candidates and awards diplomas (F.R.I.B.A., A.R.I.B.A., L.R.I.B.A.). It absorbed the Society of Architects in 1925.

The Architectural Association, affiliated to the Institute, was founded in London in 1847 to provide social intercourse among architects, especially for the younger men and students; and it conducts a large architectural school in Bedford Square, London.

Since the enactment in 1938 of the Architects Registration Act, architectural practice and the use of the title 'architect' has been restricted in Britain to persons duly qualified and registered, as in certain countries abroad. In the United States the premier body is the American Institute of Architects, with its headquarters in Washington.

> *See* M. S. Briggs, *The Architect in History*, 1927; J. Harvey, *English Medieval Architects down to 1550*, 1954; H. M. Colvin, *A Biographical Dictionary of English Architects, 1660 to 1840*, 1954; and the current *Kalendar* of the Royal Institute of British Architects.

Architectonic, a rare term implying that a building shows a knowledge of architectural principles on the part of its designer.

Architects' Benevolent Society (with offices at 66 Portland Place, London, W.1) was founded in 1850, and provides aid for architects and their families in distressed circumstances.

Architects in Fiction, *see* FICTIONAL ARCHITECTS.

Architects Registration Council of the United Kingdom (offices at 68 Portland Place, London, W.1) was appointed under the Architects Registration Acts of 1931 and 1938 to set up and maintain a register of architects. It awards a number of scholarships annually. *See* ARCHITECT.

Architects, Royal Institute of British, *see* ARCHITECT.

Architects, Society of, founded in 1884, was amalgamated with the Royal Institute of British Architects in 1925. *See* ARCHITECT.

Architectural Association, with its offices and school at 34–6, Bedford Square, London, W.C.1, was founded in 1847. *See* ARCHITECT.

Architectural Publication Society, under the editorship of Wyatt Papworth (q.v.), published, at intervals from 1853 to 1892, a *Dictionary of Architecture* in eleven volumes.

Architecture. *Definition.* The word 'architecture' was first used about 1563, so is not very old as English words go; but is derived from Lat. *architectura*, and that in turn from Gk *architektōn*, literally 'chief craftsman' or 'master builder.' Hence architecture means building designed by a competent person (*see* ARCHITECT) as distinct from building not so designed. This is not a very clear distinction, and is so difficult to explain that most of the attempts made for three or four centuries past are all unsatisfactory. An English writer in 1581 defined architecture as 'the scyence of building.' Ruskin in the nineteenth century wrote that it is 'nothing but ornament applied to buildings,' a dictum that is universally rejected to-day, when many stark and austere buildings devoid of ornament are accepted as excellent architecture. It is something more than 'good building' in the sense of sound construction with good materials. An often quoted definition by Sir Henry Wotton, an amateur critic, in his book, *The Elements of Architecture*, 1624, comes very near the truth. He says that it must fulfil three conditions, 'Commoditie, Firmenes, and Delight,' meaning that, to constitute architecture, a building must not only be conveniently planned for its purpose ('commodity'), and be soundly built of good materials ('firmness'), but must also give pleasure to the eye of a discriminating beholder ('delight'). It is this third quality, added to the other two essentials, that differentiates 'architecture' from mere 'building.'

Some very primitive buildings, such as rude huts or wigwams in all ages, cannot be counted as architecture; and to these may be added primitive stone circles (such as Stonehenge), megaliths, and barrows; also, perhaps, the Egyptian pyramids, and, in modern times, bridges and other structures which are now commonly regarded as 'civil engineering' rather than architecture or even building.

Bibliography. GENERAL: J. Ruskin, *The Seven Lamps of Architecture*, 1849; R. Sturgis, *Dictionary of Architecture* (3 vols.), 1901–2; H. M. Robertson, *Principles of Architectural Composition*, 1924, and *Architecture Explained*, 1926; A. S. G. Butler, *The Substance of Architecture*, 1926; T. D. Atkinson, *A Glossary of Architecture* (4th ed.), 1928. GENERAL HISTORY OF ARCHITECTURE: J. F. Durm (ed.), *Handbuch der Architektur*, 1885 onwards; J. Fergusson, *History of Architecture* (5 vols.), 1891–3; A. Choisy, *Histoire de l'Architecture* (2 vols.), 1899; F. M. Simpson, *History of Architectural Development* (3 vols.), 1905–11; W. R. Lethaby, *Architecture*, 1912; T. G. Jackson, *Architecture*, 1925; A. L. N. Russell, *Architecture*, 1927; A. D. F. Hamlin, *History of Architecture*, 1928; A. E. Richardson and H. O. Corfiato, *The Art of Architecture*, 1938; N. Pevsner, *Outline of European Architecture*, 1942; M. S. Briggs, *Architecture*, 1947; H. H. Statham, *A Short Critical History of Architecture* (3rd ed.), 1950; P. L. Waterhouse and R. A. Cordingley, *The Story of Architecture* (3rd ed.), 1950; B. F. Fletcher, *History of Architecture* (latest ed.), 1958. (For histories of special periods and of the architecture of individual countries, e.g. AMERICAN ARCHITECTURE, ENGLISH ARCHITECTURE, *see* bibliographies at end of articles on each.)

Architecture, Periods of. The following article briefly describes the various 'periods' or stages in the general world development of architecture up to the present time, excluding regions outside the main stream of evolution, such as CHINESE, JAPANESE, INDIAN, and MUSLIM ARCHITECTURE (qq.v.). For the distinctive national characteristics of the architecture of each of the principal countries of the western and Mediterranean world, with its chief buildings and the names of their architects (where known), *see* the separate articles on each, e.g. ENGLISH, FRENCH, SPANISH, and UNITED STATES ARCHITECTURE.

1. *Pre-Classical Architecture*, up to *c.* 700 B.C. (i.e. older than the classical or Hellenic architecture of Greece, the first classical period

in Europe).   Before that date buildings of some pretensions had been erected in western Asia—including Persia, Mesopotamia, and India— and in Egypt, Greece, and the Aegean Islands; some of them as far back as *c.* 4000 B.C.

1(*a*). *Egypt.* Because no importance was attached to man's life upon earth and great importance to his future life, dwelling-houses were constructed of relatively impermanent materials, and hardly any have survived (but *see* HOUSE).   Temples and tombs, however, were built so massively that numbers of them survive to-day in excellent condition.   The Pyramids themselves (*see* PYRAMID) were, in fact, gigantic royal tombs, originating from a primitive type of tomb, the Mastaba (q.v.).   The story of Egyptian architecture begins about 4000 B.C., or earlier, and extends to about 30 B.C., the year when Egypt became a Roman province.   All through those centuries, and even after the Roman conquest, it retained its distinctive national features, right up to the Arab invasion in A.D. 640, after which Egypt formed part of the Muslim dominions (*see* MUSLIM ARCHITECTURE).

Egyptian temples were usually built of granite and had 'battered' (i.e. tapering) walls, squat and clumsy columns, and flat roofs. Outside each of the greater temples stood pairs of obelisks (*see* OBELISK).   The chief examples are the Temple of the Sphinx (4th millennium B.C.) at Giza near Cairo; the great group of temples at Karnak (*c.* 2466 B.C. onwards); and the single temples at Abydos (1350–1330 B.C.), Abu Simbel (1330 B.C.), Edfu (237 B.C.), Philae, and Dendera.

> See E. Bell, *The Architecture of Ancient Egypt,* 1915; Sir W. Flinders Petrie, *Egyptian Architecture,* 1938; W. Stevenson Smith, *The Art and Architecture of Ancient Egypt,* 1958.

1(*b*). *Western Asia.* The three dynastic and architectural periods are generally described as Babylonian, *c.* 2630–1275 B.C.; Assyrian, 1275–538 B.C.; and Persian, 538–331 B.C.   In the seventh century the whole region was conquered by the Arabs (*see* MUSLIM ARCHITECTURE).   The once enormous and magnificent city of Babylon, with its palaces and temples, is now entirely in ruins, and hardly anything remains.   From the Assyrian period some ruined palaces survive, e.g. Nimrud, ninth century B.C.; Khorsabad, 722–705 B.C.; and Nineveh, seventh century B.C. (*see* ZIGGURAT).   For the Persian period, coeval with Hellenic Greek architecture, *see* PERSIAN ARCHITECTURE.

> See also E. Bell, *Early Architecture in Western Asia,* 1924.

1(*c*). *Primitive Greece, the Aegean, and Crete.* This is commonly called the 'Aegean Period.'   Although evidence exists of still earlier civilization in the area, the first palaces at Knossos and Phaistos in Crete were built about 2000 B.C., and restored or rebuilt a few centuries later after damage by fire and earthquakes.   The ruined palace at Knossos displays an impressive sequence of rooms and staircases, with coloured mural decorations and an elaborate drainage system. Mycenae, on the mainland of Greece, was already powerful *c.* 1400 B.C., when its inhabitants conquered Crete and made Mycenae the chief power in the Aegean until about 1100–1000 B.C.; then Dorian invaders from the north ended its rule. (*See* MINOAN and MYCENEAN ARCHITECTURE.) The great palace of Mycenae, now ruined, contains a famous domed tomb, the so-called 'Treasury of Atreus' (*c.* 1185 B.C.), and the 'Lion Gate' (*c.* 1200 B.C.). A feature of this palace, as also of the neighbouring palace or citadel of Tiryns, is the use of colossal masonry blocks. It is now known that there was frequent contact between these Aegean peoples and Egypt.

See E. Bell, *Pre-Hellenic Architecture of the Aegean*, 1926, and J. D. S. Pendlebury, *A Handbook to the Palace of Minos, Knossos*, 1955.

2. *Greece*. The Classical or Hellenic period in Greece began about 700 B.C., and lasted till the Roman occupation, 146 B.C.; but its later phases, from the death of Alexander the Great, 323 B.C. until 146 B.C., are generally described as 'Graeco-Roman' or 'Hellenistic' architecture. The so-called 'Golden Age' in Greece, from 480 B.C. to 323 B.C., saw the erection of all the finest Greek buildings. These comprised temples, theatres, tombs, formal colonnades or *stoae* (qq.v.), and, of course, dwelling-houses (*see* HOUSE), but hardly any palaces. Much has been written about the architecture of Greek temples, which have been classified in various ways: (i) according to the type of column or 'Order' employed (*see* ORDERS); (ii) according to the number of columns in the portico; (iii) according to the arrangement of columns surrounding the building; (iv) according to the plan, though that was simple enough.

(For ii, iii, and iv *see* TEMPLE ARCHITECTURE, GREEK AND ROMAN. That article also gives references to the numerous terms used in describing architectural details of a Greek temple.)

Generally speaking, the walls, columns, and lintels were either of fine Pentelic or other marble, or else of limestone. The design of the temples was based upon timber prototypes, a fact which explains many curious features. The roofs were of low pitch, and were covered with tiles of burnt clay or marble. Especially in the Parthenon at Athens (*see* below), one of the most highly finished buildings in the world, the architects achieved a remarkable subtlety in their correction of optical illusions (*see* OPTICAL REFINEMENTS, CALLICRATES, ICTINUS). Some fine Greek temples exist, though ruined, in Sicily and South Italy (*see* ITALIAN ARCHITECTURE). Of those in Greece and Asia Minor, the following are of outstanding importance (all dates B.C.): *Doric Order:* The Heraion, Olympia (*c.* 640); Temple of Apollo, Corinth (*c.* 625); Temple of Zeus, Olympia (*c.* 460); the Parthenon, Athens (447–432); the 'Theseion,' Athens (*c.* 428); Temple of Poseidon, Sunium (*c.* 425); Temple of Apollo, Bassae (*c.* 420); Tholos (circular temple) at Epidauros (360–330). *Ionic Order:* Older Temple of Artemis or Diana, Ephesus (*c.* 560); Temple on the Ilissos, Athens (*c.* 450); Temple of Niké Apteros, Athens (*c.* 421); later Temple of Artemis, Ephesus (*c.* 356). *Corinthian Order:* the Olympieion, Athens (*c.* 170).

Besides temples, theatres, *stoae*, and houses, Athens contains an immense stadium (q.v.) and a beautiful little Choragic monument (q.v.) from the Hellenic age.

See E. Bell, *Hellenic Architecture*, 1920; D. S. Robertson, *Greek and Roman Architecture*, 1929; W. B. Dinsmoor, *Architecture of Ancient Greece* (3rd ed.), 1950; H. Plommer, *Ancient and Classical Architecture*, 1956; A. W. Lawrence, *Greek Architecture*, 1957.

3. *Rome.* The earliest Roman architecture is called 'Etruscan' after the primitive Etruscans who occupied Etruria, the area north of Rome and south of Florence. These people may have arrived in Italy as early as *c.* 1000 B.C., but their surviving tombs are judged to be much later; and none of their temples exists, though the Villa Giulia at Rome contains an interesting hypothetical reconstruction of one. Rome was reputedly and probably founded in 753 B.C., but such scanty remains of buildings older than *c.* 100 B.C. that now survive are called 'Etruscan,' not 'Roman.' Etruscan temples were usually of wood, covered with plates and ornaments of terra-cotta (q.v.). The example at the Villa Giulia is a rustic version of the Doric Order (*see* ORDERS).

The story of Roman architecture begins about 100 B.C., and ends with the collapse of the Empire in the fifth and sixth centuries A.D. Although many of its features were derived from the 'trabeated' (i.e. column and beam) system of construction used by the Greeks, the Romans introduced arches freely, and thus were the first people to employ 'arcuated' construction on a large scale. Their arches were always semicircular, not only in their famous aqueducts (q.v.), but also in their theatres, amphitheatres (e.g. the Colosseum), and triumphal arches. They constructed great vaults and domes over their larger public buildings, e.g. the Pantheon, the *thermae* or public baths, the basilicas, etc., making extensive use of concrete for this purpose and employing a volcanic ash, *pozzolana* (q.v.), as an important ingredient. Their favourite stone was travertine (q.v.). The chief difference between Greek and Roman architecture is that whereas the Greeks used the Orders (q.v.) as structural features, the Romans preferred arcuated structure, and used the Orders as pure decorative features. Their normal Order was the Corinthian, but they also used the Doric and Ionic; and they invented a fourth Order, called the 'Composite' because it was a combination of the Ionic and the Corinthian. The writings of the architect Vitruvius (q.v.), first century B.C., give us an admirable detailed account of Roman buildings, materials, and methods. At the height of its splendour, in the fourth century A.D., when the population is said to have reached a million, the city contained some 400 temples. Of those still surviving, all ruined, the chief examples are the temples of Fortuna Virilis (*c.* 40 B.C.); Mars Ultor (2 B.C.); Concord (7 B.C.–A.D. 10); Castor and Pollux (A.D. 6); Vespasian (*c.* A.D. 80); Venus and Rome (A.D. 135); Antonius and Faustina (A.D. 141); and Saturn (*c.* A.D. 320). The two temples of Vesta, in Rome (A.D. 205) and at Tivoli, not far away (*c.* 80 B.C.), are both circular, as is the immense Pantheon in Rome (27 B.C.–A.D. 124). The enormous public baths of Rome (*see* THERMAE), the numerous aqueducts (q.v.), the Flavian Amphitheatre or Colosseum (q.v.), the basilicas (q.v.), and the ordinary dwelling-houses in Rome and at its seaport of Ostia (*see* HOUSE) are all mentioned in separate articles, as are various Roman

B

amphitheatres and other buildings outside Rome itself.   For these provincial examples *see* the articles on the various countries which originally formed part of the Roman Empire, e.g. ENGLISH, FRENCH, GERMAN, ITALIAN, and SPANISH ARCHITECTURE.

> *See* W. J. Anderson, R. P. Spiers, and T. Ashby, *Architecture of Ancient Rome*, 1927; D. S. Robertson, *Greek and Roman Architecture*, 1929; H. Plommer, *Ancient and Classical Architecture*, 1956.

> *See also* articles on APOLLODORUS and HADRIAN.

4. *Early Christian and Byzantine.* After the Emperor Constantine transferred the capital of his empire from Rome to Byzantium or Constantinople in A.D. 324, having accorded official recognition to Christianity in A.D. 313, there was a great change in the course of Roman architecture; for the building of a number of basilican churches began in Rome itself, while other types of building activity languished.   The period between *c.* A.D. 330 and the establishment of the Lombard kingdom of Italy in A.D. 568 is usually described as the 'Early Christian Period,' followed by the 'Lombard Period'— itself the first phase of the 'Romanesque Period' (*see* next section). No churches survive from a date earlier than 313, or even 330, because Christian worship had hitherto been proscribed, and for nearly three centuries its devotees had had to meet in secret.   Of the group of famous basilican churches erected in Rome after 330 (*see* ITALIAN ARCHITECTURE), St Paul-without-the-Walls is the most typical, but is in fact a comparatively modern replica of the old church, which was built in 380, and rebuilt in 1823 after a fire. Most of these early basilican churches have an aisled nave, separated from each of its aisles by a range of Corinthian columns (often rifled from old temples); round-headed windows in the wall above them to light the interior of the church; an apse at one end (*see* ORIENTATION); and a narthex (q.v.) or vestibule at the other end, where one enters the church through an open courtyard or atrium (q.v.).   Some circular churches were also erected in Rome at the same period— S. Costanza (330); the Baptistery of Constantine (430–40); S. Stefano Rotondo.

Outside Italy Constantine rebuilt the Church of the Nativity at Bethlehem on a basilican plan in 330; and several others at Constantinople, of which one, S. Sophia, when rebuilt on the grand scale by Justinian (*see* below), became, in its new form, the noblest example of Byzantine architecture.   Mention is made, under ENGLISH, FRENCH, and SPANISH ARCHITECTURE, of sundry other Early Christian churches; and at Ravenna in Italy are two fine basilican churches—S. Apollinare Nuovo (*c.* 526) and S. Apollinare in Classe (534–9).

These were coeval with the splendid Byzantine churches erected by the Emperor Justinian in the sixth century A.D.   The most famous is S. Sophia at Constantinople, rebuilt in 532–7, by the architects Anthemius (q.v.) and Isodorus (q.v.).   After the Turkish conquest of Constantinople in 1453, it was converted into a mosque, and furnished with minarets (*see* TURKISH ARCHITECTURE).   Other domed Byzantine churches in the city are SS. Sergius and Bacchus

(527); St Irene (740); and St Saviour-in-the-Chora (*c.* 1050). Justinian also built the small but important domed church of S. Vitale at Ravenna (526–47). St Mark's at Venice, though much altered externally by florid additions, is a late Byzantine work of 1042–71.

Byzantine architecture was adopted in the countries under the rule of the Greek or Orthodox Church, including Greece and Syria. There are Greek Byzantine churches at Athens, Daphni, Mistra, and Salonika. Later the style penetrated Russia (*see* RUSSIAN ARCHITECTURE). Byzantine churches are characterized by the use of domes, in contrast to the simple span roof of the Early Christian basilica. These domes generally rise on pendentives (q.v.) from a square base. The churches are centrally planned to form a 'Greek Cross,' whereas the typical Roman Catholic medieval church had a 'Latin Cross' plan, with a long nave. Mosaics (q.v.) were plentifully used as decoration. A new feature was the 'dosseret' (q.v.), a block placed upon the top of the capital of a column, to give support to the arch above, invariably semicircular in form.

See C. Diehl, *Manuel d'art byzantin*, 1910; O. M. Dalton, *Byzantine Art*, 1911, and *East Christian Art*, 1926; T. G. Jackson, *Byzantine and Romanesque Architecture*, 1920; J. A. Hamilton, *Byzantine Architecture* (2nd ed.,) 1956; C. Stewart, *Byzantine Legacy*, 1947, and *Early Christian, Byzantine and Romanesque Architecture*, 1954.

5. *Romanesque Architecture* is a term covering all the variants of a style which prevailed in western Europe from the collapse of Roman rule in the sixth century A.D. to the emergence of the Gothic style (q.v.) about A.D. 1200. It thus embraces several regional variants, e.g. 'Lombard' in Italy, 'Saxon' and 'Norman' in England, 'Carolingian' and 'Rhenish' in Germany. Although it spread over all the former western provinces of the Roman Empire, it also penetrated Scandinavia and Poland, which were never ruled by Rome. In south-east Europe, as already noted, 'Byzantine' held the field. This regional division also reflected a religious division; for Romanesque architecture was used in the Roman Catholic countries, and Byzantine in countries following the Greek Orthodox rite.

In the first centuries after the fall of Rome, very little building took place anywhere in eastern Europe. Examples of so-called 'Lombard' (or Early Romanesque) architecture in Italy include a few churches in Rome, parts of S. Ambrogio at Milan, and the cathedral at Torcello—all erected while Lombard kings ruled in Rome. In Germany there is Charlemagne's cathedral at Aachen (796–804), which may be regarded as the first important Romanesque building in central Europe.

The period *c.* 800–*c.* 1200 was the age of monasticism in Europe. The oldest Order was the Benedictine (founded in the sixth century), followed between 900 and 1100 by the Cluniac, Cistercian, Augustinian, Premonstratensian, and Carthusian Orders (*see* MONASTERY). The total amount of monastic building done in those centuries was prodigious; and there was also great activity in the erection of cathedrals and churches. Hardly less striking was the energy expended in castle-building (*see* CASTLE), for this was the heyday of feudalism. Of ordinary dwelling-houses, however, very few examples survive, because they were seldom substantially built. (For the names of Romanesque buildings in various European countries *see* the separate articles on BELGIAN, ENGLISH, FRENCH, GERMAN, IRISH, ITALIAN, SCANDINAVIAN, SCOTTISH, SPANISH, and SWISS ARCHITECTURE.)

Romanesque architects adopted from their Roman predecessors the semicircular arch, the groined cross-vault (*see* VAULT), and a debased form of the Corinthian capital; but they also developed vaulting and buttressing beyond Roman practice. Their churches were usually of basilican plan, sometimes with the addition of transepts, and with an ambulatory (q.v.) continuing the aisles round the east end. Towers of various types were popular, those of the Rhineland usually terminating in gables. Some circular churches were also built, following the precedent of the Early Christian baptistery; and the circular churches of the Knights Templars, in England and elsewhere, were modelled upon the Church of the Holy Sepulchre at Jerusalem. Rows of decorative arcading (q.v.) ornamented the exteriors of many churches. The tympanum (q.v.) over the entrance doorway was a favourite place for sculpture. The art of stained glass (q.v.) made its appearance in several countries.

> *See* the books by T. G. Jackson and C. Stewart cited at the end of the previous section; *also* A. K. Porter, *Medieval Architecture*, 1909; W. R. Lethaby, *Medieval Art*, 1912; G. T. Rivoira, *Lombardic Architecture* (2nd ed.), 1933; A. W. Clapham, *Romanesque Architecture in Western Europe*, 1936; K. J. Conant, *Carolingian and Romanesque Architecture*, 1959; *also* works cited at the end of each of the articles on the various European countries.

6. *Gothic Architecture* prevailed in western Europe from about 1200 to the beginning of the Renaissance (*see* section 7) of Roman architecture, which started in Italy in the fifteenth century, and elsewhere in the sixteenth. Gothic, it must be realized, is a nickname or term of opprobrium, though nowadays we accept it as a description of an architectural style of great splendour and beauty. It was first used in the seventeenth century to label a mode of building which was then considered uncouth and barbarous, because it was known that the Goths (and Vandals) were savage tribes insensitive to beauty, who had destroyed Rome, the centre of classical civilization. That was true; but in fact the Goths of the fourth to sixth centuries had nothing to do with 'Gothic' architecture of the twelfth to sixteenth centuries, and indeed produced hardly any buildings themselves.

Gothic architecture was adopted by all those countries (*see* section 5) who had adopted Romanesque; also by Hungary, Portugal, and Poland; and it was carried farther east by the Crusaders to Palestine and Cyprus. It attained its highest excellence in England and France—the Gothic buildings of Germany, Spain, Belgium, Holland, and Switzerland being strongly influenced by France. In Italy, because of the powerful Roman tradition, it never reached so high a level—whatever Ruskin may have thought and written. (For the chief Gothic buildings in the various countries of Europe *see* the separate articles devoted to their national architecture.)

The most obviously distinctive feature of Gothic architecture in general is the pointed arch, the origin of which is now universally ascribed to the Middle East, where it has been found in Syrian buildings of the sixth century A.D., as well as in the great mosques of Samarra in Iraq (mid ninth century) and Ibn Tulun at Cairo (876–9) (*see* MUSLIM ARCHITECTURE). Its introduction into western Europe was probably due to the Crusaders. The pointed arch was not, however, merely an ornamental form: it enabled Gothic architects to solve problems of vaulting which had long perplexed the Romanesque builders (*see* VAULT).

By concentrating the weight of vaulted roofs on to stone ribs, and counteracting the outward thrust of the ribs by means of bold buttresses, it became possible to reduce the thickness of walls between buttresses, and to pierce these thin walls with large windows. As the desire for stained glass (q.v.) grew urgent, these enlarged and pointed windows—divided by mullions (q.v.) and tracery (q.v.)—became one of the most beautiful features of Gothic architecture, so much so that its various phases came to be classified according to window design. In England the now familiar 'periods'—Early English, Decorated, and Perpendicular—were accepted in Victorian days as standards for differentiating the successive phases of Gothic (*see* ENGLISH ARCHITECTURE); but they do not apply equally to continental countries. Thus France had a 'Flamboyant' phase coeval with English 'Perpendicular.' Flying buttresses (q.v.), common in France, were seldom used in England, whereas fan-vaulting (q.v.) was peculiarly English.

Gothic architecture was never confined to churches: there are many beautiful Gothic town halls abroad, and a few great palaces, such as that of the popes at Avignon. It was the contemporary way of building, not a special 'style' for churches. It persisted in England long after the first waves of the Renaissance reached our shores; and even in the United States there is an authentic Gothic building—the little brick church of St Luke in Virginia, erected by English colonists in 1632.

See E. Corroyer, *L'Architecture gothique*, 1891; A. K. Porter, *Medieval Architecture*, 1909; G. H. West, *Gothic Architecture in England and France*, 1911; W. R. Lethaby, *Medieval Art* (2nd ed.), 1912; T. G. Jackson, *Gothic Architecture in France, England, and Italy*, 1915; J. Harvey, *The Gothic World*, 1950; *also* books cited at the end of each article on the architecture of various countries.

7. *Renaissance, to c. 1820*. The Renaissance (Fr., rebirth) was a revival of interest in classic culture and art. It began in Italy early in the fifteenth century so far as architecture was concerned. At that time Rome was in a deplorable state—a small town with probably no more than 20,000 inhabitants, mostly living in squalor around the fallen and ruined buildings of antiquity, overgrown with weeds. In 1401–7 Filippo Brunelleschi (q.v.) of Florence made a prolonged visit to Rome to study those buildings, partly with the purpose of obtaining ideas for completing the cathedral at Florence, for which competition designs had been invited. In 1420 or thereabouts

he built the Pazzi Chapel at Florence, commonly considered the first architectural work of the Renaissance in Italy. For the next thirty years Florence was the centre of the new movement; but the lead in spreading the fashion gradually passed to the writers of architectural manuals: Alberti, Vignola, Serlio, Palladio, and Scamozzi (qq.v.). All these men quoted extensively from the manual *De Architectura*, by the Roman architect Vitruvius (q.v.), so that Renaissance architecture has been sarcastically described as 'the architecture of a book,' and *De Architectura* as 'the architect's Bible.' Thus architectural design in Italy, and later in France and England, became a matter of following rules formulated by scholars on the basis of ancient Roman precedent.

In the other countries of western Europe, where the Gothic tradition was far stronger than in Italy, the Renaissance took root very slowly. It was first adopted as a novel fashion in court circles, and was confined to the purely decorative use of classical ornament and the classical Orders (*see* ORDERS), much of the work being executed by imported Italian craftsmen. During the Elizabethan and Jacobean (qq.v.) periods which followed in England, 1558–1625, a clumsy but very picturesque blending of Gothic and Renaissance was the result. In France the same period produced the ornate *châteaux* of Touraine, and in Germany, Holland, and Belgium many quaint town halls, market halls, and dwelling-houses were built. (All these stages are described in the articles on ENGLISH, FRENCH, GERMAN, and BELGIAN AND DUTCH ARCHITECTURE.)

Returning to Italy, we find that the Renaissance movement already described had been widely accepted, and is exemplified in the work of Bramante, Peruzzi, Palladio (qq.v.), and others; but it soon entered upon the phase recently christened Mannerism (q.v.), in which the chief architects were Michelangelo, Alessi, Tibaldi, and Vignola (qq.v.), who produced a more original type of architecture between *c.* 1530 and *c.* 1590 (*see* ITALIAN ARCHITECTURE).

This tendency, especially in the work of Michelangelo—who regarded architecture pictorially, having been a sculptor and painter before he turned to architecture—led to the Baroque (q.v.) phase. It spread from Italy all over western Europe, and was especially popular in Austria, Belgium, Spain, South Germany, Portugal, and in the new countries of Latin America, but also reached Poland and Scandinavia. It made little impression upon England or France, though it appears in the work of Wren (q.v.), as well as in the buildings of Archer, Hawksmoor, and Vanbrugh (qq.v.), who may fairly be called Baroque architects. It was bold, unconventional, often highly eccentric, but had the merit of relating buildings to their surroundings; and Baroque planning was magnificent.

In England and France, however, there was a reaction against the picturesque mingling of Gothic and Classical elements, and this new movement towards formal classicism was led in England by Inigo Jones (q.v.) between *c.* 1620 and *c.* 1650, and in France by F. Mansart (q.v.) at the same period. They reverted to a stricter rendering of classical architecture according to the rules of Palladio, hence much subsequent English architecture of the early eighteenth century is called Palladian (q.v.). Wren was hardly a Palladian, his training as a scientist rather than as an architect making his outlook unconventional.

The next important change in European architecture was from the Baroque and the Palladian to Rococo (q.v.), which originated in France, and was particularly favoured in Austria, Germany, and Switzerland, but not in England, during the latter half of the eighteenth century. At this period Adam (q.v.) was designing buildings in England in an original style influenced by his study of late-Roman work in Pompeii, etc.

> On Renaissance and Baroque architecture in general *see* L. Palustre, *L'Architecture de la Renaissance*, 1892; M. S. Briggs, *Baroque Architecture*, 1913 (also in German, 1914); T. G. Jackson, *The Renaissance of Roman Architecture* (3 vols.), 1921–3; Geoffrey Scott, *The Architecture of Humanism*, 1924; *also* books cited at the end of each article on the architecture of the individual countries.

8. *The Age of Revivals, c.* 1800–*c.* 1900. The last phase of Renaissance architecture in France was the Empire style (q.v.) of the early years of the nineteenth century; and in England the Georgian style (q.v.) which is sometimes held to include the delightful Regency style (q.v.), in vogue about 1820–30. All these were, in a sense, revivals of classical architecture; but the years which followed saw a conflict and competition between two rival schools of revivalism—the Greek and the Gothic—which lasted to the end of the nineteenth century in England, continental Europe, the United States, and the British colonies—Canada, Australia, even British India.

The Greek Revival, mainly in the second quarter of the century, was led in England by Wilkins, Burton, and Inwood (qq.v.); in Scotland by Playfair and 'Greek Thomson' (qq.v.); in Germany by Schinkel and Von Klenze (qq.v.); elsewhere by other architects.

Abreast of the Greek Revival flourished the Gothic Revival, which started long before with the ornate and picturesque villa known as Strawberry Hill, near Twickenham in Middlesex, built in 1753 by Horace Walpole, the famous writer and connoisseur. It was merely the hobby of a rich eccentric, but was soon followed by other eccentric noblemen who decorated their parks with sham ruins. Gothic architecture for churches had almost fallen into disuse for two centuries, very few churches being built in England between 1550 and 1660 (*see* CHURCH); and those designed by Wren, as well as the Nonconformist meeting-houses erected especially from 1680 onwards (*see* NONCONFORMIST CHURCH ARCHITECTURE), being in the classical style. In 1818, however, Parliament voted a million pounds for new Anglican churches, and three-quarters of these were designed in a pseudo-Gothic style. Once started, the fashion spread like wildfire; and from 1818 onwards, for nearly a century, almost all new churches in England, and many overseas, were in the Gothic style.

For public buildings there was some reluctance to introduce Gothic, but its adoption for the new Houses of Parliament in London (1834), where the proximity of Westminster suggested some form of

Gothic design, broke the spell. The town halls of Birmingham (1832–50) and Leeds (1853–8) were classical, as was the noble St George's Hall at Liverpool (1842); but that at Manchester (1868) was Gothic. There was a terrific 'Battle of the Styles' in Parliament during 1855–72, when the respective merits of Gothic and Classic for the new Foreign and India Offices in Whitehall were argued *ad nauseam*. This phase (dealt with more fully under ENGLISH ARCHITECTURE, q.v.) was matched in most other countries.

In the last quarter of the nineteenth century England indulged in Jacobean and so-called 'Queen Anne' revivals (*see* SHAW). Attempts at a Romanesque revival were made in America by H. H. Richardson (q.v.) and in England by A. Waterhouse (q.v.); but in 1900 all the revivals were nearly played out. A brief and curious interlude known as Art Nouveau (q.v.) followed; meanwhile pioneers such as Mackintosh, Voysey, and Philip Webb (qq.v.) were steadily feeling their way towards an escape from all forms of revivalism, and a similar process was taking place abroad. In that movement the development of steel construction, and the rapid emergence of reinforced concrete as a new material capable of great possibilities, were important factors.

> *See* Sir K. Clark, *The Gothic Revival* (2nd ed.), 1950; R. Turnor, *Nineteenth Century Architecture in Britain*, 1950; H. S. Goodhart-Rendel, *English Architecture since the Regency*, 1953; *also* books cited at the end of each article on the architecture of individual countries, including England.

9. *The Twentieth Century*. The absurd title of the 'Modern Movement'—absurd because 'modern' is a relative term, always becoming out of date—is constantly used to describe the change from the revivals to functional design (*see* FUNCTIONALISM), which made itself felt just before the First World War. Reference is made to the national characteristics of the movement in separate articles on the architecture of each of the principal countries, where the principal exponents and practitioners are mentioned, short biographies of each of them, with his buildings, being also provided in alphabetical order. Among the most active apostles of *Modernismus* have been 'Le Corbusier' and Perret (qq.v.) in France; Behrens, Gropius, Mendelsohn, and Van der Rohe (qq.v.) in Germany; Berlage and Dudok (qq.v.) in Holland; F. L. Wright (q.v.) in the United States. (For England *see* ENGLISH ARCHITECTURE.) In conclusion it must be emphasized that, although in most countries there has been a great deal of building—especially post-war reconstruction—in the so-called 'Contemporary Style,' the tendency remains for many people to cling to traditional forms of architectural design.

> *See* C. Marriott, *Modern English Architecture*, 1924; 'Le Corbusier,' *Towards a New Architecture*, 1927; G. A. Platz, *Die Baukunst der neuesten Zeit*, 1930; Sir R. Blomfield, *Modernismus*, 1934, an amusing but bigoted attack on the Modern Movement; W. Gropius, *The New Architecture and the Bauhaus*, 1935; N. Pevsner, *Pioneers of the Modern Movement*, 1936; F. R. S. Yorke and C. Penn, *A Key to Modern Architecture*, 1939; J. M.

Richards, *An Introduction to Modern Architecture*, 1940; M. S. Briggs, *Building To-day* (2nd ed.), 1948.

Architrave. (1) In any of the Greek and Roman 'Orders' (q.v.), the lowest member of the entablature (q.v., *illustrated*), resting directly upon the capitals of the supporting columns.   (2) A moulding surrounding or framing a doorway or a window opening, inside or outside a building.

Archivolt, a moulding or architrave curving round an arch.

Arcuated, a style of architecture in which the structure is supported on arches; in contrast to 'trabeated' architecture (q.v.) where vertical posts and horizontal beams are used structurally throughout.

A.R.C.U.K., abbreviation for Architects Registration Council of the United Kingdom (q.v.).

Arena (Lat., sand), the central open space in an amphitheatre where gladiatorial combats took place: so called because it was usually strewn with sand, for obvious reasons.

A.R.I.B.A., abbreviation for Associate of the Royal Institute of British Architects. *See* ARCHITECT.

Arnolfo di Cambio, or **Di Lapo** (*b*. Colle di Val d'Elsa, **1232**; *d*. Florence, 1302), Italian architect, designed the following buildings in Florence: the cathedral of S. Maria del Fiore (1294 onwards); the church of S. Croce (1294 onwards); and, according to Vasari, the Palazzo Vecchio (1298–1314); also refaced and altered the Baptistery (1290 onwards).

Arras, tapestry originally made at Arras in Artois (France), and much used for lining the stone walls of important rooms in medieval houses before the introduction of wood panelling.

Arris, the sharp edge produced by the angular contact of two plane surfaces, usually of wood.

A.R.S.A., abbreviation for Associate of the Royal Scottish Academy. *See* ACADEMY.

Arsenal, a building or group of buildings for the storage and manufacture of naval or military munitions of war.

Art Nouveau (Fr., new art), a term loosely applied to a curious phase of decoration which prevailed in continental Europe *c*. 1893–1905 but had little effect upon architecture in England.   It originated suddenly and spontaneously in Belgium in 1893, in the design of a house at Uccle near Brussels by the young architect Victor Horta (*b*. 1861), and was then popularized by H. Van de Velde (*b*. 1863) (q.v.), who was in touch with William Morris (q.v.) in England. From about 1895 to about 1900, the style was chiefly favoured in Germany and Austria, as the *Jugendstil*. It was essentially an aesthetic movement, bearing no relation to architectural structure or planning, and had some kinship with the work of Aubrey Beardsley in England. Art Nouveau decoration consisted chiefly in a prodigal use of curving lines and shapes, based on plant forms such as the tulip or on the antennae of insects. It was delicate and effeminate. Although Mackintosh and Voysey (qq.v.) produced many designs having Art Nouveau features, it remains uncertain whether they influenced it more than they were influenced by it. Three buildings in London by the architect C. Harrison Townsend (*d.* 1928) have often been cited as examples of Art Nouveau. They are the Bishopsgate Institute (1892–4); the Whitechapel Art Gallery (1897–9); and the Horniman Museum, Forest Hill (1900–1).

Art Workers Guild, The, founded by William Morris (q.v.) in 1884, has many architects among its members, and several have served as Master. Meetings are held at 6 Queen Square, London, W.C.1.

Ashlar, masonry walling formed of accurately squared stones with a smooth face, laid in regular courses with fine joints.

Ashlaring, or **Ashlering,** an arrangement of short vertical timbers cutting off the angle formed at the intersection of a sloping wooden roof with a floor, and forming a support for lath and plaster. This term, used in carpentry, is confusing because it has no connection with 'ashlar' (q.v.) in masonry.

Aslin, Charles Herbert (*b.* Sheffield, 15 Dec. 1893; *d.* 18 April 1959). After training in Sheffield, and a municipal appointment there, he became architect to Rotherham County Borough, 1922–6; deputy county architect of Hampshire, 1926–9; borough architect of Derby County Borough, 1929–45; and county architect of Hertfordshire, 1945, in which post his ingenious design of school buildings to comply with difficult post-war circumstances made his reputation. He was appointed C.B.E. in 1951, and served as President of the R.I.B.A., 1954–6.

Asplund, Gunnar (*b.* Stockholm, 22 Nov. 1885; *d.* there, 20 Oct. 1940), Swedish architect; Professor of Architecture at Stockholm, 1931–40. The principal buildings designed by him are extensions of the Law Courts, the railway station, the central library, the Skandia Cinema, the crematorium—all in Stockholm; extensions of the Gothenburg Town Hall (1934); numerous schools; the Swedish pavilion at the Paris Exhibition (1923).

See monographs by B. Zevi, 1948; G. Holmdal and others, 1950; E. de Maré, 1953.

Assyrian Architecture, *see* ARCHITECTURE, PERIODS OF, 1(*b*).

Astragal, a small bead or convex moulding of semicircular section, used as a necking for classical columns and also elsewhere; sometimes carved with a 'bead and reel' enrichment (q.v.).

Astylar (Gk *a* + *stulos*; literally 'without columns'), a term applied to classical façades which have no columns or pilasters.

Asymmetry, lack of balance between the elements of a façade or of a plan; the opposite of 'symmetry.'

Atelier (Fr.), an artist's studio; a workshop. In France the system of architectural training is controlled by the S.A.D.G. (q.v.), and carried out by the École des Beaux Arts, whose architect professors conduct private tuition in their *ateliers*. The first Atelier of Architecture was opened in London in 1913 by the Society of Architects (q.v.), with distinguished French and English support. The first English professor was Arthur Davis, R.A. (q.v.), and his first English assistant or *sous-patron* was H. O. Corfiato (q.v.). The *atelier* was closed in 1923.

Atlantes (plural of Atlas, name of the Greek deity who was supposed to carry the world on his shoulders), a term applied in architecture to carved stone figures of men or half-men, used instead of columns to support an entablature, in the same way that female figures known as 'caryatides' (q.v.) were used for a similar purpose at the Erechtheum at Athens, and at St Pancras Church, London.

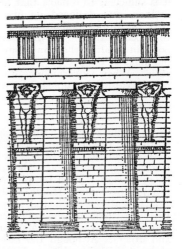

ATLANTES at the Greek Doric temple of Zeus Olympios, Agrigentum (c. 470 B.C.)

Atrium. (1) In Greek and Roman houses, an open central court. (2) In early Christian churches, a forecourt. (*Illustrated* CHURCH.)

Attic. (1) In classical and monumental architecture, a stage or storey (properly the 'attic storey'), above the principal entablature of the Order or building, often decorated with 'Attic pilasters,' hence the name. (2) Derived from the above specific usage, an attic in modern speech, since the early eighteenth century, has been a garret, i.e. a room partly or wholly in the sloping roof of a house, lit by dormers or skylights. (3) Used as an adjective, the 'Attic base' occurs in the Ionic and Corinthian Orders, and consists of two convex toruses separated by a concave scotia, resting upon a plain square plinth.

Auditorium, in any theatre, church, or other place of assembly, the area of seating which is occupied by the audience or congregation.

Aula (Lat.). (1) A Roman hall. (2) In modern Germany, the assembly hall of a university or other scholastic building.

Aumbry, *see* ALMERY.

Austin, George (*b.* Woodstock, 1786; *d.* Canterbury, 26 Oct. 1848), English architect. After having been appointed resident architect to Canterbury Cathedral, he proceeded in 1834 to demolish the dilapidated Norman north-west tower, and then to rebuild it in the Perpendicular style to match the south-west tower. This action, often cited as sheer vandalism, is regarded by other critics as entirely legitimate because of the resultant harmonious grouping of the two towers and the great central tower.

Australian Architecture began as an unexpected by-product of the British penal colony established in 1788 at Botany Bay, a few miles south of modern Sydney. Among the felons who landed there in 1813 was one Francis Greenway, a Bristol architect, who had been condemned to death for forging a document, his sentence then being reduced to banishment. His astounding subsequent career in Australia is outlined in a separate article (*see* GREENWAY), and here it is sufficient to remark that he made the town plan of the future Sydney, and designed its first hospital and some churches. In 1835 the site of Melbourne was selected: its population had grown to 24,000 by 1842. The discovery of gold in 1851 led to a tremendous boom in building, there and elsewhere. The few surviving Australian buildings of the period *c.* 1820–50 are mostly in a pleasant Regency style. When Government House, Melbourne, was built (*c.* 1856) by W. Wardell, he copied Osborne House, but made its ball-room just one foot longer, a fact which is said to have made Queen Victoria 'very cross.'

The Gothic Revival (q.v.), which had already spread from England to its colonies by that time, was represented by Sydney Cathedral (1819–68); Government House, Sydney (1837); Sydney University by Edmund Blacket; St Mary's Roman Catholic Cathedral, Sydney (1868–1905), and St Patrick's Roman Catholic Cathedral, Melbourne (1849 onwards), both by W. Wardell, a pupil of A. W. N. Pugin (q.v.); Government House, Hobart, by W. Porden-Kay; Adelaide Roman Catholic Cathedral (1870) by A. W. N. Pugin and others; Brisbane Roman Catholic Cathedral (1901) by J. L. Pearson (q.v.); and St Paul's Cathedral, Melbourne (1850), by W. Butterfield (q.v.) and others. Although the last three buildings were designed by eminent English architects, local talent was generally employed from about 1870 onwards. In 1911, however, the international competition for the new federal capital at Canberra was won by an American architect, W. B. Griffin.

Among many notable buildings erected since 1910 may be mentioned the Parliament House, Administrative Offices, National Library, Governor-General's House, School of Forestry, Institute of Anatomy, and War Memorial, all at Canberra, and all erected 1925–1941; the Anzac War Memorial, Sydney; Newman College, Melbourne (1916), and the Capitol Theatre, Melbourne (1924), both by Griffin; the Shrine of Remembrance, Melbourne (1933); the City Hall, Brisbane (1928), by Hall and Prentice; the Residential Hall at Canberra University (1952) by B. B. Lewis; the block of flats at Pott's Point, New South Wales (1951), by A. M. Bolot; several buildings by the firm of Stephenson & Turner, including the huge Royal Hospital at Melbourne (1942); the General Hospital at Concord, New South Wales (1942–5); the Vacuum Oil Refinery at Altona, Victoria (1954); and some handsome office blocks in Sydney. The Royal Gold Medal of the R.I.B.A. for 1954 was awarded to Sir Arthur Stephenson.

See M. Herman, *Early Australian Architects and their Work*, 1954.

Austrian Architecture, included in GERMAN ARCHITECTURE (q.v.).

Axonometric Projection, a method of pictorial drawing which shows a building or other object in three dimensions. The plan is set up to scale to a true angle of either 45 degrees or of 30 degrees and 60 degrees; and verticals are also drawn to scale; but by this method diagonals and curves are distorted (*Illustrated* DRAWING). For other methods of drawing *see* ISOMETRIC, ORTHOGRAPHIC, and PERSPECTIVE PROJECTION.

B

Babylonian Architecture, *see* ARCHITECTURE, PERIODS OF, 1(*b*).

Badia (Ital.), an abbey, e.g. the famous Badia di Fiesole near Florence.

Bagnio (from Ital. *bagno*, Lat. *balneum*, a bath), either (i) a bath or bathing establishment; or (ii) an oriental prison for slaves; or (iii) a brothel.

Baguette (Fr.), a small moulding.

Bailey, a term first applied to the external wall surrounding a medieval castle or keep; later to one of the internal courts of the castle, e.g. the outer bailey, inner bailey, etc. In London the Central Criminal Court is commonly called the 'Old Bailey,' from its situation in the street of that name, which was a part of the medieval bailey between Lud Gate and New Gate. *See* CASTLE.

Baker, Sir Herbert, R.A. (*b*. Cobham, Kent, 1862; *d*. in same place, 4 Feb. 1946), English architect, R.I.B.A. Royal Gold Medallist, 1927. He was educated at Tonbridge School, 1875–81, and then articled to his cousin Arthur Baker, studying in his evenings at the Royal Academy Schools and at the Victoria and Albert Museum. In 1884 or 1885 he went as assistant to Ernest George, R.A. (q.v.), and had risen to the post of chief assistant when Edwin Lutyens (q.v.) arrived in the office as a pupil. During the next few years these two young men became close friends and had many sketching tours together, so it is sad that in later life, when both had become famous, professional squabbles at New Delhi led to their estrangement. Continuing to study in his evenings, Baker undertook a few small commissions on his own account, while with George; but in 1892 went to South Africa where his brother had just started fruit farming. Baker began visiting the surviving old Dutch houses of South Africa, and thereby came to the notice of Cecil Rhodes, who soon entrusted him with the restoration of his old house, Groote Schuur, near Cape Town. He did this work so successfully that Rhodes exerted his great influence on his behalf, and soon Baker had created a large practice in Cape Town. In 1902 he moved to Johannesburg, then a shabby but rising town. During the ten years that he was there he built the railway station, St John's College, a girls' school, the Research Institute, and many houses. He was next commissioned to design the large Government buildings for the new Government of South Africa, at its new capital, Pretoria. In 1912 he was appointed joint architect with Lutyens for the new capital of India at Delhi, the various buildings required being shared between them. Baker's work included the secretariat buildings. His other major commissions included the cathedral, railway station, and Government House at Pretoria; cathedrals at Cape Town and Salisbury

34

(Rhodesia); the Union Club, Johannesburg; Government House, Mombasa; Government House, the Law Courts, and other important buildings at Nairobi; the Rhodes Memorial near Cape Town; Rhodes House, Oxford; and the following in London, where he worked during his later life: India House, Aldwych; South Africa House, Trafalgar Square; the premises of the Royal Empire Society, Northumberland Avenue; Ninth Church of Christ Scientist; Church House, Westminster; London House, Guilford Street; and the rebuilding of the Bank of England. He also designed many war memorials and cemeteries for the Imperial War Graves Commission after the First World War. In all his public buildings, whether in England, India, or South Africa, he was strongly influenced by the classical tradition.

See his reminiscences, *Architecture and Personalities*, 1944; *also* his book, *Cecil Rhodes, by his Architect*, 1934.

Balcony. (1) A platform projecting from the face of a building, outside windows, and supported either by brackets or, in modern multi-storey flats, by cantilever construction. A balcony is usually protected by a railing, or by a wall, waist high, and may have a roof. (2) In a modern theatre, the portion of the auditorium which is above the dress-circle.

Baldaquin, or **Baldachin** (Ital. *baldacchino*), a Spanish term originally applied to rich brocade made in Baghdad; then to a canopy of such brocade, hung over an altar, tomb, or doorway in a church; finally to an isolated canopied structure over an altar. The most notable example is at St Peter's, Rome (1633), with huge bronze pillars. It was Wren's intention to erect a similar structure at St Paul's, London. His wish was never realized; but the destruction of the elaborate (modern) marble reredos by bombing in the Second World War has led to a decision to replace it by a baldaquin on the lines of Wren's design.

Balistraria (med. Lat.), a cruciform opening in the battlements or wall of a medieval fortress, through which a crossbow could be discharged.

Ball-flower, in English Gothic architecture of the thirteenth to fourteenth centuries, and occasionally in France at a somewhat earlier date, an ornament carved at regular intervals along a hollow moulding, and resembling a spherical three-lobed flower, opened to show an enclosed sphere or ball. (*Illustrated* MOULDINGS, ENRICHED (GOTHIC).)

BALDAQUIN. St Peter's, Rome

Balloon-framing, a form of framed timber construction much used to-day in building timber houses in Scandinavia and the U.S.A. The vertical members ('studs') run continuously from sill to eaves, the horizontal members being nailed to them.

Baluster, one of a row of vertical members supporting a handrail (if on a staircase) or a coping (if forming an external parapet): such a row constitutes a balustrade (q.v.). Balusters may be of stone, terracotta, wood, or iron. Italian writers of the Renaissance period laid down rules for the design of stone balusters, and these have since been followed for monumental buildings in stone, and even occasionally for internal work in wood. Cast-iron balusters came into use in the late eighteenth century, in conjunction with mahogany handrails. About the beginning of the twentieth century plain wood balusters about one inch square came into fashion for small houses, in order to decrease dusting and painting. A still more recent tendency is to substitute a plywood panel for balusters, but some loss of light may result. *See* STAIRCASE.

BALUSTER. Three 18th-century examples: centre, in stone; right and left, in wood

Baluster Shafts, sturdy stone circular pillars, resembling balusters, and used instead of mullions to divide Early Romanesque (or 'Saxon') church windows into 'lights'; as at Worth, Sussex.

Balustrade, normally, a row of balusters (q.v.), supporting a handrail or coping; but in several ornate English mansions of the seventeenth century the place of balusters was taken by pierced and elaborately carved panels, e.g. at Ham House, Hatfield House, Castle Ashby, Sudbury Hall. In the eighteenth century ornamental panels of wrought iron were similarly used. At the De Grey Rooms, York, there is a particularly beautiful cast-iron panel containing a design of vine leaves (late eighteenth century).

Band. (1) A plain or moulded flat strip or string-course running horizontally across the face of a building. (2) A moulding round the shaft of a column. (Cf. ANNULET.)

Banister, Bannisters, a corruption of Baluster, Balustrade (qq.v.).

Banquette (rare), either (i) a raised walk inside the parapet of a bridge; or (ii) a recessed window-seat.

Baptistery, in modern times, either (i) a bay, corner, or chapel,

reserved for baptisms in an Anglican or other church; or (ii) a sunk
tank for total immersion, as used by the Baptist denomination.   In
such cases the minimum size of the tank should be 7 feet by 4 feet,
and steps leading down to it are required.

Detached buildings of some size, where large numbers of persons
could be baptized at a central font or in a sunk tank for immersion,
adjoin certain important historic churches in Italy, e.g. the Baptistery
of Constantine in the Lateran at Rome; and those at Nocera (350);
Ravenna, late fourth century; Pisa (1153–1278); and Florence (date
uncertain).

Bar-tracery has its curved members carved into the same mouldings as the mullions from which it springs; its patterns may therefore
be more flexible than those of the earlier and heavier plate tracery.
See TRACERY, *illustrated.*

Barbican, an outwork or detached feature of a castle, sometimes
provided with a tower, and planned to protect the drawbridge or
approach to the main entrance gateway.   English examples at
Alnwick, Carlisle, Scarborough, and York.   The street named
'Barbican' in London recalls a similar feature in the City Wall.
(*Illustrated* CASTLE.)

Barge-board, or **Verge-board,** a projecting inclined board, often
decoratively pierced and carved, fixed beneath the eaves of a gable
to cover the rafters.   (*Illustrated* ROOF.)

Barn, a building for the storage of hay and corn.   Many surviving
English examples are of great age, size, and beauty, e.g. (in stone)
Torquay, Devon (probably thirteenth century); Glastonbury (early
fourteenth century);   Bradford-on-Avon,   Wiltshire   (fourteenth
century); Preston Plucknett, Wiltshire (fifteenth century); Abbots-
bury, Dorset; Cherhill, Wiltshire (fifteenth century); Ombersley,
Worcestershire (1376); Maidstone, Kent (fourteenth century).   In
flint: Paston, Norfolk (1581).   In brick: Bredon, Worcestershire
(fourteenth century).   In timber: Avebury, Wiltshire (fifteenth
century); and the magnificent example at Harmondsworth, Middlesex
(fourteenth or fifteenth century).   Many of these were ecclesiastical
tithe barns.

See M. S. Briggs, *The English Farmhouse*, 1953.   *See also*
DUTCH BARN.

Baroque Architecture (originally from Port. *barroco*, a misshapen
pearl), a phase of architecture specially prevalent in the Catholic
countries of Europe (Italy, Spain, Portugal, Austria, South Germany,
Belgium), and of Latin America (Brazil, Mexico, etc.) during the
seventeenth to eighteenth centuries.   *See* ARCHITECTURE, PERIODS
OF, 7: *also* articles on the architecture of the various countries
concerned, and M. S. Briggs, *Baroque Architecture*, 1913.

Barozzi da Vignola, *see* VIGNOLA.

Barrel Vault, or **Tunnel Vault,** a continuous semicircular arch or
tunnel of brick, stone, or concrete, used from very early times in
Roman and Romanesque architecture.   *See* VAULTING, *illustrated.*

Barry, Sir Charles, R.A. (*b*. London, 23 May 1795; *d*. there, 12 May 1860), English architect, designer of the Houses of Parliament, London; R.I.B.A. Royal Gold Medallist, 1850; F.R.S., 1849; knighted, 1852. He was articled at the age of fifteen to Messrs Middleton & Bailey of Lambeth, a firm engaged in surveying rather than architecture; but this somewhat pedestrian training proved invaluable to him in later life. Between 1817 and 1820 he spent three years of travel and study in Greece, Italy, Egypt, and Palestine. His first success, however, was in a competition for St Peter's Church, Brighton, built 1823–6, which was one of the earliest examples of the English Gothic Revival (q.v.); and in 1833–6 he built King Edward's Grammar School, Birmingham, in Tudor Gothic. Most of his buildings were nevertheless in the classic style that he preferred. They included the Royal Institution of Fine Arts (1824–35) and the Athenaeum (1837–9), both in Manchester; the Travellers' Club (1829–31); the Reform Club (1837–41); Bridgewater House (1847–9, since demolished); part of Stafford House, now Lancaster House (1843)—all close together in London; Trentham Park, Staffordshire (1838, since demolished); Clifden or Cliveden, Buckinghamshire (1837); and Halifax Town Hall (1859–62), completed after his death. His winning design for the new Houses of Parliament, in Tudor Gothic, was the result of a competition held in 1836, after the previous buildings had been destroyed by fire. There were ninety-seven competitors, who were bound by the stipulation that designs must be 'Gothic' or 'Elizabethan,' to harmonize with the adjoining Abbey and with Westminster Hall, which was to be incorporated in the scheme. Though the plan and general idea were certainly Barry's, he was greatly and ably assisted in the design and execution of the elaborate Gothic details by A. W. N. Pugin (q.v.); and the work was completed, after Barry's death, by his son E. M. Barry, R.A.

See biography by his son, the Rev. Dr Alfred Barry, 1867.

Bartizan, a turret projecting from a medieval tower.

Barton, a name used in Devon and Cornwall for a large farmhouse with its ancillary buildings; originally it signified a threshing-floor, then a farmyard.

Base. (1) The lowest course of masonry in a stone building. (2) The projecting member between the shaft of a column and its plinth. *See* ORDERS OF ARCHITECTURE. (3) The lowest stage of panelling in a panelled room. *See also* DADO, PLINTH, SKIRTING.

Base-block, or **Plinth-block,** a flat or bevelled block at the intersection of a skirting with the architrave around a doorway or other opening in a wall.

Base-court (from Fr. *basse cour*, low court), the outer court of a medieval castle or, later, of a country mansion, containing the servants' quarters.

Basement. (1) The lowest storey of a building, whether wholly or partially below ground level. (2) In classical architecture, the lowest storey beneath the Orders (q.v.) of columns or pilasters

decorating the upper part of the façade. In such buildings the
basement was sometimes 'rusticated' (q.v.) in order to create an
impression of great strength.

Basevi, George (*b.* London, 1 April 1794; *d.* Ely, 16 Oct. 1845),
English architect, was a pupil of Sir John Soane (q.v.). He travelled
and studied in Italy and Greece, 1816–19. His principal building
was the Fitzwilliam Museum, Cambridge (1836–45). In London he
laid out part of Belgravia, including Belgrave Square (1825), Thurloe
Square, Sydney Place, and Pelham Crescent. Among his other
works were the Conservative Club, St James's Street, in collaboration
with S. Smirke (q.v.); country mansions at Gatcombe Park and
Taplow; and several Gothic churches, including St Thomas, Stockport (1822–5); Holy Trinity, Twickenham (1839–41); St Jude,
Chelsea (1843–4). He was killed by falling from a tower at Ely
Cathedral while inspecting it.

Basilica (Gk *basilikē*, a royal building or palace) may be either
(i) a public hall for the administration of justice and the transaction
of business in a Roman city, usually adjoining the Forum or market-
place; or (ii) an early Christian church, somewhat resembling a
secular basilica in its general plan and arrangements. The chief
Roman basilicas were built in Rome itself, and provided shelter from
rain and freedom from disturbance, essential requirements for the
orderly conduct of legal and commercial business. The earliest
recorded example, the Porcian basilica, was erected in 184 B.C., and
may have been inspired by the Stoa (q.v.) at Athens. It no longer
survives, and the oldest remaining example is at Pompeii (*c.* 100 B.C.).
In Rome the Basilica Aemilia (*c.* 54–34 B.C.) was followed by the
Basilica Julia (31 B.C. to A.D. 14) and the Basilica Ulpia (A.D. 112).
The Basilica Nova, begun by Maxentius, was finished by Constantine
after A.D. 313. There were basilicas in all the principal Roman
cities, including a large one in London on the site of modern Gracechurch Street, and smaller examples have been excavated at Cirencester and Silchester. The typical Roman basilica, excluding the
latest examples, consisted of a long and wide open space or nave,
flanked on either side by aisles, which were separated from the nave
by a range of columns. Above the aisles were often galleries with
flat roofs, and above these again were ranges of windows lighting the
nave. The normal Roman secular basilica did not possess an apse,
but there was a throne for the judge at the end facing the entrance.
For the basilican type of church *see* CHURCH.

Bastide (Fr.), one of the small fortified towns, laid out during the
Middle Ages on a rectilinear or chess-board plan, by the English in
the parts of France occupied by them. Monpazier in Dordogne
(1284) is a typical example. Winchelsea in Kent, laid out in 1281,
is an English counterpart.

Bastion, one of a series of projections from the main curtain wall
(q.v.) of a fortress, placed at intervals in such a manner as to enable
the garrison to enfilade besiegers attacking the intervening stretches
of wall. Bastions are usually pentagonal or semicircular on plan,
but may be triangular (e.g. at Famagusta, Cyprus).

Baths, Roman Public, *see* THERMAE.

Batten, a thin and narrow strip of wood; as used in slating, tiling, and plastering; also in the construction of a 'batten door.' *See* DOOR.

Batter, a slight inward inclination or tilt of a wall from its base upwards. The purpose is either (i) to increase the strength of the base, as in retaining walls (q.v.); or (ii) to add to the defensive strength of the wall of a fortress; or (iii) occasionally as an optical refinement, as in the Cenotaph, London. The batter of walls and pylons in ancient Egyptian temples is probably a superfluous translation into stone of primitive mud construction, when walls had to be battered to ensure stability.

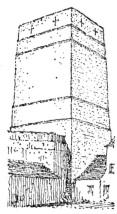

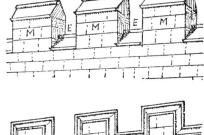

BATTER. St George's Tower, Oxford Castle (c. 1070)

BATTLEMENTS. Above, early type; below, late type. M=*merlon;* E=*embrasure or crenel*

Battlement, a form of parapet which is indented or crenellated so that archers could shoot through the indentations (crenels or embrasures) between the protecting solid portions (merlons), as well as through arrow slits in the merlons. In medieval practice it was usual to make the crenel or embrasure half the width of the merlon; but battlements were used in the East long before the Middle Ages, indeed almost from the beginnings of military architecture.

After the invention of gunpowder had made them obsolete, they continued in use in England for purely ornamental purposes, not only around the stone parapets of churches and quiet collegiate buildings, but were even imitated in wood, to a miniature scale, in the decoration of church screens, etc. *See* CRENELLATION.

Bauhaus, *see* GROPIUS.

Bay. (1) A compartment or section in the length of a building, between each pair of roof-trusses or transverse vaulting-ribs and their supporting buttresses, if any. (2) A similar compartment of a framed floor, between girders.

Bay-window, a window projecting from the face of a building at ground level, and either rectangular or polygonal on plan. The name seems to have been derived from the fact that a large bay-window normally was placed in the bay of the medieval 'great hall' in which the daïs and 'high table' stood (*see* HALL). A bay-window may be of one or more storeys; but if it projects on corbelling (q.v.), or brackets from an upper floor, it is called an 'oriel' (q.v.); and if it is curved on plan it is called a 'bow window' (q.v.).

Bazaar (from Persian *bāzār*, market), strictly speaking, an oriental market or market-place, lined with booths or stalls. (*Suq* in Arabic).

Bazhenov, Vasily (*b.* Moscow, 1 Mar. 1737; *d.* St Petersburg, 2 Aug. 1799), Russian architect. After his training at the Academy of Fine Art, Moscow, he travelled in Italy with a scholarship, and then worked in France. Returning to St Petersburg in 1765, he was commissioned to build the palace of Kamenostrovski at St Petersburg for the Empress Catherine. His other commissions included the Arsenal (1769), now mostly destroyed; designs for an enormous palace of St Michael at St Petersburg, ultimately carried out by Brenna; the imperial palace at Caricyno near Moscow; and a design for remodelling the Kremlin at Moscow, never executed. He worked mostly in the Italian Palladian style, though deriving some ideas from the Russian medieval tradition and making a few attempts at reviving Gothic forms.

Bead, a small convex moulding. (*Illustrated* MOULDINGS, CLASSICAL.)

Bead and Reel, or **Reel and Bead,** in classical architecture, a moulding enriched with alternating 'beads' and 'reels.' (*Illustrated* MOULDINGS, ENRICHED (CLASSICAL).)

Beak-head, in English Romanesque architecture, a grotesque ornament vaguely suggesting a head with a beak, and sometimes called a 'cat's head' if the tongue is hanging out. Used in rows on mouldings framing richly decorated doorways of churches. (*Illustrated* MOULDINGS, ENRICHED (ROMANESQUE).)

Beam, originally a tree trunk or log which has been squared; then any large horizontal timber in a building. In structural mechanics a beam is, more precisely, any horizontal structural member, of any material, resting upon two or more supports, and subject to a transverse load. *See also* CANTILEVER, COLLAR-BEAM, GIRDER, JOIST, LINTEL, TIE-BEAM.

Bearer, in carpentry, a small and subsidiary wooden joist, used to support the boarding of a lead gutter, the winders of a staircase, etc.

Beaux Arts, École des, the oldest and most celebrated centre of architectural education in the world. Its premises are situated on the Quai Malaquais in Paris. The origin of the school is to be found in the Académie d'Architecture established by Colbert in 1671, but all the academies (*see* ACADEMY) were abolished in 1793 during the revolution. The Académie des Beaux Arts was then founded in 1807, and regular courses in architecture were instituted in 1819. A system of school *ateliers* (*see* ATELIER) was introduced in 1863, under a director. To obtain admission a candidate has to pass a stiff entrance examination in elementary drawing and design, as well as in mathematics, geometry, and history. Once admitted, the length of his course varies, and attendance is not strictly prescribed for all lectures and examinations. Instruction is free, and is open to foreigners. The work consists mainly of graded exercises in design (*projets*) carried out in isolated cubicles (*en loge*) six times a year. The course culminates in an examination for a diploma, obtained by only a small proportion of candidates.

The famous *Grand Prix de Rome*, offered annually in each of the principal arts (painting, sculpture, and architecture), enabling prizemen to study at the French Academy in the Villa Medici at Rome, has been awarded in architecture since 1720, and the roll of its winners includes the chief French architects. Foreigners are not eligible for this prize; but the influence of the École des Beaux Arts on several foreign countries, especially the United States, has been profound for more than a century, as will be noted in many of the short biographies of American architects included in this book.

Bed Mould, properly **Bed Moulding,** in classical architecture, the moulding or group of mouldings immediately beneath the corona (q.v.) of a cornice.

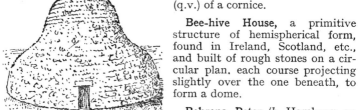

BEE-HIVE HOUSE. Lewis, Scotland

Bee-hive House, a primitive structure of hemispherical form, found in Ireland, Scotland, etc., and built of rough stones on a circular plan, each course projecting slightly over the one beneath, to form a dome.

Behrens, Peter (*b.* Hamburg, 14 April 1868, *d.* Berlin, 27 Feb. 1940), German architect; a pioneer of the 'Modern Movement' in architecture. After working in Munich, Darmstadt, and Düsseldorf he moved, about 1907, to Berlin and in 1922 to Vienna. He designed many notable industrial buildings in and near Berlin; also some admirable housing schemes; and in 1924 a monastery near Salzburg. Among his pupils and assistants were Gropius (q.v.), 'Le Corbusier' (q.v.), and M. van der Rohe (q.v.).

See monographs by F. Hoeber, 1913, and P. J. Cremers, 1928.

Belcher, John, R.A. (*b.* London, 10 July 1841; *d.* there, 8 Nov. 1913), English architect, son of an architect of the same name. President R.I.B.A., 1904–6; awarded R.I.B.A. Royal Gold Medal, 1907. He was educated partly in Germany, and also studied architecture in Paris; then joined his father. His earliest work shows the influence of the Gothic Revival then in vogue; but all his later buildings have a Roman and monumental character, the natural result of the great book he was compiling, jointly with Mervyn Macartney (q.v.), entitled *Later Renaissance Architecture in England* (published 1901). His first important commission was the Royal Insurance Company's office (since demolished) in Lombard Street, London, in French Renaissance style. Among notable works which followed were the Institute of Chartered Accountants, Moorgate Street (1890); Electra House, Finsbury Pavement (1902); Whiteley's Store, Bayswater (1912)—all these in London; and Colchester Town Hall (1902). His *Essentials in Architecture* (1907) is an unusual and thoughtful little book.

Belfast Roof-truss, a segmentally shaped timber roof-truss, having a curved principal rafter and a horizontal tie-beam forming the chord. These two members are connected by a diagonal lattice of light wooden ties. (*Illustrated* ROOF-TRUSS.)

Belfry (probably from late Lat. *berfredus*, a defensive place of shelter). Originally the name had no reference to bells, and meant a movable wooden tower used in medieval warfare; but later it came to mean, as it still does, either (i) a bell-tower or campanile; or (ii) the stage of a church tower in which the bells are hung; or (iii) a lower

BELFRY. Left, in stone; right, in timber

chamber of the tower, in which the ringers stand. The medieval *Beffroi* in the market-place of Bruges in Belgium is a famous example, with a fine carillon of bells. *See also* CAMPANILE.

Belgian and Dutch Architecture may be considered here as a whole, for the present state of Belgium only dates from 1830, when it was separated from the kingdom of the Netherlands, established in 1815. Before that date the two countries had formed part of larger empires from time to time, and were subject to architectural influence from France on the south and from Germany on the east. Both became rich during the Middle Ages, but both, especially Belgium, have suffered much damage to historical buildings during times of war. Ever since the Reformation Holland has been predominantly Protestant, whereas Belgium has remained predominantly Catholic.

Though both countries were included in the Roman Empire, no Roman buildings of note survive. Christianity arrived late on the scene, and the earliest important historical monument is the nave of the cathedral at Tournai (1070). The transept and towers of that cathedral are about eighty years later. Other Romanesque buildings are very scarce. The principal surviving Gothic buildings are the cathedrals of Antwerp, Bruges, Brussels, Ghent, Louvain, Malines, and Ypres; the town halls of Bruges, Brussels, Ghent, Louvain, and Oudenarde; the battered Cloth Hall at Ypres; the lovely church of Notre-Dame du Sablon at Brussels; and the collegiate church at

Huy—all these in Belgium; the cathedrals of Dordrecht, Haarlem, and Utrecht; the town halls of Middelburg and Veere—all in Holland; also picturesque gabled houses in both countries.

The Renaissance movement from Italy reached Belgium and Holland late. It is natural that its earlier works closely resemble our 'Elizabethan' and 'Jacobean' buildings, for English architects of that period derived many of their ideas from Flemish, Dutch, and German books. Picturesque examples of this style are to be found in gabled house fronts all over the two countries, and also in some civic buildings, e.g. the meat market at Haarlem (1603), the town hall at Leyden (1579), and the steeples of many churches. The town hall of Antwerp (1565) is a more conservative design, but its central gable, its mullioned windows, and its bold eaves give it a Flemish picturesqueness. The Mauritshuis (1630) at The Hague, the Huis ten Bosch (1645) not far away, and many of the quiet streets of Haarlem, Amsterdam, and other Dutch cities, recall the dignified domestic architecture of Wren, built in the days of 'Dutch William.' *See* FLORIS, KAMPEN, KEY, KEYSER, POST.

Baroque architecture, favoured in all the Catholic countries of Europe, made little appeal to the Dutch, who stripped all trappings from inside their churches after they became Protestant at the Reformation; but in Catholic Belgium there was great activity, not only in building new churches at Antwerp (Jesuit church, 1614–21), Brussels (Notre-Dame du Béguinage, 1664), Louvain (St Michel, 1650), Namur (St Loup, 1621–53), but in decorating existing churches internally with ornate pulpits, confessionals, and altar-pieces. *See* FAYD'HERBE, RUBENS, VINGBOOMS.

The wonderful row of guild houses in the Grande Place at Brussels, erected between 1697 and 1752, are baroque or rococo in character.

Belgian and Dutch architecture of the nineteenth century calls for little comment. The Bourse at Brussels (1874) is typical of French architecture of the period. Neither the overpowering Palais de Justice at Brussels (1866–83), nor the railway station at Amsterdam (1889, by Cuypers), nor the grandiose Palace of Peace at The Hague (finished 1913) can find many admirers to-day. From Holland, however, has come some of the impulse that created the so-called 'Modern Movement in architecture' early in the present century. One of the pioneers of that movement was H. P. Berlage (q.v.), designer of the Bourse at Amsterdam (1899–1903); and a prominent leader of the movement was W. M. Dudok (q.v.), most of whose work was done in Hilversum. The extensive housing schemes carried out in Holland after the First World War aroused great interest, as did some of the factories and department stores built at the same period. The rebuilding of Rotterdam since the Second World War has been notable. *See* OUD.

> *See* M. Laurent, *L'Architecture en Belgique*, 1928; M. Schmitz, *L'Architecture moderne en Belgique*, 1937; S. Sitwell, *The Netherlands*, 1948; M. Beasley, *The Architecture of the Netherlands*, 1959.

Belgiojoso, Lodovico Barbiano (*b.* Milan, 1909), Italian architect;

senior surviving partner of the firm of Banfi, Belgiojoso, Peressuti, & Rogers, practising in Milan. Gian Luigi Banfi (*b.* 1910) died in 1945. The three other partners all graduated in architecture at the Milan Polytechnic in 1932. The principal buildings designed by the firm include numerous blocks of flats in Milan; the pavilion of the Italian Merchant Navy at the Paris Exhibition (1937); buildings at several other exhibitions in Milan and Rome (1936 onwards); the Sun Treatment Centre at Legnano (1939); the town plan for Aosta; and the Central Post Office at Rome.

Bell, in classical architecture, the core or solid central portion of a Corinthian capital, surrounded and partially concealed by carved acanthus leaves.

Bell, Henry, commonly called 'Bell of Lynn' (*b.* King's Lynn, *c.* 1653; *d.* there, 17 April 1717), English architect and engraver. He is known to have designed the Exchange, now the Customs House (1683), and the Duke's Head Inn (1685) in the Tuesday Market Place; also possibly Clifton House in Queen Street—all at Lynn; and may have been responsible for the rebuilding of North Runcton Church, Norfolk (1703–13). His Customs House is a picturesque and attractive building.

Bell-tower, *see* CAMPANILE.

Belvedere (Ital., fine view), a structure erected upon the roof of a palace or house, open to the air on three sides, and commanding a view. There are many examples in Italian Renaissance architecture.

Bema (Gk *bēma*, a step, hence a raised place for speaking from). Originally a low platform used by Athenian orators; later the raised sanctuary or chancel of an early Christian church, between the apse and the chancel steps.

Bench End, the end of a bench or seat in a church, often carved with great imagination and beauty in English churches of late Gothic date. *See also* PEW.

Benjamin, Asher (*b.* Greenfield, Massachusetts, 15 June 1773; *d.* there, 26 July 1845), American architect and writer on architecture. For some time he lived at Windsor, Vermont, where he designed two houses and, apparently, the Old South Congregational Meeting House. He also did some teaching

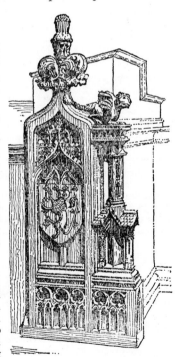

BENCH-END. Manchester Cathedral

of architecture. Buildings attributed to him include the First Congregational Church at Bennington, Vermont (1806); the West Church, Boston (1806); the Parish Church, Bedford, Massachusetts; and the Old Congregational Church at Northampton, burnt down many years ago. He is best known, however, for his books: *The Country Builder's Assistant*, 1797; *The American Builder's Companion* (with D. Reynard), 1806; *The Rudiments of Architecture*, 1814; and *The Practical House Carpenter*, 1830.

Bennett, Sir Thomas Penberthy (*b.* London, 14 Aug. 1887), English architect; Chairman of Crawley New Town since 1947, and of Stevenage Development Corporation, 1951–3. He was trained in London, and was chief assistant to A. J. Davis (q.v.) in 1919–20. For many years he was head of the School of Architecture at the Northern Polytechnic, London. During both world wars he was in Government service, becoming Director of Works at the Ministry of Works during the Second World War. His very extensive private practice has included large blocks of offices in London (Great Westminster House, Neville House, Cleland House, Atlantic House, Sentinel House, etc.); large blocks of London flats, in the design of which he is a recognized specialist (Eyre Court, Prince's Gate Court, Dorset House, Westminster Gardens, Marsham Court, etc.); the Saville Theatre; John Barnes's Store, Hampstead; housing schemes at Greenwich and Hornsey; several factories and banks; flour-mills; King Edward VII Hospital for Officers; and Old People's Homes for the Linen and Woollen Drapers' Association.

Bentley, John Francis (*b.* Doncaster, 30 Jan. 1839; *d.* Clapham, 2 Mar. 1902), English architect, was the designer of Westminster (Roman Catholic) Cathedral. He was originally trained as an engineer and builder. In 1862 he joined the Church of Rome and, having had some training in architecture under H. Clutton, started practice as an architect. Up to 1895 his work consisted mainly of houses, schools, and churches in the Gothic style, notably the fine Church of the Holy Rood at Watford (1887). In 1895 he was appointed architect for the great new Roman Catholic Cathedral at Westminster. The authorities having decided that the building must be Byzantine in style—to avoid rivalry with the Gothic of Westminster Abbey not far away—Bentley made an extensive tour of south-eastern Europe to study Byzantine architecture. His design, as carried out, shows an original treatment of that style; but he did not live to see the completion of the building, and the decoration is still (in 1959) unfinished. His other new churches were St Mary, Cadogan Street, Chelsea (1875–9); Our Lady of the Holy Souls, Kensal New Town (1880–2); Corpus Christi, Brixton Hill (1886–7); and St Luke, Chiddingstone Causeway (1897–8)—the last-named Anglican, the others Roman Catholic. He also built St Thomas's Seminary, Hammersmith (1876–88); the Redemptorist Monastery, Clapham (1891–3); and St John's Preparatory School, Beaumont College, Old Windsor (1883–8).

See biography by his daughter, Winifred de L'Hôpital, 1919.

Berettini, or **Berrettini, Pietro,** commonly called **'Pietro da Cortona'**

(*b.* Cortona, 1 Nov. 1596; *d.* Rome, 16 May 1669), Italian architect and painter; one of the early exponents of Baroque architecture (q.v.). He was the son of a carver, and was apprenticed to the Florentine painter Commodi with whom he went to Rome in 1613 and there painted some frescoes for Cardinal Barberini. His first work in architecture was a large pavilion, since demolished, in the Villa del Pineto (1625–30). As a result of his successful design of the church of SS. Luca e Martina, Rome, he was appointed in 1634 to be Director of the Accademia di S. Luca, an institute of artistic design. From 1640 to 1647 he worked in Florence, and executed the decorations of the Pitti Palace there. Returning to Rome in 1647, he designed new façades for the churches of S. Maria della Pace (1657), a particularly beautiful work, and of S. Maria in Via Lata (1656 62); also a new dome for S. Carlo al Corso (1665), etc.

See monograph by A. Muñoz, 1921.

Berlage, Hendrik Petrus (*b.* Amsterdam, 21 Feb. 1856; *d.* The Hague, 12 Aug. 1934), Dutch architect, became a pioneer of the 'Modern Movement' in architecture. After being trained in Switzerland and travelling in Italy, he started independent practice about 1882 in Amsterdam, where his most important building was the Bourse or New Exchange (1899–1903), which greatly influenced subsequent architecture throughout western Europe. He was awarded the R.I.B.A. Royal Gold Medal in 1932.

See monographs by M. Eisler, 1921, and J. Gratama, 1925.

Bernini, Giovanni Lorenzo (*b.* Naples, 7 Dec. 1598; *d.* Rome, 28 Nov. 1680), Italian architect and sculptor, was, with the possible exception of Borromini (q.v.), the leading figure of the Baroque movement in Rome. The son of a Florentine sculptor working in Naples, he went to Rome in 1604; and there, while still a boy of only fourteen or fifteen, carved or modelled two portrait busts of such surprising excellence that he soon earned the patronage of several influential cardinals and ultimately came to be employed by the Pope himself, and took a prominent part in the transformation of Rome. His chief architectural works there included the completion of St Peter's, notably the baldaquin (q.v.) over the high altar; the *Scala Regia*, with its ingenious use of distorted perspective to increase the apparent length; the magnificent colonnaded *piazza* (1656–1667); the church of S. Andrea al Quirinale (1678); and many beautiful fountains. In 1665 he visited Paris to advise Louis XIV on the rebuilding of the Louvre, and there met Wren (q.v.). Of his theatrical but marvellously competent sculpture, the finest examples are the 'Apollo and Daphne' in the Borghese Gallery, and the 'Ecstasy of St Teresa' in the church of S. Maria della Vittoria—both in Rome.

See monographs by F. Baldinucci, 1682 (reprinted 1948); S. Fraschetti, 1900; C. Ricci, 1910; M. Reymond, 1911; M. von Boehn, 1912; A. Muñoz, 1925; E. Benkard, 1926; R. Pane, 1953; R. Wittkower, 1955.

Berruguete, Alonso (*b.* Parades de Nava, 1480; *d.* Toledo, 1561), was a Spanish architect and sculptor, excelling in both of these arts.

He went to Italy about 1503, studying especially the work of Michelangelo and Bramante. Returning to Spain in 1520, he designed the portal of the Hospital of S. Juan Bautista, Toledo; the courtyard of the Irish College, Salamanca; and, in part, the tower of the cathedral, Murcia.

See monograph by Orneta, 1917.

Bevel, a sloping surface, usually on an edge. *See also* CANT, CHAMFER, SPLAY.

Bianco, Baccio di Bartolomeo (*b.* Como, *c.* 1580; *d.* Genoa, *c.* 1651), Italian architect. He started work as a painter, but soon attracted the attention of members of the powerful family of Balbi in Genoa, for whom he erected, from 1609 onwards, three fine palaces in the Via Balbi in that city, viz. the Universitá (1623); the Palazzo Balbi-Durazzo-Pallavicini (1620); and the Palazzo Balbi-Senarega. These palaces, of which the Universitá was severely damaged in the Second World War, were magnificently planned; and their splendid staircases served as a model for those in many great mansions and London club-houses built by Barry (q.v.) and other architects in the nineteenth century. Bianco, who became the city architect of Genoa in 1620, also built the Villa Durazzo, east of that city.

Bibiena Family of Italian architects (seventeenth to eighteenth centuries), notable as designers of theatres and theatrical scenery in Italy, Austria, France, and the small princely court capitals of Germany. They derived their name from Bibiena or Bibbiena in the Casentino. The chief members of the family were FRANCESCO BIBIENA (1659–1739), who built theatres at Verona and Nancy; and his nephews ANTONIO BIBIENA (1700–74), who built theatres at Bologna, Livorno, Mantua, Pistoia, Rome, and Siena, and GIUSEPPE GALLI BIBIENA (1696–1756), who published many magnificent drawings of theatrical designs.

See monograph by C. Ricci, 1915.

Billet Moulding, an ornamental moulding used in Byzantine and Romanesque architecture, and consisting of small cylindrical blocks arranged in a sunk moulding. Its name originated in the supposed resemblance of these blocks to 'billets' of wood. (*Illustrated* MOULDINGS, ENRICHED (ROMANESQUE).)

Binder, in a framed 'double' timber floor (*see* FLOOR), a large transverse beam supporting the joists.

Bird's beak moulding, in Gothic architecture, a moulding used beneath the abacus of a capital, and supposed to resemble, in its sectional contour, the downward-curving beak of a bird.

Blind storey, in medieval architecture, an alternative name for the Triforium (q.v.), sometimes called a 'blind storey' in contradistinction to the Clear Storey or Clerestorey (q.v.) because the latter is pierced with windows, whereas the triforium arches open into a dark enclosed space beneath the sloping roof over the aisle.

Blind tracery, in Gothic architecture, an imitation of actual window tracery on a flat surface, carved in solid wood or stone, e.g. on internal wooden chancel screens, or on external walls of churches, etc.

Blocking course, in classical architecture, a course of solid masonry built upon the top of a projecting cornice; and, incidentally, serving to neutralize any tendency of the cornice to overturn the wall.

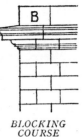

BLOCKING
COURSE
(marked B)

Blomfield, Sir Arthur William, A.R.A. (*b.* London, 6 Mar. 1829; *d.* Broadway, Worcestershire, 30 Oct. 1899), English architect; R.I.B.A. Royal Gold Medallist, 1891; son of the Bishop of London; articled to P. Hardwick (q.v.), and began practice 1856. He restored several English cathedrals, including Canterbury, Chichester, Lincoln, and Salisbury. In 1887 he became architect to the Bank of England and designed the Law Courts Branch. His other works include the Royal College of Music, Kensington (1883); St Mary's Church, Portsea; the nave and transepts of Southwark Cathedral (1890–7); the Cathedral Library, Hereford; school chapels at Malvern and Haileybury; the Whitgift School, Croydon; the Bancroft School; Selwyn College, Cambridge; Sion College Library, London, etc.

Blomfield, Sir Reginald Theodore, R.A. (*b.* Bow, Devon, 20 Dec. 1856; *d.* Hampstead, 27 Dec. 1942), English architect and writer on architecture; President R.I.B.A., 1912–14; R.I.B.A. Royal Gold Medallist, 1913; son of a clergyman. After leaving Oxford he was articled to his uncle, Sir A. W. Blomfield (q.v.). His first two books—*The Formal Garden in England,* 1892, and *A History of Renaissance Architecture in England,* 1897—led to a practice which included the remodelling of several country mansions and their gardens, e.g. Brocklesby Park, Apethorpe, Chequers, and Mellerstain. Among his other important works were a large warehouse in Westminster for the Army and Navy Stores; the Usher Art Gallery, Public Library, and Water Tower—all at Lincoln; Lady Margaret Hall, Oxford; the United University Club, the refacing of the Carlton Club, Lambeth Bridge, the Quadrant in Regent Street—all in London; the 'Cross of Sacrifice,' the Menin Gate, and several cemeteries for the War Graves Commission (1918–26); 'The Headrow' (a new street) in Leeds. Besides the books mentioned above, he produced several other scholarly volumes, including his *History of French Architecture from 1494 to 1774,* in four volumes, and *Memoirs of an Architect,* 1932.

Blondel, François (*b.* Ribemont, 1617, *d.* Paris, 21 Jan. 1686), French architect and writer on architecture. He resembled Wren (q.v.), Vanbrugh (q.v.), and Perrault (q.v.) in the fact that he turned to architecture late in life. Previously he had commanded a galley, travelled through Europe as a nobleman's tutor, undertaken a diplomatic mission, and carried out civil engineering work of some importance. Yet in 1671, at the mature age of fifty-two, he was suddenly appointed director of the newly founded Academy of Architecture. His only buildings of any importance were three gates in Paris—the Portes St Bernard, St Antoine, and St Denis—the last-named a fine design.   All were built in 1672–3; and, after this brief experience of actual practice, he devoted himself to writing about architecture for the rest of his life.   His chief book was the *Cours d'Architecture*, 1675–8, composed of his various professorial lectures at the Academy, and dealing with the artistic theory of design (based upon Vitruvius, q.v.) as well as with planning and construction.

Blondel, Jacques-François (*b.* Rouen, 8 Jan. 1705; *d.* Paris, 9 Jan. 1774), French architect and writer on architecture.   He seems to have been no relation to François Blondel (q.v.), but was the nephew of yet another architect Blondel, JEAN-FRANÇOIS BLONDEL (*b.* 1683; *d.* 1748), whose work was relatively unimportant but included the Bourse at Rouen (*c.* 1725), the Château de Saussure (1723), and other houses near Geneva.   Confusion between the three Blondels is increased by the fact that Jacques-François, as well as François, wrote a separate and later *Cours d'Architecture*, published 1771–7, in addition to two other books: *Architecture Française*, 1771–7, and *Maisons de Plaisance*, 1737–8.   He too served as professor of architecture at the Academy, 1762–74.   His actual buildings were few, as he devoted most of his time to writing and to the conduct of an *atelier*, where Ledoux (q.v.) was one of his pupils.

See monograph by A. Prost, 1860.

Blore, Edward, F.R.S. (*b.* Derby, 13 Sept. 1787; *d.* London, 4 Sept. 1879), English architect, draughtsman, and writer on architecture. He was employed for many years in illustrating books on architecture and topography, his father having been interested in topography as a hobby; and Edward's work included illustrations to his father's *History of Rutland*.   It was in the course of such work that he met Sir Walter Scott, for whom he designed Abbotsford in 1816.   From that moment his success was assured, and he had an enormous practice.   He completed Buckingham Palace, begun by John Nash (q.v.), and restored Windsor Castle and Hampton Court Palace as architect to the Crown.   Other restorations included Peterborough, Norwich, Ely, and Glasgow cathedrals; Westminster Abbey; Merton and St John's College chapels at Oxford; and Lambeth Palace. Among his new buildings were the Pitt Press, Cambridge (1831–2); Worsley Hall, Lancashire (1840–6); Goodrich Court, Hereford (1828); Latimers, Buckinghamshire; Merevale Hall, Worcestershire; Pull Court, Worcestershire; Ramsey Abbey, Huntingdonshire; Government House, Sydney, Australia (1837); and a large number of churches.   In 1824 he published *Monumental Remains of Eminent Persons*.   He was a founder member of the R.I.B.A.

Boasting, in masonry, means the rough shaping of a block of stone by means of a broad chisel called a ' boaster,' preliminary to ornamental carving, e.g. of a statue or a sculptured capital.

Bodley, George Frederick, R.A. (*b.* Hull, 14 Mar. 1827; *d.* Water

Eaton, 21 Oct. 1907), English architect. A pupil of Sir George Gilbert Scott (q.v.), he became the most distinguished exponent of revived fourteenth-century Gothic. His work, mostly in partnership with Thomas Garner (1839–1906), included new buildings at Magdalen and University Colleges, Oxford; Queen's College Chapel and a new block at King's College, Cambridge; Marlborough College Chapel; Holy Trinity Church, Kensington; Eton Mission Church, Hackney Wick; churches at Eccleston, Hoar Cross, Pendlebury, Clumber, Burton, Chapel Allerton (Leeds), All Saints at Cambridge, St Faith's at Brentford; the offices of the London School Board, etc.; also the marble reredos at St Paul's Cathedral, London, destroyed in the Second World War. In collaboration with James Vaughan, he designed the cathedral at Washington, U.S.A., and the cathedrals at San Francisco and at Hobart (Tasmania). He acted as assessor in the Liverpool Cathedral competition in 1903, and subsequently as advisory architect after Giles Scott (q.v.) had won it.

Boffrand, Germain (*b.* Nantes, 7 May 1667; *d.* Paris, 18 Mar. 1754), French architect, went to Paris in 1681 and was at first apprenticed to Girardon, the sculptor. Turning, however, to architecture, he became an assistant to J.-H. Mansart (q.v.). In 1709 he was elected to the Academy of Architecture. His large practice included numerous mansions in Paris, among them the Hôtel de Tourcy (1714) and the Hôtel Amelot; also the decoration of the Hôtel Soubise (*c.* 1740). Outside Paris he designed mansions at Nancy and Luneville in France, and the château at Bouchefort near Brussels. He followed contemporary fashion in producing a *Livre d'Architecture,* 1745.

Bolection Moulding, in architecture of the later Renaissance, and especially in wood panelling, a moulding which projects in front of the face of the framing. Used with great effect by Wren.

Bond, in walling of brickwork or masonry, an arrangement of bricks or of stone blocks in such a manner as to give the maximum strength and stability. *See* ENGLISH BOND, FLEMISH BOND.

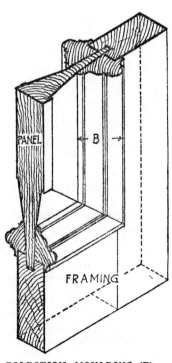

BOLECTION MOULDING (B) *on a panelled wooden door*

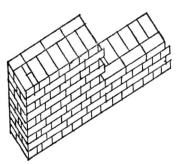

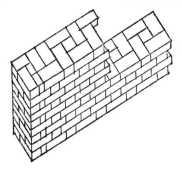

BOND, ENGLISH, for a 1½-brick wall   *BOND, FLEMISH, for a 1½-brick wall*

Bonnet Tile, the curved or bonnet-shaped tiles used to cover the junction of plain tiles at the hip (q.v.) of a hipped roof.

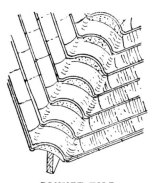

BONNET TILE

Bonomi, Joseph, A.R.A. (*b.* Rome, 19 Jan. 1739; *d.* London, 19 Mar. 1808), Italo-English architect, was educated at the Collegio Romano in Rome, and then became the protégé of an Italian nobleman who practised as an amateur architect. He was invited by the brothers Adam (q.v.) to join them in London in 1767, and remained with them for several years. After a further period as assistant to Thomas Leverton (q.v.), he established a flourishing practice of his own in London, and was elected A.R.A. in 1789. He became so fashionable as a designer and remodeller of country houses that he figures in that capacity in Jane Austen's *Sense and Sensibility*. His younger son, also named Joseph (1796–1878), after training as a sculptor, became interested in the then new science of Egyptology, and acted as assistant curator of Sir John Soane's Museum, 1861–78. The elder Joseph's country mansions included Dale Park, Madehurst (1784–8); Ashtead Park, Surrey (1790); Eastwell Park, Kent (1793–1800); Longford Hall, Shropshire (1794–7); Barrells, Warwickshire (*c.* 1795); Roseneath, Dunbartonshire (1803–6).

Borromini, Francesco (*b.* Bissone, in Canton Ticino, 1599; *d.* Rome, 1667), an Italian Baroque architect who arrived in Rome as a youth about 1617, and worked first for Maderno (q.v.) and then for Bernini (q.v.), whose immense prestige as leader of the Baroque movement in Rome he was eventually to rival. Bernini, however, was as talented a sculptor as an architect, whereas Borromini's brilliant genius was confined to architecture. His chief buildings were the churches of S. Carlo alle Quattro Fontane (1634–67), of S. Agnese in the Piazza Navona (1652–7) (except the two *campanili* added by Carlo Fontana, q.v.), and of S. Filippo Neri (1637–50)—all these in Rome; the Propaganda Fide, Rome (1646–57); the Palazzo Falconieri, Rome; and also additions to the Villa Falconieri at Frascati (1638–41). He committed suicide in 1667.

See monographs by A. Muñoz; H. Sedlmayer, 1930; G. C. Argan, 1952.

Borrowed Light, a window inside a building—usually in a partition between a passage without external windows and a room which has external windows, giving light 'borrowed' from the latter.

Boss, in medieval architecture, a keystone (q.v.), ornamentally carved and often also painted and gilded, at the intersection of ribs in a vaulted roof. There are fine examples in the cloisters of Canterbury and Norwich cathedrals. Carved wooden bosses were also used at the rectangular intersection of beams in open wooden ceilings.

BOSS. (R=*ribs of vaulting*)

Boulevard (Fr.), a broad avenue planted with trees. This term, first used in the eighteenth century, has, however, a more specific application, and meant originally the wide avenues laid out on the site of ramparts, demolished as they became obsolete. Paris provides the most notable example, with two circuits of boulevards representing two concentric rings of fortifications; but many other continental cities can show a similar history, and this factor has greatly influenced and facilitated their modern town-planning.

Boullée, Étienne Louis (*b.* Paris, 12 Feb. 1728; *d.* there, 6 Feb. 1799), French architect, whose designs marked a reaction from current tradition and an approach to archaeology. He became a member of the Academy in 1762, and for a time he was chief architect to the King of Prussia. His principal buildings in Paris were the Hôtel Brunoy (1772), the Hôtel Thun, and the Hôtel de Monville. Elsewhere he built the châteaux of Tassé at Chaville, Perreux at Nogent-sur-Marne, and Chauvry at Montmorency. Many other gigantic and fantastic projects remained only designs on paper.

See H. Rosenau, *Boullée's Treatise on Architecture*, 1953.

Bow-string Truss, a Belfast truss (q.v.). (*Illustrated* ROOF-TRUSS.)

Bowtell (rare; and occasionally **Boltel**), either (i) a rounded moulding, torus (q.v.), or bead (q.v.); or (ii) a small shaft on a clustered pillar.

Bow-window, a curved bay-window (q.v.).

C

Brace, in any framed structure, but more especially in timber-framing, a diagonal strut serving to stiffen the horizontal and vertical members.

Bracket, a support projecting from a wall or column. In classical architecture it is usually called an ancon, a console, or a modillion (qq.v.); in medieval building, a corbel (q.v.); in modern construction, a cantilever (q.v.).

Bramante, Donato (*b.* Monte Asdruvaldo, near Urbino, 1444; *d.* Rome, 14 Mar. or 1 April 1514), Italian architect; a leader of the Early Renaissance in Rome. From about 1480 to 1499 he worked in Milan; thereafter in Rome. Before 1482 he was chiefly employed in painting. His principal buildings were S. Maria presso S. Satiro, Milan (1482); the apse and sacristy of Pavia Cathedral (1488); the apses of S. Maria delle Grazie, Milan (1494 onwards); the Canonico and Monastery of S. Ambrogio, Milan (1492–8); the portico of the cathedral of Abbiategrasso (1497); the *Tempietto* at S. Pietro in Montorio, Rome (1503); the cloister of S. Maria della Pace, Rome (1504); the remodelling of the Vatican Palace, Rome, with the great niche, staircase, and colonnade of the Belvedere, and the Cortile di S. Damaso. His precise share in designing the Palazzo della Cancelleria, Rome (1483–1511), is uncertain. From 1504 onwards he was chiefly engaged in rebuilding St Peter's, Rome.

See monographs by P. L. Pungileoni, 1836; H. Semper, 1879; H. von Geymüller, 1884; F. Malaguzzi-Valeri, 1924; C. Baroni, 1945.

Brasses, Memorial. These interesting examples of medieval craftsmanship are found in far larger numbers in England than in any other European country, and are particularly useful for their recording of contemporary armour, costume, heraldry, and lettering. The 4,000 examples estimated to survive in English churches date from the thirteenth to the mid seventeenth centuries. As they are let into stone slabs in the floor, especially of the chancel, many are badly worn, but to-day most are protected by mats or carpets. They are engraved plates of brass, formerly called 'latten.' The eastern counties are particularly rich in examples. These include fine effigies of knights at Stoke d'Abernon, Surrey; Trumpington, Cambridge; Acton Burnell, Shropshire; and St Mary's, Warwickshire; of clerics at Horsemonden, Kent, and New College, Oxford; of noble ladies at Cobham, Kent, and Trotton, Sussex.

See monographs by C. Boutell, 1849; J. G. Waller, 1864; H. W. Macklin, 1890 and 1907; J. S. M. Ward, 1912.

Brattice, in medieval military architecture, a temporary wooden gallery for use in a siege.

BRATTICE or HOARDING

Brattishing, a form of ornamental cresting used in English late Gothic architecture on the top of a screen, and composed of 'Tudor flowers' (q.v.) and conventional leaves, together with miniature battlements (q.v.).

Brazilian Architecture. When Brazil was discovered and annexed by the Portuguese in 1500, that vast territory contained none of the Indian architecture found in Mexico (q.v.) or Peru; and the first notable buildings were churches and convents erected by Jesuit missionaries. By the middle of the eighteenth century these included the cathedral at Belem do Para; the great church at Recife (1729); the church of the Conceicão da Praia at Bahia, a notable example (sent over from Portugal in numbered sections); and many large Baroque churches in the mining districts (*Minas Geraes*). Rio de Janeiro was developed rather later, but its cathedral and vice-regal palace date from the latter part of the eighteenth century. The following century was marked, as in Mexico, by the importation of revived historical styles from Europe; but after about 1920 Brazilian architecture forged ahead, and the cities of Rio, São Paulo, Belo Horizonte, etc., abound in examples of advanced modern architecture. The leader of this movement was Oscar Niemeyer (q.v.).

See monographs on recent architecture in Brazil by G. E. K. Smith, 1943; E. Graeff and others, 1947; H. E. Mindlin, 1956. *See also* G. Bazin, *L'Architecture religieuse baroque au Brésil*, 1955.

Breast, *see* CHIMNEY BREASTS.

Bressummer, properly **Breastsummer** (Fr. *sommier*, a beam), a massive beam, spanning a wide opening, such as a fire-place opening between the chimney breasts (q.v.).

Brettingham, Matthew (*b.* Norwich, 1699; *d.* in the same place, 1769), English architect, was the son of a bricklayer. He acted as clerk of works or resident architect under William Kent (q.v.) during the building of Holkham Hall, Norfolk (1734 onwards), and after its completion remained in charge of the building till 1759. In 1761 he published a book describing and illustrating this enormous mansion without regard to Kent, though it seems certain that Kent and his patron, Lord Burlington (q.v.), were really responsible for it. So far as can be ascertained, Brettingham did design the following: Benacre Hall, Suffolk (1763–4); Gunton Hall, Norfolk (after 1742, since gutted by fire); the north-east wing of Kedleston Hall, Derby (1758); the nave, crossing, and transepts of St Margaret's Church, King's Lynn (1742–6); the Shirehouse, Norwich (1749, since demolished); several houses in Norwich; and four large houses in London, of which York House, 86 Pall Mall, for the Duke of York (1760–7), and Norfolk House, St James's Square, for the Duke of Norfolk, (1747–56) have been demolished in recent years. The names of these two clients show that the bricklayer's son had climbed a long way, indeed he had become a popular member of White's Club. His son Matthew (1725–1803) was therefore able to make the 'Grand Tour' of Italy and Greece in leisure and comfort (1747–54). He continued his father's practice for a time, but then accepted a sinecure from Lord North, and retired to spend his remaining years at Norwich in slippered ease.

Breuer, Marcel Lajos (b. Pécs, Hungary, 1902), architect. After studying at the Bauhaus at Weimar, Germany, 1920-4, he joined the staff under Gropius (q.v.); worked there 1925-8 after the Bauhaus had been moved to Dessau; then went to Berlin and carried out numerous commissions for interior decoration and furniture. From 1931 to 1935 he practised in London in collaboration with F. R. S. Yorke (q.v.), one of their buildings being a remarkable house at Angmering, Sussex. In 1937 he went to America as associate professor under Gropius (q.v.) (formerly his chief at the Bauhaus) at Harvard, and also practised as his partner, 1937-42. His buildings include the Civic Hospital at Bogotá, Colombia (1947-8); airport at Fairbanks, Alaska, and a store at New York (1950); a theatre at Bronxville and public library at Grosse Pointe, Michigan (1951); library, etc., at Hunter College, New York (1952-4); church and convent of St John, Collegeville, Minnesota; several schools in Connecticut; the Bijenkorf Store, Rotterdam (1953); housing at Princeton University (1954); dormitory block at Vassar College (1952); joint architect of U.N.E.S.C.O. Building, Paris (1958).

See monographs by P. Blake, 1949, and G. C. Argan, 1957.

Brick-nogging, the filling with bricks of the spaces between the vertical 'studs' (posts) of a timber partition.

Bricks and Brickwork. The most primitive method of building with clay is in clay-lump, represented in recent times by 'cob' (q.v.) and *pisé* (q.v.). In the earliest homes of civilized man—Egypt and Mesopotamia—clay or mud bricks, moulded by hand and mixed with straw to make them tough (*vide* references in the Old Testament), were dried in the sun, and lasted a surprisingly long time; but, even in those ancient lands, kiln-dried bricks were used at a very early date. Over most of western Asia (*see* ASSYRIAN, BABYLONIAN, and PERSIAN ARCHITECTURE) good building stone is scarce, so the use of brick has always been traditional there, for arches and vaults and domes as well as for walls; but these were often cased with glazed and coloured tiles if in palaces, etc. The Greeks used bricks only for their humbler buildings, and sometimes as a core in walls. Roman bricks and brickwork were excellent, as may be seen in many English ruins and museums. The chapters in Vitruvius (q.v.) on brickwork are worth reading. From the fifth century to the fourteenth, bricks were hardly ever used in England, but were then introduced into East Anglia from the Continent, mainly by Flemish refugees. Examples are Queen's College, Cambridge (c. 1450); the church at St Osyth, Essex (early sixteenth century); Hampton Court Palace (Tudor portion) (early sixteenth century); Eastbury Manor House, Barking (c. 1550). Wren's handling of brickwork was excellent, e.g. at Chelsea Hospital and Hampton Court. From the late eighteenth century onwards yellow 'stock' bricks became popular in London.

The size of a brick has been standardized to various dimensions at intervals ever since 1477, and is now $8\frac{3}{4}$ inches by $4\frac{3}{16}$ inches by $2\frac{5}{8}$ inches to $2\frac{7}{8}$ inches. Outside England there is much notable historical brick architecture in Prussia and the Low Countries. A modern master of architectural brickwork was Sir Edwin Lutyens (q.v.).

See N. Lloyd, *A History of English Brickwork* (2nd ed.), 1935; *also* articles on ARCH, BOND, BRICK-NOGGING, GAUGED BRICK-WORK.

Brise Soleil (Fr., from *briser*, to break, *soleil*, sun: literally 'sun-break,' generally translated as 'sun-baffle'), a form of screen designed to diminish the glare of the sun upon windows in a building. Some such contrivance has been used in hot countries for centuries, e.g. in the form of *shish* (q.v.) and *mushrabiyyah* (q.v.) lattices, and *qamariyyah* (q.v.) pierced stone screens or grilles. (This type was also used in India, e.g. at the Taj Mahal.) Venetian blinds (q.v.) fulfil the same purpose, and modern types with semi-transparent plastic slats give a pleasant diffused light. The French architect 'Le Corbusier' (q.v.) introduced a more substantial type of baffle in 1933, but development of the *brise soleil* since that date has been most notable in Brazil, where he became consultant architect to the Ministry of Health and Education in 1937. Their new offices at Rio were furnished with adjustable horizontal baffles manipulated with a crank. The later example, however, illustrated here, from the A.B.I. (Associação Brasiliera de Imprensa) building at Rio, has adjustable vertical concrete baffles—each 32 inches deep and 2¾

ELEVATION

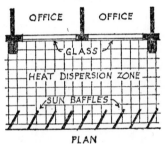

PLAN

BRISE SOLEIL. A Brazilian example

inches thick—diagonally set on the outer face of the building and separated from the office windows by a wide verandah or 'heat dispersion zone.' Many other types of baffle are used in Brazil, including the fixed lattices and grilles and the Venetian blinds mentioned above.

British School at Athens, Speusippe Street, Athens (London Office: 31–4 Gordon Square, W.C.1), was founded in 1886 'to promote the study of Greek archaeology in all its departments,' including Greek architecture. It is maintained by corporate and personal subscriptions, and also receives an annual grant from the British Treasury. The R.I.B.A. is represented upon its Managing Committee. There is a resident director, a residential hostel, and an excellent library. The Athens Bursary of the R.I.B.A. was first awarded in 1930, and the Florence Bursary (1933) also allows architects an opportunity for study in Athens.

British School at Rome, Valle Giulia, Rome, 51 (London Office:

1 Lowther Gardens, Kensington, S.W.7), was founded in 1901 and is financed from the funds of the 1851 Exhibition Commissioners. Up to 1916 it occupied rooms in the Palazzo Odescalchi in the Corso, Rome, Dr Thomas Ashby being director and Mrs Eugénie Strong sub-director. There was no residential accommodation for students. After the Rome Exhibition of 1910 the city authorities offered the school a fine site in the Valle Giulia, opposite the Borghese Gardens, for a new building (including hostel accommodation for twenty-four students), to be a replica of the British Pavilion designed for the exhibition by Sir E. L. Lutyens (q.v.). Work on this new building began in 1912, but was delayed by the First World War, and was not completed till 1916. Subsequent additions were made in 1923 and 1928. There is a resident director. The R.I.B.A. is represented on the school's Faculty of Architecture. The first Rome Scholarship in Architecture was awarded to H. C. Bradshaw in 1913.

British Standard Specifications, specifications for various building materials and components, etc., issued by the British Standards Institution (founded 1901) from its offices at 2 Park Street, London, W.1, and continually brought up to date.

Broach, the half-pyramid of masonry formed by the intersection of an octagonal stone spire with a pyramid rising from a square tower beneath. Where broaches are used the square tower has no parapet. The broach spire is especially characteristic of English Gothic churches of the thirteenth to fourteenth centuries in Northamptonshire. (*Illustrated* SPIRE.)

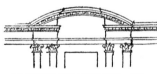

BROKEN PEDIMENT. Three 18th-century examples

Brodrick, Cuthbert (*b. c.* 1822; *d.* Gorey, Jersey, C.I., 1905), English architect; designer of the Town Hall, Leeds (1853–8); also of the Corn Exchange (1860–3) and the Mechanics' Institute, both in Leeds; and of Hull Town Hall (1862–6).

Broken Pediment. Whereas a normal pediment (q.v.) is the gable-end of a classical building, and has its moulded cornice carried up from its base to its apex, a broken pediment is a perverse variant from the normal, adopted in late Roman (e.g. at Petra) and in Baroque architecture, where the apex is deliberately omitted or 'broken,' together with its cornice mouldings.

Brown, Lancelot, who was commonly called 'Capability Brown' (*b.* Kirkharle, Northumberland, 1716; *d.* Hampton Court, 6 Feb.

1783), was a pioneer of the landscape garden or *jardin anglais* (Fr.), supposedly a return from formal gardening to nature, but in reality very artful. His early years, 1732–49, were spent as a working gardener at Kirkharle, at Wotton near Aylesbury, and at Stowe, where he met William Kent, the architect (q.v.), the real father of landscape gardening. In 1749 Brown gave up his post at Stowe and started practice as a landscape architect, soon becoming busy, famous, and rich. He now began to undertake the design of stables, summer-houses, and other ancillary buildings in the parks and gardens that he was laying out. The actual erection was done by a builder named Holland, whose son Henry (q.v.) became an architect, joined Brown as junior partner about 1772, and married his daughter in 1773. Brown's work included some substantial architectural commissions, among them Croome Court, Worcestershire (1751–2); Spring Hill, Worcestershire (1763); Claremont House, Surrey (1772); Benham Park, Berkshire (1772–5); and many other mansions since demolished.

See monograph by D. Stroud, 1950.

B.R.S., abbreviation for Building Research Station (q.v.).

Bruand, Libéral (*b.* Paris, *c.* 1637; *d.* there, 22 Nov. 1697), French architect, elected one of the *architectes du Roi*, was a founder member of the French Academy of Architecture in 1671. He goes down to history as the designer of two enormous hospitals in Paris— the Hôpital de la Salpêtrière (1656–68), with 3,818 beds in wards communicating with a central octagonal domed church, and the even larger Hôtel des Invalides (1670–5), built to accommodate 7,000 military patients. Of the two churches included in this vast group of buildings, that of St Louis-des-Invalides was designed by Bruand, but the magnificent Dôme des Invalides is by J.-H. Mansart (q.v.). These two huge commissions must have brought him a fortune, but he died in poverty.

Bruce, Sir William, Bart., M.P. (*b. c.* 1630; *d.* 1710), Scottish architect, was an extremely pushful person who was granted a lucrative sinecure and created a baronet in 1668 (but not for his architectural work). Little is known of his early career, except that he designed the Gothic tower of the Merchants' House, Glasgow. In 1671 he was appointed King's Surveyor, and proceeded to remodel the royal palace of Holyrood (1671–9). He built himself a small country house at Balcaskie about 1675. Then followed Moncreiffe House (*c.* 1679) and the façade of Drumlanrig (*c.* 1686). Next he built for himself a mansion, Kinross House (1684–95). His largest building, Hopetoun House, West Lothian, was completed in 1703, but afterwards greatly extended by William Adam, Sen. (q.v.). Other work by Bruce included a small house at Auchendinny, 1707. He was elected M.P. for Kinross-shire in 1681.

Brunelleschi, Filippo (*b.* Florence, 1377; *d.* in the same place, 1446), Italian architect and sculptor, generally regarded as the founder of the Renaissance movement in Italian architecture. He started his working life as a goldsmith's apprentice, then tried his hand at sculpture; but was soon inspired to visit Rome, with the idea of reviving some of the glories of classical architecture on returning home. Back at Florence in 1407, he submitted in competition a design for the completion of the cathedral of S. Maria del Fiore with a dome. Although his design was successful in the competition, it was not carried into effect till 1420, and the crowning lantern—for which he left a wooden model, still extant though worm-eaten—was not finished until after his death. Other buildings designed by him included the churches of S. Lorenzo (1420–5) and S. Spirito (1444); the Pazzi Chapel (c. 1430); the Ospedale degli Innocenti (1421); and the Pitti Palace (begun 1435)—all these are in Florence.

See monographs by C. V. Fabriczy, 1892; Leader Scott, 1901; P. Fontana, 1920; A. Venturi, 1923; G. L. Luzzatto, 1926; G. C. Argan, 1955.

Brydon, John McKean (*b*. Dunfermline, Scotland, 1840; *d*. London, 25 May 1901), British architect. After being trained in Liverpool, he studied in Italy, and then became an assistant—first to David Bryce in Edinburgh, and then to Nesfield (q.v.) and Norman Shaw (q.v.) in London. His success in the competition for Chelsea Town Hall (1885) was followed by commissions to design the Chelsea Public Library and Chelsea Polytechnic (1889). In 1891 he won the competition for Bath Municipal Buildings, work which led to his designing the Bath Technical School, Art Gallery, Library, and Pump Room. He built St Peter's Hospital, Henrietta Street (1883–1884); the New Hospital for Women, Euston Road (1889); and the School of Medicine for Women, Handel Street (1896); and in 1898 was selected to design the large block of government offices at the corner of Great George Street and Whitehall, but died before their completion.

BUCRANIUM

B.S.S., abbreviation for British Standard Specifications (q.v.).

Buckling, the bending of a structural member under pressure.

Bucranium (Lat., from Gk *boukranion*), a carved ox-head or ox-skull, used decoratively in classical architecture, generally in combination with garlands.

Buhl (Ger.), or **Boule,** or **Boulle** (Fr.), an ornamental inlay of brass, tortoiseshell, etc., used in French furniture. Derived from the name of a French wood-carver, André Charles Boulle (1642–1732), who worked in the reign of Louis XIV.

Builder, a person who builds: in modern usage and more precisely, (1) a master-builder or building contractor, who employs all 'trades' or categories of building craftsmen, including masons, bricklayers, plasterers, plumbers, and painters; and, for all important building contracts, works under the direction of an architect. The master-builder or building contractor did not make his appearance until the late eighteenth or early nineteenth century; previously each craft had worked under its own master, as is still the custom on small contracts in the north of England, etc.; but this practice has disadvantages, as it leads to friction and divided responsibility. (2) A speculative builder, who erects houses or other buildings at his own risk as a speculation, with a view to making a profit on the site as well as on the building. Speculative builders operated in London as early as the seventeenth century. (3) the term 'builder' is sometimes misapplied to the person who pays for the building—properly the 'building owner'; and also to bricklayers and masons as opposed to carpenters, plumbers, etc.

The Builders' History, by R. W. Postgate, 1923, is chiefly concerned with labour conditions within the industry.

Building Board, a term covering a wide range of artificial products used internally in modern building. All building boards are manufactured in sheets of standard size, and may be classified as (i) fibre board, composed of wood or other fibrous material, shredded and compressed to a uniform consistency, and used for insulating purposes; (ii) built-up or laminated board, consisting of several layers, and used for insulation against damp, noise, heat, and vermin; (iii) plaster board, composed of gypsum or similar materials, faced with cardboard, etc.; and specially useful for fire resistance and as a substitute for ordinary plaster ceilings.

Building By-laws vary greatly in different localities, but are all derived from powers granted to local authorities under Section 157 of the Public Health Act of 1875, and subsequent legislation. They govern most matters of building construction and hygiene which affect the safety, health, and well-being of the community and of individuals. Some by-laws are sadly in need of revision to comply with changed methods of construction, etc.

Building Centre, The, 26 Store Street, London, W.C.1, was founded in 1931 to provide a central showroom or permanent exhibition where architects, their clients, and the public generally can see a wide range of building components and materials exhibited by manufacturers. The centre's reference library contains all the standard building directories, a list of more than 50,000 trade names, and a comprehensive catalogue library. The centre is in constant touch with its counterparts overseas.

Building Research Station, The, Bucknall's Lane, Garston, near Watford, Hertfordshire, is a branch of the Department of Scientific and Industrial Research (set up during the First World War), and was established in 1920, moving from Acton to its present premises in 1925. Later 'The Thatched Barn,' a roadhouse on the Barnet by-pass, was acquired for a 'Building Operations Research Unit.' The work of the station embraces two main fields of study: (i) general research into 'the fundamental qualities of building materials'; and (ii) the application of 'the information so obtained to the solution of special problems submitted to them by various inquirers.'

* C

The publications of the station are very numerous, including *Annual Reports*; *Special Reports*, 'intended primarily for the building industry'; *Bulletins*, 'written for the most part in non-scientific language'; *Technical Papers*, 'generally of the nature of scientific memoirs'; *Building Science Abstracts* from the world's technical press; and *The Building Research Station Digest*, issued at frequent intervals. These publications are obtainable *only* through H.M. Stationery Office, not from the Building Research Station.

Bulfinch, Charles (*b*. Boston, Massachusetts, 8 Aug. 1763; *d*. there, 4 April 1844), American architect. He graduated at Harvard in 1781; then travelled extensively to study architecture in Europe; returned to Boston in 1787, and is believed to have been the first architect to practise there professionally. He was a follower of the style of Robert Adam (q.v.), and also followed his example in venturing into speculative building, which was unsuccessful. His chief works were the State House at Boston (1798); a number of fine houses in Beacon Street, Boston; and the Maine State House (1828). He also completed the Capitol at Washington (1817–30), which had been begun by Latrobe (q.v.) in 1814, following designs made originally by Thornton (q.v.) in 1793.

Bullant, Jean (*b*. Écouen, France, 1515; *d*. 13 Oct. 1578), French architect, first appears as the designer of alterations to the château of Écouen for its owner, the Duc de Montmorency (*c*. 1545), then for further work for him at the Châtelet at Chantilly (*c*. 1547), and a new gallery (now in ruins) at La-Fère-en-Tardenois. Having previously studied classical architecture in Italy, he published in 1568 a folio treatise entitled *Reigle générale d'architecture des cinque manières de colonnes*. As *architecte du Roi* he added a pavilion to the Tuileries palace in Paris, 1570–2; and may also have designed the chapel at Anet (*c*. 1560–6), as a memorial to Diane de Poitiers, and the 'Arc de Nazareth,' now at the Musée Carnavalet, Paris, 1550.

Bull's-eye Window, a circular window (cf. Fr. *œil-de-bœuf*).

Bungalow (from Hind. *banglā*, belonging to Bengal). A lightly built dwelling of one storey, as used in the East. The ironical term 'bungaloid growths' was coined in the twentieth century to describe badly designed and badly built suburban outcrops along our coasts and highways. *See* SUBTOPIA.

Buonarroti, M. A., *see* MICHELANGELO.

Buontalenti, Bernardo (*b*. Florence, 1536; *d*. there, June 1608), Italian architect. Most of his principal buildings were erected in Florence. They include the façade of S. Trinita; a grotto in the Boboli Gardens; a theatre; Palazzo Riccardi all' Annunziata (1565); alterations to the Uffizi; portico of the hospital of S. Maria Nuova (1574); Casino S. Marco (1576); Casino and Giardino Mediceo (1576); fortress of S. Giorgio (1590); Palazzo Nonfinito (1592). Outside Florence he built the Villa Petraia; the Palazzo Reale at Siena; and the Palazzo Ducale at Pisa (1603).

Burges, William, A.R.A. (*b*. London, 2 Oct. 1827; *d*. there, 20 April

1881), English architect, was a pioneer of the Gothic Revival (q.v.), who carried his enthusiasm to the point of eccentricity in his extraordinary house, No. 9 Melbury Road, Kensington (1875–80), where he tried to live a medieval life. His other buildings included the cathedral of St Finbar, Cork, Ireland (1863–70); the mansion of Castle Coch in Wales (c. 1875); the picturesque restoration of Cardiff Castle (1865); the speech-room of Harrow School (1877); and two small but richly decorated churches in Yorkshire—at Skelton and at Studley Royal—both built in 1871.

Burlington, Richard Boyle, 3rd Earl of, and 4th Earl of Cork (b. 25 April 1695; d. 4 Dec. 1753), architect, inherited, after his father's death in 1704, large estates in Yorkshire and Ireland, Burlington House in Piccadilly, and a house at Chiswick. At the age of twenty-one he was already a privy councillor, Lord Lieutenant of the West Riding, and Lord High Treasurer of Ireland; but his taste was for architecture, of which he became not only a noble patron, but also, to a considerable extent, a practitioner. After lengthy visits to Italy in 1714–15 and in 1719, he acquired a warm admiration for the work of Palladio (q.v.), which he popularized in England, and published an edition of his *Fabbriche Antiche* in 1730. From Italy in 1719 he brought home with him young William Kent (q.v.), who lived with him at Burlington House, which they then proceeded to transform internally, Gibbs (q.v.) and Campbell (q.v.) having begun remodelling its exterior. Although there is still some doubt as to Burlington's dependence upon Kent, it now seems that the earl must be given credit for Chiswick House, Middlesex (c. 1725); the dormitory of Westminster School (1722–30); the Assembly Rooms, York (1731–2); Lord Monteath's house, 29 Old Burlington Street, London; and several other buildings.

Burnet, Sir John James, R.A. (b. Glasgow, 1857; d. Colinton, near Edinburgh, 2 July 1938), Scottish architect, R.I.B.A. Royal Gold Medallist, 1923, was the son of a Glasgow architect whom he joined as partner after his training at the École des Beaux Arts in Paris. In later years he became senior partner in the firm of Sir John Burnet, Tait, & Lorne. His large practice in Scotland included extensions to the university and the Western Infirmary at Glasgow; Messrs Forsyth's premises in Princes Street, Edinburgh; and a number of churches, houses, commercial buildings, and railway stations. In 1904 he was appointed architect for the Edward VII Galleries of the British Museum, erected 1905–14. His other works in London included General Buildings, Kingsway (1909–11); Kodak Building, Kingsway (1910); Institute of Chemistry, Bloomsbury (1914–15); extensions of Selfridge's Store (1919–28); Adelaide House, London Bridge (1921–4). As one of the chief architects of the Imperial War Graves Commission, he designed several war cemeteries in Palestine and Gallipoli, including that at Jerusalem. *See also* TAIT, T. S.

Burnham, Daniel Hudson (b. Henderson, New York, 4 Sept. 1846; d. Heidelberg, Germany, 1 June 1912), American architect. After his training in Chicago he began practice in partnership with J. W.

Root. On Root's death in 1891 Burnham formed, with C. B. Attwood, a new partnership—D. H. Burnham & Co. With one or other of his two partnerships, Burnham was responsible for planning the World's Fair at Chicago (1893); the Great Northern Hotel, the Masonic Temple, and the Railway Exchange in Chicago; the 'Flat-iron' Building and Wanamaker's Store in New York; the Pennsylvania railway station at Pittsburgh; Filene's Store, Boston; the Union railway station, Washington; and Selfridge's Store in London. He was elected President of the American Institute of Architects in 1894; was made chairman of the committee for beautifying Washington; and prepared plans for improving the cities of Cleveland (1903), San Francisco (1905, after the earthquake), Chicago (1909), Baltimore, and Manila in the Philippines. Thus he was a pioneer of civic design as well as of steel construction.

See monograph by C. H. Moore.

Burton, Decimus (*b.* ? London, 1800; *d.* there, 14 Dec. 1881), English architect, was the son of a London builder, by whom he was trained. He then entered the Royal Academy schools to study architecture, started practice at a very early age, was befriended by John Nash (q.v.), and ultimately became a leading figure of the Classical Revival, although he never studied architecture first hand in Italy or Greece till late in life. His father's name is commemorated in the name of Burton Street (Bloomsbury), part of an estate which the elder Burton developed in 1807, and where he built himself a house on the site of the later British Medical Association headquarters. Decimus designed much of the London work built by his father, including 'The Holme' in Regent's, Park (*c.* 1818), and in 1821 Cornwall Terrace, Regent's Park, was being erected from his designs. Grove House, Regent's Park, followed in 1822–4. In 1825 he designed the beautiful screen and the 'Pimlico Arch' at Hyde Park Corner, and the various lodges in Hyde Park; also St Dunstan's Lodge and sundry buildings for the Zoological Society—all in Regent's Park. His enormous practice included many notable buildings since demolished, but mention must be made of some of the survivors: Charing Cross Hospital (1831–4); the Palm House and Winter Garden at Kew (1844–66); a great number of large country houses, chiefly in Kent and the other home counties; and several important building estates, including the Calverley Estate, Tunbridge Wells (1828–52); Adelaide Crescent, Brighton (1830–4); the new town of Bournemouth (1845–59); the Radnor Estate, Folkestone (1843); and, farther afield, an estate at Liverpool (1834–5), another at Howth in Ireland, and the Kelvinside Estate, Glasgow (1839–40). Strange to say, Burton also built eight neo-Gothic churches. His masterpiece is the Athenaeum Club in London (1827–30), the appearance of which was much altered when a new storey was added in 1899.

Butterfield, William (*b.* London, 7 Sept. 1814; *d.* there, 23 Feb. 1900), English architect, awarded the R.I.B.A. Royal Gold Medal, 1884, was the most original designer in the English Gothic Revival (q.v.), but has been criticized for his excessive fondness for 'polychromy,' i.e. the use of strongly contrasting colours in materials and

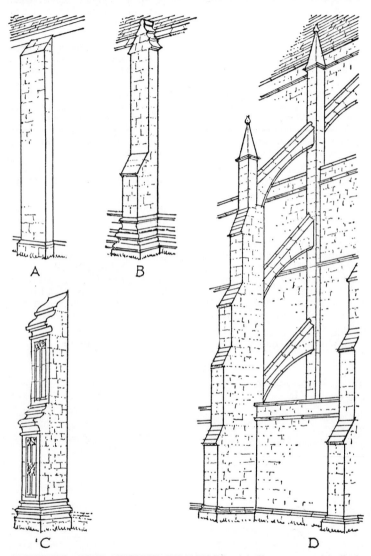

BUTTRESS: FOUR ENGLISH EXAMPLES. (A) *Romanesque;* (B) *Early Gothic;* (C) *Late Gothic;* (D) *Flying Buttresses, Westminster Abbey*

decoration, whereas his contemporary, G. F. Bodley (q.v.), used colour as freely, but with the utmost restraint and taste. Criticism is particularly severe of his design of Keble College, Oxford (1870–5), a very fine design in itself, but in brick, and out of harmony with the prevailing tradition of stone building in Oxford; and to many eyes his church of All Saints, Margaret Street, London (1859), appears strident in its interior colour scheme. His other buildings in Oxford —additions to Merton College (1864), and the chapel at Balliol College (1857)—are also somewhat alien to the *genius loci*. After he had been trained at Worcester, his first notable commission was the restoration of St Augustine's College, Canterbury (1845), a picturesque and skilful design. Other work by him includes St Alban, Holborn, London (1863); St Matthias, Stoke Newington (1851); and the chapel of Rugby School (1875).

Buttery, in a medieval house or college, a store-room for bottles of wine and other liquor (from Fr. *bouteillerie*). The word has no connection with butter.

Buttress (Old Fr. *bouterez*, from *bouter*, to thrust), a vertical mass of masonry or brickwork, projecting at intervals from the external face of a wall, to resist the outward thrust of a vault of a roof-truss, or merely to stiffen the wall. Buttresses were seldom used in classical architecture; and even in Romanesque architecture they were relatively slight in bulk and projection; but throughout the Gothic period they were progressively increased in size, thus enabling the intervening lengths of wall to be reduced in thickness and to be pierced with large windows. Hence buttressing is a most important feature of Gothic architecture. *See* FLYING BUTTRESS and VAULTING.

Byzantine Architecture, *see* ARCHITECTURE, PERIODS OF, 4.

C

Cabin, a small hut, usually of timber, and generally isolated, e.g. a forester's cabin. Shakespeare, in *Twelfth Night* (I. v. 287), says: 'Make me a willow Cabine at your gate.'

Cabinet (cf. Ital. *gabinetto,* a study or small room; dim. of 'cabin).' (1) A small room, cabin, summer-house, or bower. (2) A piece of furniture with a glazed front, for the display of china, curios, etc. (3) In modern France a water-closet.

Cable Moulding, in Romanesque architecture, a convex moulding or bead, carved spirally to imitate a cable or rope. (*Illustrated* MOULDINGS, ENRICHED (ROMANESQUE).)

Caisson (Fr.). (1) In architecture, a sunk panel or coffer (q.v.) in a ceiling or vault. (2) In civil engineering, a water-tight cylinder or tank sunk in deep water to facilitate the construction of foundations.

Caldarium (Lat.), a hot room in a Roman bathing establishment. *See* THERMAE, *illustrated.*

Callicrates (fifth century B.C.), Greek architect. With Ictinus (q.v.) he designed the Parthenon at Athens (447–432 B.C.); also the temple of Nike Apteros at Athens (*c.* 425 B.C.).

Camber, the slight curved rise given to a beam of wide span or to the underside of a 'flat arch' (q.v.), to avoid sagging or the appearance of sagging.

Camber Arch, a 'flat arch' (q.v.) with a 'camber' as above. (*Illustrated* ARCH, TYPES OF.)

Cambio, Arnolfo di, *see* ARNOLFO DI CAMBIO.

Came, one of the small grooved lead bars used in glazing a leaded or 'latticed' window.

Cameron, Charles (*b. c.* 1740; *d.* 1812), Scottish architect, worked intermittently in Russia from 1779 almost up to the date of his death. He is believed to have studied under the French architect Clérisseau, but nothing is known of his early life or training.

Some time before 1772, however, Cameron must have made an intensive study of the Roman *thermae* (q.v.), for in that year he published a book in French on the subject, followed in 1775 by an English version, *The Baths of the Romans.* He was then living in London, where he was befriended by Sir William Chambers (q.v.). In 1779 the Empress Catherine invited him to Russia. He was commissioned to decorate the royal palace at Tsarskoe Selo built by

Rastrelli (q.v.), and erected a house near by for himself.   At Pavlovsk
he laid out the park of the royal villa, which he then rebuilt, together
with two temples, an aviary, and a colonnade.   At Baturin he built
another palace.   After a spell in England, 1796–1800, he returned to
Russia as chief architect to the Admiralty.   His work was classical
in spirit and very scholarly, but unfortunately much of it was
destroyed in the Second World War.

See monograph by G. Loukomski, 1943.

Campanile (Ital., from Lat. *campana*, a church bell), a bell-tower,
whether forming an integral part of a church or detached from it.
Although the earliest known use of a bell as a summons to Christian
worship dates from A.D. 604, the existing *campanili* at Ravenna are
slightly older, but it is possible that they were originally erected as
watch-towers.   Several picturesque brick examples in Rome date
from the eighth to eleventh centuries.   The fine brick *campanile* in
St Mark's Piazza, Venice, begun in 902, suddenly collapsed exactly
1,000 years later, but has since been rebuilt in its original form.
Other notable Italian examples, both in marble, are 'Giotto's Tower'
at Florence (1334–87) and the 'Leaning Tower' at Pisa (1174).   In
England the detached *campanile* at Chichester Cathedral (*c.* 1410–
1440) still survives, but that at Salisbury Cathedral was demolished
in 1789.   *See also* BELFRY.

Campbell, Colin (*b.* Scotland; *d.* London, 13 Sept. 1729), was an
architect whose early life and career are unknown before he suddenly emerges as the author of an immense book of architectural
engravings, the *Vitruvius Britannicus*, of which the first volume
appeared in 1715, the others in 1717 and 1725.   This monumental
publication—for the most part illustrations of designs for noblemen's
mansions by fashionable contemporary British architects, tactfully
interspersed with a few of his own designs—is a *ballon d'essai*.   He
followed similar tactics in his edition of Palladio's *Architecture* in
1729.   This was too late to benefit him, for he died in that year; but
the fruits of the earlier book, due in part to the patronage of Lord
Burlington (q.v.), appear in the important architectural commissions
that he obtained between 1715 and 1729.   Besides several early
houses in Scotland, etc., they include Wanstead House, Essex (1715,
demolished 1824); the Rolls House, Chancery Lane, London
(demolished 1895–6); alterations (since demolished) to Burlington
House, Piccadilly (1718–19); Newby (now Baldersby) Park, Ripon
(1720–1); his *magnum opus*, Houghton, Norfolk, for Sir Robert
Walpole (1721–32); Stourhead, Wiltshire (1722, since altered);
Mereworth Castle, Kent (a copy of one of Palladio's villas in Italy)
(*c.* 1722–5); Waverley Abbey, Surrey (*c.* 1725); Compton Place,
Eastbourne (1726–7).

Campo Santo (Ital., holy field), the name given to any Italian
cemetery.   There is a notable example (thirteenth century) at Pisa,
and a notorious one at Genoa, where the neighbourhood of the
Carrara marble quarries has encouraged a blatant display of realistic
funerary sculpture.   The chief cemetery at Rome is the Campo
Verano.

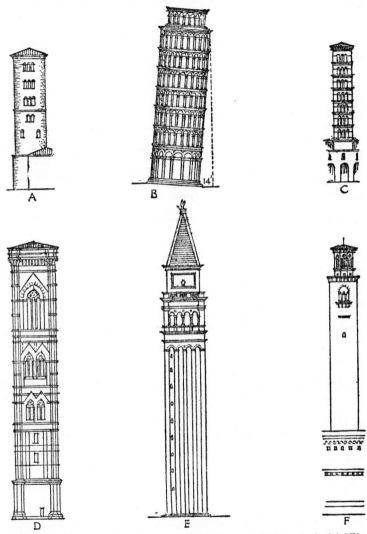

CAMPANILE. (A) *S. Apollinare in Classe, Ravenna (? 6th century);* (B) *'The Leaning Tower,' Pisa (1174);* (C) *S. Maria in Cosmedin, Rome (12th century);* (D) *'Giotto's Tower,' Florence (1334–87);* (E) *S. Marco, Venice (902, rebuilt after 1902);* (F) *Palazzo dei Signori, Verona (1172 onwards)*

Canadian Architecture began with the French, more than a century before the British conquest of Canada ('New France') in 1760–3. The first French traders and missionaries who built a village on the site of modern Quebec in 1608 found no architecture in Canada, but merely Indian huts. Settlement was slow, and the colonial population was only about 6,000 in 1666; but the Jesuits had then already erected a hospital and a convent for girls, both still in existence. Montreal was founded in 1642, and its picturesque Château de Ramezay is now a museum. The early French buildings in Canada were simple in design, and mostly constructed of stone. The French tradition, especially in Quebec, remained strong after the British conquest, and appears in many small eighteenth-century churches surviving on the Île d'Orléans, Gothic in form but classical in detail. The nineteenth century witnessed the arrival from England of the Greek, Gothic, and other architectural revivals. The Gothic Revival (q.v.), in its earliest and most inept form, produced the gimcrack church of Notre-Dame, Montreal (1824), and, much later, the Parliament Buildings at Ottawa (1859–75), which resemble contemporary work by Sir G. G. Scott (q.v.) in England, though he did not design them. The lofty tower, in the same style, was added as a war memorial in 1919. The Governor's House at Spencerwood, Quebec, is a classical building, and the cathedral or 'basilica' at Montreal (1868) is a copy, half-size, of St Peter's at Rome. The city hall of Toronto recalls the Romanesque favoured by Waterhouse (q.v.) in England and by H. H. Richardson (q.v.) in the United States; but, meanwhile, the French architectural tradition, which still persisted in eastern Canada, had produced many buildings and streets which echo Rouen and other French provincial towns, and the Legislative Building at Quebec (1878–92) is a feeble exercise in French Renaissance. While skyscrapers and industrial buildings in the style of Chicago or New York began to multiply in Toronto and Montreal at the end of the century (e.g. the Sun Life Building, Montreal), the two great rival railway companies decided to adopt the highly picturesque style of the sixteenth-century châteaux of Touraine for two gigantic new hotels—the 'Château Frontenac' at Quebec (1893) and the much later 'Château Laurier' at Ottawa (1910), by D. H. Macfarlane. Among more recent buildings are the Canadian Bank of Commerce, Toronto (1930), by Darling and Pearson; the Commonwealth Building at Ottawa (1954) by Alra and Balharrie; and others by R. C. Morris (q.v.) and his partners. In 1958 he was awarded the R.I.B.A. Royal Gold Medal, as was Frank Darling in 1915.

See R. Traquair, *The Old Architecture of Quebec*, 1947, and A. Gowans, *Looking at Architecture in Canada*, 1959.

Cancelli (Lat., bars), in early Christian architecture, marble or wooden or metal barriers or railings separating the nave (q.v.) or body of a church from the sanctuary or presbytery reserved for the priests, i.e. the 'chancel' (q.v.), deriving its name from *cancelli*.

Candela, Felix (*b.* in Spain, 1910), architect and engineer, was trained in Madrid, and in 1938 settled in Mexico, where he designed—mostly in partnership with other architects—many remarkable buildings in reinforced concrete. These included churches, ware-houses, and the Cosmic Ray Pavilion at Mexico University. (*Illustrated* Plate 18.)

Canephora (Gk), sculptured female figure with a basket on its head.

Canopy (derived ultimately from Gk *kōnōpeion*, a bed with mosquito-netting, *konops* meaning a gnat; then a carving suspended over a bed, couch, or throne), hence, in architecture, a roof-like projecting cover over a niche, window, door, etc. *See also* BALDAQUIN, MARQUISE, TESTER.

Cant, an oblique line cutting off the corner of a rectangle, usually at forty-five degrees. *See also* BEVEL, CHAMFER, SPLAY.

Canteen (Fr. *cantine*; Ital. *cantina*, a cellar), originally a regimental dining-room or refreshment-room; then an institutional dining-room where food is served from a counter or hatch.

Cantilever (derivation uncertain), a beam projecting, like a bracket, from a wall, held down at that end either by the superincumbent weight of the wall or in some other way, and capable of carrying a weight on the remainder of its length. The principle of the cantilever, though by no means new, has been widely developed in architecture of the twentieth century, partly due to the advances made in reinforced concrete construction; and the results appear in the generous provision of cantilevered balconies for modern flats (q.v.), as well as in roofs for island platforms on railway stations, and many other purposes.

Cantoris, in an Anglican cathedral, the north side of the choir, on which the 'cantor' or precentor sits facing the dean. For that reason the north and south sides of the choir are named respectively 'Cantoris' and 'Decani' (Lat. *decanus*, dean).

Cap. (1) The topmost member of a pedestal, in classical architecture. (2) The protective metal top of a wooden post. (3) An abbreviation of capital (q.v.).

Capital, the moulded or carved top of a column, serving to concentrate the superincumbent load on to the shaft of the column, and often treated with great richness of ornament. The types of capital used in the several Greek and Roman 'Orders of Architecture' (q.v.), and later in the various Romanesque (q.v.) and Gothic (q.v.) periods, are distinctive features of each style. (*Illustrated*, p. 72.)

Capping, protective covering, usually of metal, for the top of a vertical stone or timber member. *See also* Cap.

Caravanserai (from Persian), in countries of the Middle East, an inn with accommodation for merchants, their camels or other beasts, and their goods.

Carcass, the shell or skeleton of a building. The term is normally applied to buildings complete structurally, but lacking internal services, finishes, and fittings.

Carpenter, Richard Cromwell (*b.* 21 Oct. 1812; *d.* London, 27

CAPITAL. (A) *Roman Doric;* (B) *Roman Ionic;* (C) *Roman Corinthian;* (D) *Byzantine;* (E) *English Romanesque (Norman),* (F) *Early English Gothic;* (G) *Middle (decorated) English Gothic;* (H) *Late (Perpendicular) English Gothic*

Mar. 1855), English architect, was a leading figure of the Gothic Revival (q.v.). His work included the following new churches: St Alban, Kemerton (1845); St Paul, Brighton (date unknown); St Peter, Chichester (1848); St John, Bovey Tracey (1852); Christ Church, Milton (1854); and St Mary Magdalene, Munster Square, London (1849–52). He also restored Chichester Cathedral and Sherborne Abbey, and designed the large public schools of Hurstpierpoint (1851) and Lancing (1854); the houses in Lonsdale Square, Islington (c. 1842–52); and the cathedrals for Inverness, Jamaica, and Ceylon.

Carpentry, the cutting, framing, and working of structural woodwork in a building, as opposed to 'joinery' (q.v.), which comprises the lighter woodwork, e.g. panelling and cupboards. Wooden doors, windows, and staircases are usually reckoned as joinery; roofs, floors, partitions, and shoring as carpentry. To-day there is no industrial demarcation between them; but in times past the guilds of the two crafts were often in dispute in London, where two separate livery companies still recall the medieval distinction.

Carr, John (b. Horbury, Yorkshire, May 1723; d. Askham, Yorkshire, 22 Feb. 1807), English architect, commonly called 'Carr of York,' was twice lord mayor of that city. He began his career as a working mason, and moved to York before 1750. His first architectural work was there, and included the grandstand on the Knavesmire racecourse, as well as several houses. Then followed a long series of great country mansions, most but not all in Yorkshire. They included Kirby Hall, Ouseburn (c. 1750); Arncliffe Hall (1753–4); Abbot Hall, Westmorland (1759); Constable Burton (c. 1762–8); Harewood House (1759–61, afterwards decorated by R. Adam, q.v., and altered by C. Barry, q.v.); the model village of Harewood; Thoresby Park, Nottinghamshire (1768, since demolished); the stables at Castle Howard (1771–82); Colwick Hall, Nottinghamshire (1776); Basildon Park, Berkshire (1776); Denton Park (1778); the colossal stables at Wentworth House (c. 1780); probably Gledhow Hall (Leeds) and Gledstone Hall, Skipton—all in Yorkshire unless otherwise stated above. His town houses included Thornes House, Wakefield (1779–1801). Among his other works were the County Lunatic Asylum and the Assize Courts at York; the town halls at Newark, Nottinghamshire (1776) and Chesterfield, Derbyshire (1790); the infirmary (1780–1) and prison (1786–8) at Lincoln; and Horbury Church, Wakefield (1791–3).

Carrel, a small bay or enclosure for private study, much used in medieval monastic libraries and often introduced into modern libraries, where the divisions between the bays are formed by bookcases projecting at right angles from the outer walls.

Carrère, John Merien (b. Rio de Janeiro, 9 Nov. 1858; d. New York, 1 Mar. 1911), American architect, studied at the École des Beaux Arts, Paris. He then worked in New York in the office of Messrs McKim (q.v.), Mead, & White (q.v.). In 1885 he started practice in partnership with Thomas Hastings (q.v.), this arrangement lasting until Carrère's death in 1911. Their chief buildings during this period were two large hotels in Florida (1887-8); the public library (1897, won in competition), the Century Theatre, and the approaches to Manhattan Bridge—all in New York City; the offices of the Senate (1906) and the Carnegie Institution (1909)—both in Washington.

Carton Pierre (Fr., literally 'cardboard stone': also known as papier mâché; Fr., literally 'pulped paper'), a material formerly used for making casts for plaster mouldings and enrichments. It consists of boiled paper pulp, whiting, and size. In 1829 Blore (q.v.) erected vaulting of this material over the transept of Ripon Cathedral. It was replaced with oak vaulting by Sir G. G. Scott in the restorations of 1862-70.

CARTOUCHE
Badsey (1683)

Cartouche (Lat. *carta*, paper). (1) In architectural ornament of the Renaissance period, a carved or painted panel resembling a sheet of paper with the edges turned over, or a scroll. (2) In ancient Egyptian hieroglyphics, a small panel enclosing royal or divine names and titles.

Caryatid (Gk), in Greek architecture, a sculptured female figure used instead of a column to support an entablature, as at the Erechtheum at Athens (*c.* 421 B.C.). Modern examples are to be seen in the porch of St Pancras Church, London (A.D. 1819-22).

Casemate, in military architecture, a vaulted chamber, with embrasures for defence, built in the thickness of the walls or ramparts of a fortress.

Casement (derivation uncertain), a window hung to a frame by hinges on one of its vertical sides, and opening inwards or outwards. If hung on its bottom edge it is called a 'hopper' (q.v.); if made to slide horizontally a 'Yorkshire light' (q.v.). Casements were in general use until the introduction of the sash-window (*see* SASH) in the seventeenth century.

Casino (Ital., a little house). (1) A small ornamental pavilion or summer-house, the most ornate example being Lord Charlemont's 'Casino' at Clontarf, near Dublin (1755), designed by Sir W. Chambers (q.v.). (2) A building for public gaming, etc., e.g. at Monte Carlo.

Cassels, or **Cassel**, or **Castle**, **Richard** (*b.* Hesse, Germany; *d.* Carton, near Dublin, 19 Feb. 1751), German-Irish architect, was invited to Ireland by Sir Augustus Hume about 1727, and remained there until his death. He designed the printing house and the dining-hall of Trinity College, Dublin (1740-5, since rebuilt); the Rotunda Hospital, Dublin (1751), but the cupola was added later; Tyrone House,

Clanwilliam House, 85 St Stephen's Green, and Leinster House—all in Dublin; Powerscourt House, Co. Wicklow (north front, 1728–1743); Carton, Co. Kildare; Summerhill, Co. Meath, etc.

Casson, Sir Hugh Maxwell (*b.* London, 23 May 1910), English architect, was educated at Cambridge and at University College, London; travelled in Greece as Craven Scholar, 1933; was then articled to T. D. Atkinson of Winchester, and started practice in 1937. During the Second World War he served as camouflage officer under the Air Ministry; then in the Ministry of Town and Country Planning, resuming his private practice in 1946. He was Director of Architecture for the Festival of Britain, 1948–51; designed the street decorations of the City of Westminster for the Coronation, 1953; and, in collaboration with N. Conder, prepared plans for developing the Sidgwick Estate for Cambridge University. In 1953 he became Professor of Interior Design at the Royal College of Art.

He has written *New Sights of London*, 1937; *Bombed Churches*, 1946; *Homes by the Million*, 1947.

Castellan (from Lat. *castellanus*), the governor or custodian of a castle. The modern French equivalent is *châtelain* (f. *châtelaine*, hence applied to the mistress of a household).

Castellation. (1) The building of castles. (2) More precisely and usually, the furnishing of a house with battlements (q.v.). *See also* CRENELLATION.

Castle (from Lat. *castellum*, dim. of *castrum*, a fort; cf. Fr. *chastel*, later *château*; It. *castello*), a fortress or fortified building. The term is usually restricted to medieval buildings and, in England, to those erected after the Norman Conquest, 1066; but is applied loosely to certain ancient strongholds such as 'Maiden Castle,' Dorset, which was fortified about 350–100 B.C. Long before that date massive fortified palaces such as Tiryns and Mycenae (*see* ARCHITECTURE, PERIODS OF, 1(*c*)) had been built of colossal masonry, but at Maiden Castle the defences consisted of earthen ramparts and rows of palisades on a naturally strong eminence, difficult of access and commanding extensive views in all directions. Richborough 'Castle' in Kent, Pevensey 'Castle' in Sussex, and Portchester 'Castle' in Hampshire are all Roman fortresses built in the third and fourth centuries A.D. as part of a chain known as the 'forts of the Saxon shore,' to defend the south-eastern coast of England against Saxon incursions.

The building of castles in England began in earnest immediately after the Norman Conquest, under orders from William I, as a means of establishing stable government, each under one of his Norman lords, but in some cases a castle became a centre of oppression as well as a refuge in case of hostile risings.

Up to A.D. 1100, out of some eighty-five castles erected in England since 1066, only six or seven were of stone. These included the castles of London ('The White Tower'), Pevensey (rebuilt), Colchester, and Richmond (Yorkshire). All the rest followed the normal type then in vogue, viz. either the '*motte*' type (the *motte*

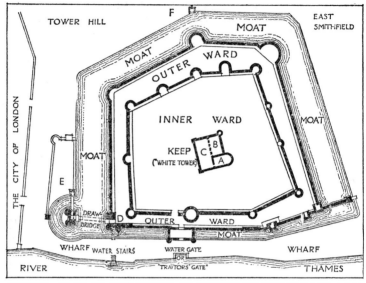

CASTLE: PLAN OF THE TOWER OF LONDON IN THE MIDDLE AGES
A=St John's Chapel; B, C=Guard Rooms; D=Gate Tower; E=Barbican
or Outwork; F=End of the (Roman) Wall surrounding London

being not a moat but a truncated conical mound of earth surrounded by a ditch and crowned with a timber palisade) or the '*motte* and bailey' type, i.e. having a *motte* provided with an outer court or bailey, enclosed by walls. The finest surviving English *motte* is at Thetford in Norfolk. When a tower came to be erected on the *motte* it was called the *donjon* or 'keep,' hence the name 'Dane John' at Canterbury. The site of a Norman castle was always carefully chosen for its defensive strength, was usually on raised ground, and where possible on the bank of a river.

Norman castles in England resembled those (e.g. Falaise) erected in France at about the same period. They are generally classified according to the type of keep, viz.: (i) rectangular (Castle Hedingham, Castle Rising, Dover, London, Middleham, Newcastle upon Tyne, Norwich, Portchester as rebuilt, Rochester, Scarborough); (ii) polygonal (Orford in Suffolk); (iii) circular (Conisborough, Pembroke); (iv) irregular 'shell-type' keep, following the natural shape of the site (Arundel, Carisbrooke, Exeter, Ludlow, The Peak, and, especially, Windsor, where the famous 'Round Tower,' which forms the keep proper, owes much of its present height to an extension at the beginning of the nineteenth century). Among other notable castles of various types are those of Beaumaris, Caernarvon, Caerphilly, and Harlech in Wales; Edinburgh and Stirling in Scotland; Carrickfergus in Northern Ireland; Castle Ruthen in the Isle of Man.

Important French examples are Château Gaillard in Normandy

(1196); Carcassonne (eleventh to thirteenth centuries); and Pierrefonds (1390). The two latter were drastically restored by Viollet-le-Duc (q.v.). Of the numerous picturesque castles on the Rhine, none compare in architectural interest with those in France just mentioned.

The keep, which formed the last refuge of the garrison after the outworks had been captured, also served as the lord's dwelling. It generally had store-rooms and a prison ('dungeon') at ground level. Stone steps led up to the first floor, which was occupied by the soldiers of the garrison, and had very narrow windows or arrow slits. The next storey was usually higher, and contained the baronial hall where the lord dined with his family and retainers. A chapel was often provided in the keep (e.g. at Dover). Latrines, in the thickness of the outer wall (e.g. at Orford), were called 'garderobes' (q.v.).

The top of the keep was often crowned with crenellated parapets or 'battlements,' consisting of solid portions ('merlons') alternating with narrow openings ('embrasures'), through which a defending soldier could shoot arrows while sheltering behind a merlon. Often this crenellated parapet projected on a row of stone corbels or brackets, and between each pair of these was a square hole closed by a lid, through which, when opened, the defenders could pour boiling water or oil, or molten lead, on to the heads of enemies attempting to mine the base of the wall far below. This arrangement, known as 'machicolation' (q.v.), is one of many military devices borrowed by the Crusaders from their 'Saracen' foes.

The outer walls of the bailey were also strongly fortified in the same way, and every important entrance gateway was furnished with one or more portcullises (q.v.). The outer enclosing wall was also often provided with towers and bastions, allowing of cross-fire on all parts of the wall; and the entrance to the castle, across the moat by a drawbridge, was also further defended by an outwork or tower—a 'barbican' (q.v.). Somewhere within the castle, and often inside the keep itself, was a deep well. (There is a notable example at Dover.) The military effectiveness of castles had greatly declined before the end of the Middle Ages; and those erected during the fourteenth to fifteenth centuries were fortified houses rather than castles, e.g. Bodiam (1383), Tattershall, Hurstmonceux (1440), Raglan (1465). Few castles were capable of conversion into convenient dwellings, so many were sold, for the value of their materials, in the sixteenth century (e.g. Wallingford). Of the remainder, a number were deliberately 'slighted' (i.e. blown up) by both contending armies during the civil war of 1642–5. (On this *see* M. S. Briggs, *Goths and Vandals*, 1952.) Most important castles in Britain are now in the care of the Ancient Monuments Branch of the Ministry of Works.

See BAILEY, BARBICAN, BARTIZAN, BASTION, BATTLEMENTS, CRENELLATION, DONJON, EMBRASURE, GARDEROBE, KEEP, MACHICOLATION, MERLON, PORTCULLIS, POSTERN.

See also Sir C. Oman, *Castles* (in western England and Wales), 1926; H. Braun, *The English Castle*, 1936; B. H. St J. O'Neil, *Castles of England and Wales*, 1953; S. Toy, *The Castles of Great Britain*, 1953 (2nd ed., 1954); R. A. Brown, *English Medieval Castles*, 1954; S. Toy, *A History of Fortification*, 1955.

Catacomb, a subterranean gallery used for the burial of the dead. Originally derived from Gk *kata*, down, and *kumbē*, a hollow, the term was first applied to a locality near Rome where there were burial vaults under the famous early Christian basilica of S. Sebastiano. This cemetery was called, in Latin, *coemeterium ad catacumbas*; then *catacumbas* for short; and, about the ninth century A.D., this term was applied to Christian burial vaults in general. Most of the Christian catacombs in Rome date from the third to fourth centuries A.D., and this form of interment ceased after Alaric's sack of Rome in 410; but there was nothing secret about it, as is commonly believed, nor was it confined to Christians. During the period of persecution Christians did undoubtedly take refuge, on occasion, in the intricate labyrinth of the underground galleries, extending in all for many hundreds of miles. Although they contain a number of interesting tombs, chapels, and *cubicula*, as well as some mural decorations, the catacombs around Rome are not of architectural importance. There are other examples, on a smaller scale, elsewhere, e.g. at Naples, Malta, Syracuse, and Alexandria (Egypt). Certain points of resemblance exist between the Christian catacombs and the far older pagan underground cemeteries at Cerveteri in Etruria, etc.

Catafalque, a movable timber structure, often richly decorated and resembling a tomb; used at funeral ceremonies in a church to support the coffin.

Cathedral (from Lat. *cathedra*, Gk *kathedra*, a chair), the principal church in a diocese, containing the chair or throne of the bishop. In the early basilican churches this was in the apse behind the altar, so that the bishop faced the congregation; later the usual position came to be on the south side of the choir. The term 'cathedral' has no relation to the mere size of the church: many English parish churches are larger than the smallest cathedrals. Of forty-five Anglican cathedrals in England, only eighteen are medieval foundations. These were originally either 'secular,' i.e. served by canons (Chichester, Exeter, Hereford, Lichfield, Lincoln, London, Salisbury, Wells, York), or 'monastic,' i.e. served by monks (Bath, Canterbury, Carlisle, Coventry, Durham, Ely, Norwich, Winchester, Worcester). After the dissolution of the monasteries in 1536–9 new cathedrals were established in formerly monastic churches (Bristol, Chester, Gloucester, Oxford, Peterborough), and, during the nineteenth to twentieth centuries, more formerly monastic churches have become cathedrals (St Albans, Southwark), together with formerly collegiate churches (Manchester, Ripon, Southwell); and numerous formerly parish churches have been enlarged or rebuilt to make them worthy of their new rank (Chelmsford, Newcastle, Sheffield, Wakefield, etc.). Guildford Cathedral is, however, an entirely new foundation as well as a new building. The administration of a cathedral is carried on by a chapter, i.e. an assembly of canons, under the presidency of a dean.

Bibliography. (i) Books on English cathedrals in general: by T. Perkins, 1901; T. D. Atkinson, 1912; T. F. Bumpus, 1925; F. Bond, 1925; A. H. Thompson, 1925; P. H. Ditchfield, 1930;

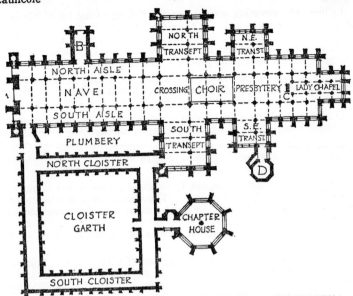

PLAN OF A TYPICAL ENGLISH CATHEDRAL: SALISBURY
A=*West Door*; B=*North Porch*; C=*High Altar*; D=*Sacristy*

H. Batsford and C. Fry, 1935; D. H. S. Cranage, 1948; K. Edwards, 1949; H. Felton and J. Harvey, 1956; E. Vale, 1956; G. H. Cook, 1957. (ii) Handbooks on individual cathedrals: *see* Bell's Cathedral Series and similar series published by J. M. Dent & Sons Ltd, John Murray, and the S.P.C.K.
The above information applies to Anglican cathedrals. Among Roman Catholic cathedrals in England mention must be made of those at Westminster (designed by J. F. Bentley, q.v.); Southwark (by A. W. N. Pugin, q.v.); Liverpool (by Sir E. Lutyens, q.v., but much modified since his death); and Leeds (by Eastwood and Greenslade).
(Reference is made to many famous cathedrals in the introductory article on architecture, and in other articles describing the architecture of Scotland, Ireland, the various European and American countries, Australia, etc.)

Caulicole (Lat. *cauliculus*, dim. of *caulis*, a stalk), in classical architecture, one of several fluted stalks springing from the greater stalks of the Corinthian capital, and terminating in acanthus leaves.

Cavetto (It. dim. of Lat. *cavus*, a hollow), a concave moulding, approximately a quadrant in section. (*Illustrated* MOULDINGS, CLASSICAL.)

C.C.C.C., abbreviation for Central Council for the Care of Churches (q.v.).

Ceiling, the covering over a room. Ceilings may be of plaster, wood, or other materials. If there be a timber floor over the room the ceiling hides the floor joists from view. A ceiling may be flat, segmental, or semicircular in section, groined or otherwise vaulted, and may have a cove at its junction with the walls.

Ceiling Light, a glazed frame in a ceiling, admitting light to a room from a lantern light (q.v.) or skylight (q.v.) fixed on the outer surface of a roof. Obscured glass is generally used in a ceiling light.

Cella (Lat.), the central portion (enclosed by walls, and roofed) of a Roman temple, excluding any portico or surrounding colonnades.

Cellar (Lat. *cellarium*, a set of cells), a store-room for wine and provisions, usually below ground. More loosely, any underground room.

Cenotaph (Gk *kenotaphion*, empty tomb), a tomb erected to honour a person whose body is elsewhere. The famous modern example in Whitehall, London (designed by Sir E. Lutyens, q.v.), commemorated the British fallen in the First World War, 1914–18, and is the scene of an annual service of remembrance on Armistice Day (11th November).

Central Council for the Care of Churches (Fulham Palace, London, S.W.6) was founded shortly after the Ancient Monuments Act of 1913 was passed (excluding any 'ecclesiastical building for the time being used for ecclesiastical purposes') as a result of a promise then made by the Archbishop of Canterbury that the Anglican Church herself would set up efficient machinery for the care of her ancient churches. After some delay due to the First World War, the new body obtained statutory recognition in 1938. It confined its work to parish churches, but in 1950 an independent advisory committee for cathedrals was formed. The council issues annual reports on its work.

Centre (or **Center**); **Centering,** a temporary support of timber or of metal tubing, erected to facilitate the construction of a brick or stone arch, and removed when the mortar of the arch has set.

Cerceau, J. A. Du, *see* DU CERCEAU, J. A.

Chair Rail, a moulded strip of wood fixed to an internal wall at the height where a chair back might damage the plaster, paint, paper, or panelling of the wall. Also called a 'dado rail.' (*Illustrated* PANELLING.)

Chaitiya (Sanskrit), in Indian architecture, a Buddhist chapel, sanctuary, or place of worship.

Châlet (Fr.), the name given in Switzerland to a herdsman's hut; then to any cottage in the mountains; and, later, to a villa or small house built in imitation of the Swiss style.

Chambers, Sir William, R.A., F.R.S. (*b.* Gothenburg, Sweden, 1723; *d.* London, 8 Mar. 1796), British architect, was the son of a Scottish merchant in business at Gothenburg. He was sent to school in England, at Ripon, where he had relatives, in 1728. Returning to

Sweden, he entered the service of the Swedish East India Company, and in 1740 sailed in one of the company's vessels as a cadet. He made a second voyage in 1743–5, and a third (to Bengal and China) in 1747–9 as a 'supercargo.' His duties being light, he had ample time to indulge his taste for drawing by sketching Chinese costumes and buildings; but, as he wrote later, 'chiefly civil architecture, for which latter I have from my earliest years felt the strongest inclination.' Between these voyages he visited England, Scotland, France, and Flanders, worked under J. F. Blondel (q.v.) in Paris, and decided to become an architect.

Between c. 1750 and c. 1755 he spent five years studying architecture in Italy, and shortly after returning to England was appointed architectural tutor to the Prince of Wales (afterwards George III). He was then commissioned by the Princess Dowager of Wales to lay out Kew Gardens, which he proceeded to embellish with the well-known Chinese Pagoda, the Orangery, and sundry 'classical' temples. Meanwhile he had built stables at Harewood, for Lord Lascelles, in 1755. His first book, *Designs of Chinese Buildings, Furniture, Dresses, etc.*, appeared in 1757; the first instalment of his *Treatise on Civil Architecture* in 1759. In 1761, already a flourishing practitioner, he became one of the two architects to the Crown, the other being Robert Adam (q.v.), and in 1782 he became Surveyor-General. He was one of the founders, and the first treasurer, of the Royal Academy. His masterpiece is Somerset House in London (1776–86), which shows the difference between his own severe classical taste and the lighter style of his lifelong rival Robert Adam, as exhibited in the Adelphi, etc. From the long list of his other notable buildings, the following deserve special mention: the town hall at Woodstock (1766); the theatre and chapel at Trinity College, Dublin (1775); the stables, etc., at Goodwood, Sussex (1757–63); the Casino at Marino, near Dublin (c. 1761–80), Duddingston, near Edinburgh (1763–4); Peper Harow, Surrey (1765–75); Roehampton Villa, Surrey, now a Jesuit college (c. 1767); Hothfield Place, Kent (1773); a number of London houses, now mostly demolished; Charlemont House, Dublin, now the Municipal Gallery of Modern Art (1763–70).

Chamfer, an angle or edge cut off diagonally. *See also* BEVEL, CANT, SPLAY.

Champneys, Basil (*b*. London, 17 Sept. 1842; *d*. there, 5 April 1935), English architect; awarded the R.I.B.A. Royal Gold Medal, 1912. After leaving Cambridge University in 1864 he was articled to John Prichard of Llandaff, and began practice in 1867. His principal buildings were the Indian Institute (1884), Mansfield College (1889), extensions at Merton and Oriel Colleges, the library of Somerville College (1903), and the church of St Peter-le-Bailey (1872–4)—all at Oxford; the Archaeological Museum (1883), the Divinity and Literary Schools (1879), extensions of Newnham College—all at Cambridge; Bedford College, Regent's Park, London (1910–13); King's Lynn Grammar School; the Butler Museum, Harrow School (1886); the chapel of Mill Hill School (1898); the Quingentenary Buildings at Winchester College; the Harpur Girls' School, Bedford; several churches, including St Luke, Hampstead (1898); the Royal Palace Hotel, Kensington; and his masterpiece, the John Rylands Memorial Library at Manchester (1890–9). This fine stone building, in late Gothic style, is said to have been the result of Mrs Rylands' admiration for his earlier work at Mansfield College, another of his successes. He was happier designing in stone than in brick, in lavish Gothic than in Jacobean.

Chancel (from Lat. *cancelli*, q.v.), also called the 'sanctuary' and the 'presbytery,' is the eastern portion of a church, reserved for the clergy. It is generally raised by several steps above the level of the nave, and is sometimes separated from it by a screen—a relic of the *cancelli* or low balustrades that separated the judge and council from the public in a Roman basilica or court of law. (*Illustrated* CHURCH.)

Chandelier (from Fr.), an ornamental frame, generally of metal and circular in shape, hung from a roof or ceiling, originally to hold candles which to-day are replaced by electric lamps.

Channel, either (i) a groove or fluting in a column or a plane surface; or (ii) a rolled steel section used in modern building.

Chantry (from Fr. *chanter*, to sing), in medieval architecture, a small chapel (attached to a church) in which masses were sung for the soul of the person who had originally endowed the chantry. The term originally applied to the endowment itself. The addition of chantry chapels to a larger parish church sometimes changed its plan from cruciform to rectangular. *See* CHURCH, *illustrated*.

Chapel (from late Lat. *cappella*, a monk's cloak), originally a small sanctuary for relics, such as the cloak of St Martin; then any small place of worship other than a church, e.g. a chantry (q.v.), a cemetery chapel, a college chapel, a royal chapel in a palace, a private chapel in a mansion, the chapel of an embassy. In the nineteenth century, when 'religious' feeling ran high in England, Nonconformist places of worship, hitherto known as 'meeting-houses' (q.v.), were described as 'chapels' to distinguish them from Anglican 'churches'; but this disparaging term has tended to fall into disuse. (*Illustrated* CHURCH.) *See* NONCONFORMIST CHURCH ARCHITECTURE.

Chapelle Ardente (Fr.) is not, as might appear, an architectural term, but means an arrangement of lights around a coffin, for a lying-in-state.

Chapter-house, the meeting-room of the chapter (i.e. the governing body) of a monastery or a cathedral, presided over, in the case of an Anglican cathedral, by the dean. Most chapter-houses in the medieval English cathedrals are polygonal in plan with a vaulted roof and a central pillar (e.g. Lichfield, Lincoln, Salisbury, and York cathedrals; also Westminster Abbey). Others are oblong (e.g. Canterbury, Chester, Exeter, and Gloucester cathedrals), and that at Worcester (*c.* 1120) is circular. (*Illustrated* CATHEDRAL and MONASTERY.)

Charnel-house (from late Lat. *carnale*, 'flesh house'), a depository for human bones, especially bones discovered when digging new graves. It may be located in the crypt of a church, as at Hythe, and at Gloucester and Ripon cathedrals, or in a separate building.

Chase, a groove cut in a brick or stone wall to accommodate pipes, wires, etc., or to receive the edge of a concrete or stone landing.

Château (Fr., from Old Fr. *chastel*; Lat. *castra*), originally a medieval castle; in later times, any large French country house.

Cheek, the vertical side of a dormer (q.v., *illustrated*) in a roof.

Chequer-work, or **Checker-work,** patterns of contrasting materials (brick, stone, flint, etc.) built into external walls for the sake of ornamental effect, e.g. in East Anglican churches where flint and limestone are so used.

Chevet (Fr.), the apsidal east end of a medieval church, including the aisle or ambulatory round the apse, girdled with chapels. The *chevet* was usual in France, but very rare in England, Westminster Abbey providing the most notable example.

Chevron (Fr.), an ornamental moulding much used in Romanesque architecture, especially around arches, doors, and window-heads, and based on the form of an inverted **V.** Also known as a 'zigzag' moulding. (*Illustrated* MOULDINGS, ENRICHED: ROMANESQUE.)

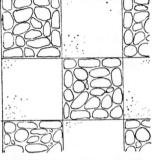

CHEQUER-WORK (East Anglian) of flint and limestone alternating

Chimney (from Old Fr. *cheminée*, late Lat. *caminata*), a vertical structure of brick or stone to carry up smoke from a fire-place. In England chimneys were not used before the Norman Conquest, and for long after that date the 'great halls' of large houses had a central hearth on the floor, from which smoke escaped through a 'louvre' (q.v.) in the ridge of the open timber roof. Fire-places against walls and chimney-stacks (q.v.) both came into use during the sixteenth century. At first the flues were very large, causing the chimney to smoke. (*Illustrated*, p. 84.)

Chimney Breasts, the solid mass of brick or stone on either side of a fire-place opening.

Chimney-corner, the space on either side of the fire-place and within the wide fire-place opening in old houses, used as a warm corner by the old and infirm, and often furnished with a seat. Sometimes called the 'ingle-nook.'

Chimney-piece, or **Mantelpiece,** an ornamental frame of wood, metal, or stone around and above a fire-place, often having an 'overmantel' above it. Elaborate and richly carved chimney-pieces, with overmantels extending up to the ceiling, were a feature of Elizabethan and Jacobean architecture in England.

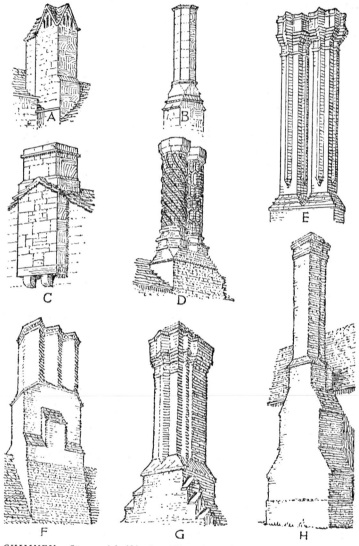

CHIMNEY. *Sione:* (A) *Abingdon Abbey* (c. 1250); (B) *Wells* (15th century);
(C) *Stainforth, Yorks.* Brick: (D) *from Essex;* (E) *Sussex;* (F) *East Anglia;*
(G) *Surrey;* (H) *Kent*

[PLATE I

ARCHITECTURE: (A) GREECE. *The Temple of Hephaistos, or 'Theseion,' at Athens (c. 428 B.C.)*

By courtesy of the French Government Tourist Office

ARCHITECTURE: (B) ROME. *The 'Maison Carrée' at Nîmes, France (16 B.C.)*

PLATE 2]

AUSTRALIAN ARCHITECTURE. Flats at Potts Point, New South Wales
(1951). *A. M. Bolot, architect*

[PLATE 3

BELGIAN AND DUTCH ARCHITECTURE (I). *The Hôtel de Ville at Brussels*
(1402; *tower* 1449)

PLATE 4]

*BELGIAN AND DUTCH ARCHITECTURE (II). The Vleeschhal (Meat Market)
at Haarlem, Holland (1603)*

[PLATE 5

By courtesy of 'The Concrete Quarterly'

BRAZILIAN ARCHITECTURE. The Press Association Building, Rio de Janeiro, showing the use of brise soleil (q.v.)

PLATE 6]

CANADIAN ARCHITECTURE. The Queen Elizabeth Hotel, Montreal (1958). *Webb and Knapp, architects*

[PLATE 7

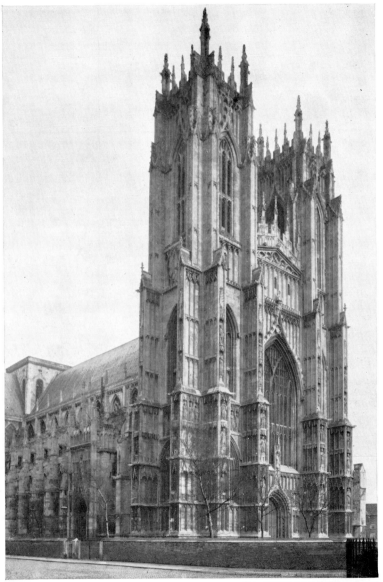

ENGLISH ARCHITECTURE: (I) GOTHIC. Beverley Minster, Yorkshire, West Front (c. 1380–c. 1430)

PLATE 8]

ENGLISH ARCHITECTURE: (II) RENAISSANCE. Above: Coleshill House, Berkshire (c. 1650–62). Below: Long Gallery, Aston Hall (1618–35)

[PLATE 9

*ENGLISH ARCHITECTURE: (III) REGENCY. Chester Terrace, Regent's Park,
London (1825), by J. Nash*

PLATE 10]

Photo: G. Welin

By courtesy of the Finnish Tourist Association

FINNISH ARCHITECTURE. Above: Sanatorium at Paimio (1933), by Aalto (q.v.). Below: Railway station at Helsinki (1904–14), by Saarinen (q.v.)

[PLATE 11

Photo: Neurdein

FRENCH ARCHITECTURE: (1) FLAMBOYANT STYLE.
West Portal of the Church of Notre Dame at Caudebec, Normandy
(1426)

PLATE 12]

FRENCH ARCHITECTURE: (II) RENAISSANCE. Above: Aerial view of the Palace of Versailles (17th–18th centuries). Below: The Petit Trianon at Versailles (1762–6), designed by A.-J. Gabriel (q.v.)

[PLATE 13

GERMAN ARCHITECTURE: RENAISSANCE. The Gewandhaus, or Drapers' Hall, Brunswick. The West Front, with gable of c. 1590

PLATE 14]

INDIAN ARCHITECTURE. The Buland Darwaza ('High Gate') in the Great Mosque
at Fatehpur Sikri (begun in 1569)

[PLATE 15

ITALIAN ARCHITECTURE (*I*).   *Siena Cathedral*

PLATE 16]

Copyright: Alinari

ITALIAN ARCHITECTURE (II). Above: Church of S. Sabina, Rome (425). Below: Villa di Papa Giulio, Rome (1550–5), by Vignola (q.v.)

[PLATE 17

ITALIAN ARCHITECTURE (III). The Baroque Church of S. Maria della Salute at Venice (1631), by Longhena (q.v.)

PLATE 18]

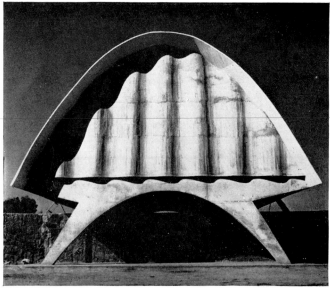

Photos by courtesy of 'The Concrete Quarterly'

MEXICAN ARCHITECTURE. Mexico City University. Above: The Library. Below: The Cosmic Rays Pavilion

[PLATE 19

MUSLIM ARCHITECTURE (I). Sabil (q.v.) of Qayt-Bay in the Harām ash-Sharīf at Jerusalem (c. 1445). In the background, the 'Dome of the Rock' (7th–8th centuries)

PLATE 20]

MUSLIM ARCHITECTURE (II). Interior of the Madrasah (q.v.) of Al-Ghury at Cairo (c. A.D. 1503)

[PLATE 21

RUSSIAN ARCHITECTURE (I). Above: The Cathedral of the Annunciation, Moscow.
Below: The Sklifasovsky Institute, Moscow

PLATE 22]

RUSSIAN ARCHITECTURE (II). Moscow State University

[PLATE 23

SCANDINAVIAN ARCHITECTURE (I). The *medieval timber-built church at Borgund, Norway*

PLATE 24]

SCANDINAVIAN ARCHITECTURE (II). *The Grundtvig Memorial Church at Copenhagen, Denmark* (1921)

[PLATE 25

Photos by courtesy of the South African Government

SOUTH AFRICAN ARCHITECTURE. *Above: Rhône, at Groot-Drakenstein.*
Below: Groot Constantia

PLATE 26]

SPANISH ARCHITECTURE: (I) PLATERESQUE. Portal of the Hospital of
Santa Cruz, Toledo

[PLATE 27

SPANISH ARCHITECTURE (II). The Baroque façade (1737–90) of Murcia Cathedral, by Jaime Bort

PLATE 28]

SWISS ARCHITECTURE. High-tension Electrical Laboratory at Baden, Switzerland. R. Rohn, architect

By courtesy of Swiss Federal Railways

SWISS ARCHITECTURE. The Benedictine Abbey of Einsiedeln (1704–70)

[PLATE 29

TURKISH ARCHITECTURE.   *A fountain at Damascus*

PLATE 30]

By courtesy of Topsfield Historical Society

UNITED STATES ARCHITECTURE. The Parson Capen House at Topsfield, Massachusetts (1683)

By courtesy of Virginia State Chamber

UNITED STATES ARCHITECTURE. The restored Governor's House at Williamsburg, Virginia

[PLATE 31

UNITED STATES ARCHITECTURE (II).   The Capitol, Washington, D.C.

PLATE 32]

UNITED STATES ARCHITECTURE (III). The Empire State
Building, New York City

Chimney-stack, a mass of brickwork or masonry containing groups of flues and rising above roof level. During the Tudor and Stuart periods in England chimney-stacks became picturesque, elaborate, and sometimes eccentric, their brick shafts being spirally carved or fluted.

Chinese Architecture. The early Chinese were cave dwellers, but ruins of palaces (attributed to the fourteenth century B.C.) have been discovered, which suggest timber framing. Temples are chiefly of wood, on a tall stone base, and decorated in bright colours with glazed tiles, etc., and the construction is remarkable in that the roof is not supported by the walls, but by a wooden framework. It is, in fact, put on before the panels of the wall are filled in. Wood carving plays an important part in the interior of a Chinese building. The use of brick and stone has been known to the Chinese since very early times; the latter has been used chiefly for city walls, embankments, bridges, and pagodas. The stone arch was known in ancient China and some of the long bridges have as many as over ten arches.

> *See* G. D. Mirams, *A Brief History of Chinese Architecture*, 1940, and L. Sickman and A. Soper, *The Art and Architecture of China*, 1956.

Chinoiserie (Fr.), a phase of taste for Chinese fashions in wall-paper, fabrics, furniture, and, to some extent, architectural ornament. It was particularly prevalent in the middle of the eighteenth century in England, when it was fostered by the famous furniture designer, Thomas Chippendale; but the architect Chambers (q.v.) also had some share in the movement through his book, *Designs of Chinese Buildings, Furniture, Dresses, etc.*, published in 1757.

Choir, that portion of a church which is specially reserved and furnished for choristers. This is usually, but not invariably, in the eastern part of the church, occupying the western part of the chancel (q.v.) or sanctuary. Hence the terms 'choir' and 'chancel' have come to be almost synonymous; but this usage may be incorrect, e.g. at Westminster Abbey, where the choir is in the nave. (*Illustrated* CATHEDRAL.)

Choir Stalls, canopied and carved seats for the choir and the officiating clergy. They are often of great magnificence, e.g. at St Paul's Cathedral, London.

Choragic Monument (from Gk *choragos*, leader of the chorus), a pedestal, sometimes highly ornamental, used in ancient Athens to display a trophy won by a chorus in competition. There is one famous surviving example: the monument of Lysikrates at Athens (334 B.C.)

Church (from Gk *kuriakon*, 'belonging to the Lord'; hence 'the Lord's house'), a building for Christian public worship. The following is a brief description of the types of building erected by Christians for various forms of their worship in successive periods of history. (For the architectural style of these churches *see* the article on ARCHITECTURE, PERIODS OF, 4–9; *also* the articles on the architecture of the various Christian countries.)

D

CHORAGIC MONUMENT of Lysikrates, Athens (restored)

In the first centuries of Christianity, when persecution often prevailed in the Roman Empire, the small congregations met secretly in private houses, or in the catacombs (q.v.) outside Rome. The oldest surviving Christian churches were erected in Rome, either just before or just after Constantine's edict of 313 had permitted freedom of worship throughout the Empire. (For a list of them *see* ITALIAN ARCHITECTURE.) They are now all known as 'basilican churches' or 'Christian basilicas,' because their general form resembles, and may have been suggested by, the secular basilicas used in Rome, Pompeii, and elsewhere, from the second century onwards, as covered places of assembly for the transaction of legal and commercial business (*see* BASILICA). The early 'basilican' churches usually had an aisled nave, separated from its flanking aisles by a range of columns; round-headed windows in the wall above (later called the 'clerestory,' q.v.) to light the nave; an apse at the east end; and a narthex or vestibule at the west end.

While this type of church, often with added transepts forming a cruciform or 'Latin Cross' plan, was adopted in most of western Europe during the Romanesque period, the Byzantine or Greek or Orthodox Church in eastern Europe and Asia Minor favoured a 'Greek Cross' plan with a central dome and four short arms of equal length, in contrast to the long nave and choir and the short transept of the Roman Catholic West. (*See* ARCHITECTURE, PERIODS OF, 4.) The cruciform plan was not adopted in the West, as has been sometimes supposed, to symbolize our Lord's crucifixion; and the curious deflection sometimes apparent in the axis of the choir, alleged to symbolize the drooping of Christ's head upon the cross, is now believed to have been entirely unintentional, and due to inaccurate setting out of the foundations by the builders. The chancel derives its name from Lat. *cancelli* (barriers provided in secular basilicas to protect the judge in the apse from the public in the nave). In the early Christian basilicas there was a range of seats around the apse for the bishop and the officiating clergy, who thus had their backs to the east and faced the congregation.

As the elaboration of services increased, space was needed for a choir as well as for the clergy; and the chancel or presbytery reserved for the priests was therefore lengthened and divided from the congregation by a screen, at first low and often of marble; centuries later of Gothic traceried woodwork, allowing a view of the altar but yet maintaining a sharp distinction between the nave and the chancel. The chancel is often called the 'choir,' though in some churches (e.g. Westminster Abbey) the choir is actually seated in the nave, and in some others, of later date, in a western gallery, which gives good acoustic results. Eventually England discarded the Romanesque apse, and most English churches after *c.* A.D. 1200

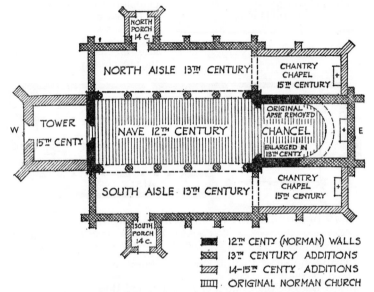

NORTH PORCH 14 C.

NORTH AISLE 13TH CENTURY

CHANTRY CHAPEL 15TH CENTURY

TOWER 15TH CENTY

W

NAVE 12TH CENTURY

ORIGINAL APSE REMOVED

CHANCEL

ENLARGED IN 13TH CENTY

E

CHANTRY CHAPEL 15TH CENTURY

SOUTH AISLE 13TH CENTURY

SOUTH PORCH 14 C.

▰ 12TH CENTY (NORMAN) WALLS
▨ 13TH CENTURY ADDITIONS
▧ 14-15TH CENTY ADDITIONS
▥ ORIGINAL NORMAN CHURCH

Plan showing the growth of a typical English parish church

have a square east end. Pulpits (q.v.) were seldom provided before the seventeenth century, and benches were rare, while closed pews (q.v.) were an innovation of the seventeenth century.

Although the largest English churches were cruciform, few of the smaller ones were. They often consisted of a nave and chancel only, without porches, aisles, or transepts. As local population grew, most churches were enlarged gradually. The usual procedure was to add one or two porches (south and north), a western tower, one or two aisles, and occasionally a transept; also to lengthen the chancel, often substituting a square east end for a Norman apse. Chantry chapels were frequently added at the cost of pious or penitent parishioners, and such chapels often filled up the angle between chancel and transept, so that the whole plan of the church was altered between Norman and Tudor times. Fixed fonts were usually provided in medieval churches, but organs (q.v.) were almost

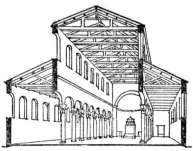

Sectional elevation of a typical basilican church or Christian basilica

unknown and were rare even in 1700 in London.

Besides the normal type of church just described, a few circular churches were erected in western Europe (including England), mainly by the Knights Templars, who took as their model the church of the Holy Sepulchre at Jerusalem. A few so-called 'hall churches,' without chancel, aisles, or transepts, were also erected by the friars for preaching purposes.

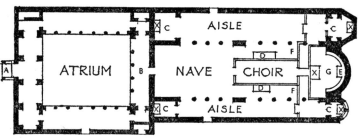

PLAN OF THE BASILICAN CHURCH OF SAN CLEMENTE, ROME
A=*Entrance;* B=*Narthex;* C=*Chapels;* D=*Ambos (pulpits);* E=*Bishop's seat;* F=*Marble screens ('cancelli');* G=*Apse;* X=*Altars*

The evolution of English church architecture was sharply interrupted by the Reformation, when, in 1531, Henry VIII proclaimed himself head of the Church of England, and thus severed the connection with the Papacy in Rome. For the next century and a quarter very little church building took place, and much damage was done to the interior of existing churches. Thomas (not to be confused with Oliver) Cromwell led the official 'Protestant' campaign on behalf of the newly reformed Church of England, and removed from the churches, or destroyed, all objects which were considered 'idolatrous.' The list included representations of Christ, the Virgin Mary, the saints, the Cross, and even religious texts and inscriptions, whether painted on glass or plaster, carved in wood or stone, or engraved upon metal. This 'iconoclasm' (q.v.) continued through the reigns of Edward VI and Elizabeth I, but under Mary there was a brief reaction, and carvers worked overtime to replace the destroyed images, many of which were very beautiful. Archbishop Laud in the early seventeenth century took steps to restore order and seemliness into the churches, but his bigotry in other directions led to the final wave of iconoclasm during the Commonwealth. The part played by Oliver Cromwell in this phase is uncertain, and has been exaggerated. (On all this iconoclasm *see* M. S. Briggs, *Goths and Vandals*, 1952.)

When church building was resumed under Wren (q.v.) on a large scale after the Great Fire of London, 1666, he introduced entirely fresh ideas into religious architecture, abandoning the medieval type of ritual arrangement together with the Gothic style which had been used up to the Reformation. Himself the son of a dean and the nephew of a bishop, he accepted the 'Protestant' outlook, and frankly planned his new London churches as preaching-houses, brilliantly designed, and admirably decorated with superb craftsmanship. At St Paul's Cathedral, however, he had to compromise with the clerical demand for a 'Latin cross' plan. In many of his City churches, on cramped sites, he was constrained to provide galleries, much as he disliked them, in order to bring all the congregation within range of the preacher's voice.

The type of church thus designed by Wren between 1666 and *c.* 1710 was imitated by other architects throughout the eighteenth and early nineteenth centuries, though from *c.* 1720 to *c.* 1820 comparatively few churches were built.

Before the Toleration Act of 1689, only a few Nonconformist meeting-houses had been erected; but during the next eleven years over 2,000 buildings were registered for worship by Congregationalists, Baptists, and Presbyterians, who had become very numerous since their beginnings under Elizabeth I. Of these licensed premises, only a proportion were built for their purpose (and of these a number still survive—*see* NONCONFORMIST CHURCH ARCHITECTURE), somewhat in Wren's style, but simpler and smaller, owing to lack of funds. No Roman Catholic churches, however, were permitted until the Catholic Emancipation Act of 1829. There was a great boom in church building in 1818, when Parliament voted a million pounds for new Anglican churches, most of which were in the newly revived Gothic style (*see* GOTHIC REVIVAL). For another century Gothic held the field, but during recent years more original ideas of design have appeared. Though the above brief account relates only to England, a somewhat similar course of development took place in the other mainly Protestant countries of north-west Europe, and in North America.

See AISLE, ALTAR, AMBULATORY, APSE, ANTE-CHAPEL, ATRIUM, AUMBRY, BALDAQUIN, BAPTISTERY, BELFRY, CAMPANILE, CATAFALQUE, CHANCEL, CHANTRY, CHAPEL, CHARNEL-HOUSE, CHEVET, CHOIR, CLERESTORY, CLOISTER, EASTER SEPULCHRE, FERETORY, FONT, GALILEE, HAGIOSCOPE, ICONOSTASIS, JESSE WINDOW, JUBÉ, LADY CHAPEL, LECTERN, LICH-GATE, LOW-SIDE WINDOW, MINSTER, MISERICORD, MONASTERY, NARTHEX, NAVE, ORATORY, ORGAN, ORIENTATION, PARCLOSE SCREEN, PARVISE, PEW, PISCINA, PLUMBERY, PORTICUS, PREDELLA, PRESBYTERY, PULPIT, PULPITUM, REREDOS, RETRO-CHOIR, ROOD-LOFT, ROOD-SCREEN, SACRISTY, SANCTUARY, SEDILIA, SOUNDING-BOARD, SQUINT, STALL, STEEPLE, STOUP, TABERNACLE, TRANSEPT, TRIFORIUM, VESTRY, WATCHING CHAMBER; *also* ABBEY, BASILICA, CATHEDRAL, 'C.C.C.C.,' ECCLESIOLOGICAL SOCIETY, PRIORY.

Bibliography. A. H. Thompson, *The Ground Plan of the English Parish Church*, 1911, and *The Historical Growth of the English Parish Church*, 1911; A. L. Drummond, *The Church Architecture of Protestantism*, 1934; J. C. Cox and C. B. Ford, *The Parish Churches of England*, 1935; G. W. Addleshaw and F. Etchells, *The Architectural Setting of Anglican Worship*, 1936; E. H. Short, *A History of Religious Architecture*, 1936; H. Batsford and C. Fry, *The Greater English Church*, 1940; Incorporated Church Building Society, *Fifty Modern Churches*, 1947; G. H. Cook, *The English Mediaeval Parish Church*, 1954; J. D. O'Connell, (R.C.) *Church Building and Furnishing*, 1955; E. D. Mills, *The Modern Church*, 1956. *See also* bibliographies under the long article on ARCHITECTURE, PERIODS OF, 4–9, and at end of other articles on the architecture of various countries.

Churriguera, José de (*b.* Madrid, 1650; *d.* Salamanca, 1723), Spanish architect, was the leading member of a large family of architects, to whom has been wrongly ascribed much of the so-called 'Churrigueresque' work—very fantastic and exuberant—of the Baroque period in Spain. In fact, his work was much less flamboyant than that of his followers, Pedro de Ribera and Narciso Tomé. So far as it is possible to distinguish his own buildings, the chief examples are the façades of the churches of S. Cajetano and S. Tomás at Madrid;

the Palacio Goyeneche at Madrid, later the Real Academia de San Fernando, built for a newspaper proprietor; a town plan, palace, and church at Nuevo Bastan for the same patron (1709–13); the Ayuntamiento (town hall), the tower and courtyard of the Jesuit College, and probably the general layout of the Plaza Mayor (1720–33)—all at Salamanca, which has been called 'a town of the Churrigueras.'

C.I.A.M., abbreviation for Congrès Internationaux d'Architecture Moderne, founded in 1928, with Dr Giedion (q.v.) as general secretary.

Ciborium (Lat., from Gk *kibōrion*), either (i) a small ornamental receptacle, often made of precious materials, for the reservation of the Eucharist, which Sir Gilbert Scott (q.v.) said may possibly

CIBORIUM (9th century) in the church of S. Apollinare in Classe, Ravenna, Italy

have given him the idea for his immense Albert Memorial (1863–72); or (ii) a canopied structure over a high altar, e.g. at S. Apollinare in Classe, Ravenna (ninth century), as illustrated. In later years such a *ciborium* became known as a baldaquin as at St Peter's, Rome.

Cincture, a ring or fillet around the shaft of a column.

Cinquecento (Ital., fifteen hundred), 'the fifteen hundreds,' i.e. the sixteenth century, not the fifteenth.

Cinquefoil (Fr. *cinq*, five), in medieval architecture, an arch or circular opening divided into five lobes or leaves by projecting 'cusps' (q.v.).

Circus (Lat., from Gk *kirkos*). (1) In ancient Rome a large building, normally oblong (with one or both ends rounded) or oval; with tiers of seats for spectators, encircling a flat open space for races, public spectacles, etc. (cf. ARENA and STADIUM). In Rome the former Circus Flaminius is ruined and the former Circus of Domitian (about 700 feet by 180 feet) is represented by the Piazza Navona, but the Circus Maximus (about 2,000 feet long) still remains in a rather dismal condition, though the gasworks on the site have been removed recently. (2) A circular

CINQUEFOIL. Two varieties

range of houses. The most notable examples in Britain are the Circus at Bath (1764), and Royal Circus and Moray Place (both 1767) at Edinburgh. (3) A more or less circular space at the junction of two main thoroughfares at right angles, e.g. Oxford Circus in London.

Cistern (Lat. *cisterna*), a tank or artificial reservoir for the storage of water. In modern houses, served by a municipal water supply, this is a comparatively small metal tank in the roof; in ancient times, however, vast underground cisterns for water were provided, notably at Constantinople (Istanbul), and in the Roman settlements along the north coast of Africa.

Cladding, an old English version of 'clothing,' applied in modern architecture to a thin external covering of various materials over a hidden structure of other materials, e.g. reinforced concrete.

Clapboard, a thin narrow board, usually of cleft oak, but to-day often of sawn deal, used for covering the exterior of timber-framed buildings, especially in the New England states of America, where the fashion, as well as the name, was introduced from England in the seventeenth century and still persists. In modern England the term generally used is 'weather-boarding.'

Classical Architecture, strictly speaking, the architecture of Hellenic Greece and of imperial Rome, from *c.* 500 B.C. to *c.* A.D. 450; also extended to cover the revival of classical forms during the Renaissance in Europe and America, especially the formal classical or 'Palladian' type (q.v.), introduced by Inigo Jones (q.v.) from Italy, early in the seventeenth century.

Clerestory, Clerestorey, or **Clearstory,** a term of which the meaning is evident, as it implies the stage or storey of an aisled basilica or church above a range of arches or columns (the Arcade or Colonnade) and also above the blank stage (the Triforium) concealing the lean-to roof of the aisle, because the clerestory contains a row of large windows to light the interior of the church—this fact explaining the word 'clear.'

Clock. Many famous clocks with moving figures or other remarkable features are found in various parts of Europe, e.g. at the Torre dell' Orologio at Venice (1496–99); in the cathedral at Roskilde, Denmark (*c.* 1500); in Wells Cathedral (*c.* 1523); and at Hampton Court Palace (1500). 'Big Ben' (1851), at Westminster, was designed by Lord Grimthorpe (q.v.), a versatile lawyer who was an expert horologist as well as an amateur architect. There are fine bracket clocks, projecting over the street, on the Guildhall at Guildford (1683), and on the tower of St Mary-le-Bow, London (about the same date).

Cloister (Lat. *claustrum,* an enclosed place or enclosure), a covered walk or arcade in a monastery or college, usually around all four sides of a square area of grass—the 'cloister garth.' There are fine medieval vaulted cloisters in several English cathedrals, e.g. Canterbury, Gloucester, Lincoln, Norwich, and at Westminster Abbey. (*Illustrated* CATHEDRAL and MONASTERY.)

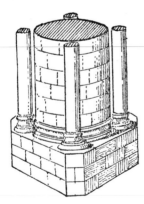

CLUSTERED COLUMN
From Westminster Abbey
(13*th century*)

Close, an enclosure; more precisely, the precinct of a cathedral, enclosed by buildings belonging to the cathedral (e.g. the deanery and the houses of the canons), and often by formerly monastic buildings. The close, with its pleasant lawns and trees, is a feature particularly distinctive of English cathedrals, and is seldom found abroad.

Closet, originally any small private room; occasionally a monarch's private apartment; later a small store-room for provisions or utensils, or a 'powder closet'; but applied to a water-closet after the invention of that appliance, its predecessor having been known as a 'privy.'

Clustered Column, an apparently single column formed of several stone shafts or pillars attached to each other.

Coade Stone, a form of artificial stone, resembling terra-cotta, manufactured from *c.* 1769 onwards at a factory in Lambeth, London, owned by Mrs Elizabeth Coade. It was largely used in London for 'dressings' (q.v.) on brick buildings, e.g. in Bedford Square, where it has weathered well.

Cob, a mixture of clay and chopped straw, formerly much used in Devon and Dorset as a walling material. It requires periodical lime-washing. The top of cob walls must be protected from rain and frost by an overhanging 'hat' of thatch, tiles, brick, or stone, and their base by 'shoes' in the form of a brick or stone plinth.

Cockerell, Charles Robert, R.A. (*b.* London, 28 April 1788; *d.* there, 17 Sept. 1863), a learned English architect and writer on architecture, was the first R.I.B.A. Royal Gold Medallist in 1848, and the first professional President of the R.I.B.A. in 1860. He was trained at first by his father, an architect, and then under Robert Smirke (q.v.). He travelled extensively in Greece and Italy, 1810–17, and wrote an amusing journal of his adventures. He started independent practice on returning to London, 1817; succeeded his father as surveyor to St Paul's Cathedral in 1819, and became architect to the Bank of England after the resignation of Sir John Soane (q.v.) in 1833. From 1840 to 1857 he was Professor of Architecture at the Royal Academy. He was a superb draughtsman as well as a competent archaeologist and a successful lecturer on classical architecture. In 1838 he exhibited at the Royal Academy a wonderful drawing entitled 'A Tribute to Wren,' showing all that great man's buildings in a single group. Cockerell's own chief buildings were the Literary and Philosophical Institution (now Freemasons' Hall) at Bristol (1821–3); St David's College, Lampeter—in Gothic style (1822–7); Hanover Chapel, Regent Street, London (1823–5, demolished 1896); Holy Trinity Church, Bristol (1829–33); alterations to the Bank of England (1834–5 and 1848–50); branches of the Bank of England at Plymouth (1835), Bristol (1844), Liverpool (1845), Manchester (1845–6), the north part of the Cambridge University Library (1837–40); the completion of the Fitzwilliam Museum, Cambridge (begun by Basevi, q.v.) (1845–62), and of St George's Hall, Liverpool (begun by H. L. Elmes, q.v.) (1851–4); and, most important of all, the Ashmolean Museum and Taylorian Institute at Oxford (1841). He competed unsuccessfully for several other large buildings in London. His researches in Greece (at Aegina and Bassae, 1810–17) were not published till 1860, and his journal of his travels in Greece not until 1903.

Coffering, a series of deep panels sunk in the surface of a ceiling, vault, or dome.

COFFERING. A coffered ceiling

* D

Collar-beam Roof, a timber pitched roof having its sloping rafters tied together by a collar-beam at a point well above their spring. It is inferior in strength to a roof of which the rafters are tied at their base or 'spring' by a tie-beam but it gives more internal head-room. (*Illustrated* Roof.)

Collcutt, Thomas Edward (*b.* Oxford, 16 Mar. 1840; *d.* 7 Oct. 1924), English architect; President R.I.B.A., 1906–8; R.I.B.A. Royal Gold Medallist, 1902. He was articled to E. W. Armstrong, and then became assistant to G. E. Street (q.v.). His principal buildings were Blackburn Public Library (1872); Wakefield Town Hall (1880); Royal Opera House (now Palace Theatre), London (1891); the Imperial Institute, London, with its fine tower (1893); extensions to the Savoy Hotel, London; boarding-houses at Harrow School and at Mill Hill School.

Colonnade, a row of columns supporting an entablature.

Colonnette, a small column.

Colosseum, sometimes spelt **Coliseum** (e.g. by Byron: 'While stands the Coliseum, Rome shall stand'), a term derived from Lat. *colosseus* (gigantic), commonly applied to the Flavian Amphitheatre at Rome, built *c.* A.D. 75–82.

Columbarium (Lat., from *columba*, a dove or pigeon). (1) A dove-cote or pigeon-cote, of which a number of historical examples still exist in England, some with nests for over a thousand birds each (*see* M. S. Briggs, *The English Farmhouse*, 1953). (2) In ancient Rome the name was also given to sepulchral chambers containing numerous niches for cinerary urns.

Column (Lat. *columna*). (1) A cylindrical and slightly tapered pillar, serving as a support to some portion of a building. (2) A similar pillar standing isolated as a monument, e.g. Trajan's Column at Rome, A.D. 112 and Nelson's Column in London. (*Illustrated* Orders.)

Commode Step, a curved step at the foot of a flight of stairs.

Common Rafters, the sloping rafters carrying slates or tiles in any type of sloping roof (q.v., *illustrated*).

Comper, Sir John Ninian (*b.* Aberdeen, 10 June 1864; *d.* London, 22 Dec. 1960). Noted for his successful decoration of churches and their accessories. He was articled to Messrs Bodley (q.v.) & Garner. Among his new churches are St Margaret, Braemar, and St Barnabas, Ilford (1898); New Hinksey (1899); St George, Mexborough (1900); St Cyprian, Marylebone; St Crispin, Yerendawna, India; Kirriemuir-Angus; St Gilbert and St Hugh, Gosberton (1903); St Mary, Welling, borough (1906); St Giles, Wimborne; St Mary, Rochdale; St Michael, Newquay (1911); Rosyth, Fife (1919); St Philip, Cosham (1937). Other church work includes the Lady Chapel of Downside Abbey (1893); the Warriors' Chapel at Westminster Abbey (1931–2); a long list of decorative work in Southwark Cathedral and elswhere. He also designed the Welsh National War Memorial at Cardiff (1928). Comper was knighted in 1960.

Competitions, Architectural. A competition is recorded as early as 448 B.C., when the Boulē (Senate or Council) of Athens invited designs from architects for a war memorial on the Acropolis, and even prescribed the scale for designs. There are a few instances in the Middle Ages (e.g. for the layout of the Piazza della Signoria at Florence, 1355, according to Vasari), and during the sixteenth century in Italy (*see* BRUNELLESCHI) and Spain (e.g. for the Escurial, 22 architects taking part). The competition for the completion of the Louvre in Paris, 1665, was a sordid example of intrigue. In Britain the first authentic and organized competitions seem to have been those for the Royal Exchange at Dublin, 1768, with 64 competitors taking part; for the 'Lunatic Hospital' (New Bedlam) in Southwark, 1776; and for the Bank of England, 1788, won by Soane (q.v.) against 13 competitors. During the past century and a quarter the following have been the most notable competitions in Britain, the names of the winners being given in brackets: University of London, now University College (Wilkins, q.v.), 1826; Cambridge University Library (Cockerell, q.v.), 1830; National Gallery, London (Wilkins), 1832; Fitzwilliam Museum, Cambridge (Basevi, q.v.), 1835; Houses of Parliament, London, 97 competitors (Barry, q.v.), 1835; St George's Hall, Liverpool, 86 competitors (Elmes, q.v., aged twenty-four), 1839; Royal Exchange, London (Tite, q.v.), 1840; Foreign Office and India Office, London, 219 competitors (Gilbert Scott, q.v.), 1856; Albert Memorial, London (Scott), 1863; St Pancras Hotel, London (Scott), 1865; Law Courts, London (Street, q.v.), 1866; Town Hall and Law Courts, Manchester (Waterhouse, q.v.), 1868; Edinburgh Cathedral (Scott), 1873; Cardiff City Hall and Law Courts (Lanchester and Rickards, qq.v.), 1897; Victoria and Albert Museum, London (A. Webb, q.v.), 1899; Liverpool Cathedral (Giles Scott, q.v., aged twenty-two), 1903; Wesleyan Central Hall, London (Lanchester and Rickards), 1905; Belfast City Hall (A. B. Thomas, q.v.), 1906; London County Hall (R. Knott, q.v.), 1908; Welsh National Museum, Cardiff (A. D. Smith and C. Brewer), 1910; Port of London Building (Cooper, q.v.), 1912; New Royal Horticultural Hall, London (Easton and Robertson, qq.v.), 1926; Leeds University Extensions (Lanchester, 1927); new R.I.B.A. Headquarters, London (Wornum, q.v.), 1932; Guildford Cathedral (Maufe, q.v.), 1936; Coventry Cathedral (Spence, q.v.), 1951. Among international competitions in recent years, the most notable have been those for the layout of Canberra, Australia (won by W. B. Griffin of U.S.A.) and for the League of Nations Headquarters at Geneva, 1927.

Some of the competitions in the mid nineteenth century, especially those for the Royal Exchange and for the Foreign Office, were so scandalously manipulated that a much more rigorous system of control was found to be necessary. At the present day the R.I.B.A. (q.v.) is generally able to insist upon the appointment of a professional and impartial assessor, the issue of clear conditions in advance, the absolute anonymity of competitors, the award to the competitor placed first, and other desirable requirements. Competitions may be either (i) public, open to all comers; or (ii) limited, open only to selected and invited architects of known experience; or (iii) in two stages: senior architects being invited to compete in the second stage with others competitively selected in the first stage; as in the competition for the London County Hall.

Composite Order, The, *see* ORDERS OF ARCHITECTURE.

Conant, Kenneth John (*b.* Neenah, Wisconsin, 28 June 1894), architectural writer and teacher. He graduated A.B. at Harvard in 1915, M.Arch., 1919, Ph.D., 1925. He joined the staff of the Faculty of Architecture at Harvard in 1920, becoming professor in 1936. He took part in the Carnegie Expedition to Yucatan in 1926, and was also associated with the excavation of the Abbey of Cluny in France. He served in the First World War, 1917–19. He has written several books, including a history of the famous cathedral at Santiago de Compostela in Spain, published 1926.

Concrete (Lat. *concretus*, from *concrescere*, to grow together). A form of concrete was much used by the Romans, and contributed largely to the strength of their most famous buildings (*see* ARCHITECTURE, PERIODS OF, 3). It depended for its efficiency upon a cement made of volcanic ash, pozzolana (q.v.). The introduction of scientifically prepared concrete into modern building began early in the nineteenth century, chiefly as a result of the invention of Portland cement, patented in 1824, and it is now one of the most important of all building materials. It is composed, according to requirements, of an 'aggregate' (broken brick or stones, ballast or gravel, etc., with sand) together with a carefully graded 'matrix' of Portland cement. *See also* REINFORCED CONCRETE and PRE-STRESSED CONCRETE CONSTRUCTION.

See A. C. Davis, *Portland Cement*, 1934; W. H. Glanville (ed.), *Modern Concrete Construction*, 1939; H. L. Childe, *Concrete Products, etc.*, 1940; F. M. Lea and C. H. Desch, *The Chemistry of Cement and Concrete*, 1956.

Conduit (Fr., from Med. Lat. *conductus*), pronounced 'cundit,' an artificial channel for the conveyance of water, service pipes, cables, etc.

Confessio (Lat.), a crypt (q.v.) under a church, specially built to contain the tomb of a saint or martyr, e.g. at St Peter's, Rome, but found in many other Italian churches. It is usually placed under the high altar. There are English examples in several pre-Conquest Romanesque or 'Saxon' churches, e.g. at Wing, Buckinghamshire; Repton, Derbyshire; Brixworth, Northamptonshire; Ripon Cathedral, and Hexham.

Confessional, in Roman Catholic churches, a small box or enclosed stall in which a priest hears confessions from a person kneeling outside. In Baroque churches of the seventeenth to eighteenth centuries the confessional boxes are of woodwork richly carved with statuary and emblems, notably at Brussels and Louvain in Belgium.

Console. (1) In classical architecture, an ornamental bracket of slight projection but of much greater height, with two reversed volutes (q.v.); as used at the Erechtheum at Athens, a Greek temple of the Ionic Order; also occasionally called an 'ancon.' (2) A detached and isolated desk or fitting containing the keyboards and stops of an organ, and placed at some distance from the organ itself.

Conurbation, a term in town-planning, invented by Sir Patrick Geddes (*c.* 1937) to describe a group of previously separate but adjoining townships which have grown together to form one huge inchoate mass of population. The chief examples in Britain are Greater London, the Birmingham area, Merseyside including Liverpool, the Manchester area, Leeds-Bradford, Tyneside, and the Glasgow area. In the six English 'conurbations' live 40 per cent of the population of England; in Scotland 40 per cent of the nation live in the Glasgow area.

See P. Self, *Cities in Flood*, 1947.

Convent, *see* MONASTERY.

CONSOLE

Cooley, Thomas (*b.* in England, 1740; *d.* at Dublin, 1784), an architect whose career was astounding. He was apprenticed as a carpenter, and as a boy won a prize at the Royal Society of Arts; then, in 1769, won the important competition for the Royal Exchange at Dublin, and went to Ireland to supervise its building, which was finished in 1779. He made the preliminary plans for the Four Courts in Dublin (afterwards completed by Gandon, q.v.), and designed Newgate Jail (since demolished) and the tower of Armagh Cathedral.

Cooper, Sir Edwin, R.A. (*b.* Scarborough, Yorks, 1873; *d.* London, 24 June 1942), English architect, R.I.B.A. Royal Gold Medallist, 1931, had a sensationally successful career. He was articled in Yorkshire, travelled abroad, came to work in London as an assistant, and started independent practice in 1897, the year in which he won the first two of a long series of public competitions. For some years he was in partnership with Messrs Hall & Davis, then with S. B. Russell; but from 1910 he worked alone, and the series of successes in competitions continued with Marylebone Town Hall in 1911 and the Port of London Authority's huge building on Tower Hill in 1912. The chief items in his enormous subsequent practice were the Star and Garter Home at Richmond (1924); the Guildhall and Law Courts at Hull; the new Lloyd's Building (1929); Royal Mail Buildings, Leadenhall Street (1929); the National Provincial Bank, Lothbury (1931)—the last three in the City of London; a number of important buildings at Tilbury and in the Docks for the Port of London Authority; the Holker Law Library, Gray's Inn, London (1930); the Devonport School of Pathology and Nurses' Home at Greenwich (1929); the Riddell Home at St Thomas's Hospital, London (1937); the

College of Nursing in Cavendish Square, London (1922–6); extensions
to St Mary's Hospital, London (1933); the South London Hospital for
Women; additions to Cranleigh School and Bedale's School; the
chapel at Bryanston School; the library at St Hilda's College, Oxford;
and, among a long list of country houses, Gatton Park in Surrey.
His buildings were splendidly planned, dignified, scholarly, very
Roman in character, and displayed the proud swagger of the prosperous Edwardian period. He was knighted in 1923.

Coping, a protective capping or covering of brick or stone on the
top of a wall. It usually projects slightly over the wall face, and has
a throating or groove to prevent rain-water from running down the
wall face.

Corbel, a projection, usually of stone but occasionally of brick or

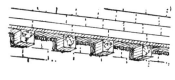

iron, built into a wall and projecting from its face, as a bracket
to support a beam or a roof-truss.

Corbel Course, a course of bricks
projecting from a wall as a continuous corbel, to carry a superincumbent weight.

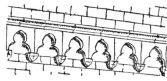

Corbel Table, a parapet or projecting course of stone, resting
upon a series of corbels.

*CORBEL TABLE. Above, Norman;
below, Gothic*

Corbett, Harvey Wiley (*b.* San
Francisco, 8 Jan. 1873; *d.* New
York, 22 April 1954), American
architect; designed Bush House,
Strand, London, delayed by the
First World War but completed in
1935. After graduating at the University of California in 1895, he
studied at the École des Beaux Arts in Paris, and started independent
practice in New York in 1901. From 1903 to 1912 he worked in
partnership with F. L. Pell; from 1912 to 1922 with F. J. Helme;
from 1922 to 1941 with Messrs Harrison & MacMurray; thereafter
alone. The principal buildings in the United States designed by
these partnerships or by him alone were the Maryland Institute at
Baltimore; Municipal Buildings at Springfield, Massachusetts; the
Bush Terminal Building; part of the Rockefeller Centre (1931);
the Criminal Courts Building (1936); the Fifth Avenue Hotel; the
Community Church (1935); the Riverside Health Centre (1949);
buildings at Brooklyn College (1935); two branch libraries—all these
in New York; and the Bushnell Library at Hartford, Connecticut.
Bush House, London, presented a difficult problem, on an island site
with a substantial drop in level from Kingsway to the Strand.

Corbie Steps, or **Crow** Steps (from 'corbie,' a raven or crow), a
series of steps or indentations in the coping of a gable. Much used
in Flanders and Holland, introduced into eastern England during the
fifteenth century, and also popular in Scotland.

Corfiato, Hector Othon (*b.* Kafr
az-Zaiyat, Egypt, 22 Dec. 1892;
d. London, 3 May 1963), architect;
Prof. of Architecture, University
College, London, 1946-1960. He
studied at the École des Beaux
Arts and in the Atelier Daumet-
Jaussely, Paris. His principal
buildings are the churches of
Notre Dame de France, Leicester

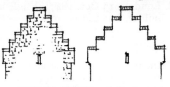

*CORBIE STEPS. Left, stone;
right, brick*

Square, and of the Perpetual Adoration, Chelsea; large additions to
University College—all these in London; several buildings in Burma;
the layout and buildings of the Colleges of Technology at Zaria and
Enugu, and the School of Pharmacy at Ibadan—all these in Nigeria
(1954–9). He has written, jointly with Sir A. E. Richardson (q.v.)
The Art of Architecture, 1938.

Corinthian Order, The, *see* ORDERS OF ARCHITECTURE, *illustrated.*

Cornice. (1) A projecting horizontal feature, usually moulded,
which crowns an external façade, or occurs internally at the junction
of a wall and a ceiling. (2) In classical architecture, the topmost
member of the entablature (q.v., *illustrated*).

Corona (Lat., crown), in classical architecture, a vertical member
forming part of a cornice (q.v.), between the cymatium (q.v.) and
the bed-moulding.

Corridor (from Ital. *corridore*, literally 'a running-place'), a wide
passage in a building.

Cortile (Ital.), an internal courtyard in a palace or in a large
building.

Cortona, Pietro da, *see* BERETTINI.

Cottage (a word of uncertain derivation but in use so long ago as
Chaucer's time), a small or humble dwelling, in country or town.
Early in the twentieth century, however, the invention of the week
end and the motor-car caused the term to be applied (or misapplied)
to much larger buildings, which came to be known as 'country
cottages' in contrast to their owners' 'town houses.' Such a dwelling
often contains six bedrooms, a couple of bath-rooms, and three
sitting-rooms, in addition to ancillary accommodation.

For old English country cottages *see* S. R. Jones, *The Village
Homes of England*, 1912, and *English Village Homes*, 1936, and
B. Oliver, *Cottages of England of the 16th–18th Centuries*, 1929.
For Regency examples *see* W. Barber, *Designs for Cottages*,
1802, and R. Elsam, *Designs for Cottages*, 1816. *See also*
reports on design of modern cottages published by the R.I.B.A.
(1918), Ministry of Agriculture (1914–15) and other Government
departments, especially *Design of Dwellings* (Ministry of Health),
1944.

Cottingham, Lewis Nockalls (*b.* Laxfield, Suffolk, 24 Oct. 1787;

d. London, 13 Oct. 1847), English architect. He was apprenticed to a builder, but turned to architecture and worked as an assistant in a London architect's office until he started practice in 1814. He was appointed surveyor to the Cooks' Company in London in 1822; and in 1825 was commissioned by the dean and chapter of Rochester Cathedral to restore the fabric. Among his many other restorations were St Albans Abbey (1833); Magdalen College Chapel, Oxford (1830–5); Hereford Cathedral (1841); and an almost complete rebuilding of Armagh Cathedral (1834). He designed Snelston Hall in Derbyshire (1830–5), and laid out an estate on the south side of Waterloo Bridge, London (*c*. 1825). He formed a private museum of Gothic carvings, casts, etc., which became the nucleus of the Royal Architectural Museum (*see* MUSEUMS), and published several books on architecture and ornament.

Council for the Preservation of Rural England (4 Hobart Place, London, S.W.1). The C.P.R.E., as it is commonly called, was founded in 1926 by a group of patriotic idealists, including Sir Guy Dawber (q.v.), the architect, and Sir Patrick Abercrombie (q.v.), best known as a town-planner. Although its interests are not restricted to preserving beautiful or historical buildings, for which the S.P.A.B. (q.v.) already exists, the C.P.R.E., in its proclaimed purpose of organizing 'concerted action to secure the protection of rural landscape and of country and town amenities from disfigurement and injury,' is concerned with buildings in so far as they form part of the landscape, as also with posters, electric pylons, petrol stations, and any other features which, if badly designed, or unsuitably sited, may disturb rural charm.

Couple Roof, a timber roof of small span, which has only its two sloping rafters, without any tie-beam or collar-beam (q.v.). (*Illustrated* ROOF.)

Course, a continuous layer of bricks, or of stones of equal thickness, in a wall.

Court (cf. Fr. *cour*; Ital. *cortile*; Ger. *hof*; Sp. *patio*), an open space or yard surrounded by walls or buildings.

C.P.R.E., abbreviation for Council for the Preservation of Rural England (q.v.).

Craig, James (*b*. ? 1740; *d*. Edinburgh, 23 June 1795), Scottish architect and town-planner, was trained by Sir Robert Taylor (q.v.). In 1767 he won a competition for planning the 'New Town' of Edinburgh, where he also designed the Physicians' Hall (1774, since demolished) and other buildings as part of the scheme.

Cram, Ralph Adams (*b*. Hamilton Falls, New Hampshire, 16 Dec. 1863; *d*. Boston, Massachusetts, 22 Sept. 1942), American architect. He began practice in 1889, joining in partnership with Wentworth from 1890, Goodhue (q.v.) from 1895, and Ferguson from 1899, Goodhue leaving the firm in 1914. Both he and Cram were enthusiasts in reviving Gothic architecture for churches and colleges, and both men wrote books on its history. Cram was Professor of

Architecture at the Massachusetts Institute of Technology from 1914 to 1921. The firm's large practice included West Point Academy, won in competition (1903); All Saints' Church, Brookline, Massachusetts (1905); Trinity Church, Havana—in Spanish Baroque style (1905); the cathedral of St John the Divine, New York (1906); Calvary Church, Pittsburgh (1907).

Crazing, a defect often seen in cement surfaces, in the form of very fine cracks. This may arise from various causes, especially from an unsuitable mixture of ingredients for the cement.

Crematorium, or **Crematory** (from Lat. *cremare,* to consume by fire), a building for the incineration of corpses.

> *See* F. C. Fidler, *Cremation,* 1930, and P. H. Jones and G. H. Noble, *Cremation in Great Britain,* 1931.

Crenellation (from Old Fr. *crenel,* a notch), either (i) the act of furnishing a house with notched or indented battlements (q.v., *illustrated*); or (ii) such a battlement itself. In feudal England licences 'to crenellate' (i.e. to fortify their houses) were issued only to approved persons.

Crepidoma, the stepped base of a Greek temple. *See* STYLOBATE.

Cresting, a line of ornament on the ridge of a roof or on the top of a screen. *See also* BRATTISHING.

CRESTING

Crocket, in Gothic architecture, a carved ornament somewhat resembling a curved leaf; used especially on the angles of spires and on canopies over niches.

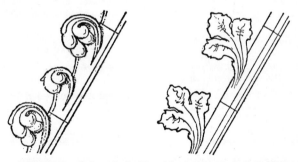

CROCKET. Left, early Gothic; right, late Gothic (both English)

'Cronaca, Il,' properly **Simone del Pollaiolo** (*b.* Florence, 30 Oct. 1457; *d.* there, 27 Sept. 1508), Italian architect and sculptor. He studied in Rome, then returned to Florence, and in 1491 was commissioned to complete the great Strozzi Palace there. His work included the famous cornice. He took charge of the cathedral about 1495, and of the Palazzo Vecchio, where in 1495–7 he added the Cinquecento Hall, afterwards altered by Vasari (q.v.). Another work in Florence was the church of S. Salvatore al Monte, 1504.

Crossing, in any cruciform church, the space where the nave and chancel are crossed by the transept. Many English cathedrals (e.g. Canterbury, Durham, Gloucester, Lincoln, St Albans, Salisbury, Worcester, York) have a tower over the crossing.

Cross Vault, the intersection of two vaults at right-angles. (*Illustrated* VAULTING.)

Crown. (1) The highest point of a semicircular arch or vault (corresponding to the 'apex' of a pointed arch). (*Illustrated* ARCH, PARTS OF AN.) (2) The open-work spire of certain churches,

CRUCKS. A cottage on crucks at Dymock, Glos.

e.g. Newcastle Cathedral, in the shape of a crown. (*Illustrated* SPIRE.)

Crow Steps, *see* CORBIE STEPS.

Crucks, curved or roughly shaped tree trunks, used in primitive timber-framed construction, at each end of a building and also intermediately, to serve the dual function of vertical posts and sloping rafters.

Crypt (from Gk *kruptos*, hidden place), an underground chamber or vault. The term is usually applied only to churches. Crypts are often provided with altars and used for worship.

Cryptoporticus (Lat.), an enclosed or concealed portico; or, occasionally, an underground passage.

Cupola (Lat. *cupula*, dim. of *cupa*, a cask), a curved or domical roof over a circular, square, or polygonal space. The term is almost synonymous with 'Dome' and 'Rotunda' (qq.v.); but over the town hall at Leeds (1853–8) is a steeply curving domical roof which could be more accurately described as a cupola rather than as a dome.

Curtail Step, a step with its curved end shaped like a scroll, at the foot of a flight of stairs.

Curtain Wall. (1) In medieval military architecture, a length of wall between two towers or bastions. (2) In a modern framed building, a thin wall between, and often in front of, the main structural members of steel or of reinforced concrete, and bearing no load. *See also* CLADDING.

Cushion Capital, in Romanesque architecture, a cubical capital with its lower corners cut away and rounded to resemble a cushion.

Cusp, in Gothic architecture, a projection carved on the underside of an arch. Cusps divide the arch into a series of 'foils' (q.v.), and are purely ornamental. They are moulded, and sometimes terminate in a flower.

CUSHION CAPITAL

Cyclopean Masonry, a term originally restricted to the Mycenaean and other primitive Aegean masonry of huge and irregular stone blocks, the supposition being that this was the work of a mythical race of giants (Gk *kuklops*). The term has since been loosely extended to describe any masonry of large-sized polygonal blocks.

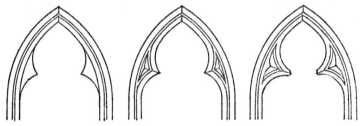

CUSP. Left, early or primitive type; middle, chamfer cusp; right, late type

Cyma Recta (first word spelt SIMA in U.S.A.), in classical architecture, a moulding which is concave above and convex below; also called an 'ogee' moulding. (*Illustrated* MOULDINGS, CLASSICAL.)

Cyma Reversa, in classical architecture, a moulding which is the converse of the Cyma Recta (q.v.), being convex above and concave below. (*Illustrated* MOULDINGS, CLASSICAL.)

Cymatium, in classical architecture, the crowning member of a cornice, usually in the form of a cyma recta or cyma reversa (qq.v.).

Cyprus, Architecture in. Before its occupation by Britain in 1878, Cyprus had a long series of rulers; but only three periods have left any substantial remains. When Richard Cœur-de-Lion captured it in 1191, it already contained some Byzantine castles, now ruined, e.g. at Kantára, Kyrenia, St Hilarion, and Buffavento. The French crusader, Guy de Lusignan, became King of Cyprus soon afterwards; and the fine cathedral of Famagusta, in French mid Gothic style, is only one of many churches erected during the period 1192–1489, among them the now ruined abbey of Bella Pais. The Venetians occupied Cyprus in 1489, and constructed the fortifications and town gates of Famagusta and Nicosia. The Turks conquered the island in 1571, and retained it until 1878. Their buildings were mediocre, and their conversion of the Gothic churches into mosques was deplorably clumsy. Under British rule the Turkish vandalism and neglect was remedied, the historical monuments being carefully preserved.   The Governor's House, after its destruction by a mob in 1931, was rebuilt from designs by Maurice Webb.

See G. B. Jeffery, *Historical Monuments of Cyprus*, 1918.

Czechoslovakian Architecture, *see* GERMAN ARCHITECTURE; *also* two books by M. S. Briggs on the buildings of Prague: *City of Baroque and Gothic*, 1946, and *Magic in Stone*, 1947.

D

Dado. (1) In a room, the lower part of a wall, up to a height of 2 to 3 feet above floor level. Usually the top of the dado is capped with a moulding—the 'dado rail' or 'chair rail' (q.v.)—or by a line of paint, and the dado itself is often painted dark or covered with panelling or some protective material to avoid damage. (2) In classical architecture, the plain part of a pedestal between its base and its cornice. An alternative term is 'die.' (*Illustrated* PANELLING.)

Dado Rail, *see* DADO above; *also* CHAIR RAIL.

Dais. (1) In the 'hall' of a large medieval or Tudor house, a raised platform (at the end farthest from the kitchen quarters) on which sat the owner, his family, and his guests, at a long dining-table. (2) In a modern college dining-hall, a similar platform. (*Illustrated* HOUSE.)

Dance, George, the Elder (*b.* 1695 or 1700; *d.* London, Feb. 1768), English architect, son of Giles Dance, a mason. George also began his career as a 'stone-cutter,' and by 1735 had become 'Clerk of the City Works' in London. In that capacity he submitted a design for the New Mansion House in 1737—in competition with Gibbs, James, and Leoni (qq.v.), a formidable trio of rivals—and was successful. Besides this important work, completed in 1752, he also built the churches of St Leonard, Shoreditch (1736–40); St Matthew, Bethnal Green (1740–6, gutted 1940); and St Botolph, Aldgate (1741–4); the Fleet Market (1737); Surgeons' Hall, Old Bailey (1745); the Corn Exchange, Mark Lane (1749–50); and, in partnership with Sir R. Taylor (q.v.), London Bridge (1756–60)—these last five buildings since demolished; also, possibly but improbably, St Luke, Old Street, which seems to have been actually designed by John James (q.v.).

Dance, George, the Younger, R.A., F.R.S. (*b.* London, 20 Mar. 1741; *d.* there, 14 Jan. 1825), English architect. He was the fifth and youngest son of George Dance the Elder (q.v.), and had a much better start in life. He travelled and studied in Italy, 1763–5, obtaining several distinctions in Rome; returned to England in 1765, and succeeded to his father's City appointment in 1768. He then designed his masterpiece, Newgate Prison (1770–8), a really noble building, demolished in 1902. His other work included All Hallows Church, London Wall (1765–7); St Luke's Hospital, Old Street (1782–4); additions to St Bartholomew's Hospital (1793); the 'Gothic' front of the Guildhall (1788–9); the mansion of Wilderness Park, Sevenoaks, since demolished. Among his pupils was John Soane (q.v.).

Danish Architecture, *see* SCANDINAVIAN ARCHITECTURE.

Darwaza (Persian), in Indian architecture, a gateway or doorway.

Davis, Arthur Joseph, R.A. (*b.* London, 21 May 1878; *d.* there, 22 July 1951), English architect. He studied at the École des Beaux Arts in Paris. While there he met a leading French architect, Charles Mewès, and assisted him in his practice, becoming a partner in 1900 for Mewès's work in England. Their first important commissions in London were two splendid buildings of very French design—the Ritz Hotel (1900–6) and the *Morning Post* offices in the Strand. Mewès died in 1914. Other work by the partners, or later by Davis alone, included the Royal Automobile Club, the remodelling of the Carlton Club, Cunard House, Hudson Bay House, the Westminster Bank in Lothbury, the Armenian Church in Iverna Gardens —all these in London; and the remodelling of Luton Hoo. Generally speaking, Davis's work shows the Beaux Arts tradition at its best.

Dawber, Sir (Edward) Guy, R.A. (*b.* King's Lynn, 3 Aug. 1861; *d.* London, 24 April 1938), English architect, was President R.I.B.A., 1925–7, and Royal Gold Medallist, 1928. He was articled in King's Lynn; then worked as assistant to Sir T. Deane (q.v.) in Dublin, and next to Ernest George (q.v.) in London, for several years. During that period overwork strained his eyesight, so George sent him to the Cotswolds in 1887 as a clerk of works. The traditional architecture of the Cotswolds so impressed him that he published a book on the subject in 1905, a sequel to another on the old houses of Kent and Sussex in 1900. Thus he acquired a love of rural England and its buildings which led to his share in founding the C.P.R.E. (q.v.) in 1926; and also influenced his own practice, which consisted chiefly of charming country houses in traditional English style, several of them in the Cotswolds.

Deane, Sir Thomas (*b.* Cork, 1792; *d.* Monkstown, Dublin, 2 Sept. 1871), Irish architect. For part of his career he assisted his father, a builder, and in 1830 he became mayor of Cork and was knighted. Turning to architecture rather late in life, he designed a number of buildings in Cork, including Queen's College, now University College (1849), and the classical portico of the Court House; also Killarney Asylum. In partnership with Benjamin Woodward, he designed the museum at Trinity College, Dublin (1853–7), and also the much criticized and often ridiculed Oxford Museum (1854–60, won in competition), in which Ruskin took such an active and deplorable interest. With this venture was also associated Deane's son, Thomas Newenham Deane (q.v.).

Deane, Sir Thomas Newenham (*b.* near Cork, 15 July 1828; *d.* Dublin, 8 Nov. 1899), Irish architect, was the son of the last named. He entered his father's office in 1850 and continued his practice. His chief buildings were in Dublin, viz. the National Library and Museum (1860–90, won in competition), and St Anne's Church (date unknown), but he also designed the Clarendon Laboratory at Oxford. His eldest son, Sir Thomas Manly Deane (1851–1933), continued the family practice and was knighted in 1911.

Death-watch Beetle (*Xestobium*), one of several insects making a noise supposed to portend death: thus Goldsmith writes: 'I listened for death-watches in the wainscot.' This beetle attacks timber, especially hardwoods, and has caused untold damage in the roofs of old churches, and notably at Westminster Hall.

De Brosse, Salomon (*b.* Paris, 1562; *d.* there, 9 Dec. 1626), French architect. He was the son of a clerk of works and was trained by his grandfather, J. A. du Cerceau (q.v.). He was appointed *architecte du Roi* in 1616. His chief buildings were the 'Protestant Temple' at Charenton (1606, destroyed 1621); the Aqueduct of Arcueil (1612); the Hôtel de Bouillon (1613); the châteaux of Coulommiers (1613) and Blérencourt (1614); the façade of St Gervais (1616–21) and the Luxembourg Palace (1615–24)—both in Paris; the Capuchin Church at Coulommiers (1617–25); the Parliament House at Rennes (1618); and possibly the royal hunting-lodge at Versailles (1624).

Decani, *see* CANTORIS.

Decastyle (Gk *deka*, ten; *stulos*, a column), in classical architecture, a portico having ten columns in a row.

Decorated Style, sometimes called the 'Middle Pointed' or 'Mid-Gothic' style, was the phase of Gothic prevailing in England during the fourteenth century, when the lancet windows of the so-called 'Early English' style were replaced by tracery—at first geometrical, afterwards flowing.

Deflection, or **Deflexion,** the bending of a beam or column under pressure.

Deinocrates, a Greek architect of the fourth century B.C., who worked for Alexander the Great, planned the city of Alexandria in Egypt on geometrical lines, and evolved sundry daring or eccentric schemes which, fortunately, never came to fruition.

De L'Orme, Philibert (*b.* Lyons, *c.* 1512–15; *d.* Ivry, 8 Jan. 1570), French architect and writer on architecture. After training by his father, a builder, he studied in Italy 1533–6, and returned to work in Paris about 1540. About that date he designed the château of St Maur-les-Fosses, and took charge of the royal palace at Fontainebleau. His later work included the tomb of François I at St Denis (1547); the château of Anet (1552–9); extensions of the château of Chenonceaux (1557); an extension of the Tuileries Palace in Paris (1565). He also compiled some important books on architecture and building construction, especially *Nouvelles inventions pour bien bastir et a petits fraiz,* 1561.

See monograph by A. Blunt, 1958.

Dentil (from Lat. *denticulus,* dim. of *dens,* a tooth), a small block used in rows, resembling a row of teeth, in the cornices of Greek and Roman buildings, for purely ornamental purposes. (*Illustrated* MOULDINGS, ENRICHED (CLASSICAL).)

Dentil Course, a row of dentils.

Design, the architect's graphical solution of a project or programme —economically, structurally, and aesthetically.

Devey, George (*b*. London, 1820; *d*. Nov. 1886), English architect, was a notable figure in domestic architecture of the mid nineteenth century, far ahead of his time, and anticipating the change of fashion created by Norman Shaw (q.v.). He began his career as a student of painting, but turned to architecture, and started practice early in Victoria's reign. His work at the historic Penshurst Place in 1851 was his first important commission, and soon led to a long series of country mansions, including Betteshanger (1856); Coombe Warren, Surrey; Killarney House, Ireland; Goldings, near Hertford; St Alban's Court, near Dover; Hall Place, near Tonbridge; and Worth Park (later to be Milton Mount College), near Crawley, Sussex.

Diaconicum (Lat., from Gk *diakonikon*), in ecclesiastical architecture, a sacristy or vestry (qq.v.) adjoining a church, and used for the storage of vestments and sacred vessels.

Diaper, a regular surface pattern, carved in stone (e.g. at Westminster Abbey) or painted, in early Gothic work. It consists of rows of flowers, each framed in a square, and is derived from textile patterns. One theory finds the derivation of the name as 'd'Ypres,' where a cloth with such patterns was made; another suggests *diaspros* (Gk, 'thoroughly white').

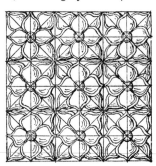

DIAPER. Lincoln Cathedral   *DIAPER. Westminster Abbey*

Diastyle, in classical architecture, the spacing of columns 2¾ to 4 diameters apart. (This is rather wide spacing: cf. EUSTYLE.)

Die, in classical architecture, the part of a pedestal between the base and the cornice.

Dientzenhofer, family of architects, practising in Prague during the seventeenth to eighteenth centuries in the Baroque style. The two most prominent of them were: (1) KILIAN IGNAZIO DIENTZEN-HOFER (*b*. Prague, 1 Sept. 1689; *d*. there, 18 Dec. 1721), who was trained by Fischer von Erlach (q.v.), and built numerous churches and convents in and around Prague, including those of St Nikolaus (1732), SS. Peter and Paul, St Charles Borromeus, and St Johann am Felsem; also the Kinsky Palace at Prague (1755–66), completed by Anselmo Lurago, and the St Maria Magdalenkirche at Karlsbad

(1733–6); (2) JOHANN DIENTZENHOFER (d. Bamberg, 1726), who designed the cathedral (1704–12) and Schloss at Fulda, and the Schloss at Pommersfelden (1711–18).

See monographs by H. Schmerber, 1900, and O. A. Weigmann, 1902.

Diglyph (Gk, rare), in classical architecture, a projecting tablet with two vertical grooves or channels.   (Cf. TRIGLYPH.)

Dikkah (Arabic), in Muslim architecture, either (i) a tribune from which certain parts of the service are said, in the sanctuary of a mosque; or (ii) a settee in a house.

Dipteral, in Greek architecture, a temple having a double peristyle.   (*Illustrated* TEMPLE.)

Distyle (Gk, two columns), in Greek architecture, a portico having two columns.   (*Illustrated* TEMPLE.)

Dīwān-I-Am (Persian), in Indian architecture, a hall for public or private audience.

Dīwān-I-Khas (Persian), in Indian architecture, a hall for public or private audience.

Dodecastyle (Gk *dōdeka*, twelve; *stulos*, column), a temple having twelve columns in its portico.

Dog-legged Staircase, a staircase (q.v., *illustrated*) which has no well-hole between parallel flights running in opposite directions.

Dog-tooth Moulding, an ornamental moulding much used around arches in England during the thirteenth century.   It consists of a row of pyramidal projections, each carved into four leaves.   (*Illustrated* MOULDINGS, ENRICHED (GOTHIC).)

Dome, a convex roof, of approximately hemispherical form, erected over a square, octagonal, or circular space in a building.   Cupola (q.v.) is an almost synonymous term (*see also* ROTUNDA).   A 'saucer dome' has a flat curve, less than a hemisphere.   Domes may be constructed wholly or partially of stone, brick, concrete, reinforced concrete, hollow tiles, steel or aluminium framing, and may be covered externally with lead, copper, or other materials.   For ideal visual effect a dome needs to be steeper than a hemisphere externally, or it appears insignificant.   Hence, certain famous domes are of double construction (e.g. St Peter's, Rome) or even of triple construction (e.g. St Paul's, London, where the heavy stone lantern is carried by a brick cone entirely concealed between the outer and inner domes, the former being of timber-framing covered with lead, the latter of brick 18 inches thick).

Domes were used by the Assyrians many centuries B.C., but the first important historical example is the Pantheon at Rome, *c*. A.D. 112, of brick and concrete, 142 feet 6 inches diameter (*illustration* 'A').   The famous Byzantine dome of S. Sophia at Constantinople, 107 feet in diameter, erected A.D. 537–52, is of brick (*illustration* 'B').

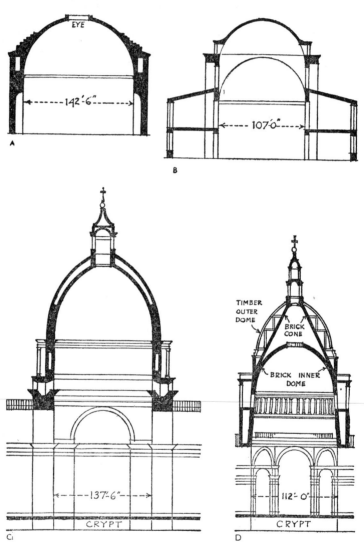

EYE

142'-6"

A

107'-0"

B

TIMBER
OUTER
DOME

BRICK
CONE

BRICK INNER
DOME

137'-6"

CRYPT

C₁

112'-0"

CRYPT

D

COMPARATIVE SECTIONS OF FOUR FAMOUS DOMES. (A) *The Pantheon, Rome;* (B) *S. Sophia, Istanbul;* (C) *St Peter's, Rome;* (D) *St Paul's, London*

In Muslim architecture (q.v.), and in India both before and after the Muslim conquest, domes were largely used for mosques and tombs, often rising above a square base with pendentives (q.v.) or squinches (q.v.) in each angle.

Though seldom found in Gothic or Romanesque architecture, the dome was reintroduced after the Renaissance. Famous examples are Brunelleschi's steep dome (1420–34) at Florence Cathedral; Bramante's little 'Tempietto' (1502–10), only 15 feet in internal diameter, adjoining S. Pietro in Montorio at Rome; and four churches at Paris—the Sorbonne (1635–49), by Lemercier, 40 feet diameter; the Val-de-Grâce (1645–50), by F. Mansart, 56 feet diameter; the Invalides (1706), by J. H. Mansart, 91 feet diameter; and the Panthéon (1757–90) by Soufflot, 69 feet diameter. Among more modern examples are the dome over the reading-room at the British Museum, London (1857), 140 feet diameter; the extraordinary stone dome over the church at Musta in Malta (1864), 118 feet diameter; and the aluminium 'Dome of Discovery' at the 1951 Exhibition in London (demolished 1953), 365 feet diameter.

Donjon (Fr., originally from Lat. *dominus,* lord; hence, the dwelling of a lord), the keep or central fortress in a castle (q.v.).

Door, a movable barrier closing the entrance ('doorway') to a building or a room. It may be hinged at the side by strap hinges or butts, or pivoted at top and bottom, or made to slide. It may be secured by locks, latches, or bolts. Doors are normally made of wood, occasionally of steel to resist fire, and in a few ancient tombs were made of stone. There are magnificent bronze doors at the Pantheon, Rome (A.D. 112), each of the two leaves measuring *c.* 24 feet high by 7 feet wide, and other famous examples of the Baptistery in Florence (1401).

Probably the oldest wooden door in England is an example, some 3,000 years old, from Egypt, now in the British Museum. Its survival is due to the dry climate of Egypt. It measures 8 feet by 4 feet, and consists of five vertical boards, $2\frac{1}{2}$ inches thick, held together by three horizontal battens. This simple type, still used for sheds, etc., in modern practice everywhere, is a 'ledged door.' The addition of diagonal braces to prevent the door sagging from its hinges produces a 'ledged and braced door.'

During the Middle Ages 'framed doors,' where the horizontal 'rails' are tenoned into the vertical 'styles,' were introduced, and in Tudor times panelled doors followed. These consist of a framed structure filled with thin panels, the latter becoming progressively larger during the seventeenth to eighteenth centuries (*see* PANELLING). A modern innovation is the factory-made 'flush door,' which has a rough framework entirely concealed by a thin veneer of hardwood with a flush face.

Door Furniture, the fittings, generally of metal, for hanging, opening, and securing a door, i.e. hinges, locks, latches, and bolts; but, more precisely, handles, knobs, escutcheons, and finger-plates.

Doric Order, *see* ORDERS OF ARCHITECTURE, *illustrated.*

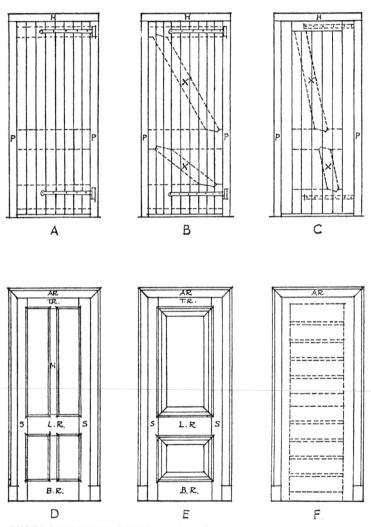

TYPES OF WOODEN DOORS. (A) *Ledged;* (B) *Ledged and braced;* (C) *Framed and braced;* (D) *Four-panel, moulded;* (E) *Two-panel, bolection-moulded, with fielded panels;* (F) *Flush, with plywood faces.* AR=*architrave;* B.R.=*bottom rail;* H=*head;* L.R.=*lock-rail;* P=*door post;* M=*muntin;* S=*stile;* T.R.=*top rail;* X=*brace*

Dormer (from Lat. *dormitorium*, a sleeping-room), a vertical window projecting from the sloping roof of a house, and having vertical sides ('cheeks') and a flat or sloping roof.

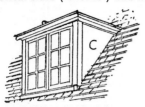

DORMER. With flat lead roof and lead 'cheeks' (C)

DORMER. With hipped tiled roof and tiled cheeks

Dormitory (Lat. *dormitorium*), a sleeping-room containing a number of beds, in a monastery, school, or other institution.

Dosseret, in Byzantine architecture, a block placed upon the top of a capital of an arch in an arcade, to assist in supporting the voussoirs (q.v.).

Dovecot, *see* COLUMBARIUM.

Dowel, a peg made of wood, metal, or slate, let into sockets in two adjoining blocks of stone to hold them together.

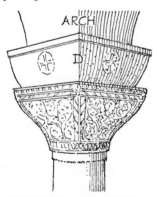

DOSSERET or PULVIN (D)

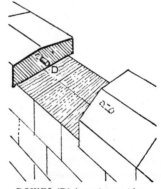

DOWEL (D) *in a stone coping*

Drawing, Architectural. There is irrefutable evidence that architects used drawings in the very earliest days. In ancient Egypt, thousands of years ago, plans were made on papyrus, and one such is preserved in the museum at Turin. In a competition for a war memorial at Athens in 448 B.C., drawings were required to a prescribed scale. Roman architects made plans on parchment, and Aulus Gellius mentions an example where competition designs for public baths were concerned. In Victorian England the absurd idea somehow took root that medieval architects never used plans:

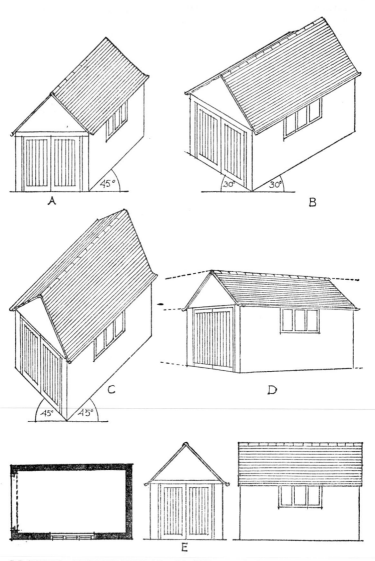

DRAWING, ARCHITECTURAL. (A) *Oblique projection* (*q.v.*); (B) *Isometric projection* (*q.v.*); (C) *Axometric projection* (*q.v.*); (D) *Perspective* (*q.v.*); (E) *Orthographic projection* (*q.v.*)

indeed that medieval buildings were erected without preliminary designs by architects. The comparative scarcity of surviving drawings is due to the impermanence of the material used, to the prevalent belief that a drawing had no artistic value or historical importance, and to the practice of erasing a drawing after a building was complete in order to re-use the precious parchment. Nevertheless a substantial number of medieval drawings have survived, though few in England. Many plans and details were prepared in the drawing office ('trasour') on the site, on thin boards rather than on parchment. The earliest medieval drawings known are picture plans of the monastery of St Gall in Switzerland (ninth century A.D.) and of Canterbury Cathedral (c. 1165); but these are hardly working drawings. The famous sketch-book of Villard de Honnecourt (q.v.), thirteenth century, now preserved in the Bibliothèque Nationale at Paris, contains many plans and architectural details; but, again, they cannot be reckoned as working drawings. From the fourteenth century, however, we have the very large and magnificent drawings of the west front of Cologne Cathedral, and a number of other drawings from Germany and Italy, including a competition drawing of 1339 at Siena, where there are several fine examples. In England the designs for King's College Chapel, Cambridge (fifteenth to sixteenth centuries), are now in the British Museum; but the finest late Gothic examples are to be seen in the Academy of Fine Art in Vienna. The Smithson (q.v.) and Thorpe (q.v.) collections of English drawings date from the late sixteenth and early seventeenth centuries. From that period onwards architectural drawing reached a high level in Italy (see BIBIENA FAMILY, BRAMANTE, D. FONTANA, PALLADIO, PERUZZI, POZZO, SERLIO) and France (see DE L'ORME, DU CERCEAU, MAROT, etc.). Among English architects of the eighteenth and nineteenth centuries who were notably fine draughtsmen are: Campbell, Cockerell, Gandon, E. George, Gibbs, A. W. N. Pugin, T. Sandby, and Soane (qq.v.).

See R. Blomfield, *Architectural Drawing and Draughtsmen*, 1912, and M. S. Briggs, *The Architect in History*, 1927.

Drawing-room, a modern shortened form of 'withdrawing-room,' i.e. a private sitting-room, also called a *solar* (q.v.), for the family in a large medieval house.

Dressings (from Fr. *dresser*, to straighten, to smooth), blocks of smooth stone, used at the angles ('quoins') of buildings, or as a frame for doors and windows in a building of brick or stone.

Drew, Sir Thomas (*b.* Belfast, 8 Sept. 1838; *d.* Dublin, 13 Mar. 1910), Irish architect. President of the Royal Hibernian Academy, 1900–10, and of the Royal Institute of Architects of Ireland, 1892–1901. He was articled in 1854 to Sir Charles Lanyon (q.v.) of Belfast, and after 1862 worked as an assistant in Dublin, until he started independent practice there in 1865. He was consulting architect to four Irish cathedrals, and took a keen interest in the preservation of Irish antiquities. His principal buildings were the town hall at Rathmines, 1889; the law library at the Four Courts, Dublin; and St Anne's Cathedral at Belfast, a most original building,

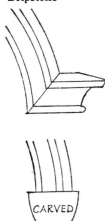

DRIPSTONE. Two types of termination

begun in 1899, but not completed until several years after his death.

Dripstone, or **Label Moulding,** in medieval and Tudor masonry, a stone moulding projecting over and round the heads of doorways and window openings, in order to throw off rainwater.

Drops. (1) In classical architecture, the *guttae* (Lat., drops) or small projections under the triglyphs (q.v.). (2) In Elizabethan and Jacobean architecture, carved wooden pendants on the feet of the newel-posts of a staircase.

Drum. (1) One of the cylindrical sections forming a stone column if it is not a monolith. (2) The cylindrical lower part of a dome.

Dry Rot (*Merulius lacrymans*), a most insidious fungoid growth liable to develop in infected timber which is inadequately ventilated and subject to damp. It can penetrate through brick joints. Though it is difficult and often expensive to eradicate, drastic action is often successful.

Du Cerceau, Jacques Androuet (*b.* Paris, *c.* 1510; *d.* near Annecy, *c.* 1585), French architect. He studied in Italy from 1530 to 1533, and on returning to France he settled at Orléans, where he began preparing the collection of drawings of architectural subjects, afterwards engraved and published in 1576–9 as *Les Plus Excellents Bastiments de France,* on which his reputation chiefly rests. His only known buildings were erected late in his career and included the large châteaux of Verneuil-sur-Oise (begun 1565) and of Charleval (begun 1572 and now mostly demolished). Two of his sons and one grandson became architects. BAPTISTE DU CERCEAU (*d.* 1590) designed the Pont Neuf (1578–1604), the oldest surviving bridge in Paris.

See monograph by Geymüller, 1910.

Duct (from Lat. *ducere,* to lead, to convey), in modern building, any channel for the conveyance of pipes, cables, etc., or a metal ventilating flue.

Dudok, Willem Marinus (*b.* Amsterdam, 6 July 1884), Dutch architect, R.I.B.A. Royal Gold Medallist, 1935. In 1915 he was appointed director of works at Hilversum, where he designed the town hall (1938–51) and other buildings which have greatly influenced European architecture. His work also includes the first Bijenkorf Store at Rotterdam (1929–30); the Dutch Hostel at the Cité Universitaire, Paris (1927–8); several housing schemes; and many commercial and industrial buildings.

Dungeon may mean either donjon (q.v.) or an underground chamber or prison in a castle.

Durqa'ah (Arabic), the central portion of the reception hall (*mandarah*) of any Muslim mansion in Cairo.

Dutch Architecture, *see* BELGIAN AND DUTCH ARCHITECTURE.

Dutch Barn, a hay barn with open sides. If the roof is capable of being raised and lowered it is called a 'Derbyshire hay barn.'

E

Early English Style, the name given by Rickman (q.v.) to the first phase of English Gothic architecture, prevailing in the thirteenth century (c. 1190–c. 1310). Its most characteristic feature is the lancet window, without tracery. *See* ENGLISH ARCHITECTURE, 4.

Easter Sepulchre, in medieval churches, a recess—either of wood if temporary, or carved in stone if permanent—sheltering a representation of the burial and resurrection of Christ: usually placed on the north side of the chancel.

Easton, John Murray (b. Aberdeen, 30 Jan. 1889), British architect; R.I.B.A. Royal Gold Medallist, 1955. He was articled in Aberdeen, then came to London. He started practice in London in partnership with H. M. Robertson (q.v.) in 1919. From 1929 to 1940 they were associated with E. Stanley Hall. Important buildings designed by the firm of Easton & Robertson include the British Pavilion at the Paris Exhibition (1925); the Royal Horticultural Society's new hall in Westminster (1926); exhibition pavilions at Johannesburg, Brussels, and New York (1936–9); numerous scientific, administrative, and collegiate buildings for Cambridge University (1932 onwards); blocks of residential flats in St John's Wood and Marylebone, London; several large hospitals; Hatfield Technical College (1948); new buildings for Reading University (1949); the University of Malaya (1953); South Bank Development Scheme, London (1953); Watling House, London (1954).

Eaves (plural of 'eave,' but the singular is seldom used), the lower edge of a sloping roof, overhanging the face of the wall. Normally a gutter is fixed to the eaves. The feet of the rafters may be left open so that they show, or may be covered by an 'eaves board' or 'fascia' (q.v.). (*Illustrated* ROOF.)

Ecclesiological Society (7 Mellows Road, Wallington, Surrey), founded as the Cambridge Camden Society in 1839, played a prominent part in the bitter controversy, during early Victorian times, about matters of church ritual, planning and decoration; and is still interested in all these questions.

Echinus, in classical architecture, a convex or ovolo moulding beneath the abacus of a Doric capital. (*Illustrated* MOULDINGS, CLASSICAL.)

École des Beaux Arts, *see* BEAUX ARTS, ÉCOLE DES.

Edge Roll, in Gothic architecture, a bead moulding on an external angle.

Efflorescence, an unsightly white crystalline deposit, often seen on the red brickwork of new buildings; caused by the evaporation of alkaline salts.

118

Egg and Dart Moulding, in classical architecture, an ornament carved on an ovolo moulding (q.v.) and consisting of alternate eggs and arrow-heads. (*Illustrated* MOULDINGS, ENRICHED (CLASSICAL).)

Egyptian Architecture, *see* ARCHITECTURE, PERIODS OF, 1(*a*).

Elizabethan Architecture, English architecture of the reign of Queen Elizabeth I 1558–1603. *See* ENGLISH ARCHITECTURE, 5.

Ell (American), a one-storey lean-to addition to a framed and weather-boarded house in New England, usually made in the latter part of the seventeenth century after the 'Pilgrim Fathers' and other early immigrants from England had established themselves. The ell contained the kitchen, etc.

Elliptical Arch, *see* ARCH, TYPES OF, *illustrated*.

Elmes, Harvey Lonsdale (*b.* Oving, Sussex, 1814; *d.* in Jamaica, 26 Nov. 1847), English architect, was the son of James Elmes, an architect and writer on architecture. In 1839, when only twenty-five years of age, he won the important competition for St George's Hall at Liverpool against seventy-five rivals. Between 1839 and 1842 the design was greatly modified to include Assize Courts, not provided for in the first competition programme. Although the erection of the building began in 1842, his health broke down, and he died before its completion.

Embrasure, *see* BATTLEMENTS, *illustrated*.

Emerson, Sir William (*b.* Whetstone, 1843; *d.* Shanklin, 26 Dec. 1924), English architect, President R.I.B.A., 1899–1902. He was articled to William Burges (q.v.). In 1864 he went to India, where he designed a number of buildings, including the Markets at Bombay (1865–71); and, after returning to England, Allahabad University, Lucknow Cathedral, and the imposing Victoria Memorial at Calcutta (1906–21)—a typical example of Edwardian ostentation and lavish expenditure. His works in England included St Mary's Church, Brighton; the ornate Clarence Wing of St Mary's Hospital, Paddington (1892); and the Royal Caledonian Hospital.

Empire Style, the style of design, for French architecture and furniture, in vogue after Napoleon became emperor in 1804. As a result of his Egyptian campaign in 1798–9, and the craze for Egyptian art that followed the publication of the magnificent *Description de l'Égypte* in 1809–22, it included Egyptian as well as classical features.

Encaustic Tiles, tiles inlaid with decorative patterns in differently coloured clays, afterwards burnt in; used for flooring and wall covering.

Enceinte (Fr., a girdle; an enclosure), in military architecture, the line of the wall, ditch, etc., enclosing a fortress.

Engaged Column, a stone column which is partially built into a wall, usually for half of its diameter.

English Architecture. This article, like those on the architecture of other countries, deals only with the *special* national characteristics of the various periods, with typical buildings in each, and the names

of their architects where those are known. For the *general* charac-
teristics *see* ARCHITECTURE, PERIODS OF; *also* CASTLE, CATHEDRAL,
CHURCH, HOUSE, MONASTERY, RESTORATION, TEMPLE, TOWN-
PLANNING; and on structural details: BUTTRESS, COLUMN, DOOR,
TRACERY, VAULT. (Separate articles describe IRISH, SCOTTISH,
and WELSH ARCHITECTURE.)

Excluding primitive hut dwellings, and such prehistoric monu-
ments as Stonehenge and Maiden Castle, the oldest buildings in
England that merit the name of architecture were erected during the
Roman occupation of Britain, terminating *c.* A.D. 410. They
resemble Roman architecture of other provinces of the Empire, and
are somewhat less ambitious and elaborate than those of the city of
Rome itself. Most of them are to be found in certain of the larger
Roman towns—Camulodunum (Colchester), Verulamium (St Albans),
Aquae Sulis (Bath), Calleva Atrebatum (Silchester), Viriconium
(Wroxeter), and Isca Silurum (Caerwent). Other important towns—
e.g. Londinium (London), Eboracum (York), Ratae (Leicester),
Lindum (Lincoln), Glevum (Gloucester), and Corinium (Cirencester)
—have yielded comparatively fewer remains; usually because later
building has smothered or destroyed the Roman work, or because
they have not yet been thoroughly excavated.

1. Roman buildings in Britain comprise (i) amphitheatres (an
especially fine example is at Caerwent, Monmouthshire); (ii) theatres
(the best being at Verulamium); (iii) secular basilicas, including a
large one under Gracechurch Street, London, and smaller examples
at Cirencester, Silchester, Wroxeter, and Caerwent; (iv) public
baths, especially at Bath, but also at Leicester, Silchester, and
Wroxeter; (v) temples; none now remaining above ground level but
foundations of a large one at Colchester; also numerous temples to
the eastern deity, Mithras, e.g. the remarkable example recently
discovered in Walbrook, London; (vi) Christian churches, the only
survivor being a fragment of a small basilican church at Silchester,
c. 410 (public buildings were generally grouped round the forum or
market-place, as at Verulamium); (vii) town houses, best studied at
Verulamium, where the streets form a chess-board pattern, with
houses centrally heated by hot air, equipped with baths, and provided
with mosaic floors; (viii) villas or country houses from which farming
was carried on, some of them having over fifty rooms, and most
having central heating, baths, and mosaic floors. They are chiefly
situated south and east of a line from York to Exeter, the best
examples being at Bignor (Sussex), Brading (Isle of Wight), Chedworth (Gloucester), Folkestone (Kent), Northleigh (Oxfordshire),
and Woodchester (Oxfordshire).

2. Little evidence remains of the buildings which the first Anglo-
Saxon settlers must have erected during the period *c.* 410–597.
The next phase began with the landing of St Augustine in Kent in
597. His speedy conversion of the Kentish king resulted in the
erection of Christian churches in Canterbury (SS. Peter and Paul,
597; St Pancras, *c.* 600; St Mary, *c.* 620); also St Andrew, Rochester,
(604); St Mary, Lyminge (*c.* 633); St Mary, Reculver (669)—all these in
Kent. St Peter, Bradwell (Essex), was built *c.* 660; and at Brixworth

(Northamptonshire) was erected a large church (*c.* 670) which still survives, and has been described by a leading authority as 'perhaps the most imposing monument of the seventh century yet surviving north of the Alps.' It has a long aisled nave with semicircular brick arches, a small apsidal chancel, and a timber roof.

Only a few years later a second group of Christian churches was erected in the former 'kingdom of Northumbria,' as a result of missionary activity by Benedict Biscop, who had studied in Rome. His three churches, all very small and roughly built, are at Monkwearmouth (*c.* 675), Jarrow (chancel only, *c.* 685), and Escomb (about same date). In Hexham Abbey and Ripon Cathedral are crypts of this period, built *c.* 675 by St Wilfrid, Archbishop of York.

During the eighth and ninth centuries, mainly because of Danish invasions, there was another lull in church-building. The next phase began early in the tenth century.

Between that date and the Norman conquest of England in 1066, a number of churches were erected. They used to be called 'Saxon,' but, because they represent only a ruder form of continental 'Romanesque,' they are now generally classified under that head as 'Pre-Conquest Romanesque,' whereas those built after 1066 are 'Post-Conquest Romanesque' (not 'Norman' as they were commonly called a generation ago). Nothing remains to-day of Pre-Conquest domestic architecture, and the following are the chief surviving Pre-Conquest Romanesque churches.

Tenth century. Deerhurst (Gloucestershire); Bradford-on-Avon (Wiltshire); Wing (Buckinghamshire); Worth (Sussex); Earl's Barton (Northamptonshire); Barton-on-Humber (Leicestershire); St Benet, Cambridge; Wittering (Northamptonshire); Breamore (Hampshire). (St Mary-in-Castro, Dover, may be of either the tenth or the eleventh century.)

Eleventh century. Bosham (Sussex); Sompting (Sussex); the foundations of North Elmham Cathedral, and of St Augustine's Abbey, Canterbury; also possibly the curious little timber church at Greenstead, near Ongar in Essex. The first abbey-church at Westminster was begun *c.* 1050 and dedicated in 1065.

3. Surviving buildings of the Post-Conquest Romanesque (or 'Norman') period, 1066–*c.* 1200, consist almost entirely of churches and castles. The feudal lords lived in castles, the peasantry in wretched shacks of wood, or of wattle-and-daub, which have perished long ago, and there were hardly any middle-class people requiring houses. The so-called 'Jews' Houses' at Lincoln are among the few that remain.

Of the various types of castle (*see* CASTLE) the chief English examples are: (i) *Motte* type: Thetford in Norfolk; (ii) *Shell-keep* type: Arundel, Carisbrooke, Clifford, Exeter, Ludlow, Peak; (iii) *Rectangular keep:* London ('The Tower'), Castle Rising, Dover, Hedingham, Middleham, Newcastle upon Tyne, Norwich, Portchester, Rochester, Scarborough; (iv) *Twelve-sided keep:* Orford in Suffolk; (v) *Round keep:* Conisborough, Pembroke, and Windsor (but the so-called 'Round Tower' at Windsor was considerably raised in height during the nineteenth century).

Post-Conquest Romanesque may be studied in the following cathedrals: Chichester, Durham, Ely, Exeter, Gloucester, Hereford, Norwich, Oxford, Peterborough, St Albans, Winchester; in Tewkesbury and Waltham abbeys; and in parish churches at Adel (Yorkshire), Barfreston (Kent), Iffley (Oxfordshire), Kilpeck (Herefordshire), Melbourne (Derbyshire), St Peter at Northampton, Stewkley (Buckinghamshire); also in the wonderful little chapel of St John in the Tower of London.

In England, as elsewhere, round arches were invariably used throughout the Romanesque period. The flow of architectural influence into England continued to be from France, as it had been before the Conquest; but the Normans had only recently become skilful builders and designers. When they invaded Normandy from Scandinavia in the ninth century they were barbarous pirates like the Danes who ravaged England, and it was not until the eleventh century that they began to produce architecture of any importance in Normandy. Hence the progress of Romanesque architecture in England and Normandy moved on parallel lines until the end of the twelfth century when, in both countries, the pointed arch was introduced and the Gothic period began. From that date fundamental differences began to appear between French architecture (q.v.) and English, these differences becoming progressively more marked up to the end of the Gothic period (*c.* 1540 in England).

4. The successive stages of English Gothic architecture may be classified as: (i) Early English, or Early Pointed, *c.* 1200–*c.* 1300; (ii) Decorated, or Middle Pointed, *c.* 1300–*c.* 1370; (iii) Perpendicular, or Late Pointed, *c.* 1370–*c.* 1540. There was no abrupt line of change between these various periods; each merged into the next by a gradual transition, as new structural or decorative features were introduced, and sometimes they overlapped. One of the simplest ways of distinguishing them is by the design of their windows (*see* Tracery); but more important is the gradual development of vaulting and buttressing, whereby the thick walls and heavy barrel vaults, the flat buttresses, and the narrow windows of the twelfth century came to be replaced by bolder buttresses, thinner walls between them, thinner vaults supported on stone ribs, and much larger windows filled with tracery; until, in such late examples as King's College Chapel at Cambridge (1446–1515) and Henry VII's Chapel at Westminster (1503–19), the walls have become a mere panelled screen, mostly filled with glass—all the weight of the thin vaulted roof being carried by stone ribs converging on to very bold buttresses capped with tall pinnacles which help to neutralize the downwards and outward 'thrust' of the vaulting ribs, or (if there is no vaulting) of the timber roof-trusses.

Following are the chief examples of the three Gothic periods.

(i) *Early English.* Cathedrals: most of Salisbury; most of Lincoln except the choir and west front; the west fronts of Peterborough and Ripon; the choirs of Lichfield, Southwark, Southwell, and Worcester; most of Wells, including the west front; the nave of York; the 'Chapel of the Nine Altars' at Durham. Other buildings: the choirs of

Westminster Abbey and of the Temple Church in London; the choir and transepts of Beverley Minster.

(ii) *Decorated*. Cathedrals: the naves of Exeter and Lichfield; the choirs of Bristol, Lincoln, and St Albans; the choir, west front, and chapter-house of York; the chapter-houses of Salisbury, Southwell, and Wells. Other buildings: the nave of Beverley Minster; the parish church of Heckington, Lincolnshire.

(iii) *Perpendicular*. Cathedrals: the naves of Canterbury, Manchester, and Winchester; the choirs of Gloucester and York; the cloisters of Gloucester; the west fronts of Winchester and Gloucester. Other buildings: Sherborne Abbey; the west front of Beverley Minster; St George's Chapel, Windsor; King's College Chapel, Cambridge; Henry VII's Chapel, Westminster; the roof of Westminster Hall; several of the older colleges at Oxford and Cambridge.

5. The Renaissance movement in Italy began to influence English architecture early in the sixteenth century, but at first was confined to small ornamental details imported from Italy (e.g. the terra-cotta busts of Roman emperors at Hampton Court, *c.* 1520) or carried out by imported Italian craftsmen (e.g. Torrigiano's tomb for Henry VII in Westminster Abbey, 1512). Italian ornamental features soon came to be copied by English craftsmen, and books of engravings of the 'Orders' (q.v.) and other Roman architectural details were compiled, mainly in Germany and the Netherlands, and were studied in England. The first stage of transition from Gothic to Renaissance is sometimes called 'Tudor,' the period 1558–1603 is commonly known as 'Elizabethan,' and that from 1603 to *c.* 1630 as 'Jacobean.'

Church-building was almost in abeyance from *c.* 1540 to *c.* 1660, owing to religious turmoil and to the existence of a surplus of medieval churches—partly the result of over-building during the 'Age of Faith,' partly owing to the dissolution of the monasteries. The most important example is St John's Church, Leeds (1634), which is entirely Gothic in structure and general design, but contains magnificent 'Jacobean' (strictly 'Carolean') interior woodwork fittings. The Tudor, Elizabethan, and Jacobean periods, however, saw a great boom and revolution in the building of houses and of grammar schools and colleges. An extreme example of the application of Roman features is the 'Tower of the Five Orders' (1613–18) at the Bodleian Library, Oxford, where the classic Orders are applied as mere decoration to a building with mullioned windows, battlements, and pinnacles erected at the same time.

5*a*. A sudden and violent change to full-blown Italian Renaissance architecture occurred early in the seventeenth century, when Inigo Jones (q.v.) appeared upon the scene, and designed the Queen's House at Greenwich (1617–35) and the Banqueting House in Whitehall (1619–22). Gothic architecture died very slowly, especially in Oxford; but, from *c.* 1640 onwards up to *c.* 1830, all English architecture was based on that of Rome, save for a few exceptions that led to the 'Greek Revival' and the 'Gothic Revival' towards the end of that period. The 'Georgian' period lasted from 1714 to 1820, strictly speaking, and therefore includes the 'Regency' period of 1810–20; but both are commonly extended to 1830 or even to 1837.

'Palladian' architecture includes not only the work of Inigo Jones (q.v.), but also that of many architects of the eighteenth century who followed Palladio (q.v.) rather than Wren (q.v.). Buildings of the period include many vast aristocratic mansions, such as Blenheim, Castle Howard, Holkham, Kedleston, Harewood, Kenwood, and Chatsworth; many charming Georgian houses; St Paul's Cathedral, many churches of the new 'Protestant' type, and Nonconformist meeting-houses; important public buildings such as Greenwich Hospital, Chelsea Hospital, and Somerset House. For the leading architects of the period and their works (in addition to JONES and WREN already mentioned) see ADAM (J. and R.); ALDRICH, H.; ARCHER, T.; BELL, H.; BONOMI, J.; BOYLE, R. (Lord Burlington); BRETTINGHAM, M.; BROWN, L.; BURTON, D.; CAMPBELL, C.; CARR, J.; CHAMBERS, SIR W.; COCKERELL, C. R.; COTTINGHAM, L. N.; DANCE, G. (2); ESSEX, J.; FLITCROFT, H.; GANDON, J.; GANDY, J.; GIBBS, J.; GWYNN, J.; HALFPENNY, W.; HAWKSMOOR, N.; HOLLAND, H.; HOOKE, R.; INWOOD, H. W.; IVORY, T.; JAMES, J.; JERMAN, J.; KENT, W.; LANGLEY, B.; LEONI, G.; LEVERTON, T.; MAY, H.; MYLNE, R.; NASH, J.; PAIN, J.; PAINE, J.; REPTON, H.; RIPLEY, T.; SMIRKE, SIR R.; SMIRKE, S.; SOANE, SIR J.; TALMAN, W.; VANBRUGH, SIR J.; VARDY, J.; WARE, I.; WEBB, J.; WHITE, T.; WILKINS, W.; WILSON, SIR W.; WOOD, J.; WYATT, J.; WYATT, SIR B. D.; WYATT, SIR M. D.; WYATT, T. H.; WYATVILLE, SIR J.

6. The period c. 1830 to c. 1900 may be called the 'Victorian' phase, and was notable for a continuous struggle between the supporters of revived Classic (i.e. Greek and Roman) and revived Gothic architecture, as explained in the article ARCHITECTURE, PERIODS OF, 8. For the leading architects of the Victorian period and their buildings see AUSTIN, G.; BARRY, SIR C.; BASEVI; BELCHER, J.; BENTLEY, J.; BLOMFIELD, SIR A. and SIR R.; BLORE; BODLEY, G.; BURGES, W.; BUTTERFIELD, W.; CARPENTER; CHAMPNEYS; DEVEY; ELMES, H. L.; FERREY; GEORGE, SIR E.; HANSOM; HARDWICK; HARE; JACKSON, SIR T. G.; JONES, O.; LAMB; MOUNTFORD; NESFIELD; NEWTON; PEARSON, J. L.; PENNETHORNE; PENROSE; PUGIN, A. W. N.; SALVIN, A.; SAVAGE, J.; SCOTT, SIR G. G., Sen.; SEDDING, J. D.; SHARPE, E.; SHAW, R. N.; STREET, G. E.; TITE, SIR W.; WATERHOUSE, A.; WEBB, P. See also GRIMTHORPE, LORD; MORRIS, W.; PAXTON, SIR J; RUSKIN, J.

7. The movement towards a less imitative and more 'functional' architecture is described in ARCHITECTURE, PERIODS OF, 9. For leading architects of the twentieth century and their buildings see ABERCROMBIE, SIR P.; ASLIN, C. H.; BAKER, SIR H.; BENNETT, SIR T. P.; BURNET, SIR J.; CASSON, SIR H. M.; COLLCUTT, T. E.; COMPER, SIR J. N.; COOPER, SIR E.; CORFIATO, H. O.; DAVIS, A.; DAWBER, SIR E. G.; EASTON, J. M.; EMERSON, SIR W.; FLETCHER, SIR B. F.; FRY, E. M.; GIBBERD, SIR F.; GOODHART-RENDEL, H. S.; GOTCH, J. A.; HARRIS, E. V.; HOLDEN, C. H.; HOLFORD, LORD; HORDER, P. M.; KNOTT, R.; LANCHESTER, H. V.; LETHABY, W. R.; LORIMER, SIR R.; LUTYENS, SIR E.; MACKINTOSH, C. R.; MARTIN, SIR J. L.; MATTHEW, SIR R. H.; MAUFE, SIR E.; REILLY, SIR C. H.; RICHARDSON SIR A. E.; RICKARDS, E. A.; ROBERTSON, SIR H. M.;

SCOTT, SIR GILES; SPENCE, B.; STOKES, L. A.; THOMAS, SIR A. B.; THOMAS, SIR P.; THORNELY, SIR A.; TUBBS, R.; UNWIN, SIR R.; VOYSEY, C. F. A.; WEBB, SIR A.; WORNUM, G. G.; YORKE, F. R. S.

See Sir R. Blomfield, *Short History of Renaissance Architecture in England*, 1900; E. S. Prior, *History of Gothic Architecture in England*, 1900; J. A. Gotch, *Renaissance Architecture in England*, 1901; F. Bond, *Gothic Architecture in England*, 1906; *English Church Architecture* (2 vols.), 1913; W. H. Godfrey, *Story of Architecture in England* (2 vols.), 1928–31; A. W. Clapham, *English Romanesque Architecture* (2 vols.), 1930–4; F. R. S. Yorke and C. Penn, *A Key to Modern Architecture*, 1939; S. Sitwell, *British Architects and Craftsmen, 1600–1830*, 1945; M. S. Briggs, *Building Today*, 1945; A. H. Gardner, *Outline of English Architecture*, 1945; R. Turnor, *Nineteenth Century Architecture in Britain*, 1950; J. H. Lees-Milne, *Tudor Renaissance*, 1951; G. Webb, *Architecture in Britain: The Middle Ages*, 1956; E. A. Fisher, *Anglo-Saxon Architecture*, 1959.

English Bond, in brickwork, a form of bond (q.v.) in which alternate courses consist entirely of headers and entirely of stretchers.

Enneastyle (Gk *ennea*, nine; *stulos*, a column), in classical architecture, a portico which has nine columns in a row.

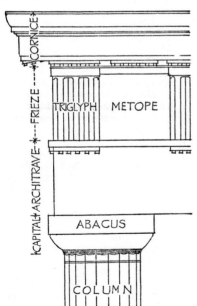

ENTABLATURE of the Greek Doric Order, from the Parthenon at Athens

Enrichment, the decoration of surfaces and architectural features with carved, modelled, or painted ornament.

Entablature (from It. *intavolatura*, something laid upon a table; hence, something laid flat upon something else), in classical architecture, the arrangement of three horizontal members—architrave, frieze, and cornice—above the supporting columns in any of the classical Orders (q.v.).

Entasis (Gk), in classical architecture, the almost imperceptible and amazingly subtle convex swelling of a column, in order to correct the optical illusion of concavity created by simple tapering.

Entresol, *see* MEZZANINE.

Epistle Side, the south side of the chancel of a church, from which the epistle is read.

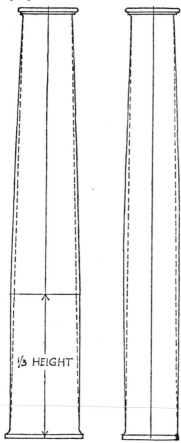

ENTASIS of columns, according to G. B. Vignola (q.v.). Left (Doric column): entasis beginning at one-third of height of column above base. Right (Corinthian column): entasis for whole height. N.B. Dotted lines show the effect if columns were merely tapered, without entasis

⅓ HEIGHT

Epistyle (Gk *epi*, on; *stulos*, a column), in classical architecture, the architrave (q.v.) of one of the Orders (q.v.).

Equilateral Arch, a pointed arch with its radius equal to its span. *See* ARCH, TYPES OF, *illustrated*.

Escutcheon. (1) In heraldry, a shield displaying armorial bearings. (2) A small pivoted metal plate over the keyhole of a door.

Espagnolette Bolt, a long vertical bolt for securing a French window. It fits into a socket at top and bottom and is operated by a knob or handle fixed at a convenient height.

Essex, James (*b.* Cambridge, Aug. 1722; *d.* there, 14 Sept. 1774), English architect, was the son of a carpenter employed chiefly on university buildings in Cambridge. Educated in the town, he then studied architecture under Sir James Burrough, and collaborated with him in designing various buildings, while continuing to practise his trade as a carpenter. In the latter capacity he built (but did not design) the wooden bridge at Queens' College (1749–50). He was one of the first architects to take an interest in the then despised Gothic style, and in later years to design neo-Gothic buildings. His work in Cambridge included the Ramsden Building of St Catherine's Hall (1757); chambers at Queens' College (1756–60); the stone bridge at Trinity College (1763–5); the completion of the Senate House (1766–8); the street front of Emmanuel College (1769–75); the chapel, library, and Master's Lodge at Sidney Sussex College; and the Guildhall. Outside Cambridge he did a good deal of work at Canterbury, Ely, Lincoln, and Winchester cathedrals.

His published writings include numerous papers on archaeology and historical architecture.   He also wrote, but never published, *A History of Gothic Architecture in England.*

Etruscan Architecture, *see* ARCHITECTURE, PERIODS OF, 3.

Eustyle (Gk *eu*, well; *stulos*, a column), in classical architecture, the formula for columns which the Greeks considered well spaced, viz. a space of $2\frac{1}{4}$ diameters between columns.

Exedra (Lat.), originally the portion of a gymnasium reserved for disputation, or the vestibule of a dwelling-house; later (occasionally) a porch, chapel, or recess in a wall projecting externally.

Exonarthex, the outer vestibule of a Greek (Byzantine) church. *See* NARTHEX.

Extrados (Lat. *extra*, outside; Fr. *dos*, the back), the curving upper surface of an arch or its component voussoirs.   *See* ARCH, PARTS OF AN, *illustrated.*

Eye, in classical architecture, the small disk in the centre of the volute of an Ionic capital.

F

Fabric (from Lat. and Fr.), literally 'something made' by a craftsman: hence, a building. More precisely, the structure of a building.

Façade (Fr.), the face or (principal) front of a building.

Facings, the materials used specially and solely for the external face of a wall, when the remaining thickness or core is of some other material: this applies equally to brick and stone walls.

F.A.I.A., abbreviation for Fellow of the American Institute of Architects.

Faience, glazed ceramic ware originally made at Faenza in Italy; hence the name.

Fanlight, a glazed oblong or semicircular sash over a door: so called because in the late eighteenth century, when they became popular, such windows had glazing bars radiating from the centre like a fan.

FANLIGHT in iron, copper, and brass; for Drapers' Hall, London, by R. Adam (q.v.).

Fan-vaulting, or conoidal vaulting, so called because all the ribs have an identical curvature, resembling a fan. This type is peculiar to England, and occurs only in late Gothic work. Examples are Gloucester Cathedral cloisters (1381–1412); Sherborne Abbey (1475); the Divinity School, Oxford (1480–3); Henry VII's Chapel, Westminster (1500–12); St George's Chapel, Windsor (c. 1507–28); King's College Chapel, Cambridge (begun 1512); Christ Church Hall staircase, Oxford (1630). *See also* VAULTING.

Fascia (Lat., a strip or band). (1) Most commonly, a strip of wood

128

covering the ends of the rafters at the eaves of a roof. (2) The name board over a shop window. (3) In classical architecture, one member of the architrave in the Ionic and Corinthian Orders.

Fayd'herbe, or **Faidherbe, Luc** (*b*. Malines, 19 Jan. 1617; *d*. there, 31 Dec. 1697), Flemish Baroque architect and sculptor. He was trained as a painter by P. P. Rubens (q.v.), but turned to architecture in 1662. His principal works were Notre-Dame de Hanswyck, Malines (1663–78); designs for the abbey of Lilienthal (begun 1662), and for the abbey church of Averbode (1664–70). The Béguinage Church at Brussels (1657–76) and the Jesuit Church at Malines (1669) are also attributed to him.

Fenestration (from Lat. *fenestra*, a window), the architectural arrangement of windows in a façade.

Feretory, a portable or fixed shrine, used in the Middle Ages as a repository for the relics of saints.

Fergusson, James (*b*. Ayr, 22 Jan. 1808; *d*. London, 9 Jan. 1886), the first person to compile a worthy general history of architecture, though he had no architectural training. He went to India as a merchant when young, became interested in Indian architecture, and soon after returning to London published a book on *The Rock-cut Temples of India*, 1845. Two years later appeared his *Handbook of Architecture*, and this was expanded into his much larger *History of Architecture*, 1865; followed by a more exhaustive treatment of *Indian and Eastern Architecture*, 1876. In 1871 he was awarded the R.I.B.A. Royal Gold Medal for architecture. Even after 1896, when a rival appeared (*see* FLETCHER), his massive, expensive, and learned volumes remained indispensable to serious students of architecture; and they are still useful.

Ferrey, Benjamin (*b*. Christchurch, Hampshire, 1 April 1810; *d*. London, 22 Aug. 1880), English architect, was articled to Augustus Pugin (q.v.), and made many drawings to illustrate his master's books. (Long afterwards, in 1861, he published a somewhat pedestrian biography of the two Pugins, father and son.) Ferrey went from Pugin's office to work for Wilkins (q.v.), who employed him on the drawings for the National Gallery. Ferrey's own work, after he had embarked on independent practice, included the layout of part of Bournemouth; the restoration of the cathedral and Bishop's Palace at Wells (1841–2); and the churches of St James, Morpeth (1843), and of St Stephen, Westminster (1845).

Ferro-concrete, *see* REINFORCED CONCRETE.

Festoon, or **Swag**, a carved, modelled or painted garland of fruit and flowers, bound with ribbons, and suspended from its ends. (*Illustrated* SWAG.)

Fictional Architects. One of the first English novelists to portray an architect was Charles Dickens, whose Pecksniff in *Martin Chuzzlewit* (1843) was an unfortunate advertisement for the profession. Arnold Bennett had as his closest friend E. A. Rickards (q.v.) who may have provided the prototype of one of the architects in *The Roll Call* (1919); and the charming characters of Orgreave and his son in the *Clayhanger* novels (1910–25) are as attractive as any architect could wish. H. G. Wells, on the other hand, in *Kipps* (1905), describes the whimsies of the architect who designed Art Kipps's house at Sandgate; and it must be noted that C. F. A. Voysey (q.v.) did actually build a house for Wells at Sandgate in 1899–1900. Humphrey Pakington, who spent his earlier years as an architect and then as a naval officer, before he turned finally to novel writing, pictures a very pleasant and well-bred architect in *Four in Family* (1931) and other stories. An architect is the central figure in J. M. Faulkner's *The Nebuly Coat* (1903), and Galsworthy opens *The Man of Property* (1906) with the tragic fate of Philip Bosinney, quite a different type of personality. A very different type of architect, a French itinerant consultant in the Middle Ages, appears in Charles Lowrie's *Castle Bedon*—a convincing reconstruction of the architect's status at that period. Thomas Hardy (q.v.) utilized his architectural training in describing Wessex farmhouses and barns rather than in featuring architects in his novels.

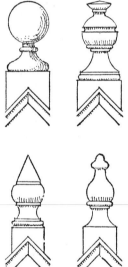

Fielded Panels, in late Renaissance architecture, panels which have the greater part of their surface projecting beyond the face of the framing. *See* PANELLING. (*Illustrated* BOLECTION MOULDING.)

Fillet (from Fr. *filet*, dim. of *fil*, a thread), a narrow flat strip between two mouldings or between two flutes of a column; or a narrow strip of wood used elsewhere. (*Illustrated* MOULDINGS, CLASSICAL.)

Fine Art Commission, Royal, *see* ROYAL FINE ART COMMISSION.

Finger-plate, a strip of metal or porcelain screwed on to a door, above or below the handle, to prevent finger marks on the paint.

Finial, an ornamental feature, generally of stone, placed on the top of a pinnacle or at the base and apex of a gable.

FINIAL. Stone finials of 16th–17th centuries (English)

Finnish Architecture. Finland was a wild and empty country of lakes and forests when, in A.D. 1157, it was conquered by Sweden and converted to Christianity. It remained under Swedish rule until it passed under the suzerainty of Russia in 1809, and it became an independent republic in 1917. Thus for the greater part of its history it has been western in its outlook. Its architecture during the Middle Ages and the Renaissance was of no great importance, the chief buildings being the cathedral of Turku (Abo) and the medieval castles of Viipuri (Viborg) and Turku. Many of the churches were decorated with frescoes. In 1812 Helsinki became the capital and was laid out on classical lines by the German architect K. L. Engel. From that period date the university (1817) and the Governor's Palace (1818–32). A phase of eclectic architecture lasted through the second half of the nineteenth century. The competition for Helsinki railway station was won in 1904 with a remarkable design by Eliel Saarinen (q.v.). Since then Alvar Aalto (q.v.) has produced a number of buildings of the first rank. The imposing Parliament House at Helsinki, finished in 1931, is by Johan Sirén.

See T. Paulsson, *Scandinavian Architecture*, 1958.

Fire-back, a cast-iron plate, often decorated with dates, initials, emblems, etc., placed at the back of a brick fire-place in English houses of the seventeenth to eighteenth centuries. Many examples, mostly made in Sussex, are exhibited in the Victoria and Albert Museum, London.

Firedogs, *see* ANDIRONS.

Fire-place, the open recess at the base of a chimney, containing the grate for the fire. This recess was very large in medieval and Stuart houses, when an open grate was used.

Fischer von Erlach, Johann Bernhard (*b.* Graz, 20 July 1656; *d.* Vienna, 5 April 1723), Austrian Baroque architect and sculptor. He was studying sculpture in Rome when he came under the influence of Borromini (q.v.) and adopted architecture as his profession.

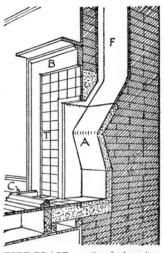

FIRE-PLACE: sectional view. A= *fireclay interior;* B=*wooden chimney-piece;* C=*curb fender;* F=*flue;* T= *tiled surround*

Returning home *c.* 1683, he was employed by the Prince-Archbishop of Salzburg, for whom he carried out work at the court stables there, followed by four churches, including the great Kollegienkirche (1694–1707). He then rebuilt the enormous Imperial Palace at Schönbrunn near Vienna (*c.* 1700). His other important buildings included the Clam-Gallas Palace, Prague (1707), and the following in Vienna: the Karlskirche (1715–37); the Trautson Palace (1710–12); the Schönbrunn Palace (1700); Prince Eugen's Palace, afterwards the Finanzministerium (1695–1710); the Schwarzenberg Palace (1696–1725); and additions to the Hofburg (Imperial Palace) (begun *c.* 1722). Some of his later buildings were completed after his death by his son Josef Emanuel (1693–1742).

See monographs by H. V. Lanchester, 1924; H. Sedlmayer, 1925; A. Ilg, 1929.

Flagstone, any large flat paving-stone, obtainable from laminated sandstone rocks found in Yorkshire, etc.

Flamboyant Style (from Old Fr. *flambe*, a flame), the last phase of French Gothic architecture, so called because the flowing lines of the tracery resemble flames in shape. This tracery also resembles English 'flowing Decorated' tracery of the fourteenth century, and is attributed to the English occupation of much of France at that period. The style is finicky in detail, and is characterized by elaborate interpenetration of mouldings. It flourished in France from *c.* 1460 onwards. *See also* FRENCH ARCHITECTURE.

FLAMBOYANT window tracery.   Snettisham Church, Norfolk

Flat. (1) An abbreviated term for a flat roof of concrete, lead, asphalt, etc. (2) A suite of rooms on one floor, forming a self-contained dwelling, in a multi-storey block of such dwellings.

Flat Arch, an arch which is almost flat, though usually given a slight 'camber' (q.v.) to avoid sagging. That defect is theoretically avoided by the wedge shape of the voussoirs, sometimes reinforced by a flat iron bar beneath them. (*Illustrated* ARCH, TYPES OF.)

Flèche (Fr., arrow), a small and slender wooden spire covered with lead. There is a fine example on the roof of the cathedral of Notre-Dame, Paris.

Flemish Bond, a form of bond (q.v.) in brickwork, in which headers and stretchers are laid alternately in every course.

Fletcher, Sir Banister Flight (*b.* London, 15 Feb. 1866; *d.* there, 17 Aug. 1953), English architect and historian of architecture; President R.I.B.A., 1929–31. He was the son of Professor Banister Fletcher, whose office he entered in 1884. He continued to practise up to the time of his death, and designed the large Gillette factory at Isleworth when he was seventy years of age. Having also qualified as a barrister, he undertook much legal-architectural work, and was, besides, an excellent lecturer. He took an active part in the affairs of the City, and was knighted as sheriff. His reputation rests, however, entirely upon his admirable *History of Architecture on the Comparative Method*, compiled originally in collaboration with his father. First published in 1896, it was repeatedly revised and enlarged, attained a deservedly phenomenal success, was translated into many foreign languages, and still remains an indispensable text-book.

Flight, the series of stairs between any two landings.

Flint Buildings in England are chiefly found in East Anglia and Hertfordshire, where building stone is scarce. Tracery, quoins (q.v.), etc., are executed in stone or brick, as flint is unsuitable for this purpose. *See also* CHEQUER-WORK.

Flitcroft, Henry (*b.* Hampton Court, 30 Aug. 1697; *d.* Hampstead, 25 Feb. 1769), English architect. He was apprenticed as a joiner and admitted to the Joiners' Company in 1719; but attracted the notice of Lord Burlington (q.v.) (hence his nickname of 'Burlington Harry'), through whose influence he obtained employment under the Board of Works. He became clerk of the works on the royal palaces in 1726, and then began simultaneous practice on his own account. His chief buildings were the church of St Giles-in-the-Fields, London (1731–4); No. 10 St James's Square, now 'Chatham House' (1734); St Olave's, Southwark (1738–9, demolished 1926); the great country mansion of Woburn Abbey (1747–61); and extensive additions to Wentworth Woodhouse, Yorkshire (*c.* 1735–70).

Floor, either (i) the under surface inside a room; or (ii) a storey (q.v.) of a house. In England the 'first floor,' however, is not the lowest above ground level: that is the 'ground floor,' and the 'first floor' is the next storey above it.

Florentine Arch, an arch which has a semicircular soffit (underside) and a pointed extrados (upper surface), with the aim of increasing its strength.

Floriated, or **Floreated,** decorated with floral ornament: applied to tracery, etc.

Floris, Cornelis, sometimes called **Cornelis de Vriendt** (*b.* Antwerp, 1514; *d.* there, 20 Oct. 1575); Flemish architect and sculptor. After studying in Italy, he designed the fine town halls of Antwerp (1561–5) and of The Hague (1565); also the Hanse Haus, Antwerp (1564–8, burnt down in 1893).

Flue, a duct of brick, stone, etc., for the conveyance of smoke in a chimney, or of hot air; in modern practice often lined with glazed pipes to facilitate sweeping.

Flush Bead, a small convex moulding flush with adjoining plane surfaces.

Fluting, the making of shallow and narrow concave grooves ('flutes') on columns, pilasters, etc.

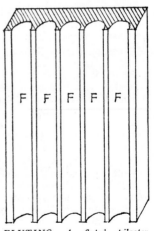

FLUTING. A fluted pilaster. (Flutes marked F)

Flying Buttress, in Gothic architecture (q.v.), a stone buttress in the form of an arched prop, supported at one end by the main wall of a building and at the other by a pier, in order to resist a lateral thrust. A pinnacle on the top of the pier increases its stability. (*Illustrated* BUTTRESS.)

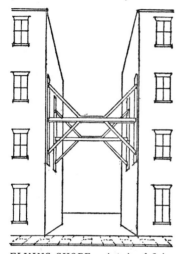

FLYING SHORE. A pair of flying shores, supporting the upper parts of two houses, between which one has been demolished

Flying Shore, a temporary timber support fixed high above ground level, between the external walls of two buildings, to prevent their collapse.

Foil, one of the small arcs between the cusps (q.v.) of tracery.

Foliation, the provision of foils (q.v.) in tracery.

Folly, a useless and generally foolish building, erected in the grounds of a wealthy eccentric, especially in the eighteenth and early nineteenth centuries.

Font, a receptacle for the water used in baptism; usually placed near the west end of a church, sometimes in a baptistery (q.v.). Normally fonts were and are made of stone, but some examples of old lead fonts still survive. Norman fonts were generally square or round; early Gothic examples were often decorated with shafts; and late Gothic fonts were normally octagonal, with traceried sides, and sometimes with elaborately carved wooden covers.

See F. Bond, *Fonts and Font Covers*, 1908.

Fontaine, Pierre François Léonard (*b.* Pontoise, 20 Sept. 1762; *d.* Paris, 10 Oct. 1853), architect and historian of architecture. During his training in Paris he met Charles Percier (q.v.) and travelled with him to Rome in 1785. He took refuge in England during the revolution. Some years later Napoleon commissioned Percier and Fontaine to restore the palace of Malmaison, and then made them his chief architects. They carried out alterations to the Louvre, the Tuileries, and the Palais Royal—all in Paris. They also compiled jointly several important books, published 1824–33, mainly illustrating historical buildings in Rome.

Fontana, Carlo (*b.* Bruciato, near Como, 1634; *d.* Rome, 5 Feb. 1714), Italian Baroque architect. He was trained in Rome, and *c.* 1660 became an assistant to the famous Bernini (q.v.). His own chief buildings in Rome were the façade of S. Marcello al Corso; the Palazzo Montecitorio; and the Dogana. He also enlarged the Palazzo Reale at Genoa, and published several books, including one on the *Templum Vaticanum* (1694).

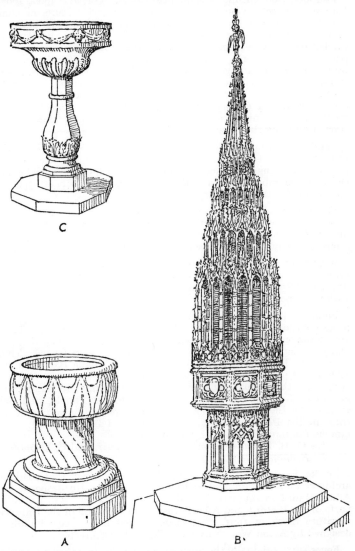

FONT. (A) *Harrow, Middlesex* (12th century); (B) *Ewelme, Oxon, with font cover*
(late Gothic); (C) **St Stephen, Walbrook, London** *(by Sir Christopher Wren,* 1679)

Fontana, Domenico (*b.* Melide, near Como, 1543; *d.* Naples, 1607), Italian architect. Going to Rome to study architecture, he came under the notice of Cardinal Montalto, who became Pope Sixtus V in 1585 and made Fontana his chief architect. For the Pope he carried important extensions to the Vatican, Lateran, and Quirinal palaces. These works were surpassed, however, in popular interest by his erection of a huge Egyptian obelisk in the Piazza di S. Pietro in 1586, about which he wrote an imposing folio volume. After the death of Sixtus V in 1590, Fontana's mad project of turning the Colosseum into a factory was rejected by the new Pope, who dismissed him. Fontana then went to Naples in 1592, and in 1600 started building the royal palace there.

Footings, the projecting courses of brick or stone at the base of a wall, so arranged as to distribute the weight over a greater area of ground. Footings are usually double the width of the thickness of the superincumbent wall, and the layer of concrete beneath them is still wider, for the same purpose.

Formwork, in modern reinforced concrete construction is the temporary casing of wood or steel into which the concrete is poured in a wet condition. The formwork is so designed that it can be removed easily when the concrete has set hard.

Forum, in every Roman town, a central open public space, surrounded by public buildings and often by colonnades. In Rome itself, besides the Forum Romanum, there were others laid out by various emperors, e.g. the Forum of Trajan.

Fountain (from late Lat. and It. *fontana*), an erection in a public place for the delivery of water; often ornamentally treated. There are examples, mostly of sixteenth to eighteenth century date, in many Italian and other cities, but the finest are in Rome. They include the Fontane dell' Acqua Acetosa (1661), della Barcaccia, del Tritone (1640), delle Tartarughe (late sixteenth century), di Trevi (1751–62); the Acqua Paola or Paolina (1612); and the magnificent groups of fountains in the Piazze Navona, del Popolo, and San Pietro. Of those named above, the first three, and also two of the three in the Piazza Navona, are the work of Bernini (q.v.). The famous Fontana di Trevi is by Salvi (q.v.).

See G. B. Falda, *Le Fontane di Roma*, 1691, and C. D'Onofrio, *Le Fontane di Roma*, 1957.

Fowke, Francis (*b.* Belfast, 1823; *d.* London, 4 Dec. 1865), British architect and captain in the Royal Engineers. He designed the Albert Hall, London (actually built in 1867–71, after his death); also parts of the Victoria and Albert Museum in 1865 and of the Imperial Institute block in 1861, afterwards merged in the new buildings designed by Aston Webb (q.v.) and Collcutt (q.v.) respectively.

Foyer (Fr.), originally the green-room of a theatre; then a retiring-oom for the audience in a theatre; more generally, the ante-room or vestibule of a theatre or other place of entertainment.

Fra Giocondo, *see* GIOCONDO, FRA.

Framed Buildings. (1) In the historical periods, buildings constructed of timber posts and beams, filled in with wattle-and-daub (q.v.) or with brickwork, and sometimes plastered or boarded over (*see* HALF-TIMBER CONSTRUCTION). (2) In modern building, structures in which the loads are carried entirely by stancheons and girders of steel or reinforced concrete, the walls consisting of thin sheets of weather-proof material. *See* CLADDING.

Frater, the refectory (q.v.) or dining-room of a monastery.

French Architecture, up to very recent times, has always been strongly influenced by that of Italy, though in both the Romanesque and the Gothic periods the French were innovators rather than followers. So also in the late nineteenth and early twentieth centuries, they were the pioneers of reinforced concrete construction and of 'functional' architecture. The Roman occupation of Gaul (France) left an important heritage of monumental buildings in Provence, including the amphitheatres at Nîmes, Arles, and Avignon; the magnificent aqueduct near Nîmes known as the 'Pont du Gard' (16 B.C.); and the little temple at Nîmes known as the 'Maison Carrée.' In Paris there are the remains of a Roman palace with baths, adjoining the Musée de Cluny. At St Rémy is a Roman monument, and at Orange and Saintes are Roman arches. These various buildings range in date from *c.* 40 B.C. to *c.* A.D. 50.

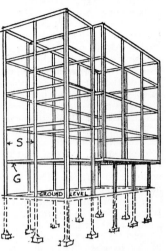

FRAMED BUILDING. S=*stancheon;* G=*girder. The projecting upper storeys on the right are carried by cantilevers (q.v.)*

Even before the evacuation of France by the Roman legions at the beginning of the fifth century A.D., a large number of Christian churches had been erected, partly owing to the energy of St Martin of Tours (*c.* A.D. 316–400); but nothing substantial remains of any of them, not even of the large church built to his memory at Tours in 472, or of other large churches at Lyons and Clermont. The oldest surviving church in France, much altered since its erection in 682–96, seems to be the so-called 'Temple of St Jean' at Poitiers, a small rectangular building with apses, incorporating a Gallo-Roman baptistery. After another long interval of time we find a rare example in the small but very interesting church at Germigny des Prés (*c.* 810), which has a Byzantine 'Greek cross' plan, and sundry Muslim details, reminding us that the victorious advance of the 'Saracens' into France was only halted by the great battle of Tours in 732. There are a few other Carolingian churches: at St Philbert de Grandlieu (*c.* 819, but much altered since), St Martin at Angers etc.; but Romanesque architecture proper in France does not begin till *c.* 1000. Examples from the eleventh century include the vaulted crypt of St Bénigne at Dijon (1001), St Hilaire at Poitiers (1018–59), St Front and St Étienne at Périgueux (1047), the Abbaye aux Dames and the Abbaye aux Hommes at Caen (1066), St Sernin at Toulouse (finished 1099), the abbeys of Cluny (1089–1131) and Vézelay (1089–1140), and Notre-Dame du Port at Clermont.

It will be noticed that few of these examples antedate the 'Norman Conquest' of England; indeed at that time few French buildings surpassed our own rather primitive 'Saxon' churches. The twelfth century saw the building of the important abbey of St Denis near Paris (1132–44) and of St Trophîme at Arles (1152); but before the end of that century the pointed arch had appeared, and, by 1215 or so, Gothic architecture was in full swing. The twelfth century also saw the erection of many stone-built fortresses (*see* CASTLE), but few substantial dwelling-houses for ordinary people.

The principal early Gothic churches in France are the cathedrals of Amiens, Bayeux, Bourges, Chartres, Coutances, Laon, Paris (Notre-Dame), Rheims, and Rouen, and the Sainte Chapelle at Paris (1244–7). Compared with English examples, they are shorter, wider, and loftier. They have a *chevet* (ring of chapels) round an apsidal east end, whereas in England the typical east end is square. They usually have west towers, and seldom a central tower. When tracery came to be introduced into windows, it was composed of geometrical forms until the 'flamboyant' type (possibly derived from English 'flowing decorated' tracery during the English occupation in the fourteenth century) became popular: there are examples at St Wulfram, Abbeville; and at St Ouen, Rouen. The English 'Perpendicular' style had no counterpart in France. Fine examples of late Gothic houses are those of Jacques Cœur at Bourges (1443), the Hôtel de Bourgthérolde at Rouen (1475), and the Hôtel de Cluny at Paris (1485), now a museum. The Château of Pierrefonds (1396) is a magnificent castle, in excellent preservation; as is the noble Palace of the Popes at Avignon (1316–70). Notable fortified towns are Aigues Mortes, Avignon, Carcassonne, and Mont St Michel.

The Renaissance entered France from Italy late in the fifteenth century, at first replacing Gothic very gradually, as in England. François I introduced a number of Italian architects at Fontainebleau, Amboise, Blois, etc. Among them was Serlio (q.v.). French architects soon acquired the new Italian fashions in design, and during the sixteenth century built the first part of the New Louvre in Paris, the château of St Germain, and many of the picturesque châteaux in the Loire valley, e.g. Chambord, Azay-le-Rideau, Chenonceaux (*see* BULLANT, DE L'ORME, P., LESCOT). Early in the sixteenth century Lemercier (q.v.), who had studied in Rome, designed the older part of the palace at Versailles, the Palais Royal, and the churches of the Sorbonne and St Roch—all in Paris; and laid out the remarkable little town and château of Richelieu for the cardinal of that name.

François Mansart (q.v.) enlarged Lescot's Carnavalet Museum and built the fine church of Val-de-Grâce, both in Paris; also the beautiful château at Maisons near Paris, his masterpiece, in 1642–51, and the Orléans wing at Blois.

He was followed by his kinsman J. H. Mansart (q.v.), the favourite architect of Louis XIV, who made Versailles one of the largest palaces in the world, designed the cathedral there and the church of the Invalides in Paris, and planned the Place des Victoires and the Place Vendôme—both in Paris. During the eighteenth century the two most talented architects in France were J. J. Gabriel (q.v.) and his son A. J. Gabriel (q.v.). Their work is more scholarly and refined than that of J. H. Mansart. Their principal buildings, mostly outside Paris, are listed under their respective names.

After the French Revolution, and under Napoleon, there ensued the 'Empire' phase in French architecture, when inspiration was derived from Pompeian, Greek, and even Egyptian sources. During the middle years of the nineteenth century France experienced the 'Gothic Revival' (*see* VIOLLET-LE-DUC) and the 'Free Classic Revival,' though still retaining some of her native architectural tradition; but towards the close of that century began to take the lead in Europe in developing reinforced concrete construction, a form of building which soon began to revolutionize her architecture, notably in the work of A. G. Perret (q.v.). His brilliant pupil, the Swiss architect 'Le Corbusier' (q.v.), settled in Paris in 1922, and became the leader and prophet of the so-called 'Modern Movement' in architecture. The work of both men is summarized under their respective names.

See also ANTOINE, BLONDEL (2), BOFFRAND, BRUAND, DU CERCEAU, DE BROSSE, FONTAINE, GARNIER (2), GUADET, LE BRETON, LE BRUN, LEDOUX, LE MUET, LE NÔTRE, LE PAUTRE, LE VAU, MAROT, MÉTÉZEAU, MONTEREAU, NEPVEU, PERCIER, PERRAULT, SERVANDONI, SOUFFLOT, VISCONTI.

> *See* G. H. West, *Gothic Architecture in England and France*, 1911; Sir R. Blomfield, *A History of French Architecture from 1494 to 1774* (4 large vols.), 1911–21; M. Aubert and G. Verrier, *L'Architecture française*, 1941; P. Lavedan, *French Architecture*, 1956.

French Window, or **French Door,** a tall window opening in two leaves like a folding door; sometimes secured by an espagnolette bolt (q.v.).

Fresco (It., fresh), painting executed on a plastered wall before the plaster has completely dried.

Fret, or **Key Pattern,** in classical architecture, an ornament composed of combinations of straight lines, usually on a flat surface. (*Illustrated* MOULDINGS, ENRICHED (CLASSICAL).)

F.R.I.B.A., abbreviation for Fellow of the Royal Institute of British Architects.

Frieze. (1) In classical architecture, the middle member of the entablature (q.v.) in one of the Orders (q.v., *illustrated*). (2) In a panelled room, the space between the top of the panelling and the cornice or ceiling. (3) In a room with papered walls, the space between the picture rail and the cornice or ceiling.

Frigidarium (Lat.), in one of the Roman public baths (*see* THERMAE), a cooling-room or a cold-water swimming-bath.

Frontispiece (rare and archaic), a façade (q.v.) or the central feature of a façade; or a pedimented entrance doorway.

Fry, Edwin Maxwell (*b.* Wallasey, 2 Aug. 1899), English architect and town-planner. He was educated at Liverpool University. After 1927 he worked as a partner with Messrs Adams & Thompson, town-planning consultants, and from 1934 to 1936 with W. Gropius (q.v.). Together they designed the Impington village centre, Cambridgeshire. From 1943 to 1945 he was town-planning adviser in West Africa, in partnership with his wife (*née* Jane Drew). In 1951 he was appointed senior architect for the new capital of the Punjab at Chandigarh (*see* ' LE CORBUSIER '). His other work includes Kensal House and other blocks of residential flats in London; educational buildings on the Gold Coast (1946–53); and Ibadan University College, Nigeria (1954).

Fuga, Ferdinando (*b.* Florence, 1699; *d.* Rome, 1781), Italian Baroque architect, worked mainly in Rome from 1717 to *c.* 1750, and became one of the Pope's two chief architects in 1730. His principal works in Rome were the completion of the Palazzo del Quirinale (1730); additions to the Palazzo Corsini (1732–6); the Palazzo della Consulta (1736); the Palazzo Petroni; the churches of S. Maria dell' Orazione (1737), and S. Apollinare (1745–8). He was invited in 1735 to complete the royal palace at Madrid, after Juvara (q.v.) had died, but he declined to leave the Pope's service. About 1750, however, he moved to Naples where he began building the Reale Albergo dei Poveri (*c.* 1751); laid out the large cemetery of Trivice (1762–3); and designed the churches of the Incurabili (1762–3) and of S. Filippo Neri (*c.* 1780).

See monographs by R. Pane, 1956, and G. Matthiae (N.D.).

Functionalism, a term coined in the twentieth century to express an idea held among rigid exponents of aesthetic puritanism, that every detail in the design of a building should be determined by its function, regardless of ' mere ' appearance. The argument may be extended to hold that the appearance of the entire building should proclaim its purpose; e.g. that a railway station should look like a railway station, not like a Greek temple or a Flemish town hall; and that a church should look like a church, not like a cinema or a factory. The real problem remains, however: what should a church or factory or station look like, intrinsically, apart from stylistic prejudices?

Fust (archaic and rare), the shaft of a column.

G

Gable (Old Fr. *gable*), the vertical triangular portion of wall at the end of a ridged roof, from the eaves level to the apex. *See also* CORBIE STEPS, PEDIMENT, ROOF, *illustrated*.

GABLE. *Above, brick gables from East Anglia (left) and Surrey (right); below, 'Cape' gables of the 18th century from South Africa*

Gabled Hip, a hip (q.v.) with a small gable over it. (*Illustrated* ROOF.)

Gabriel, Ange Jacques (*b.* Paris, 23 Oct. 1698; *d.* there, 4 Jan. 1782), French architect, son of Jacques Jules Gabriel (q.v.). He succeeded his father as *premier architecte du Roi* in 1742, and retired in 1775. In that capacity he made alterations to the palaces of Choisy, Compiègne, Fontainebleau, Marly, and Versailles; laid out the Place de la Concorde in Paris (1749–53), and designed the École Royale Militaire (1751), the Ministère de la Marine (1767–70), and the corresponding block on the other side of the Rue Royale; the Petit Trianon (1762–6) and the Royal Opera House (1748–70)—both at Versailles.

See monographs by E. Bousson, 1894; Cte. de Fels, 1911; G. Gromort, 1923; H. Bartle Cox, 1926.

Gabriel, Jacques Jules (*b.* Paris, 6 April 1667; *d.* Fontainebleau, 23 June 1742), French architect; son of Jacques Gabriel, also an architect, and father of A. J. Gabriel (q.v.). He became *architecte*

141

du Roi in 1687 and *premier architecte* in 1735. Besides bridges at Blois, Charenton, Lyon, Pontoise, Poissy, etc., he designed the façade of the cathedral at La Rochelle (1740); the Hôtel de Ville at Rennes (1734–43); the Archbishop's Palace at Blois (1725); the Hôtel Varangeville in Paris (1707); and the Place Royale at Bordeaux (1730–60), including the Bourse.

Galilee, a porch or chapel usually at the west end of a medieval church; e.g. Durham Cathedral, Ely Cathedral.

Galilei, Alessandro (*b.* Florence, 25 July 1691; *d.* Rome, 21 Dec. 1736), Italian architect. He is said to have spent seven years in England as a youth. He later settled in Rome, where he carried out his principal works: the façades of the great church of St John Lateran (1732–6) and of S. Giovanni de' Fiorentini (1734).

Gallery (Med. Lat. *galeria*). (1) A covered space for walking in, with one side open. (2) A platform projecting from the walls of a building—e.g. a church or a theatre—to augment the seating capacity; supported on pillars or cantilevers (q.v.). (3) A long upstairs room, especially in Elizabethan and Jacobean houses, called the 'Long Gallery' (q.v.). (4) A room used for the display of works of art. (5) A separate building for the same purpose.

Galleting, or **Garreting,** the decorating of mortar joints in a wall with pebbles pressed into the mortar while soft.

Gambrel Roof (especially in U.S.A.), a roof with its lower part sloping more steeply than the upper (as in a 'mansard roof', q.v.), introduced into New England during the seventeenth century.

Gandon, James (*b.* London, 29 Feb. 1742–3; *d.* Lucan, Ireland, 24 Dec. 1823), English architect and draughtsman. After working as assistant to Sir William Chambers (q.v.), he started independent practice in 1765, and won the competition for Nottingham County Hall and Jail in 1769. He moved to Dublin in 1781, and retired from practice in 1808. His important work in Dublin included the Custom House (1781–91) and additions to the Parliament House (1785) and to the Four Courts (1786). He also designed the Court House and Jail at Waterford (1784).

Gandy, Joseph Michael, A.R.A. (*b.* 1771; *d.* 1843), British architect, was the son of an employee of White's Club in London, and the eldest of three brothers who attained some distinction in architecture. As a boy of fifteen he was noticed by James Wyatt (q.v.), then rebuilding the club-house, and entered Wyatt's office. He studied at the Royal Academy Schools, won the Gold Medal in 1790, and then was sent by the proprietor of White's to Italy. Returning to London in 1798, he was employed by Soane (q.v.) to make architectural perspectives in water-colour, and for nearly fifty years he annually exhibited 'fantasies' of this sort at the Royal Academy. He also illustrated Britton's *Architectural Antiquities*, and published two books of designs for rural cottages. His architectural practice was small, but included Storrs Hall, Westmorland, 1808 (now an hotel).

He gave some instruction to his brother Michael (1778–1862), who was mainly employed in later years as a draughtsman. Another brother, John Peter Gandy, R.A., M.P., afterwards 'Deering,' (1787–1850), carried out a fair amount of building before retiring to the life of a country gentleman.

Garage (from Fr. *garer*, to shelter), a building to shelter a car. The term was first used about 1902.

Garden City, a term invented in 1902 by Ebenezer Howard whose book *Tomorrow: a Peaceful Path to Real Reform*, 1898, appeared in its second edition (1902) as *Garden Cities of Tomorrow*. He defined the garden city of his dreams as 'a town-country magnet.' It was to occupy the central area of an estate of 1,000 acres, and to be approximately circular in form, about three-quarters of a mile in diameter, divided into six segmental 'wards' by boulevards radiating from a central park in which the various civic buildings were to be located. On its outer fringe were factories, warehouses, etc., and surrounding the whole town was a wide agricultural belt of 5,000 acres, to provide vegetables, fruit, and milk, as well as healthy country surroundings, for an assumed urban population of 30,000. As a result of intense personal activity by Howard, who was a humble shorthand reporter, the site for the 'First Garden City,' at Letchworth in Hertfordshire, was purchased by a private company in 1903. The plan of Letchworth was made by Raymond Unwin (q.v.) in collaboration with Barry Parker. Howard also took the lead in founding the second garden city at Welwyn in Hertfordshire, twenty miles from central London, in 1919. *See also* Town-planning.

Garderobe (Fr.), a privy built in the wall of a medieval castle. There are interesting examples at Orford Castle, Suffolk.

Gargoyle (Old Fr. *gargouille*, a throat), in medieval buildings, a stone spout, delivering water downwards and outwards from a parapet gutter. The end of the gargoyle was often carved to represent grotesque heads or beasts, as in the famous examples at Notre-Dame, Paris.

Garnier, Charles (*b.* Paris, 6 Nov. 1825; *d.* there, 3 Aug. 1898), French architect; studied in Rome and Athens; and in 1861 won the competition for the new Opera House, Paris, completed in 1875. He also designed the Casino at Monte Carlo, and was awarded the R.I.B.A. Royal Gold Medal in 1886.

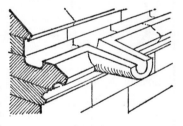

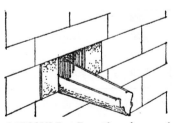

GARGOYLE. Example above, of stone; below, of lead. Both these are Gothic examples

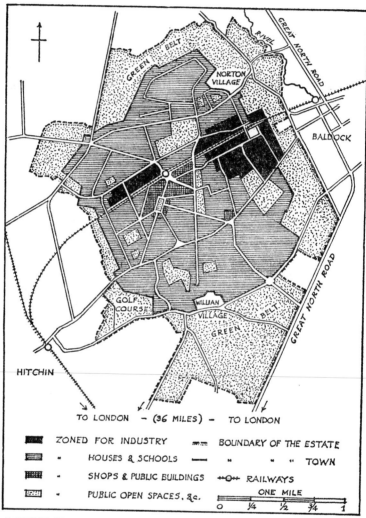

GARDEN CITY (1). *Sketch-plan of Letchworth, showing general lay-out and zoning*

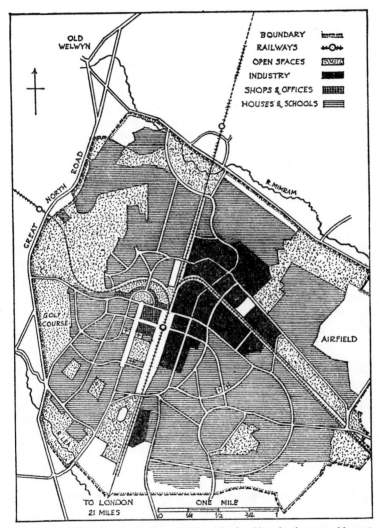

GARDEN CITY (2). *Sketch-plan of Welwyn Garden City, showing general lay-out and zoning*

Garnier, Tony (*b*. Lyon, 1869; *d*. there, 1948), French architect; studied in Paris, then in Rome; became City Architect of Lyon where he built a remarkable abattoir (1909) and stadium (1916). He published *Étude pour la Construction de Villes*, 1917.

Garret, originally a turret or watch-tower; then an attic in a roof.

Garreting, *see* GALLETING.

Gauged Brickwork, brickwork accurately built with fine joints.

GAZEBO. Holland House, London

Gazebo (derivation uncertain), usually a summer-house at the end of a garden terrace, commanding a view.

Geometrical Decorated Style, the first phase of the 'Middle Pointed' or 'Decorated' period of English Gothic architecture, in which the tracery consists of strictly geometrical forms and has not yet become 'flowing.' (*Illustrated* TRACERY.)

Geometrical Staircase, a staircase (q.v., *illustrated*) having a continuous handrail and string; usually planned around a semicircular or elliptical well.

George, Sir Ernest, R.A. (*b*. London, 13 June 1839; *d*. there, 3 Dec. 1922), English architect, President R.I.B.A., 1908–10; R.I.B.A. Royal Gold Medallist, 1896. Beginning practice in London in 1861, he had as successive partners T. Vaughan, H. Peto, and A. B. Yeates. His work consisted mainly of large country houses, among them Batsford, Motcombe, North Mimms, and West Dean, and streets of houses in West London, e.g. Collingham Gardens and Mount Street. He also designed the Royal Academy of Music (1910–11), fifty years after starting practice. For his country houses he adopted the Jacobean tradition, but his London streets display his fondness for picturesque but fussy Flemish gables, etc. His influence upon English architecture was great, for among those who worked in his office were Sir Guy Dawber (q.v.), Sir H. Baker (q.v.), and Sir E. L. Lutyens (q.v.). He was a skilful water-colour painter and etcher.

Georgian Style, strictly speaking, British architecture during the period of the 'four Georges,' 1714–1820, but usually extended up to 1830. Its earlier phase was mainly 'Palladian' (q.v.) and its last phase 'Regency' (q.v.), but throughout it followed classical tradtion. For its chief exponents *see* ENGLISH ARCHITECTURE, 5.
See also J. Summerson, *Georgian London*, 1945.

German Architecture is here assumed to include Austria and Czechoslovakia, both of which once formed part of the old German empire. At its greatest extent Roman dominion extended as far as the Danube and the Rhine, but remains of Roman buildings are chiefly confined to a few cities of the Rhineland, especially Trèves or Trier (*Augusta Trevirorum*), where there are ruins of basilicas and baths. The imposing Porta Nigra, a work of the third or fourth century, stands almost intact. Very little building took place after the Roman evacuation in the fifth century, but under Charlemagne the 'Dark Ages' became less dark than elsewhere, and at Aachen he built the Dom or cathedral in 796–804, partly to serve as his mausoleum. It is a great domed polygon. (The beautiful choir, in late Gothic style, was added in 1414.) A few minor buildings of the same period survive; then there is a gap until we reach the abbey of Gernrode in the Harz (*c.* 960); and then come a group of splendid Romanesque churches in the Rhineland—so that this has sometimes been called 'Rhenish architecture'—including the cathedrals of Worms (1016–1181), Mainz, Speyer, and Trier; the abbey-church of Laach; and in Cologne the churches of S. Maria im Kapitol, St Martin, and the Holy Apostles. Outside the Rhineland the finest Romanesque churches are the cathedral at Bamberg, and St Godehard and St Michael at Hildesheim. Several of these great churches have apses at both west end and east end, each generally flanked by gabled towers. Arcading is freely used as external decoration, this being a feature borrowed from Italy. There is little Romanesque architecture of note in Austria or Czechoslovakia.

The transition from Romanesque to Gothic may be studied at the cathedral of Limburg and the churches of St Gereon and St Cunibert, both in Cologne. German Gothic architecture, though distinctive in its later phases, is directly derived from France. Typical examples are St Elizabeth at Marburg; Cologne, Freiburg, Ratisbon cathedrals, and most of Vienna Cathedral; the nave of Strasburg Cathedral; the choir of Prague Cathedral; the Frauenkirche at Nuremberg; and several fine brick churches in North Prussia, especially the Marienkirche at Lübeck and the Marienkirche at Danzig. Germany still contains many picturesque timbered medieval houses. Neubrandenburg in Prussia has quaint medieval gates, and the towns of Rothenburg in Bavaria and Goslar in the Harz preserve a medieval aspect. The Renaissance reached Germany and Austria rather late. In Austria it followed the classical tradition more closely than in Germany, where native architects usually derived their inspiration from the same Flemish copybooks that guided our Elizabethan and Jacobean architects, so that German buildings of the late sixteenth and early seventeenth centuries resemble contemporary English examples. They include the town halls of Augsburg, Bremen, Leipzig, Molsheim, Paderborn, and Posen; the Marienkirche at Wolfenbüttel, additions to the Schloss at Heidelberg, the Schloss at Aschaffenburg, and those at Stuttgart and Wilhelmsburg. More Italian in appearance are the Schloss at Wolfenbüttel; St Michael's Church, Munich; the Hofkirche at Neuburg; the Belvedere and the Micovna in the royal castle at Prague.

Both Austria and South Germany are very rich in buildings, especially churches, of the Baroque and Rococo periods, including the huge Karlskirche (1716–36) and the University Church at Vienna; three large churches at Salzburg; the Theatine church at Munich; St Martin's, Bamberg; the Jesuit church, Mannheim; the Domkirche, Fulda; the Frauenkirche, Dresden; the great monasteries of Melk (1701–16), Wiblingen, Ottobeuren, St Florian, Gottweig; the Residenz, Würzburg; the Czernin, Clam Gallas, and Wallenstein palaces in Prague; the Kinsky and Trautson palaces as well as the great group of royal buildings in Vienna; the Zwinger palace at Dresden; Schloss Nymphenburg at Munich; and the Rococo palace of Sans Souci at Potsdam.

The 'Greek Revival' (q.v.) reached Germany early in the nineteenth century. Its chief products were the Propylaea, the Pinakothek, the Glyptothek, and the Walhalla at Munich, all designed by L. von Klenze (1784–1864), and the Brandenburg Gate, Royal Theatre, Old Museum, and Königswache in Berlin, all by K. von Schinkel (q.v.). Then followed the 'Gothic Revival' (q.v.) and next the 'Free Classic' movement, of which typical examples are the cathedral (1894–1905) and the Reichstag (1884–94), both in Berlin.

Just before the First World War a more distinctive style had begun to appear, fathered by P. Behrens (q.v.), and exemplified in the large departmental store buildings of Tietz and Wertheim in the chief cities. In the 1920's, however, a sudden change took place, and 'functional' buildings of steel, reinforced concrete, and glass were designed by a group of brilliant architects, including Gropius and Mendelsohn (qq.v.). Several of these men were Jews, and had to flee the country as Hitler came to power. They settled in England or America. Hitler himself had always intended to become an architect. Had his ambition been realized, he might have been content, and then the Second World War would never have occurred. Before it began he had managed to secure the erection of the vast Congress Hall and Stadium at Nuremberg, also the Chancellery and the Sports Centre at Berlin, all designed by his protégé Albert Speer (q.v.), who later became one of the chief Nazi ministers. Hitler's aim was to reverse the tendencies of the Jewish modernist architects, and to bring about a return to a more traditional and classic style of building.

See BREUER, DIENTZENHOFER (2), FISCHER VON ERLACH, LOOS, NEUMANN, NEUTRA, POELZIG, PÖPPELMANN, SEMPER, TAUT, VAN DE VELDE, VAN DER ROHE, WAGNER, ZUCALI.

> *See also* G. Dehio's histories of German architecture, 1922 and 1926; C. Horst, *Die Architektur der deutschen Renaissance*, 1928; G. A. Platz, *Die Baukunst der neuesten Zeit*, 1930; A. Speer, *Neue deutsche Baukunst*, 1943; and works by Gropius (q.v.).

Gibberd, Sir Frederick (*b*. Coventry, 7 Jan. 1908), English architect and town-planner. He was articled in Birmingham, and started practice in London in 1930. An early work was Pullman Court (flats) at Streatham (1934–5). It was followed by the Nurses' Home at Macclesfield, won in competition (1938); prefabricated houses for the British Iron and Steel Federation (1946); and steelworks at Frodingham (1946). Having been appointed chief architect and town-planner for Harlow New Town, he made the master-plan and designed the chief buildings there (1946 onwards). He also made the town plan for Nuneaton. His most important work is the great terminal building at London Airport (1950). Other work includes the Hull College of Technology (1951) and East Belfast Hospital.

Gibbs, James (*b.* near Aberdeen, 23 Dec. 1682; *d.* London, 5 Aug. 1754), British architect and writer on architecture. He made a protracted tour of study in Italy as a young man and, on returning to London in 1709, was soon employed by aristocratic patrons who had met him in Rome, with the result that he established a large and lucrative practice. His chief buildings in London were St Mary-le-Strand (1714–17); the steeple of St Clement Danes, Strand (1719–20); St Martin-in-the-Fields (1722–6); St Peter, Vere Street (1723–4); and St Bartholomew's Hospital (begun 1730). Outside London he rebuilt All Saints, Derby, now the cathedral (1723–5), and St Nicholas, Aberdeen (1751–5), and designed the Senate House (1722–30) and a new wing for King's College (1724–49), both at Cambridge; but his magnificent masterpiece is the domed Radcliffe Library at Oxford (1737–49). His work was both scholarly and original. He wrote two admirable books: *A Book of Architecture*, 1728, and *Rules for Drawing the Several Parts of Architecture*, 1732.
    See biography by B. Little, 1955.

Giedion, Sigfried (*b.* Lengnau, 1893), Swiss engineer and professor of the history of art, whose books on sociology and architecture have had a great influence upon contemporary thought in Europe and America. In 1928 he became general secretary of C.I.M.A. (International Congresses for Modern Architecture); in 1938 professor at Harvard University, U.S.A.; and in 1946 professor at the Federal Institute of Technology, Zürich, Switzerland. His chief published books (giving them their titles in English) have been *Late Baroque and Romantic Classicism*, 1923; *Building in France, Building in Iron, Building in Reinforced Concrete*, 1928; *Space, Time, and Architecture*, 1941; *Mechanization Takes Command*, 1948; *A Decade of Contemporary Architecture*, 1954; also a small monograph on W. Gropius (q.v.), 1931.

Gilbert, Cass (*b.* Zanesville, Ohio, U.S.A., 24 Nov. 1859; *d.* Brckenhurst, 17 May, 1934), American architect; President of the American Institute of Architects, 1908. He was trained at the Massachusetts Institute of Technology, started practice at St Paul, Minnesota, in 1883, and later moved to New York. His chief buildings were the State Capitol (1905) and two churches at St Paul; the famous Woolworth skyscraper, the United States Custom House, and the Union Club—all in New York; the Brazer Building and the Suffolk Bank at Boston; university buildings for Minnesota and Texas; public libraries at St Louis, New Haven, and Detroit.

Giocondo, Fra (*b.* Verona, *c.* 1433; *d.* Rome, 1 July 1515), Italian architect, engineer, philosopher, and antiquary. He became a Franciscan friar, and went to Rome to study archaeology. There he made a collection of ancient inscriptions. From 1489 to 1493 he

F

worked in Naples as architect to the Duke of Calabria, afterwards Alfonso II; and in 1495 went to France as architect to Charles VIII. Although he made many sketch designs for buildings, few can be confidently attributed to him; but he was probably concerned with the Loggia at Verona, the Pont Notre-Dame at Paris, and the Château of Gaillon in France. He also projected the Brenta Canal from Padua to Venice, and the fortifications between Treviso and Padua. In 1514 the Pope summoned him to Rome to assist in the building of St Peter's.

Girder, a main load-carrying beam of timber, steel, or reinforced concrete.

Glass, Stained, *see* STAINED GLASS.

Glyph (rare; from Gk *gluphē,* a carving), either (i) a sculptured feature; or (ii) a groove or channel. *See* TRIGLYPH.

Goodhart-Rendel, Harry Stuart (*b.* Cambridge, 29 May, 1887; *d.* London, 21 June 1959), architect; President R.I.B.A., 1937–9; Slade Professor of Fine Art at Oxford, 1933–6. He was educated at Eton and at Cambridge, where he took a degree in music. He served with the Grenadier Guards in both world wars. His buildings include a monastery at Prinknash; St Wilfrid's Church, Brighton; other churches at West Horsley and Ewloe (Wales); the restoration of All Souls, Langham Place, London; the extension of Dulwich Picture Gallery; Hay's Wharf, London Bridge; a factory near Kingston, Surrey; the Eton Boys' Club, Hackney Wick; and a number of town and country houses. His published work includes a witty and learned book on *English Architecture since the Regency,* 1953, and a small monograph on Hawksmoor, 1924.

Goodhue, Bertram Grosvenor (*b.* Pomfret, Connecticut, 28 April 1869; *d.* New York, 24 April 1924), American architect. After his training in New York, he went as assistant to R. A. Cram (q.v.), whose partner he became in 1895. (For buildings by this partnership *see* CRAM.) The partnership was dissolved in 1914; thereafter he practised alone. His chief buildings were the Capitol at Lincoln, Nebraska; public library, Los Angeles; National Academy of Science, Washington; chapel at the University of Chicago; the churches of St Bartholomew and of St Vincent Ferrier, New York.

Gopuram (Hindustani), gate tower of a temple enclosure.

Gospel Side, the north side of the chancel of a church, from which the gospel is read.

Gotch, John Alfred (*b.* Kettering, 28 Sept. 1852; *d.* there, 17 Jan. 1942), English architect and writer on architecture; President R.I.B.A., 1923–5. He was articled to R. W. Johnson of Melton Mowbray; began practice at Kettering in 1879, and remained there for the rest of his life, working in partnership with C. H. Saunders. His design of branch premises at Kettering for the Midland Bank led to a series of similar commissions elsewhere, culminating in the new head office building in London, where Lutyens (q.v.) was associated with the firm as consultant. Gotch's real reputation rests, however, upon his scholarly and readable books, chiefly on English architecture of the sixteenth and seventeenth centuries. They include *The Architecture of the Renaissance in England*, 1894; *Early Renaissance Architecture in England*, 1901; *The Growth of the English House*, 1909; *The English Home*, 1918; *Inigo Jones*, 1928.

Gothic Architecture, *see* ARCHITECTURE, 6.

Gothic Revival, The, a curious phase in the architectural history of England, western Europe, and the English-speaking nations overseas. Its origin was in romantic literature rather than in architecture, where its first effects were seen in Horace Walpole's mock-medieval villa at Strawberry Hill, near Twickenham, Middlesex (*c.* 1755), and in the absurd 'sham ruins' with which wealthy noblemen decorated their parks. It was not until the early nineteenth century that Gothic came to be seriously considered in building new churches, and not until 1830 that it became usual for that purpose. From *c.* 1850 to *c.* 1880 the fashion spread to town halls (e.g. Manchester), public buildings (the London Law Courts), hospitals (Leeds Infirmary), railway stations (St Pancras), and even dwelling-houses. For leaders of the movement, with their chief buildings, *see* AUSTIN, BARRY, BLOMFIELD (A. W.), BLORE, BODLEY, BURGES, BUTTERFIELD, CARPENTER, CHAMPNEYS, COTTINGHAM, FERREY, HALFPENNY, PEARSON, PUGIN (2), RICKMAN, SALVIN, SAVAGE, SCOTT (3), SEDDING, SHARPE, STREET, WATERHOUSE, WYATT, WYATVILLE; and ARCHITECTURE, PERIODS OF, 8.

> *See also* C. L. Eastlake, *A History of the Gothic Revival*, 1872; K. Clark, *The Gothic Revival*, 1928; M. S. Briggs, *Goths and Vandals*, 1952; H. S. Goodhart-Rendel, *English Architecture since the Regency*, 1953.

Graining, the imitation in paint of the natural grain of timber, practised in ancient Egypt some 5,000 years ago, and popular up to recent times.

Grand Tour, the fashionable tour through western Europe, made by noblemen's sons (usually with a tutor) in the eighteenth century, in pursuit of culture and *savoir-vivre*. Greece being inaccessible until late in that century, Italy and France were the countries chiefly visited. This habit had a profound influence upon English architectural taste in the eighteenth and early nineteenth centuries.

Grange, an outlying farm belonging to a medieval monastery.

Greek Architecture, *see* ARCHITECTURE, PERIODS OF, 2.

Greek Revival, The. A movement which arose from the publication of Stuart and Revett's *Antiquities of Athens* in 1762; from travels in Greece by Cockerell, Inwood, Robert Smirke, Wilkins (qq.v.), and other architects, soon after the country had become open, though still uncomfortable for tourists; and from the arrival in England of the Elgin Marbles in 1801. The Greek Revival lasted till *c.* 1840 in England, abreast of the Gothic Revival (q.v.).

For English architects prominent in the movement, and their buildings, *see* BURTON, COCKERELL, GANDON, GANDY, HARDWICK,

INWOOD, NASH, SMIRKE, R., SOANE, TAYLOR, and WILKINS; and for Scotland, CRAIG, PLAYFAIR, and THOMSON.

The movement also affected other countries, notably Germany (*see* KLENZE and SCHINKEL), the United States (*see* LATROBE), and the British possessions in Canada and India (*see* CANADIAN and INDIAN ARCHITECTURE).

See also ARCHITECTURE, PERIODS OF, 8.

Green Belt, an area around a new town, devoted exclusively to agriculture, in which all new building except agricultural building is severely restricted. The idea, proposed for London in the reign of Queen Elizabeth I, was revived by Ebenezer Howard in 1902 (*see* GARDEN CITY), and is now embodied in all new town-planning schemes. Much anxiety has arisen in recent years at the tendency of the London County Council to establish new urban communities in the green belt recommended by Sir P. Abercrombie (q.v.) in his *Greater London Plan*, 1944.

Greenway, Francis (christened Mangotsfield, near Bath, 20 Nov. 1777; *d.* in Australia, Sept. 1837), architect. He came from a family of masons and builders, and first appears in 1805 in an advertisement in a Bristol newspaper, where the firm offers to erect ' houses, lodges,' etc., from designs 'drawn by F. Greenway.' He and his two brothers developed much of the Clifton district of Bristol—including the Grand Hotel, Assembly Rooms, and Lower Crescent—in a pleasant Regency style. In 1809, however, he was declared a bankrupt, and in 1812 was condemned to death for forging a document. This severe sentence was reduced to banishment to Australia, which took place in 1813. Meanwhile General Macquarie, the governor of the new colony, had sent to England for a competent architect to plan Sydney and its buildings. Greenway, very prudently, carried a letter of introduction to the governor in his slender baggage, and made such good use of it that, from his landing onwards, he was employed as official architect—at first without pay—and soon became a prosperous professional man. In 1817 he made the town plan for Sydney. The following are the chief buildings designed by him, in or near Sydney, before his ambitions led to his dismissal in 1819 and his second bankruptcy in 1824: St Matthew's Church, Windsor (1817–22); St Luke's Church, Liverpool (1818–25); St James's Church, Sydney (1819–22); the Court House, Hyde Park (1820); the Governor's Stables (1819–21). His ambitious designs for the Governor's House and for St Andrew's Cathedral were never carried out.

See biography by M. H. Ellis, 1949.

Grille (from Fr.), a grating; hence a diagonal or rectangular, and often ornamental, arrangement of metal bars to enclose a space or to fill a doorway or window opening (*see* FANLIGHT). For wooden screens fulfilling the same purpose *see* LATTICE, MUSHRABIYYAH (Arabic), TRELLIS; and for their counterparts in stone, marble, or stucco *see* QAMARIYYAH (Arabic) and TRANSENNA.

Grimthorpe, Lord, 1st Baron; previously Sir Edmund Beckett,

5th Baronet (*b.* Carlton, Notts., 12 May 1816; *d.* Batch Wood, Herts., 29 April 1905), was an incredibly versatile person who, though most successful as a barrister, and hardly less so as an amateur horologist, figures prominently as a severe critic, a 'difficult' patron, and a disastrously confident amateur architect. He interfered unmercifully with Sir George Gilbert Scott (q.v.) during the latter's rebuilding of Doncaster Parish Church in 1853; but differences between the two men flared up to a crisis some years later, when Scott was restoring St Alban's Abbey, where Grimthorpe was not only the moving spirit but the chief subscriber. In the end Scott was cast adrift, and it is Grimthorpe's design that we see to-day in the hideous west front and some other features of the cathedral.

GRILLE, portion of a: from Lincoln Cathedral (c. 1200)

   See biography by P. Ferriday, 1957.

Groin, in vaulting, the line of intersection of two vaults. (*Illustrated*, VAULTING.)

Gropius, Walter Adolf Georg (*b.* Berlin, 18 May 1883), German-American architect. He was the son of an architect, was trained in Munich, and then worked under Behrens (q.v.) in Berlin. He practised independently in Berlin, 1910–14 and 1928–34. In 1919 he was appointed director of the Bauhaus (a school of applied art and building) at Weimar, in succession to Van de Velde (q.v.), but in 1925 it was transferred to Dessau. From 1934 to 1936 he worked in London, in collaboration with E. Maxwell Fry (q.v.), and in 1937 went to America as Professor of Architecture at Harvard University, meanwhile carrying on private practice in partnership with Marcel Breuer (q.v.). In 1946 he founded the Architects' Collaborative in America, and in 1956 he was awarded the R.I.B.A. Royal Gold Medal. His principal buildings are, in Germany—pavilions at the Cologne Exhibition (1914); factory at Alfeld (1914); theatre at Jena (1922); the Bauhaus at Dessau (1926); housing on a large scale at Stuttgart, Karlsruhe, and Berlin; in America—housing at Aluminium City (1943), Harvard Graduate Center (1950). His books and buildings have had an immense influence on recent architecture in all countries.

   See biographies by G. C. Argan, 1951, and S. Giedion, 1954.

Grotesque (derived indirectly from GROTTO, q.v.), in architecture, (1) a fanciful combination of human and animal forms with foliage and flowers; (2) comical, bizarre, or extravagant variations of such designs.

Grotto (It. *grotta*; Gk *kruptē*, crypt or vault), an artificial imitation of a natural cave, sometimes adorned with shells.

Grout, mortar of thin consistency, poured while still fluid into the interstices of masonry, especially in restoration work.

Guadet, Julien (*b.* Paris, 25 Dec. 1834; *d.* there, 17 May 1908), French architect and writer on architecture. He studied under H. Labrouste and J. André at the École des Beaux Arts, Paris; won the Prix de Rome, 1864; worked for some time at the French Academy in Rome; and in 1871 became a teacher at the Beaux Arts. His buildings included the Hôtel des Postes, Paris, 1880–4; the enlargement of the Théatre-Français, Paris, 1900; and numerous dwelling-houses. He is chiefly notable, however, for his standard book, *Éléments et Théorie de l'Architecture*, 1904.

Guarini, Camillo-Guarino (*b.* Modena, 17 Jan. 1624; *d.* Milan, 6 Mar. 1683), Italian Baroque architect, mathematician, monk, professor of philosophy and literature. He practised these varied activities simultaneously. His chief buildings, many of which were eccentric in design, included the façade of S. Gregorio, Messina (destroyed by earthquake, 1908); the Palazzo dell' Accademia delle Scienze, Turin (*c.* 1668–87); the Palazzo Carignano, Turin (1680); S. Lorenzo, Turin (*c.* 1668–87); the Santuario of the Madonna della Consolata, Turin (1679–1705); the Theatine Church of St Anne, Paris (1662, since destroyed).

See monograph by P. Portoghesi, 1956.

Guilloche (Fr.), in Greek architecture, a flat strip ornamented with a pattern composed of two hands interlacing to form circles. (*Illustrated* MOULDINGS, ENRICHED (CLASSICAL).)

Gumbaz (Persian), in Indian Muslim architecture, a dome or cupola.

Guttae (Lat., drops), the drop-like projections beneath the mutules and triglyphs (qq.v.) of a Doric entablature (q.v., *illustrated*).

Gwilt, Joseph (*b.* London, 11 Jan. 1784; *d.* Henley, 11 Sept. 1863), English architect and writer on architecture, was the son of George Gwilt, architect (1746–1807), who trained him. He also studied in the Royal Academy Schools, and in 1814–18 he travelled in Italy. His buildings include Markree Castle, Ireland (1843), and St Thomas's Church, Charlton, Kent (1847–50). He was a versatile man, interested in philology and music, and is remembered for his books, especially his comprehensive *Encyclopaedia of Architecture*, 1842, which had a great vogue. His other works include a translation of Vitruvius (q.v.), 1826; a new edition of Chambers's *Civil Architecture*, 1825; and, surprisingly, *Rudiments of the Anglo-Saxon Tongue*, 1829.

Gwynn, John, R.A. (*b.* Shrewsbury; *d.* Worcester, 28 Feb. 1786), English architect and writer on architecture. He appears to have started his career as a carpenter, but attained such eminence as an architect that he was one of the founders of the Royal Academy in 1768. He found employment as a draughtsman and designer before his practice developed, and in 1749 published Wren's plan for rebuilding London. His chief executed works were the English Bridge, Shrewsbury (1769–74); Atcham Bridge, Shropshire (1769–1771); Worcester Bridge and approaches (1771–80); Magdalen Bridge, Oxford (1772–82); and the markets at Oxford, since altered (1773–4).

Gynaeceum (Lat., from Gk *gunaikeion*, derived from *gunē*, a woman), in a Greek or Roman house, the apartments set apart for women, corresponding to the Arabic term *harim* (harem, q.v.). The portion of an early Christian church which was reserved for women was called a *matroneum* (q.v.).

H

Hadrian (*b.* A.D. 76; *d.* Baiae, A.D. 138), Roman emperor, A.D. 117–138, fancied himself as an amateur architect, and was so incensed by sarcastic criticism of his designs by his official architect, Apollodorus (q.v.), that he first banished him and then put him to death.

Hagioscope, a squint (q.v.).

Halfpenny, William, alias 'Michael Hoare' (*d.* 1755), English architect and writer on architecture, describes himself as 'architect and carpenter' on the title-page of one of his numerous books. His authenticated buildings are few, but include the large church of Holy Trinity, Leeds (1722–7), recently threatened with demolition; the Coopers' Hall (1743–4), and possibly the Assembly Rooms (1754–5), both at Bristol; but apparently not Redland Chapel, Bristol (1743), which has been attributed to him. Most of his published books—a score or more in all—are either pocket manuals for builders or collections of his own designs for dwelling-houses, farmhouses, and cottages, but three are unusual in their titles and scope, viz. *Rural Architecture in the Gothic Taste,* 1752; *Chinese and Gothic Architecture properly Ornamented,* 1752; and *Rural Architecture in the Chinese Taste,* 1750–5. Thus he was not only one of the first exponents of the Gothic Revival (q.v.), but also of Chinoiserie (q.v.).

Half-timber Construction is a form of building in which the external 'walls' and internal partitions are of timber-framing (generally connected to the roof timbers), and are filled with brickwork or (occasionally) stone, or covered with lath-and-plaster or weatherboarding (q.v.) or tile-hanging (q.v.). In England half-timber buildings are found chiefly in those districts where stone is scarce, i.e. the southern counties (where the timbering is simple in design) and the West Midlands (where it is generally very ornate). This type of construction was most popular from *c.* 1450 to *c.* 1650. Half-timbering was also common in parts of France and Germany.

See F. H. Crossley, *Timber Building in England,* 1951.

Hall. (1) Formerly the communal room in a medieval house, where all the inmates lived, fed, and slept. (2) The principal dwelling in a rural area. (*Illustrated* HOUSE.)

Hammam (Arabic), an oriental bath or bathing establishment.

Hammer-beam Roof, an elaborate type of roof-truss, peculiar to England and used in late Gothic and Tudor buildings. There are fine examples, richly decorated, at Westminster Hall (1395–9) and Hampton Court Palace (1530–5). In order to avoid a tie-beam across an imposing hall, short timber cantilevers ('hammer-beams') are used, but structurally they are inferior in strength to tie-beams.

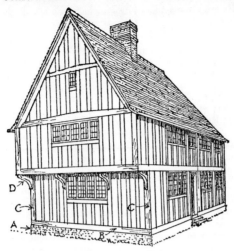

HALF-TIMBER CONSTRUCTION: traditional Kentish type. Note massiveness and close spacing of timbers. A=brick plinth; B=sill or wall-plate; C=angle-posts; D=brackets

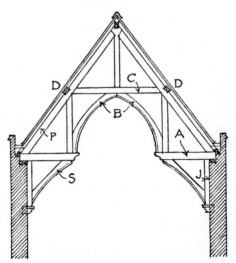

HAMMER-BEAM ROOF-TRUSS. A=hammer-beam; B=brace; C=collar; D=purlin; J=jack-leg; P=principal; S=strut

*F

Hangar (Fr.), a covered shed or shelter; used since 1902 to describe sheds for aircraft.

Hansom, Joseph Aloysius (*b.* York, 26 Oct. 1803; *d.* London, 29 June 1882), chiefly known as the inventor of the hansom-cab in 1834, was an architect, inventor, and journalist. He was articled in York, and in 1831 won the competition for the Birmingham Town Hall, which was duly built. He also designed several Roman Catholic churches, including the cathedral at Plymouth; St Walpurga, Preston; St François de Sales, Boulogne; and St Philip Neri, Arundel. He founded *The Builder* journal, and retired from practice in 1879.

Haram (Arabic), a sacred enclosure around a mosque, e.g. the Haram ash-Sharif at Jerusalem.

Hardwick, Philip, R.A. (*b.* London, 15 June 1792; *d.* Wimbledon, 28 Dec. 1870), architect, was the youngest son of Thomas Hardwick and entered his office in 1808. He travelled extensively in Italy, 1817–19, and began independent practice about 1820. He was a founder member of the R.I.B.A. in 1834, and was awarded its Royal Gold Medal in 1854. From 1850 to 1861 he was treasurer of the Royal Academy. His principal buildings, all in London, were the warehouses at St Katherine's Docks (1827–8); Goldsmiths' Hall (1829–35); Euston Station portico, hotel, and lodges (1836–9); Stone Buildings, Lincoln's Inn (1835–42); and a house in Belgrave Square (1842).

Hardwick, Thomas (*b.* Brentford, 1752; *d.* London, 16 Jan. 1829), architect, was the son of an architect of the same name, and father of Philip Hardwick (q.v.). He was articled to Sir William Chambers (q.v.), studied at the Royal Academy Schools, travelled in Italy from 1776 to 1779, and soon created a large practice on his return. His chief works were the rebuilding of St Paul's Church, Covent Garden (1795–8); St Mary's Church, Wanstead (1787–90); Galway Jail, Ireland (1802); St Pancras Workhouse (1809); Marylebone Parish Church (1813–17); St John's Chapel, St John's Wood (1814).

Hardy, Thomas, O.M. (*b.* Higher Bockhampton, Dorset, 2 June 1840; *d.* Dorchester, 11 Jan. 1928), man of letters, was an architect in his early years. After serving his articles in Dorchester, he went to London in 1862, became assistant to A. W. Blomfield (q.v.), and in 1863 won the R.I.B.A. Essay Medal for a thesis on *Coloured Brick and Terra-cotta Architecture*; also the Architectural Association's prize for design. Two years later his first short story appeared, and soon afterwards he left London for Dorset, and forsook architecture for literature, but built himself a house called 'Max Gate' at Dorchester in 1885.

Hare, Henry Thomas (*b.* Scarborough, Yorks., 1860; *d.* Farnham Common, 10 Jan. 1921), architect; President R.I.B.A., 1917–19. He was articled in Scarborough, then studied in Paris, and soon after settling in London in 1891 began practice. He was remarkably successful in competitions, which accounted for most of his work. This included County Offices, Stafford (1892); Municipal Buildings,

Oxford (1897); Westminster College, Cambridge (1897); Liverpool Technical School and Museum (1897); Henley Municipal Buildings (1898); Southend Municipal Buildings (1898) and Technical School (1899); Stafford Technical School (1900); Harrogate Municipal Buildings (1902); Crewe Municipal Buildings (1903); University College, Bangor (1907); and public libraries at Wolverhampton (1902), Southend (1903); Hammersmith (1903); Harrogate (1904); Islington (1905), and Fulham (1908).

Harem, properly **Harīm** (Arabic), in architecture, the secluded women's quarters in an Arab house.

Harling, a Scottish term for rough-cast (q.v.).

Harris, Emanuel Vincent, R.A. (*b.* Plymouth, Devonshire, 1879), architect; R.I.B.A. Royal Gold Medallist, 1951. He was articled in Plymouth and, after working as assistant to Leonard Stokes (q.v.) and Sir William Emerson (q.v.), started independent practice in London in 1908. He won a succession of important public competitions. These provided most of his work, which included Glamorgan County Hall, Cardiff (1908); Cardiff fire station (1912); the enormous block of government offices (still under construction in 1959) between Whitehall and the Embankment (1915); Sheffield City Hall (1920); Manchester Central Library and extension of Municipal Buildings (1925); Surrey County Hall (1925); Leeds Civic Hall (1926); Somerset County Hall (1932); Nottingham County Hall (1935); Bristol Council House (1935); new buildings for Durham University (1947) and for University College, Exeter (1930–54). He retired from practice in 1954.

Harrison, Peter (*b.* York, England, 14 June 1716; *d.* New Haven, Connecticut, 30 April 1775), architect, who became one of the leading figures in American colonial architecture, arrived in Rhode Island from England in 1740, and settled at Newport as a merchant. Apparently he had no training as an architect, and was simply a very gifted amateur who made full use of the published works of Palladio, Gibbs, and Batty Langley (qq.v.). Among buildings designed by him were the Redwood Library (1748–50); the Brick Market (1761); the Synagogue (1762–3)—all at Newport, Rhode Island; King's Chapel, Boston (1749–54), and Christ Church, Cambridge, Massachusetts (1761).

Harrison, Wallace Kirkman (*b.* Worcester, Massachusetts, 28 Sept. 1895), American architect. After working in the office of Messrs McKim, Mead, & White (q.v.), he began independent practice in 1927. He was appointed co-ordinating architect for the Rockefeller Center, New York, and Director of Planning for the United Nations Building at New York in 1950. His firm also designed the 'Theme Building' at the New York World's Fair and the Alcoa Building, Pittsburgh (1953). He has been Professor of Design at Columbia University and Associate Professor of Design at Yale University.

Hastings, Thomas (*b.* New York, 11 Mar. 1860; *d.* Mineola, Long Island, 22 Oct. 1929), American architect; R.I.B.A. Royal Gold Medallist, 1922. After studying at the École des Beaux Arts in

Paris, he joined J. M. Carrère (q.v. for their buildings), and worked in partnership with him from 1885 till Carrère's death in 1911. His work after that date included the offices of the Senate and House of Representatives at Washington; the Arlington War Memorial Amphitheatre; the Victory Arch; the Atlantic City War Memorial; the Standard Oil Building and the United Rubber Building in New York; and Devonshire House, London.

Haunch, the lower part of an arch.   (*Illustrated* ARCH.)

Haviland, John (*b.* in Somerset, England, 15 Dec. 1792; *d.* Philadelphia, 28 Mar. 1852), American architect. He studied architecture in London under James Elmes, father of H. L. Elmes (q.v.), and in 1816 went to Philadelphia where relatives lived. With a friend he founded a small school of architecture; and in 1818–19 they jointly produced a work in two volumes, *The Builder's Assistant,* characteristic of its period. His buildings included the First Presbyterian Church, St Andrew's Episcopal Church, and the Pennsylvania Institute for the Deaf and Dumb—all at Philadelphia; the United States Naval Asylum at Norfolk; the State Insane Asylum at Harrisburg; and county halls at Pittsburgh, Newark, Norfolk, etc.

He was chiefly notable as the inventor of the modern radiating plan for prisons. From 1821 onwards he built a number of these, among them the City Prison of New York—famous as 'The Tombs'—rebuilt in 1888. The governments of Great Britain, France, and Russia sent missions to America to study these buildings.

Hawksmoor, Nicholas (*b.* in Nottinghamshire, 1661; *d.* London, 25 Mar. 1736; architect. His birth-place was probably Ragnall, near Tuxford, Nottinghamshire. At about eighteen years of age he became 'clerk' to Wren, and at twenty-one his deputy at Chelsea Hospital. He was a talented draughtsman, assisting Wren in that capacity or in other ways at St Paul's Cathedral, Westminster Abbey, Winchester Palace, Kensington Palace, St James's Palace, Greenwich Hospital, and the City churches. He also assisted Vanbrugh (q.v.) at Castle Howard and Blenheim. In 1725 he became surveyor to Westminster Abbey. New buildings designed by him included the London churches of St Alphege, Greenwich (1712–14); St Anne, Limehouse (1712–24); St George-in-the-East (1715–23); St Mary Woolnoth (1716–27); St George, Bloomsbury (1720–30); and Christ Church, Spitalfields (1713–29). Other work included Queen's College, Oxford (1709–38); part of All Souls College, Oxford (1715–40); and the Clarendon Building, Oxford (1712–15).
See lives by H. S. Goodhart-Rendel, 1924; K. Downes, 1959.

Helladic (from Gk *Hellas,* Greece), a term applied to the early architecture of mainland Greece from *c.* 2500 to *c.* 1100 B.C., and thus including the Mycenaean architecture of mainland Greece, and corresponding to the Minoan period in Crete. For both *see* ARCHITECTURE, PERIODS OF, 1(*c*).

Hellenic Architecture, Greek architecture from *c.* 700 B.C. to *c.* 323 B.C. (the date of Alexander the Great's death). For examples *see* ARCHITECTURE, PERIODS OF, 2.

Hellenistic Architecture, or 'Graeco-Roman' architecture, prevailed from *c.* 323 B.C. onwards, in all countries influenced by Greece in the eastern Mediterranean, until the advent of distinctively Roman architecture in the first to second centuries A.D.

Helm Roof, in Romanesque architecture, an unusual form of spire with gables on each of the four faces, and a pyramidal spire rising from the apices of the gables. Examples: at Sompting in Sussex, and in several Rhineland churches.

Hemicycle, a semicircular structure.

Heptastyle (Gk *hepta*, seven; *stulos*, a column), a classical portico having seven columns in a row.

Heroum, in classical architecture, a shrine or chapel dedicated to the memory of a deified or semi-deified person.

Herrera, Juan de (*b.* Mobellon, near Santander, *c.* 1530; *d.* Madrid, 15 Jan. 1597), Spanish architect. After military service in Flanders and Italy, 1548–53, he was commissioned by Philip II in 1563 to build the Escorial palace and monastery from plans previously made by Juan Bautista de Toledo (q.v.). His other work included the Puenta de Segovia, Madrid (1584); the unfinished cathedral of Valladolid (begun 1585); additions to the Alcazar at Toledo and the palaces of Simancas and Aranjuez; and designs for the Bourse at Seville.

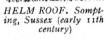

HELM ROOF. Sompting, Sussex (early 11th century)

See monograph by A. Ruiz de Ancante, 1936.

Herring-bone Brickwork, an arrangement of facing-bricks in diagonal patterns for decorative purposes, sometimes in the panels of half-timber framing; or of paving-bricks set diagonally.

Hexastyle (Gk *hexa*, six; *stulos*, a column), a classical portico having six columns in a row. (*Illustrated* TEMPLE.)

Hip, the salient angle formed by the intersection of two sloping roof surfaces. (*Illustrated* ROOF.)

Hipped Gable, a gable with its top part hipped. (*Illustrated* ROOF.)

Hitchcock, Henry Russell (*b.* Boston, Massachusetts, 3 June 1903), American architectural historian. He graduated at Harvard as

HERRING-BONE BRICKWORK in a vertical wall-panel

A.B. in 1924, A.M. in 1927. He became Assistant Professor of Art at Vassar College, 1927–8, and at the Wesleyan University, Middletown, Connecticut, in 1929. After serving as associate professor in that institution. 1941–7, and as professor, 1947–8, he became professor at Smith College in 1948. He has also acted as visiting lecturer at Yale and at the Massachusetts Institute of Technology. Among his numerous published books are *Frank Lloyd Wright*, 1928; *Modern Architecture*, 1929; *J. J. P. Oud*, 1931; *The International Style* (with P. Johnson) 1932; *The Architecture of H. H. Richardson*, 1936; *Rhode Island Architecture*, 1939; *The Nature of Materials*, 1942; *The Buildings of F. L. Wright*, 1942; *American Architectural Books*, 1946; *Painting towards Architecture*, 1948.

Hoban, James (*b.* in Ireland, 1758 or 1762; *d.* in U.S.A., 8 Dec. 1831), architect. After being trained in Dublin, he went to America, first to Charleston, then to South Carolina, and in 1792 to Washington, where he worked for the rest of his career on several important new public buildings. He designed the White House, and rebuilt it after its destruction by the British in 1814. He also supervised the erection of the Capitol from designs by Dr Thornton (q.v.).

Hoffmann, Josef (*b.* Pirnitz, Austria, 15 Dec. 1870), Austrian architect. After his training in Vienna under Hasenauer and Otto Wagner (q.v.), he became one of the founders of the 'Vienna Secession' movement in 1903, against the then fashionable flowing curves of *Art Nouveau* (q.v.). He advocated a return to straight lines in architecture. His designs included much furniture and decoration, as well as buildings. Among the latter were the Stoclet mansion at Brussels (1905–11) for a wealthy coal magnate, a number of private houses, several sanatoria, and various other commissions. He also showed his talents at numerous exhibitions from 1906 onwards.

See monographs by L. Kleiner, 1927, and A. Weiser, 1930.

Holden, Charles Henry (*b.* Bolton, 12 May 1875; *d.* 1 May 1960), architect and town-planner. Having completed his articles in Manchester, he came to London and entered the office of H. P. Adams as an assistant. In 1905 he won the important competition for Bristol Central Library. In 1907 he was taken into partnership by Adams, and in 1913 they were joined by L. G. Pearson. Adams died in 1930, Pearson in 1953. Work carried out by the firm included large hospitals at Bristol, Torquay, Valletta (Malta), and Istanbul; the British Medical Association's building in London; Sutton Valence School; the offices of the underground railways (now London Transport) over St James's Park Station; and a number of stations in the London area. During the First World War Holden was one of the principal architects of the Imperial War Graves Commission. In 1931 he was appointed sole architect for the Senate House and other buildings of London University in Bloomsbury. He was author, with W. G. Holford (q.v.), of the momentous town-planning report on the City of London, issued in 1947. R.I.B.A. Royal Gold Medallist, 1936.

Holford of Kemp Town, William Graham Holford, Baron (*b.* Johannesburg, 22 Mar. 1907), architect and town-planner; Professor of Town-planning at London University since 1948. He was trained at Liverpool University; then studied in Italy and America. He collaborated with Charles Holden (q.v.) in preparing the new plan for the City of London in 1947, and made the town plan for Cambridge in 1950. His published works include *The Future of Merseyside*, 1937, and *Civic Design*, 1949. Knight, 1953; Life Peer, 1965.

Holland, Henry (*b*. London, 20 July 1745; *d*. there, 17 June 1806), architect, was apprenticed to his father, a builder in Fulham; and in 1771 became partner of the landscape architect 'Capability Brown' (q.v.), whose daughter he married in 1773.   From 1775 to 1782 he held the post of clerk of the works at the Royal Mews in Charing Cross.   From 1771 onwards he was engaged in developing the 'Hans Town' estate in Chelsea, including Sloane Street and Cadogan Place.   He then created a very large and aristocratic practice, including the beautiful 'Marine Pavilion' at Brighton (1786–7), afterwards drastically remodelled by John Nash (q.v.); and Carlton House, London (1783–5), demolished in 1827–8. Of his other buildings, those still surviving include Claremont, Esher (1771–4); Brooks' Club, St James's Street (1776–8); Southill House, Bedfordshire (1795); Park Place, Henley (*c*. 1796); the remodelling of the Albany, London (1803–4); and a number of buildings in Bedfordshire.
  See monograph by D. Stroud, 1950.

Honnecourt, Villard, or **Wilars de** (thirteenth century), a French architect whose famous sketch-book (reproduced in facsimile 1859 and 1927) is preserved in the Bibliothèque Nationale, Paris.   He is believed to have designed the choir of St Quentin Cathedral, consecrated 1257.
  See monograph by H. R. Hahnloser, 1935.

Hood, *see* CANOPY.

Hooke, Robert (*b*. Freshwater, I. of Wight, 18 July 1635; *d*. London, 3 Mar. 1703), scientist and architect, was a contemporary and intimate friend of Wren (q.v.).   Like him, he was educated at Westminster School, and, with him, helped to found the Royal Society.   Like Wren, again, he entered architecture in middle life after being a professor at Gresham College, London, where he lived from 1665 onwards.   His inventive ability in the fields of chemistry and physics is famous, whereas his work as an architect is little known.   It began, about three years later than Wren's, when he submitted a plan for rebuilding London after the Great Fire, as Wren did also; and he was then nominated by the City to organize the rebuilding. Almost everything he designed himself has been either demolished or burnt, including the Royal College of Physicians (1672–8); Bethlehem Hospital, Moorfields, (1675–6); Montagu House, Bloomsbury (1675–1679); and Aske's Hospital, Hoxton (*c*. 1690–3); while Ragley in Warwickshire (1679–83) has been much altered.
  See monographs by R. Waller, 1705; M. 'Espinasse, 1956; and Hooke's own curious *Diary*, edited by H. W. Robinson and W. Adams, 1935.

Hopper, a small casement, forming part of a larger window, and hinged at the bottom to open inwards.

Horder, Percy Richard Morley, sometimes called **Morley-Horder** (*b.* Torquay, 18 Nov. 1870; *d.* East Meon, Hampshire, 7 Oct. 1944), architect. He was articled to G. Devey (q.v.) and began practice about 1902. His work consisted mainly of country houses in the traditional English style, notably one for David Lloyd George at Walton Heath, but also included several Congregational churches, a number of shops for Boots the chemists, and, as a result of his friendship with Sir Jesse Boot, the important buildings of Nottingham University College (1925–8); also Cheshunt College (1913), Wescott House, extensions to Jesus College, and the National Institute of Agricultural Botany (1919)—all at Cambridge; and an extension of Somerville, Oxford (1934). In the design of the London School of Hygiene, Bloomsbury (1926–9), he was associated with V. O. Rees.

Horseshoe Arch, largely used in Muslim architecture (q.v.), may be either (i) the 'round horseshoe' or 'Moorish arch'; or (ii) the 'pointed horseshoe.' For illustrations of both *see* ARCH, TYPES OF (Nos. 4 and 8 respectively).

Hosh (Arabic), the courtyard of an Arab house.

Hotel (Fr. *hôtel*, formerly *hostel*), originally signified, in France, a large town house; also used in *Hôtel de ville* (town hall) and *Hôtel-Dieu* (hospital); in modern English usage, a superior type of inn.

Hôtel-Dieu (Fr., literally 'House of God'). A name given to any large hospital in a town, being a religious foundation; e.g. the Hôtel-Dieu at Paris, originally founded *c.* A.D. 660, which contains over 800 beds.

House, a dwelling; a building for human habitation. The term therefore embraces every form of dwelling from a palace to a peasant's hut. It includes not only detached but semi-detached dwellings, and also, theoretically, such part of a larger building as is lived in by a single resident or a family. In practice, however, where a small two-storey house is planned to accommodate two families, one above the other, each storey is often called a 'maisonnette,' or, in America, 'duplex'; and where a building originally planned as a single house is let to a number of tenants, their respective groups of houses are called 'tenements'; but where the building has been specially planned or adapted for a number of separate tenancies, they are usually called 'flats,' or, in America, 'apartments.' A modern detached one-storey house is generally described as a 'bungalow' (q.v.). As will appear from the following article, all these types have a long history. 'Palace' is dealt with separately, and the most primitive types of hut dwellings, such as Skara Brae (Orkneys), Chysauster (Cornwall), and the Glastonbury Lake Village, are not described here.

Probably the oldest known houses that really merit the name are those forming the 'model village' at Kahūn in Egypt, built *c.* 2500 B.C. to accommodate workmen and officials engaged in erecting a

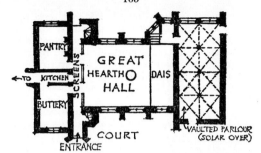

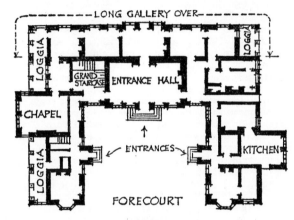

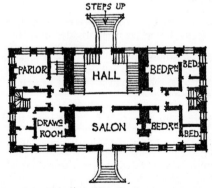

*PLANS, TO UNIFORM SCALE, OF THREE FAMOUS
ENGLISH HOUSES*

Part of Penshurst Place, Kent, 1348 (top), Aston Hall, Birmingham, 1618–35 (middle), and Coleshill, Berks., 1650 (bottom), showing the change from the discomfort of common life in the Great Hall to the increased comfort, dignity, and privacy of the Jacobean period and then to the formal and symmetrical planning of Coleshill

neighbouring pyramid. The village is laid out on a rectangular or gridiron plan. It contained some 300 dwellings for artisans, larger houses for foremen, and mansions for the chief administrative officials. The artisans' cottages contained three rooms opening off a small courtyard, from which a staircase led up to a flat roof. The foremen's dwellings had slightly larger rooms, three to five in number. The ten mansions were of uniform plan. Each contained about seventy rooms and occupied a site 198 feet by 138 feet. Each accommodated a considerable staff of servants besides the owner's family, and had two courtyards, one containing a water tank.

Rather later, c. 2000 B.C., were the large houses built at Ur of the Chaldees in Abraham's time. Externally they had blank walls facing on to narrow and probably dirty streets, but internally they were comfortable though not luxurious. Each contained thirteen or fourteen rooms on two storeys, and had brick staircases and terra-cotta drain-pipes. The imposing royal palace at Knossos in Crete (q.v.), erected before 2000 B.C., had a more elaborate scheme of drainage, one system taking away the rain-water, the other the sewage from the latrines.

In Hellenic Greece (fifth to fourth centuries B.C.), although temples and public buildings were erected on a magnificent scale, dwellings were more modest, and relatively few have survived. Even in Athens, renowned for its civic and religious architecture, the standard of domestic architecture was deplorably low in most of the squalid dwellings crowded together in narrow, tortuous, dirty, and unlighted streets. The typical Greek house was two storeys high. The external walls were blank except for the entrance doorway, all the rooms facing into an inner courtyard. A number of houses have been excavated at Olynthus in Macedonia, at Priene in Asia Minor, and on the island of Delos. At Olynthus the town was laid out on a gridiron plan, with main streets 16–23 feet wide dividing the area into *insulae* or blocks, each about 283 feet by 117 feet. Each block was bisected by an alley 4 feet 6 inches wide, and the half-blocks so formed were further divided into house lots, about 57 feet square. The walls of the houses were mostly of mud-brick on a foundation of rubble stone. The houses faced south and each had an internal courtyard paved with cobbles. There was one large room, the *oecus*, which had a central hearth. Sanitation did not exist.

The houses at Priene were somewhat similar, but most of them had a long passage running from front to back of the house. At Delos, rather later in date, many houses had a colonnade round the internal court, which usually contained a central water-tank filled with rain-water.

Pompeii (q.v.) in South Italy is a Greco-Roman or Hellenistic town, destroyed by an earthquake in A.D. 63 and then submerged in lava in A.D. 79. Its excavation in modern times has revealed a very high standard of comfort, refinement, wealth, and luxury. The Greek type of house was adopted, but the arrangement of rooms was more formal and symmetrical. Some of the larger examples included an internal garden.

The city of Rome, at the height of its glory, contained about a million people, and the palaces (now all in ruins) of the later emperors were magnificent. Outside the central area where all the splendid public buildings stood, but within the perimeter of the city walls, the bulk of the population was housed in tall 'flats' or apartment houses, all erected by private enterprise, and many of these by dishonest speculative builders.

The ground floor of each block generally consisted of shops (*tabernae*), which had hinged wooden flaps or shutters that could be let down to form a counter, projecting over the pavement. The upper storeys were of flimsy timber framing, at first faced with wattle-and-daub, later with concrete. The roofs at first were covered with wood shingles, later with tiles. Fires and collapses were frequent and fatal. In the reign of Augustus (27 B.C.–A.D. 14) new building regulations prescribed the use of solid brickwork for the lower part of such buildings, and limited their total height to 70 feet. Still more stringent regulations in the time of Nero (A.D. 54–68) insisted on fireproof materials for all external walls, and under Trajan (98–118) the maximum total height was reduced to 60 feet. These tenements had no provision for sanitation, washing, cooking, or heating; but Rome had a superb and most elaborate system of water supply. The larger private houses seem to have had baths and drainage. None of the tenement houses now remain in Rome, but at Ostia, a few miles away, there are many such, with balconies and staircases intact, all built of brick and concrete.

In Britain the foundations and basements of a large number of Roman town houses may be seen, notably at Verulamium, near St Albans. They were centrally heated by hot air from a furnace below ground level. The hot air passed through ducts in the floors and flues in the walls. Every house of any importance had its own hot bath. The principal rooms had handsome mosaic floors and gay paintings on the plastered walls. Britain also possesses about 500 examples of the Roman 'villa,' i.e. a country house or farmhouse from which an extensive estate was administered. They are mainly found in the southern half of England. The most important are at Bignor, Sussex; Brading, Isle of Wight; Chedworth, Gloucestershire; Folkestone, Kent; Northleigh and Woodchester, Oxfordshire. Some of them contain over fifty rooms, providing for all the needs of a large farm as well as accommodation for the owner's family, servants, and labourers. In them, as in the town houses, there is usually a central-heating system and some provision of baths.

After the collapse of the Roman Empire in the fifth century A.D., house building was interrupted, and Britain resembled continental Europe in the low standard of dwellings for all classes that prevailed during the next centuries. There were fortified dwellings of the feudal nobility on the one hand (*see* CASTLE), and the wretched hovels of their serfs—scarcely to be reckoned as architecture—on the other. There were no middle-class houses to speak of between the fifth century and the thirteenth, or even the fourteenth, so that hardly any early medieval dwelling-houses have survived. The so-called 'Jews' Houses' at Lincoln, 'Moyses Hall' at Bury St

Edmunds, and 'King John's House' at Southampton are rare
English examples, all in stone. The few remaining stone manor-
houses of the Middle Ages are very simple in plan, having only one
large room, the 'Great Hall,' in which the owner, his family, his
servants, and his dogs all lived, dined, and slept, keeping themselves
warm around a log fire that burned on a central hearth, the smoke
from which rose to an opening in the timber roof above. The floor
was of stone, covered with rushes which, in spite of frequent renewal,
became very foul. The windows were at first unglazed, and were
closed with wooden shutters. The kitchen, larder, and buttery were
separated from the Great Hall by wooden screens. There were no
carpets, upholstery, hangings, or panelling, and even in these upper-
class houses there was very little furniture. Progressive improve-
ments between the thirteenth century and the sixteenth included
a daïs, raised a few inches above the filth of the floor in the Great
Hall, with the 'high table' at which the owner and his family dined;
a private bedroom for the owner and his wife; bedrooms for the other
members of his family and for guests; a 'solar' or 'parlour' or private
sitting-room for the family; glazed windows; plastered ceilings;
panelled or tapestried walls; fire-places against a wall instead of in
the middle of the hall floor, and flues running up from them into
chimney-stacks; and, in fact, comfort and refinement all round.
Yet even in Elizabethan days English people must have been very
dirty, for baths and sanitary arrangements were still practically
unknown, even in the mansions of the aristocracy. All these
statements apply exclusively to upper-class medieval houses, of
which Penshurst Place, Kent (1388), and Great Chalfield Manor
House, Wiltshire (c. 1450), are typical English examples. It was not
until the Middle Ages were over that houses for yeomen and the more
prosperous artisans were built of substantial materials or provided
with the barest comforts and conveniences.

Throughout Europe, but especially in the prosperous countries of
western Europe (including England), there was a steady advance in
domestic refinement and comfort from the sixteenth century onwards,
as the civilizing influence of the Renaissance spread outwards from
Italy, and the standard of living of the upper classes began to match
that attained, long before, in Roman Britain. The 'Great Hall'
gave way to a smaller entrance hall from which the various living-
rooms opened, and in which was usually a fine staircase. Upstairs
was a magnificent 'Long Gallery,' in many great mansions a hundred
feet or more in length, which served as a family recreation-room and
sitting-room as well as for the display of pictures and fine furniture.
Mullioned windows looked out on to pleasant formal gardens with
terraces and summer-houses. There were fewer draughts, fewer
smells, far more light, and far more comfort. Examples of large
Tudor, Elizabethan, and Jacobean houses are Hampton Court Palace
(older portion, 1515–30); Sutton Place, Guildford (1523–5); Little
Moreton Hall, Cheshire (1550–9); Wollaton Hall, Nottinghamshire (1580–8); Hatfield House, Hertfordshire (1607–11); Aston Hall,
Birmingham (1618–35). The Queen's House at Greenwich (1671–
1635), by Inigo Jones (q.v.), and the château of Maisons near Paris

(1642–51), by F. Mansart (q.v.), are examples of mature Renaissance design.

The period from *c.* 1660 to *c.* 1800 in England, which included the career of Sir Christopher Wren (q.v.) and the Georgian phase, saw a certain lessening of picturesqueness in the design of the smaller houses, due in part to the substitution of sash windows for mullioned windows, and to the final abolition of pinnacles, battlements, and other romantic relics of the Gothic period, while the detail of these houses became more scholarly and their internal arrangements more refined and homely. Abreast of these charming small Georgian dwellings, however, were erected some of the largest and most over-powering mansions England has ever seen, e.g. Blenheim Palace, Castle Howard, Holkham, Houghton, designed by English 'Palladian' and 'Baroque' architects (*see* VANBRUGH and KENT), and others by Robert Adam (q.v.), e.g. Kenwood and Osterley. Similar great piles were built in France, Germany, and Spain during the eighteenth century, though there the style was more definitely Baroque. In startling contrast to these lordly seats were the rows of mean cottages erected in tens of thousands adjoining the collieries and 'mills' of north and midland England, as well as in London, as a result of the Industrial Revolution which began in the eighteenth century.

The Regency period in England (*see* ENGLISH ARCHITECTURE) was the last phase of Georgian architecture, and the Gothic Revival (q.v.) which followed it did not seriously affect domestic architecture, though John Nash (q.v.) erected some quaint Gothic houses at Park Village, near Regent's Park in London, *c.* 1824. In fact, it was not until *c.* 1850 that English house design began to assume that aspect of pretentiousness and over-ornamentation that has made the Victorian era appear ridiculous to so many modern critics. The goods displayed at the Great Exhibition of 1851 set a deplorable example of design that influenced the taste of Victorian architects for fifty years ahead, and was faithfully followed by the speculative builders who erected the vast majority of all Victorian dwellings.

William Morris (q.v.) pleaded for some simplicity and honest craftsmanship. In 1854 he employed his friend Philip Webb to design him 'The Red House' at Bexley in Kent to embody his ideals; but the most fundamental changes of taste were due to the architect C. F. A. Voysey (q.v.), who never built a cathedral or a town hall, never won a competition, and never became a Royal Academician, but who designed, between *c.* 1890 and *c.* 1914, a number of delightful and simple medium-sized houses in various parts of England. His influence was great in continental countries (especially Germany), where architecture during the nineteenth century had followed a course much like that in England.

Rather younger than Voysey was Sir Edwin Lutyens (q.v.), who began designing houses about 1888, at a very early age, in the native or rustic English tradition at first and following Voysey's lead to some extent, but later in his career turning to a more formal and Georgian style.

At the end of the First World War, when there was a clamour in England, as in other European countries, for a great quantity of 'homes for heroes,' the simple type of house originated by Voysey became the model for the government-sponsored housing schemes, which spread over agricultural land too freely outside our towns because they were laid on spacious 'garden suburb' lines, a fashion encouraged by Raymond Unwin (q.v.).

Partly as a reaction against this type of design and layout, the younger architects of the second quarter of the twentieth century tended to follow the theories of 'Le Corbusier' (q.v.), coming from France, and, later, of F. L. Wright (q.v.), coming from America. Apart from the general characteristics of construction mentioned in the article ARCHITECTURE, PERIODS OF (8, 9), the new schools of thought tends to favour, for domestic design, tall blocks of flats in preference to groups of small houses; the complete abolition of the despised Victorian 'parlour' or drawing-room; the substitution for it of an all-purpose 'lounge' or 'living-room' with a corner reserved for meals; and highly compact kitchen arrangements adapted to an age when families are small and domestic help almost unobtainable.

Bibliography. J. A. Gotch, *The Growth of the English House* (2nd ed.), 1928; P. Abercrombie, *The Book of the Modern House,* 1929; A. R. Powys, *The English House,* 1929; N. Lloyd, *A History of the English House,* 1931; S. O. Addy, *The Evolution of the English House* (2nd ed.), 1933; S. R. Jones, *English Village Homes,* 1936; F. R. S. Yorke, *The Modern House in England,* 1937, and, with F. Gibberd, *The Modern Flat,* 1937; H. Braun, *The Story of the English House,* 1940; R. McGrath, *Twentieth Century Houses,* 1940; Ministry of Health, *Design of Dwellings,* 1944; R. Dutton, *The English Interior,* 1949.

Hunt, Richard Morris (*b.* Brattleboro, Vermont, 31 Oct. 1827; *d.* Newport, Rhode Island, 31 July 1895), American architect, was one of the founders of the American Institute of Architects in 1857, and became its (third) President in 1883. He was awarded the Royal Gold Medal of the R.I.B.A. in 1893. Going to Geneva with his mother in 1843, he was articled to the architect Darier there, then worked for seven years under Hector Lefuel at the École des Beaux Arts in Paris, and in 1854 was appointed inspector of works on the new building connecting the Louvre and the Tuileries in Paris. He returned to New York in 1855, and was at first employed on the extension of the Capitol at Washington. The chief buildings subsequently designed by him were the Lenox Library (since demolished) and the Tribune Building, both in New York City; the Theological Library and Marquand Chapel at Princeton University; the Divinity College and the Scroll and Key Building at Yale University; the Vanderbilt Museum on Staten Island; the monument at Yorktown; the administration building at the Chicago Exhibition of 1893; mansions for W. K. Vanderbilt and H. G. Marquand in New York City; a country mansion for G. W. Vanderbilt at Biltmore; and several large 'cottages' on Long Island. He was a leader of the 'Beaux Arts' (q.v.) tradition of design in America, e.g. at the Lenox Library; but was equally successful in other types of design.

See memoir by B. Ferree, 1895.

Hypaethral (Gk *hupaithros*, 'open to the sky'), in Greek architecture, a building or portion of a building without a roof.

Hypocaust (Gk *hupokauston*, a place heated from below), in Roman buildings, a system of hot-air heating from a furnace below ground level.   There are examples at Verulamium and other Roman cities in Britain.

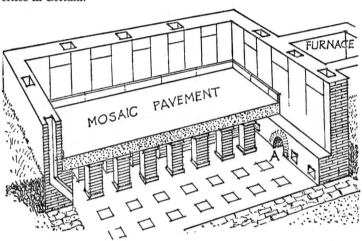

HYPOCAUST: from Silchester (2nd century A.D.).   A=inlet from furnace

Hypogeum (Lat., from Gk *hupogeion*), an underground chamber or vault.

Hypostyle Hall (Gk *hupo*, under; *stulos*, a column), in ancient temples, a large hall with its roof resting on columns, e.g. the Temple of Ammon at Karnak in Egypt.

Hypotrachelion (Gk, under the neck), a groove beneath the *trachelion* (neck) of a Greek Doric column.   (*Illustrated* ENTABLATURE.)

I

Iconoclast (Gk *eikōn*, image; *klastēs*, a breaker), applied originally to leaders of a movement in Byzantine churches in the eighth and ninth centuries, and in modern times to any person who destroys sacred images or religious objects.

Iconostasis (Gk *eikon*, image; *stasis*, a station), in Byzantine churches, a screen separating nave from chancel; statues were often placed upon it.

Ictinus (fifth century B.C.), Greek architect. He designed the Hall of the Mysteries at Eleusis; the Temple of Apollo at Bassae; and (jointly with Callicrates, q.v.), the Parthenon at Athens.

Imbrex (Lat. *imber*, a shower of rain), in Greek and Roman buildings, a convex roofing tile, covering a joint between flat or concave tiles.

Impluvium (Lat.), in Greek and Roman houses, a shallow tank for rain-water; usually placed in a courtyard, but occasionally under the floor of a room.

Impost, the upper course of masonry or brickwork upon which an arch rests.

Indian Architecture has a most complicated history. There are very ancient ruins at Harappa and Mohenjo-daro, *c.* 3500–2700 B.C.; also Buddhist shrines of the third century B.C. at Sanchi, but the chief surviving buildings elsewhere date from the third century B.C. onwards. Up to the time (*c.* A.D. 1775) when the British occupation became effective, they chiefly comprised (i) Buddhist temples; (ii) Hindu and Jain temples and palaces; (iii) Muslim mosques and palaces. The earliest Buddhist temples, e.g. at Karli and Nasik, were hewn out of the solid rock, with rows of massive stone pillars leading up to an apse containing the *chaitya* (shrine). There were also numerous Buddhist *viharas* (monasteries). Hindu temples usually contain a cell for the shrine, crowned by a curvilinear or pyramidal tower (*sikhara* or *vimana*), an entrance porch, a pillared hall (*mandapam*), and a lofty gateway (*gopuram*). After their conquest of India in 1193 the Muslims began to erect their characteristic mosques (*see* MOSQUE and MUSLIM ARCHITECTURE), more or less in the style that they had adopted in Persia; but fusion with the Hindu tradition resulted in a hybrid style, due partly to the employment of skilled Hindu craftsmen, and eventually produced the famous Mogul or Mughal style of the sixteenth to seventeenth centuries, at Delhi and elsewhere. The chief Muslim buildings in India (which contrast sharply with the shapeless and over-decorated Hindu temples, but are nevertheless often richly ornamented) are the Great Mosques at Delhi (1198), Ajmir (*c.* 1200), and Cambay; the

172

Atala Masjid at Jaunpur (1408); the
Moti Masjid at Delhi; the Great
Mosques at Jaunpur (1438), and at
Mandu (1454); and several mosques
at Ahmadabad (fifteenth century).
Among the principal Mughal examples are famous mosques, tombs,
and palaces at Agra, Delhi, Lahore,
Fatehpur-Sikri, Udaipur, and Bija-
pur. Most important among them
are the tomb of Humayum at Delhi
(1565–9); the fort at Agra (1566); the
palace and the Great Mosque at
Fatehpur-Sikri; and the Taj Mahal
at Agra (1631–53). From the middle
of the seventeenth century Mughal
architecture declined, India being
disturbed by wars. After the British
occupation (c. 1775), western styles
of architecture were introduced—
first as the 'Greek Revival' (q.v.),
then the 'Gothic Revival' favoured
by Sir George Gilbert Scott (q.v.),
then some praiseworthy attempts
to revive the Mughal tradition (see

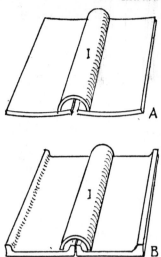

IMBREX. (A) Greek (Sicilian)
type; (B) Roman type. (Imbrex
marked I)

LANCHESTER, H. V.), then the building of the new Delhi (see BAKER,
SIR H. and LUTYENS, SIR E.), and finally the planning of a new
capital of the Punjab (see FRY, E. M. and 'LE CORBUSIER').

> See J. Fergusson, *History of Indian Architecture* (rev. ed.), 1910;
> E. B. Havell, *Indian Architecture* (2nd ed.), 1927; B. Rowland,
> *The Art and Architecture of India: Hindu, Buddhist, Jain*, 1953.

Ingeniator (Lat.), literally 'engineer,' but often used in medieval
records to denote any person in charge of building operations: hence
sometimes the 'architect' (q.v.).

Ingle-nook, *see* CHIMNEY-CORNER.

Inlay(-ing), the decoration of surfaces with thin sheets of wood or
metal let into shallow sinkings. (Cf. INTARSIA and MARQUETRY.)

Intarsia, inlay (q.v.) of a pictorial character.

Intercolumniation, in classical architecture, the spacing apart of
columns according to accepted rules. (Cf. EUSTYLE.)

Intrados, the inner curve or underside or soffit of an arch. (*Illustrated* ARCH, PARTS OF AN.)

Inverted Arch, a segmental arch (*illustrated* ARCH) reversed, and
built of brick between the foundations of brick piers, in order to
distribute the vertical downward pressure evenly over the foundations. Seldom used in modern building.

Inwood, Henry William (*b.* 22 May 1794; *d.* at sea, 20 Mar. 1843),
architect, was the eldest son of William Inwood, a London architect,

in whose office he was trained. After prolonged travel in Greece from 1819 onwards, he entered the Royal Academy Schools in 1822. The influence of his travels is to be seen at St Pancras Church, London, with its caryatid porch—one of the chief works of the English Greek Revival—where he assisted his father. Together they designed other churches. Two of his brothers also became architects. He published in 1827 a book on the Erechtheum at Athens.

Ionic Order, *see* ORDERS OF ARCHITECTURE, *illustrated.*

Irish Architecture, prior to the Anglo-Norman conquest of the country in 1169, comprised sundry small chapels or oratories erected after St Patrick's landing in A.D. 432, and numerous round towers, built as refuges or watch-towers after the Danish and Norse invasions in the eighth century, e.g. at Clonmacnoise, Glendalough, Ardmore, Cashel, Kilkenny, Kildare, Kells, and Donaghmore. Carrickfergus Castle, near Belfast, was erected soon after the conquest, and there was naturally much activity in building churches in the Romanesque style; but earlier Romanesque buildings include Cormac's Chapel at Cashel (1134); the Nun's Chapel at Clonmacnoise (c. 1168); the doorway of Clonfert Cathedral (c. 1166), and the chancel of St Saviour at Glendalough. After 1169 the building of the two cathedrals at Dublin began, Christ Church in 1172 and St Patrick's in 1190, but style did not differ substantially from contemporary work in England. The other chief Gothic churches in Ireland are Kilkenny Cathedral (mid thirteenth century) and the abbeys of Muckross, Quin, and Holycross. In 1592 Queen Elizabeth I founded Trinity College, Dublin, but building in general languished throughout the disturbed sixteenth and seventeenth centuries. Kilmainham Hospital, Dublin (1680), is a rare exception. During the eighteenth century, however, the brilliant Georgian period beautified Dublin with many notable buildings, including the Custom House, the Four Courts, Trinity College with its fine library, the House of Lords, the Bank of Ireland (formerly the Parliament House), the City Hall (formerly the Royal Exchange), and the Casino at Marino. Rich noblemen adorned the city with handsome town houses, and built splendid country mansions elsewhere, e.g. Powerscourt. Important buildings of the past hundred years include the Anglican cathedral (1863–70) and the remarkable Church of Christ the King (1928–30), both at Cork; the National Library of Ireland (1890) and the church of St Thomas (1930), both in Dublin; the Belfast City Hall (1896–1902) and the Parliament Buildings of Northern Ireland at Stormont, near Belfast (1928–32).
See BURGES, CASSELS, CHAMBERS, COOLEY, DEANE (2), DREW, GANDON, IVORY, JOHNSTON, LANYON, PEARCE, ROBINSON, THOMAS, A. B., THORNELY.

Islamic Architecture, *see* MUSLIM ARCHITECTURE.

Isodorus of Miletus (sixth century A.D.) was the architect, jointly with Anthemius of Tralles (q.v.), of the church of S. Sophia at Constantinople (A.D. 532–7.)

Isometric Projection, a method of pictorial projection of solids, so called because the three planes have their angles of inclination to the plane of projection 'of equal measure' (Gk *isos*, equal; *metros*, measure). For other methods of projection *see* AXONOMETRIC, OBLIQUE, ORTHOGRAPHIC, PERSPECTIVE. (*Illustrated* DRAWING, ARCHITECTURAL.)

Italian Architecture was the most important in Europe, and indeed in the world, during the first three centuries of the Christian era, and again during the Renaissance, from *c*. 1450 to *c*. 1650. It was also notable in some stages of the Romanesque period, but Italian Gothic architecture is inferior in quality and quantity to that of France or England.

1. Although Rome may have been founded in 753 B.C., the earliest surviving buildings of any size are of the first century B.C., and anything older is now generally described as 'Etruscan' (*see* ARCHITECTURE, PERIODS OF, 3). During those centuries, however, a great deal of building was done in the various Greek colonies (collectively known as 'Magna Graecia') around the coasts of Sicily and southern Italy, where one can still see the ruins of many Greek Doric temples (*see* ARCHITECTURE, PERIODS OF, 2), erected *c*. 575 B.C.–*c*. 430 B.C, In Sicily these include three temples at Syracuse, six at Selinus. and four at Agrigentum; on the mainland there are three at Paestum, and one each at Metapontum, Locri, and Pompeii. This last example was erected *c*. 550 B.C., but most of the other public buildings of Pompeii—including the large theatre, the basilica, the Stabian baths, and the temples of Apollo and Isis—are of the second century B.C., though the small theatre and the amphitheatre are of the following century. By that time classical Greek or 'Hellenic' architecture had given place to 'Hellenistic' or 'Graeco-Roman' architecture, i.e. Greek architecture as modified and practised after 323 B.C. In A.D. 79 Pompeii was engulfed by volcanic lava, and simultaneously the neighbouring town of Herculaneum suffered the same fate; but excavation of both sites during modern times has revealed the high standard of domestic life in these Graeco-Roman towns, and the delicacy of their decorations. The nature of Roman architecture is described under ARCHITECTURE, PERIODS OF, 3), its principal examples are noted in articles on the architecture of individual countries, so here it will suffice to mention only the principal Roman buildings surviving in Italy. Excluding Rome and its neighbourhood, they are the theatre at Aosta (*c*. 40 B.C.); the Arch of Augustus at Rimini (27 B.C.); the triumphal arches at Ancona (A.D. 115), and at Beneventum (A.D. 114–17); the amphitheatres at Verona (1st cent. A.D.), Capua, and Pozzuoli, as well as that at Pompeii already mentioned.

2. This is a very short list, and one finds a similar concentration of surviving examples when one reaches the next period (*see* ARCHITECTURE, PERIODS OF, 4), for most of the early basilican churches were in Rome. They included the basilicas of St Peter (A.D. 330, completely rebuilt in the sixteenth century), St John Lateran (330, altered out of all recognition), St Agnes-without-the-Walls (324, but rebuilt 625–38), St Paul-without-the-Walls (380, destroyed by fire 1823,

then rebuilt precisely as before); St Lorenzo-without-the-Walls (a double church—one part built 432, the other rebuilt 578); the lower church of S. Clemente (4th century); S. Sabina (425). Most of these were originally founded soon after the Emperor Constantine's recognition of Christianity in 313, and all were of basilican type, consisting of an oblong aisled nave, usually with an east apse and a west narthex or vestibule. Besides this essentially Roman 'basilican, type, there were a few circular churches, including S. Stefano Rotondo (470), the Baptistery of Constantine (430–40), S. Costanza (330), all in Rome, as well as the Baptistery at Nocera (350). This latter type of plan, with a central dome, came to be typical of Byzantine architecture. There are other examples at Ravenna, viz. the tomb of Theodoric (530—not strictly a dome) and the remarkable church of S. Vitale (526–47) with its fine mosaics. At Ravenna, however, there are also two basilican churches: S. Apollinare Nuovo (493–525) and S. Apollinare in Classe (534–9). From 404 to 476 Ravenna, not Rome, was the capital of the (western) Empire. After a period of rule by Theodoric the Goth, it became the capital again.

3. Then came the Lombard kingdom, during which 'Early Romanesque' or 'Lombard' architecture made its appearance. Originating in northern Italy, especially in Milan and Lombardy, it soon spread into Germany, Scandinavia, and elsewhere. Lombard churches are basilican in plan, usually with a crypt. They have round arches, a good deal of arcading used as external ornament, rather flat sloping roofs, picturesque *campanili* (q.v.), and often stone barrel vaulting over the aisles. Following are the principal Lombard and Romanesque churches in Italy, up to the advent of the Gothic style, *c.* 1240: S. Pietro, Toscanella (739); S. Maria in Cosmedin, Rome (772–95); S. Ambrogio, Milan (789–824, but much altered since); S. Giorgio in Velabro, Rome (827–49); Torcello Cathedral (864); St Mark's, Venice (begun 976—*see also* CAMPANILE); Pisa Cathedral (1006–1118); S. Miniato, Florence (1013); Modena Cathedral (1099–1184); SS. Giovanni e Paolo, Rome (twelfth century); S. Zeno, Verona (1138); the Baptistery, Pisa (begun 1153); the Campanile, Pisa (begun 1173); the beautiful cloisters of St Paul-without-the-Walls and of St John Lateran, both in Rome and both late twelfth century; the west front of Lucca Cathedral (1204). In southern Italy and Sicily: the abbey of S. Nicola, Bari (1087–1197); the collegiate church at Barletta; the cathedrals of Bari, Bitonto, Cefalu, Giovinazzo, Messina (destroyed by earthquake, 1908), Molfetta, Palermo, and especially Monreale in Sicily, built by the Normans (1174–82).

4. In Italy, the home of the Roman tradition, Gothic architecture never reached the standard of grace or grandeur that it attained in France and England, especially as regards boldness and logicality in buttressing and vaulting; but it was certainly picturesque in its way, as Ruskin convinced his Victorian disciples. Some of its cathedrals (e.g. Siena, Orvieto) have zebra stripes of black or red and white marble, a fashion derived from farther east; other features are of 'Saracenic' origin.

Following are the principal Italian examples. In Venice: the churches of SS. Giovanni e Paolo (1234 onwards) and of the Frari (1250–80); the Doge's Palace (1309–1424), and the Ca d'Oro, Foscari, and Pisani palaces on the Grand Canal. In Florence (*see* ARNOLFO): the cathedral (1296 onwards); the Campanile (1334–87) by Giotto; S. Maria Novella (1278–1350); S. Croce (1294–1442); Or S. Michele (1356–1404); the Bigallo loggia (1352–8); the Loggia dei Lanzi (1376); the Palazzo Vecchio (1298); the Palazzo del Podesta (1255). In Assisi: S. Francesco (1228–53). In Milan: the cathedral (1385–1435). In Orvieto: the cathedral (1280–1310). In Siena: the cathedral (1245–1380). In Pisa: the Campo Santo (1278–83), and the beautiful S. Maria della Spina (1323). In Bologna: S. Petronio (1390–1437). In Padua: S. Antonio (1237–1307). In Pavia: the Certosa (1396–1481). The town halls of Siena (1289) and Perugia (1281). In Verona: S. Anastasia (1261). The only old Gothic church in Rome is S. Maria sopra Minerva (1280).

5. As explained elsewhere (*see* ARCHITECTURE, PERIODS OF, 7) Renaissance architecture was born in Italy early in the fifteenth century, and spread thence into other countries of Europe. Its two chief centres of origin were Florence, at that time the most enlightened culturally of Italian cities, and Rome, where most of the principal monuments of antiquity were to be found. The leaders of the new movement in Italy are dealt with in separate articles, in which their various buildings are mentioned. For the fifteenth century *see* ALBERTI, BRUNELLESCHI, MAJANO, MICHELOZZO, A. DA SANGALLO, senior and A. SANSOVINO (Florence); BRAMANTE (Rome and Lombardy); GIOCONDO (Verona); PONTELLI (Rome). For the sixteenth century, besides some of those mentioned above, *see* AGNOLO, MICHELANGELO, A. DA SANGALLO, junior (Florence and Rome); PERUZZI (Rome, Bologna, Siena); FONTANA, VIGNOLA (Rome); SANMICHELE, SANSOVINO (Venice); PALLADIO (Vicenza, Venice). *See also* ALESSI, AMMANATI, BUONTALENTI, CRONACA, LEONARDO, LIGORIO, LOMBARDO, LUNGHI, LURAGO, PORTA, RAPHAEL, ROMANO, SCAMOZZI, TIBALDI.

Towards the middle of the sixteenth century books on architecture began to appear, compiled by Vignola, Palladio, and Serlio (q.v.), in which rules of design according to the ancient Roman Orders (*see* ORDERS OF ARCHITECTURE) were formulated. Concurrently with this trend towards regulated design, a more picturesque form of architecture was being evolved by Michelangelo, which resulted in the Baroque style (q.v.). For the chief Baroque buildings of Rome *see* BERNINI and BORROMINI. In Venice the finest Baroque building is the church of S. Maria della Salute (1631) by Longhena. There are other examples in Milan, and many in Turin (mainly by Guarini and Juvara). Several other buildings in Rome, including the Fountain of Trevi, the façade of S. Croce, and the 'Spanish Steps'—all of the eighteenth century—are on the border-line between Baroque and Rococo (q.v.). *See also* ALFIERI, ALGARDI, BERETTINI, BIANCO, BIBIENA, GALILEI, MADERNO, PONZIO, POZZO, RAINALDI, RICCHINI, ROSSI (G. A)., SALVI, VANVITELLI.

After *c.* 1780 a marked decline ensued in the quality as well as the quantity of Italian architecture. Neither the Greek nor the Gothic

Revival had much effect in Italy. Among many ornate buildings erected during the latter part of the nineteenth century, the most bombastic was the overpowering marble monument to King Vittorio Emanuele II in Rome (1885–1911) by G. Sacconi (q.v.). Under Mussolini's brief rule between the two world wars, although many excellent new towns were laid out in the Campagna, and although the historical monuments of Rome were judiciously restored and isolated from the mean shacks which had grown over them like a fungus, some grandiose schemes in the city, such as the Foro Mussolini and the exhibition south of Rome, were vulgar as well as gigantic. In recent years the most important buildings have been the new Central Railway Station (1948) and the university (1930), both in Rome; also the numerous fine blocks of flats in Rome and Milan, a branch of architecture in which Italy stands high among the European nations. *See* BELGIOJOSO, NERVI, ROGERS, ZEVI.

> *See* C. Ricci, *Baroque Architecture in Italy*, 1912, and *Romanesque Architecture in Italy*, 1925; T. G. Jackson, *Gothic Architecture*, vol. ii, Italy, etc., 1921; W. J. Anderson and A. Stratton, *Architecture of the Renaissance in Italy* (5th ed.), 1927; G. T. Rivoira, *Lombardic Architecture*, 1933; A. Pica, *Nuova Architettura Italiana*, 1936; C. Pagani, *Architettura Italiana Oggi*, 1955; R. Wittkower, *Art and Architecture in Italy (1600–1750)*, 1958; M. S. Briggs, *Architecture in Italy*, 1961.

Ivory, Thomas (*b.* 1709; *d.* Norwich, 28 Aug. 1779), English architect, like his Irish namesake (q.v.), started life as a carpenter, and after turning to architecture in middle age combined the practice of that profession with speculative building and the trade of a timber merchant. Buildings designed by him in Norwich included the Methodist Meeting-house, Bishopsgate (1751–3); the Octagon Chapel, Colegate Street (1754–6); the Assembly Rooms (1754); the theatre (1757), afterwards altered; the Artillery Barracks (1771–2); and several houses. He also designed the theatre at Colchester (1764).

> *See* S. J. Wearing, *Georgian Norwich and its Builders*, 1926.

Ivory, Thomas (*b.* Cork, 1732; *d.* Dublin, 1786), Irish architect, began his career as a carpenter, but turned to architecture, and for twenty-seven years was 'master of architectural drawing' to the Royal Dublin Society. His buildings included the Blue-Coat School, Blackhall Place (1773); the Marine School, Rogerson's Quay (1775); the Office of Arms, now the Genealogical Office (1756–61); and Newcomen's Bank (1781)—all in Dublin.

J

Jackson, Sir Thomas Graham, Bart., R.A. (*b.* London, 21 Dec. 1835; *d.* there, 7 Nov. 1924), architect and writer on architecture; R.I.B.A. Royal Gold Medallist, 1910. After a brilliant career at Oxford he entered the office of Sir George Gilbert Scott (q.v.) in 1858, and began practice in London in 1862. His work consisted largely of scholastic and ecclesiastical buildings. For the former he favoured the Jacobean style. His principal buildings were, in Oxford: the Examination Schools, the High School for Girls, restoration of St Mary's Church, extensions to Balliol, Brasenose, Corpus Christi, and Lincoln colleges; in Cambridge: the Sedgwick Museum, Law Library, Archaeological Museum, Physiological Laboratories; in London: alterations at Drapers' Hall and at the Inner Temple; elsewhere: Giggleswick School Chapel; sundry school buildings at Eton, Harrow, Rugby, and Winchester; important restorations at Winchester Cathedral, Bath Abbey, Great Malvern Priory Church, Christchurch Priory, Hospital of St Cross, Longleat, etc. Among his many published books was a remarkable series compiled in his old age: *Byzantine and Romanesque Architecture* (2 vols.), 1913; *Gothic Architecture* (2 vols.), 1915; and *The Renaissance of Roman Architecture* (3 vols.), 1921–3.

Jacobean Architecture (from Lat. *Jacobus*, James), English architecture of the reign of King James I (1603–25). *See* ENGLISH ARCHITECTURE, 5.

Jacobsen, Arne (*b.* Copenhagen, 11 Feb. 1902), Danish architect, was trained at the Academy of Arts in Copenhagen, graduated in 1927, and started practice in Copenhagen in 1928. With F. Lassen he won a competition for 'The House of the Future' in 1929. Other successes in competitions were for the Bellevue seaside resort near Copenhagen, including a bathing establishment, riding-school, theatre, restaurant, and houses (1930–5); stadium at Gentofte (1936); Aarhus Town Hall (with E. Møller, 1937); and Søllerød Town Hall (with F. Lassen, 1939). He escaped to Sweden in 1943 from the Nazi occupation, returning to practise in Copenhagen after the war. His later work included estates at Gentofte and Klampenborg; a factory at Aalborg (1956); town hall at Glostrup (competition, 1953); municipal offices at Rødovre (1955); sports centre at Landskrona, Sweden (competition, 1956); factory at Gladsaxe (1958); schools at Gentofte (1952) and Hårby (1951); and the great air terminal for S.A.S. with a 22-storey hotel (competition, 1957). He also designed wall-papers, fabrics, furniture, etc. In 1956 he was appointed Professor of Architecture at the Royal Danish Academy, and in 1959 was invited to advise upon the new St Catherine's College at Oxford.

See monograph by J. Pedersen, 1957.

Jalousie (Fr.), a Venetian blind (q.v.).

James, John (*b. c.* 1672; *d.* Greenwich, 15 May 1746), architect, was a carpenter in the early part of his career. In that capacity he worked at Greenwich Hospital, and in 1705 followed Hawksmoor (q.v.) as clerk of the works there under Wren (q.v.). In 1716 he became assistant surveyor of St Paul's Cathedral, and also (with Hawksmoor) surveyor of the 'Fifty New Churches' from 1715 onwards. In 1725 he was elected Master of the Carpenters' Company, and about 1736 was appointed principal surveyor of H.M. Works and also of Westminster Abbey, where he built the south-west tower. His other work included Orleans House, Twickenham (1710); St George's Church, Hanover Square, London (1710); St Mary's Church, Twickenham, except the tower (1713–15); St Lawrence's Church, Edgware (1714–16); Canons, Middlesex, in part (1714–15); possibly St Luke's Church, Old Street, London (1727–33); and several other buildings since demolished.

Jami (Arabic), a large mosque used for public or congregational worship, with a central courtyard surrounded by colonnades or arches. *See* MUSLIM ARCHITECTURE.

Japanese Architecture was based primarily upon older Chinese architecture, but developed distinctive characteristics of its own. Up to quite recent times most Japanese buildings were constructed entirely of timber, and some of them erected more than 1,200 years ago still survive. The reason for adopting timber construction is partly that it resists earthquakes more effectively than brick or stone do. Roofs were steep, with immense projecting eaves carried on carved brackets, and were either hipped or gabled. They were generally covered with tiles. Curving lines predominated throughout. The chief surviving historical examples are Buddhist temples, viz. the group in the ancient capital city of Heijo, near Nara, with a pagoda (eighth century A.D.); temples of the Heian period (784–1185) on Mount Koya and Mount Hiyei; temples of the Kamakura period (1186–1392) at Kamakura, showing Chinese influence; the temple gateway of the Muromachi period (1393–1572) at Kyoto; and the temple of the Momoyama period (1573–1614), near Sendai. In modern times reinforced concrete has largely replaced timber construction for all buildings except dwelling-houses, and western fashions of design have mainly superseded native tradition. The Imperial Hotel at Tokyo (1916), by the American architect F. L. Wright (q.v.), is a typical example. Many or most Japanese houses, however, continue to follow the native tradition in their very light construction, and have notably stark interiors free from furniture.

    See H. Kishida, *Japanese Architecture*, 1935; A. L. Sadler, *A Short History of Japanese Architecture*, 1941; A. Drexler, *The Architecture of Japan*, 1955; R. A. Paine and A. Soper, *The Art and Architecture of Japan*, 1955; M. Inoue, *Castles of Japan*.

Jeanneret, Charles Édouard, *see* 'LE CORBUSIER.'

Jefferson, Thomas (*b.* Shadwell, Virginia, 13 April 1743; *d.* Monticello, Virginia, 4 July 1826), American lawyer, diplomat, statesman, and amateur architect, best known as the author of the Declaration of Independence, 1776, and as President of the U.S.A., 1801–9. After a brilliant career at William and Mary College in Virginia, he read for the Bar, and was admitted in 1767. From 1784 to 1789 he was at Versailles as American minister to France, and made a study of French architecture. On his return to his large Virginian estates, he built for himself in 1796–1809 a charming house, 'Monticello,' which he had actually designed long before in 1779. He also made designs for remodelling the Governor's House at Williamsburg (1779); for the Capitol at Richmond, Virginia (1785–9); and for the new university of Virginia at Charlottesville, which as governor of the state he founded himself.

See monograph by F. W. Hirst, 1926.

Jenney, William Le Baron (*b.* Fairhaven, Massachusetts, 25 Sept. 1832; *d.* Los Angeles, 15 June 1907), American architect. He studied in Paris, and soon after graduating there, returned to the United States and enlisted as an engineer in the civil war, retiring in 1866 with the rank of major. He started independent practice as an architect and engineer in Chicago in 1868, and designed many blocks of office buildings in that city. Among them was the first 'framed building' or 'skyscraper' (qq.v.), viz. the Chicago premises of the Home Insurance Co. of New York, erected 1884 and entirely carried on cast-iron columns and girders of Bessemer steel.

His other buildings in Chicago included the Siegel Cooper Company's department store; the Y.M.C.A. premises; the Chicago National Bank; the New York Life Building; and the Horticultural Building at the World's Fair (1892); also the Illinois Memorial at Vicksburg.

He retired in 1905. He published *Principles and Practice of Architecture* in 1869.

Jerman, or **Jarman, Edward** (*d.* 1668), was formerly a carpenter. He resigned his office as city carpenter in 1657 and next appears as one of the three surveyors appointed by the corporation, after the Great Fire of 1666, to supervise the rebuilding of the City. He then designed the new Royal Exchange, the Fishmongers' Hall (both since rebuilt), and possibly some other city companies' halls, but most of these have since been rebuilt or destroyed, and very little of his work remains.

Jesse Window, a window depicting in stained glass the genealogical 'tree'

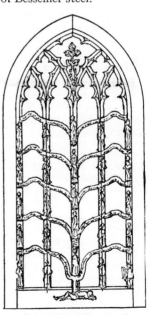

JESSE   WINDOW,   Dorchester Abbey, Oxon.

G

or 'stem' of Jesse, i.e. the descent of our Lord from the royal house of David.   There are English examples in Dorchester church, Oxfordshire (where the stone tracery forms the branches of the 'tree'); in Wells Cathedral; and at St George's, Hanover Square, London (brought from Malines in Belgium).

Jewish Architecture, *see* SYNAGOGUE.

Jib Door, an internal door, flush with the wall face, and often papered over to make it almost invisible.

Johnston, Francis (*b.* 1761; *d.* Dublin, 14 Mar. 1829),   Irish architect.   From 1786 to 1793 he lived in Armagh, where he is said to have reconstructed the cathedral, and to have designed the library, the chapel of the Archbishop's Palace, and the courthouse.   He then moved to Dublin, having been appointed 'Architect and Inspector of Civil Buildings in the Office of Public Works.'   His buildings there included St George's Church (1794–1802); the cash office of the Bank of Ireland (1804); the chapel royal in Dublin Castle (1807–16); and the General Post Office (1815–17).   He was a founder member of the Royal Hibernian Academy.

Joinery, the lighter woodwork of a building, as distinguished from carpentry (q.v.), which comprises the heavier structural woodwork. Joinery includes windows, doors, staircases, skirtings, panelling, cupboards, etc.   Most of it has always been made in a workshop, but to-day much of it is prefabricated by machinery, and often imported from abroad.

Joist, one of the timber, steel, or reinforced concrete members of a floor, upon which the actual flooring rests.   Joists may run from wall to wall, or from girder to girder in the case of large framed floors. Timber ceiling joists carry the laths and plaster of a ceiling over a room.

Jones, Sir Horace (*b.* London, 20 May 1819; *d.* there, 21 May 1887), architect; President R.I.B.A., 1882–3.   After serving his articles and travelling in Greece and Italy, he started practice in 1843.   He was appointed architect and surveyor to the City of London in 1864.   His work in that capacity included Smithfield Markets (1868–83); the Guildhall Library and Museum (1872), and new Council Chamber (1884); the Guildhall School of Music; the Griffin at Temple Bar; and (in collaboration with Sir J. Wolfe-Barry) the Tower Bridge (1882–3).

Jones, Inigo (*b.* London, 15 July 1573; *d.* there, 21 June 1652), architect, theatrical designer, and architectural draughtsman, is notable as the man who introduced mature Italian Renaissance ('Palladian') architecture into England.   Born in Smithfield of humble parents, he managed somehow to journey to Italy and to study there.   In about 1604 he entered the service of King Christian IV of Denmark, but though certain Danish buildings have been attributed to him, their authorship is quite uncertain.   On his return to England in about 1605, he started designing scenery for a series of court masques, then set off again for Italy.   His contacts with noblemen in Italy and in court circles at home led to his appointment in March 1616 as Surveyor of the Royal Works. He started building the Queen's House at Greenwich Palace in the following year, finishing it in 1635, and built the new Banqueting Hall (now the United Services Museum) in Whitehall, as part of the rambling Tudor palace, in 1619–22. His other buildings included the Chapel Royal, St James's Palace (1623–7); St Paul's, Covent Garden (since rebuilt) with the adjoining piazza (1631); the west portico of (Old) St Paul's Cathedral (c. 1633–43)—all these in London; and additions to Wilton House, Wiltshire (1649). He was imprisoned in Basing House (1643–5), and his royalist connections made him unpopular during the Commonwealth. *See also* WEBB, J.

See monographs by S. C. Ramsey, 1924; J. A. Gotch, 1928; and M. D. Whinney (*Walpole Society*, vol. xxxi, 1942–3).

Jones, Owen (*b*. London, 1809; *d*. there, 19 April 1874), architect and writer on architecture, was articled to Vulliamy (q.v.), and then spent four years of travel and study in continental Europe and the Near East. He made interior decoration his speciality after returning home in 1836, with the result that he was invited to take a leading part in the 1851 Exhibition, and subsequently in the decoration of the Crystal Palace. His published books were concerned almost exclusively with colour and decoration, and included his splendid *Grammar of Ornament* (1856). His name is perpetuated in the 'Owen Jones Studentship' of the R.I.B.A., first awarded in 1887.

Jubé (Fr.), the screen between nave and chancel in a church, known in English as the 'rood-screen' (q.v.).

Juvara, or **Juvarra, Filippo** (*b*. Messina, 16 June 1676; *d*. Madrid, 31 Jan. 1736), Italian Baroque architect. After starting on a clerical career, became a pupil of Carlo Fontana (q.v.) in Rome. He was working in Messina on the modernizing of the royal palace there when he was invited by the King of Savoy to Turin (c. 1714), and subsequently designed a number of important buildings in that city and its neighbourhood. They included the magnificent church of La Superga (1717–31); the Madama Palace (1718) and some other palaces; the small church of S. Croce; the façade of S. Cristina; the Castello Reale (royal hunting-lodge) at Stupinigi (1729–33); and the Castello at Rivoli (1718). He also designed the domes of Como Cathedral and of S. Andrea at Mantua. Outside Italy he made designs for royal palaces at Madrid in Spain (carried out by his pupil Sacchetti in 1738–64), and at Lisbon and Mafra in Portugal; also for Lisbon Cathedral.

K

Kampen, or **Campen, Jacob van** (*b.* Haarlem, 2 Feb. 1595; *d.* near Amersfoort, 13 Sept. 1657), Dutch architect. He studied in Italy and in 1621 returned to Holland, where his principal buildings were the Coymans House, Amsterdam (1624–5); the Mauritshuis at The Hague (1633–44), and the Huis ten Bosch near The Hague (1664–6)— both these in collaboration with Pieter Post (q.v.); and the town hall now the Royal Palace, at Amsterdam (1648–55).

Kazakov, Matthew Fedorovich (*b.* 1733; *d.* Moscow, 1812). Russian architect. His work in its early stages followed the Baroque style then prevailing in Russia, but his later designs were more original in character. His principal buildings, all in Moscow, were the Senate (1776–89); the university (1786–93, partly rebuilt in 1816 after his death); and the Razumovski Palace (1790–3).

Keel Arch, an unusual term for an ogee arch (q.v.). (*Illustrated* ARCH, TYPES OF.)

Keep, in medieval architecture, the central or inner tower of a castle (q.v., *illustrated*).

Kent, William (*b.* Bridlington, ? 1685 ; *d.* London, 12 April 1748) architect, decorative designer, painter, and landscape gardener seems to have been apprenticed to a coach-painter in Hull; but in 1709 was sent to Italy to study painting at the expense of three aristocratic patrons, for whom he purchased pictures and 'antiques. He actually executed a fresco himself in a Roman church in 1717 While in Rome he met the influential Lord Burlington (q.v.), who brought him back to London in 1719 as his protégé, and lodged him in Burlington House, then in process of being remodelled and redecorated. From that date onwards Kent was continuously encouraged and employed by Burlington: firstly to complete the decorations of Burlington House and of Chiswick House, Middlesex then to edit the *Designs of Inigo Jones* (published in 1727); and, from 1730 onwards, as an architect, usually to complete or execute some of Burlington's amateur architectural ideas. Kent's principal buildings were Kew Palace; the Royal Mews, Charing Cross (1732); Devonshire House, Piccadilly (1734–5)—all these three since demolished; the central part of the treasury buildings, Whitehall (1734–6); Holkham Hall, Norfolk; 17 Arlington Street (1741–50); and the Horse Guards Whitehall (1750–8)—built after Kent's death. Kent designed a great variety of costumes, etc., and the famous royal barge (1732).

See monograph by M. Jourdain, 1948.

Key, Lieven de (*b.* Ghent, *c.* 1560; *d.* Haarlem, 17 July 1627) architect, lived in London from 1580 to 1591, then moved to Holland In Leyden he designed the façade of the town hall (1593–4); the Gemeenlandhuis (1596–7) and the Latin School, now the Gymnasium

(1599). His principal buildings in Haarlem were the Weigh House (1598); the Meat Market (1601–3); the Oudemannenhuis (1608); and the tower of the Nieuwe Kerk (1613).

Key Pattern, *see* FRET.

Keyser, or **Keyzer, Hendrik de** (*b.* Utrecht, 15 May 1565; *d.* Amsterdam, 15 May 1621), Dutch architect and sculptor. He was a pupil of Cornelis Bloemaart. Going to Amsterdam in 1591, he became city architect there three years later. His principal buildings were the Zuiderkerk (1603); the East India Company's House (1605–6); the Exchange (1608); the Haarlem Gate (1615–18); the Westerkerk and the Noorderkerk—all in Amsterdam; also the town hall at Delft (1618). He visited London in 1607 while collecting ideas for the new Exchange at Amsterdam, and there met young Nicholas Stone, whom he took back to Holland as a pupil and who married his daughter. Keyser founded a family of architects, for his three sons, Pieter, Thomas, and Willem, followed his profession.
See monograph by H. Neurdenburg, 1928.

Keystone, the wedge-shaped central voussoir (q.v.) of an arch. (*Illustrated* ARCH, PARTS OF AN.)

Khaznah (Arabic), in an Arab house, a recess for a bed.

Kibla (Arabic), *see* QIBLAH.

King-post Truss, a form of timber roof-truss having an upright 'king post' from the tie-beam to the ridge. (*Illustrated* ROOF-TRUSS.)

Kiosk (Fr. *kiosque*, from Turkish *kiushk*), an open summer-house or pavilion, usually having its roof supported by pillars.

Kitchen (Lat. *cucina*, a room for cooking in), *see* HOUSE.

Klenze, Leopold von (*b.* Bockenem, near Hildesheim, 29 Feb. 1784; *d.* Munich, 27 Jan. 1864), German architect, was the leader of the 'Greek Revival' (q.v.) in Munich. He travelled in Greece and Italy; worked as court architect at Cassel from 1808 to 1813, and as architect to the King of Bavaria from 1816 until his death. His principal buildings, all in Munich, were the Glyptothek (1816–34); the Alte Pinakothek (1826–36); the War Office (1824–30); the Odeon (1826); the post office (1836–8); the Propylaea (1854–62); the Ruhmeshalle (1853); the Walhalla (1830–43); and—all in the Royal Palace—the Festsaalbau (1832–42); the Königsbau (1826–33); the Court Chapel (1837); and the Court Theatre (1823).

Knott, Ralph (*b.* London, 3 May 1878; *d.* East Sheen, 25 Jan. 1929). After serving his articles with Messrs Woodd & Ainslie in London, he entered the office of Sir Aston Webb (q.v.), and was working as an assistant there when he won the great public competition for the London County Hall in 1908. He did not live to see the completion of the whole building, but the first portion was opened in 1922.

L

Label Moulding, *see* DRIPSTONE.

Lacunaria (Lat., from *lacuna*, a hole or gap), the sunk panels in a coffered ceiling. (*Illustrated* COFFERING.)

Lady Chapel, a chapel dedicated to Our Lady, the Virgin Mary. In large churches and cathedrals it is usually situated east of the chancel and high altar; in smaller churches it is often an eastward extension of an aisle, abreast of the chancel. In either case it is used for private prayer or for very small congregations. Notable modern examples are at the new Anglican cathedrals of Liverpool and Guildford.

Laing, David (*b.* London, 1774; *d.* there, 27 Mar. 1856), architect. He was articled to Sir John Soane (q.v.) in 1790, and about 1810 was appointed architect and surveyor to H.M. Customs. He designed the present Custom House in Lower Thames Street, London, erected in 1813–17, but trouble subsequently occurred with the foundations, much rebuilding was entailed, and Laing was dismissed from office. He also designed the church of St Dunstan-in-the-East (1817–21), in collaboration with William Tite (q.v.), who was one of his pupils. He compiled two books of designs for various types of building.

Lamb, Edward Buckton (*b.* 1806; *d.* London, 30 Aug. 1869), architect, was articled to L. N. Cottingham (q.v.). He built more than thirty churches—notably at Addiscombe, Aldwark, Egham, Healey, Gospel Oak, Kentish Town, Thirkleby, and West Hartlepool —and remodelled many country houses, including Great Brickhill Manor, Holt Hall, Hughenden Manor, Mapleton and Thornham Hall. He also contributed a number of illustrations to J. C. Loudon's *Encyclopaedia of Architecture*, 1832, and published some etchings of Gothic ornament, 1830.

Lancet, a tall narrow window with an acutely pointed head, as used in 'Early English' Gothic buildings of the thirteenth century: hence also 'Lancet Arch,' which has an acutely pointed head. (*Illustrated* ARCH, TYPES OF.)

Lanchester, Henry Vaughan (*b.* London, 9 Aug. 1863; *d.* Seaford, 16 Jan. 1953), architect and town-planner; R.I.B.A. Royal Gold Medallist, 1934; editor of *The Builder*, 1910–12; one of the most distinguished figures in English architecture of the first half of the twentieth century, and a tremendous worker almost up to his death. He was trained in the office of his father, H. J. Lanchester, then worked as assistant in several other offices, and began independent practice about 1887. He won the Owen Jones studentship of the R.I.B.A. in 1889. He had several successive partners: E. A. Rickards (q.v., *d.* 1920); James Stewart (*d.* 1904); Geoffrey Lucas (*d.* 1947); and T. A. Lodge, who continued the practice after Lanchester's death. The famous partnership of Lanchester, Stewart, and Rickards sprang into prominence as a result of a spectacular series of successes in competitions: the City Hall and Law Courts at Cardiff (1899); Deptford Town Hall and Hull Art School (1901); the Wesleyan Central Hall at Westminster (1905); the Third Church of Christ Scientist, Curzon Street, London (1910). Later came the new buildings of Leeds University (1926). Other important work by the firm included technical colleges at Birmingham, Bolton, Watford, and Reading; Birmingham Hospital Centre; extensions of St Bartholomew's Hospital, London; science buildings at Oxford, Cambridge, and Belfast; town halls at Beckenham and Hackney; the Bovril Factory, London; and the Esso Refinery, Fawley. Lanchester visited India frequently: first in 1912 to report on the site for New Delhi, then to prepare town plans for several cities, including Madras; and again to design a colossal palace at Jodhpur for the Maharajah. He was a pioneer of town-planning, and a founder of the Town-planning Institute. He carried his theories into practice in Burma and Zanzibar as well as in India and England. His book on *The Art of Town-planning*, 1925, is a masterly treatment of the subject.

Landscape Architects, Institute of (offices: 2 Guilford Place, London, W.C.1), founded 1929. 'The objects of the Institute are the advancement of the art of landscape architecture; the theory and practice of garden, landscape, and civic design; the promotion of research and education therein; and the creation and maintenance of a high standard of professional qualification.'

Langley, Batty (*b.* Twickenham, 1696; *d.* London, 3 Mar. 1741), is chiefly known for his numerous books on architecture and building. He was a gardener's son, and appears to have started as a landscape gardener; but about 1740 opened a school of architectural drawing. Simultaneously he advertised his willingness to design and erect buildings of most kinds, but especially 'Grottos, Cascades, Caves, Temples, Pavilions, and other Rural Buildings of Pleasure'; also to survey estates, arrange water-supply systems, and supply statues, busts, etc., in artificial stone of his own manufacture. To these varied accomplishments he added the authorship of a long series of books—in this respect resembling his contemporary, William Halfpenny (q.v.)—ranging from tiny manuals of architecture (i.e. 'The Orders') and building construction for artisans and amateurs to more ambitious volumes of which the following has the most unusual title: *Ancient Architecture Restored and Improved by a Great Variety of Grand and Useful Designs*, 1741–2. He made a rash attempt to formulate 'Orders' of Gothic architecture.

Lantern, a turret or other small erection of stone or timber, on the top of a tower, dome, or roof, having open or glazed sides through which light is admitted to the interior of the building, e.g. at St Paul's Cathedral and at Ely Cathedral. (*Illustrated* DOME.)

Lantern Light, a glazed structure of wood or steel on a flat roof, to give light to a room below; usually in the shape of a hipped roof, but with glazed vertical sides. *See also* SKYLIGHT.

Lanyon, Sir Charles, M.P. (*b*. Eastbourne, 6 Jan. 1813; *d*. White Abbey, Ireland, 31 May 1889), architect and civil engineer. He started his career as an engineer, having been articled in Dublin, and was county surveyor of Antrim from 1836 onwards. In that capacity he laid out the beautiful coast road from Larne to Portrush, as well as railways and bridges in the Belfast neighbourhood. His numerous buildings, all in Belfast, included the county jail (1843); Queen's College (1846–8); the court house (1840–50); the Presbyterian College (1852–3); the custom-house and Inland Revenue Office (1854–7); the Ulster Institution (1854); and various banks and churches. He became Mayor of Belfast in 1862, and sat in Parliament, 1866–8.

Larder, originally a place for the storage of bacon; in modern usage, for the storage of any kind of food.

Latin-American Architecture, *see* BRAZILIAN and MEXICAN ARCHITECTURE.
  See also P. Kelemen, *Baroque and Rococo in Latin America,* 1951, and H. R. Hitchcock, *Latin-American Architecture since 1945,* 1955.

Latrobe, Benjamin Henry (*b*. Fulneck, near Leeds, 1 May 1764; *d*. New Orleans, U.S.A., 3 Sept. 1820), architect. He was the son of the head of the Moravian settlement at Fulneck, and was educated in Germany. Returning to England in 1783, he entered the Stamp Office, but then decided to become an architect. He studied architecture under S. P. Cockerell, and civil engineering under Smeaton; then carried out some building in England on his own account; but emigrated to America in 1796. There he was almost immediately successful, building the penitentiary at Richmond, Virginia; two large banks at Philadelphia, both in 'Greek Revival' style (1797–1824); the Roman Catholic Cathedral (1805) and the Exchange—both at Baltimore; and St John's Church, Washington (1816); but his chief work was the building of the Capitol there, originally designed by Thornton (q.v.). He left Washington for Baltimore in 1817.
  See monograph by T. Hamlin, 1955.

Latten, *see* BRASSES, MEMORIAL.

Lattice Window (from 'lattice,' a framework of interlacing laths), a window divided into small panes by lead bars, usually arranged diagonally.

Lavatory (Lat. *lavatorium*, a place for washing in), originally applied to arrangements for ritual or other ablutions, e.g. in a medieval cloister as at Kirkstall Abbey; in Victorian times and since, a euphemism for a water-closet because the latter apparatus is often placed in a small room containing a wash-basin.

Lay Light, *see* CEILING LIGHT.

Lazaretto (It.), or **Lazar House,** a hospital, especially for lepers.

Leaded Lights, casements divided into panes, either rectangular or diamond shaped, by grooved lead bars known as 'cames' (q.v.).

Le Blond, Alexandre Jean-Baptiste (*b*. Paris, 1679; *d*. St Petersburg, 1719), Franco-Russian Baroque architect, was a pupil of Le Nôtre (q.v.) in Paris, where he himself began practice and built some town houses; but in 1716 he went to Russia at the head of a team of French sculptors, painters, and craftsmen, to become chief architect to Peter the Great, with whom he conversed for three days after his arrival. During the remaining three years before his death, he laid out the gardens of the Summer Palace at St Petersburg, and the parks of Peterhof and Strelna, made a town plan for the central area of St Petersburg, and designed the huge palace of Peterhof, with its pavilions (now all destroyed).

Le Breton, Gilles (*d*. 1522), French architect or master-mason, was trained by his father, who was clerk of the works at Chambord. In 1527 he took charge of the conversion of the royal hunting-box at Fontainebleau into a palace. His work there, during 1527–40, included the erection of new buildings around the *Cour du Cheval Blanc* and in the *Cour Ovale*.

Le Brun, Charles (*b*. Paris, 24 Feb. 1619; *d*. there, 12 Feb. 1690), painter, decorator, and architect, rose to be virtually dictator of the fine arts in France. After studying in Rome in 1645–6, he was appointed the first rector of the Academy of Painting and Sculpture in 1648. He designed, and actually executed himself, much of the decoration at Vaux-le-Vicomte and Versailles.

See monographs by H. Jouin, 1889, and P. Marcel, 1909.

'Le Corbusier,' pseudonym of **Charles-Édouard Jeanneret** (*b*. La Chaux-de-Fonds, Switzerland, 6 Oct. 1887; *d*. Cap Martin, France, 27 Aug. 1965), architect and writer on architecture and town-planning; R.I.B.A. Royal Gold Medallist, 1953. Trained Vienna, Paris, and Berlin under Behrens (q.v.). He began independent practice in Paris about 1922. His work consisted at first chiefly of small houses. Among his later buildings were the Swiss Hostel in the Cité Universitaire, Paris (1932); several exhibition pavilions; the enormous block of flats at Marseilles known as the Unité de l'Habitation, accommodating 1,600 persons (1945–50); blocks of flats at Nantes, Algiers, and Berlin; and public buildings at Tokio, Algiers, Ahmadabad, etc. He prepared town plans for Moscow, Buenos Aires, São Paolo, Montevideo, Antwerp, Stockholm, the University City at Rio, Bogotá, Algiers, Izmir (Turkey), Saint Dié, and Chandigarh (the new capital of the Punjab). He wrote several most important books on architecture and town-planning, especially *Vers une Architecture*, 1922, and *Urbanisme*, 1924. By these books, translated into several languages and read all over the world, as well as by his own designs, he influenced current architecture everywhere more substantially than any other modern architect or writer on architecture, ever since he propounded the doctrine that 'a house is a machine for living in.' Although some of his ideas are impracticable, even absurd, his importance remains unchallenged.

* G

He was the French member of the Advisory Committee for the U.N.O. Building at New York.

See his autobiography *My Work* (English translation by J. C. Palmes, 1960); and monographs by M. Gauthier, 1943; S. Papadaki, 1948; F. Choay, 1960.

Ledoux, Claude Nicolas (*b*. Dormans, 1736; *d*. Paris, 19 Nov. 1806), French architect. After beginning as an etcher, he was trained in architecture by J. F. Blondel (q.v.). His earliest known building was a country house at Eaubonne (1762). He was appointed *architecte du Roi* in 1773, and became a member of the academy. His principal buildings were the pavilion at Louveciennes for Mme du Barry; several town houses in Paris, including the Hôtel de Thélusson (1780); the various *barrières* at the entrances to Paris (1782); and theatres at Marseilles and Besançon. He published a volume of his designs.

Lemercier, Jacques (*b*. Pontoise, *c*. 1585; *d*. Paris, 4 June 1654), architect. He was the son of an architect, Nicolas Lemercier, and studied in Rome from 1607 to *c*. 1613. He built the Pavillon de l'Horloge at the Louvre, Paris (1624); then, for Cardinal Richelieu, the town and château of Richelieu in Poitou (1625–33); the Sorbonne, Paris, with its church (1629 onwards); the Palais-Cardinal, afterwards Palais-Royal, Paris (1629–36); and the château of Rueil (*c*. 1630). He also designed the church at Richelieu; the Oratoire and St Roch at Paris; and completed F. Mansart's church of Val-de-Grâce, Paris (1646 onwards).

Le Muet, Pierre (*b*. Dijon, 7 Oct. 1591; *d*. Paris, 28 Sept. 1669), architect. After studying abroad he was appointed *architecte du Roi*. His other work included the châteaux of Ponts and Chauvigny, remodelling of the château of Tanlay; the church of Notre Dame des Victoires in Paris (1656), completed after his death; and probably the Palais Mazarin, Paris (1623)—now incorporated in the Bibliothèque Nationale. He published a translation of Palladio's *Architecture*; also *Manière de bastir pour toutes sortes de Personnes*, 1623, and *Augmentations de Nouveaux Bastiments faits en France*, 1647.

L'Enfant, Major Pierre Charles (*b*. Paris, 1754; *d*. in Maryland, U.S.A., 4 June 1825), French engineer and architect, emigrated to America and fought in the War of Independence. Having previously designed the Federal House in Philadelphia, he was commissioned by President Washington in 1791 to plan the new city of Washington, but unfortunate differences of opinion led to delay in carrying it out. Nevertheless, in spite of sundry modifications, the plan of the city to-day is substantially as L'Enfant designed it.

Le Nôtre, André (*b*. Paris, 12 Mar. 1613; *d*. there, 15 Sept. 1700), garden architect; a member of the French Academy. He was a son of the superintendent of the Tuileries gardens, and later held that post himself, from 1637 to 1692. After planning the gardens at Vaux-le-Vicomte, 1655–61, he laid out those at Chantilly, Clagny, Marly, St Cloud, Sceaux, Trianon, and Versailles, and also remodelled those of Fontainebleau, St Germain, and the Tuileries.

Leonardo da Vinci (*b*. Vinci, near Empoli, Italy, 1452; *d*. Cloux, near Amboise, 2 May 1519), painter, engineer, and natural philosopher. There is little evidence to support the claim that this 'universal man' was also an architect or a builder, for nothing proves that he ever designed or carried out a single building. On the other hand, his multitudinous notes and drawings do include many diagrams relating to structural theories and processes, fortifications, and town-planning; also a few ideal plans for churches.

See monographs by E. Müntz, 1898; E. Solmi, 1898, 1900; E. McCurdy, 1904, 1908; W. von Seidlitz, 1909; K. Clark, 1939.

Leoni, Giacomo (*b.* Venice, *c.* 1686; *d.* London, 8 June 1746), architect and engraver. He was architect to the Elector Palatine in his early career. His arrival in England, early in the eighteenth century, has been attributed to encouragement by Lord Burlington (q.v.)., but it is now known that his first patron was the Duke of Kent, to whom was dedicated Leoni's English edition, published in 1715–16, of Palladio's *Architecture*. In that book Leoni frankly offered his professional services to the public, and soon a series of aristocratic commissions came his way: Bramham Park, Yorkshire (1710); Moor Park, Hertfordshire (1720); Latham House, Lancashire (1725); Bold Hall, Lancashire (1730); Clandon Park, Surrey (1732); Burton Park, Sussex (1740); and others. In his translation (published 1726) of Alberti's *Architecture*, he makes an appreciative reference to Lord Burlington.

Le Pautre, Antoine (*b.* Paris, 1621; *d.* in the same place, 1691), architect and engraver, was appointed *architecte du Roi* in 1655. His chief buildings were the monastery of Port Royal, Paris (1646–8); the Hôtel de Beauvais, Paris (1650); two wings of the palace at St Cloud; and a mansion (since destroyed) at St Ouen, near Paris. A book of his designs was published in 1652.

'Leper Window,' *see* LOW-SIDE WINDOW.

Lescot, Pierre (*b.* Paris, *c.* 1500–15; *d.* there, 10 Sept. 1578), began his career as a painter, but turned to architecture before he was twenty-one. The original design of the Hôtel Carnavalet, Paris (*c.* 1544), is attributed to him jointly with Jean Goujon, the sculptor, but it was remodelled by F. Mansart (q.v.) in 1661. As the result of an architectural competition, Lescot began rebuilding the Louvre in Paris in 1546, again associated with Goujon, and the Fontaine des Innocents, Paris (1547–9), is also their joint work.

Lethaby, William Richard (*b.* Barnstaple, 18 Jan. 1857; *d.* London, 17 July 1931), architect, teacher, and writer on architecture. After training in provincial architects' offices, he won two scholarships with which he travelled abroad; then spent some time in the office of Norman Shaw (q.v.), and started independent practice about 1891. Compared with his other activities, his buildings are of slight importance, comprising only a few country houses, a curious little church at Brockhampton, and some business premises in Birmingham. He devoted much of his time to teaching, becoming principal of the London County Council Central School of Arts and Crafts in 1894, and first Professor of Design at the Royal College of Art in

1900. He was surveyor to Westminster Abbey from 1906 to 1928, and wrote an admirable book on it in 1906. His other numerous books included *Leadwork*, 1893; *Medieval Art*, 1904; and *Architecture: an Introduction to the History and Theory of the Art of Building*, 1912.

LICH-GATE. St Leonard's Church, Heston, Middx. (a modern reconstruction)

Le Vau, Louis (*b.* Paris, ? 1612; *d.* there, 11 Oct. 1670), architect. After studying in Genoa and Rome he settled in Paris, the earliest mention of his work there as an architect being in connection with the Hôtel Lambert, now destroyed. He succeeded Lemercier (q.v.) as *architecte du Roi* in 1654. His chief buildings in Paris were the Hôtel Lionne, since demolished; the Collège Mazarin or Collège des Quatre Nations (now the Palais de l'Institut) with its domed church (1661–5); the churches of St Sulpice (1655–70) and St Louis-en-l'Île (begun 1664); extensions eastward of the Louvre except the east façade (1668); extensions of the Tuileries Palace, now incorporated in the Louvre (1655–70). Elsewhere he built the central part of the east front of the Palace of Versailles (1661–70), around an older nucleus; the neighbouring Grand Trianon, subsequently rebuilt by J. H. Mansart (q.v.); the layout of the streets east of the palace; the large château of Vaux-le-Vicomte (1655–61); an extension of the château of Vincennes; and other châteaux at Seignelay (1662), Bercy (1670), and Le Raincy.

Leverton, Thomas (*b.* Woodford, 11 June 1743; *d.* London, 23

Sept. 1824), architect. He was trained by his father, a builder. He probably laid out Bedford Square, London, and designed some houses therein, certainly No. 1. His other work included Woodford Hall, Essex (1771); Boyles, Essex (1776); Wood Hall, Watton, Hertfordshire (1777); the Phoenix Fire Office, London (1787); Riddlesworth Hall, Norfolk (1792); Grocers' Hall, London, since rebuilt (1798–1802); Scampston House, Yorkshire (1803); and Marine Villa, Lislea, Ireland (1803).

Lich-gate, or **Lych-gate** (from 'lich,' a corpse), a roofed gateway (placed at the entrance to a churchyard), where the bier carrying a coffin could be rested, pending the arrival of the priest for a funeral.

Lierne Rib, in Gothic vaulting, a short rib connecting two main ribs. (*Illustrated* VAULTING.)

Lieven de Key. *See* KEY, L. DE.

Ligorio, Pirro (*b.* Naples, *c.* 1500; *d.* Ferrara, 30 Oct. 1583), architect and painter. He studied painting in Rome early in his career, but turned to architecture about 1549, and worked for a time at the Villa d'Este, Tivoli. His chief buildings, all in Rome, were the Palazzo Torres, later Lancellotti, in the Piazza Navona (1552); the Casino in the Vatican gardens (1555–9); and various work at the palaces of the Sapienza, the Vatican, the Quirinal, and Monte Giordano. In 1564, on the death of Michelangelo, he became architect to St Peter's; but in 1568 was summoned to Ferrara as 'chief antiquary' to the duke. His *Libro delle antichità di Roma* was published in 1553.

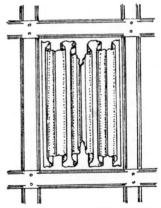

Linenfold Panelling, a form of panelling, popular in England during the Tudor period, in which the panels are carved with vertical grooves to resemble folded linen.

Lintel, a piece of stone, timber, steel, or concrete laid horizontally across a doorway or window opening, to carry superincumbent walling.

Loft, an attic or upper chamber in a roof. The word is also used in combination, e.g. 'pigeon loft,' 'hay loft,' 'organ loft.'

LINENFOLD PANEL. English (early 16th century)

Loggia (It.), a covered gallery, verandah, or portico, open on at least one side (cf. 'stoep' in South Africa; 'porch' in U.S.A.).

Lombard Architecture, *see* ITALIAN ARCHITECTURE, 3.

Lombardo, Pietro (*b.* Carona, *c.* 1435; *d.* Venice, June 1515), architect; founder of a family of architects and sculptors. His chief buildings, all in Venice, are the church of S. Maria dei Miracoli (1481–9); rebuilding of the Scuola di S. Marco (1490); remodelling of the Doges' Palace (1498 onwards) and possibly the completion of the Palazzo Vendramin-Calergi.

Long and Short Work, in early English Romanesque or 'Saxon' architecture, an arrangement of alternating horizontal and vertical stone slabs at the 'quoins' (external angles) of a building.

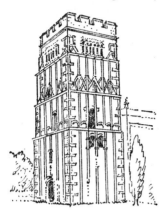

LONG AND SHORT WORK on the tower, Earls Barton Church, Northants. (10th century)

Long Gallery, in large Elizabethan and Jacobean houses in England, an upper room of great length, used for recreation and for the display of pictures and furniture, generally panelled, with florid chimney-pieces and overmantels going up to elaborately ornamented ceilings. A typical example at Aston Hall, Birmingham (1618–35), is 136 feet long, 18 feet wide, and 16 feet high. (*Illustrated* HOUSE.)

Longhena, Baldassare (*b.* Venice, 1598; *d.* there, 18 Feb. 1682), Baroque architect. He started his career as a mason, and worked on the Procuratie Nuove at Venice; then became a pupil of Scamozzi (q.v.). His first authenticated design seems to have been for the Palazzo Giustinian Lolin (*c.* 1623), followed by the Palazzo Widman (*c.* 1630). He then started his masterpiece, the magnificent church of S. Maria della Salute (1631–82). His other notable buildings included the Palazzo Rezzonico (1680); Palazzo Pesaro (1679–1710); Scuola dei Carmini (1668); Scuola dei Greci—all these in Venice; and the cathedral at Chioggia (begun in 1633).

See monograph by C. Semenzato, 1954.

Loos, Adolf (*b.* Brünn, Austria, 10 Dec. 1870; *d.* Vienna, 22 Aug. 1933), architect and writer on architecture. After training in Dresden, he worked in America; thereafter in Paris and Vienna. He became a keen advocate of 'functionalism' (q.v.) in architecture. His own buildings were chiefly houses in and around Vienna. His books included *Ornament und Verbrechen*, 1907, and *Trotzdem*, 1930.

See monograph by H. Kulka, 1931.

Lorimer, Sir Robert, A.R.A. (*b.* Edinburgh, 4 Nov. 1864; *d.* there, 13 Sept. 1929), architect. After leaving Edinburgh University he was articled to Sir R. Anderson in 1885; then became assistant to G. F. Bodley (q.v.) in London in 1889; and started practice in Edinburgh in 1892. Among many large country houses in Scotland which he built or restored were Earlshall, Rowallan, Ardinglas, Formakin, Hill of Tarvit, and Woodhill. He also restored Dunblane Cathedral, Paisley Abbey, and St John's Church at Perth; designed the beautiful Chapel of the Thistle in St Giles's Cathedral, Edinburgh (1909–11); the Scottish National War Memorial in Edinburgh Castle

(1918–27); and many local war memorials after 1918. As one of the principal architects of the Imperial War Graves Commission, he laid out cemeteries in Italy, Egypt, and Macedonia, and designed war memorials at Chatham, Portsmouth, and Plymouth. Other work outside Scotland included the restoration of Lympne Castle, Kent (1907–12), and the chapel at Stowe School (1927–30).

See monograph by C. Hussey, 1931.

Loudon, John Claudius (*b.* Cambuslang, 8 April 1783; *d.* London, 14 Dec. 1843), landscape gardener, and writer on horticulture and architecture. In addition to encyclopaedias of gardening, agriculture, trees and shrubs, and plants, and other books, he compiled *The Encyclopedia of Cottage, Farm, and Villa Architecture,* 1832, and founded *The Architectural Magazine* in 1834. He was thus a natural successor of Halfpenny and Langley (qq.v.), who both produced numerous books on architecture without having had any training in that field.

Louvre, a ventilator, usually in the form of a turret, fixed on the roof-ridge of a medieval hall or of a church, or an opening in a wall or window frame. In either case it is fitted with inclined slats to allow of the passage of air and the exit of smoke, without admitting rain or wind.

LOUVRE. A, *on the ridge of a roof* B, *in a gable*

Low-side Window, a small window near ground level, at the western end of the external wall of the chancel in some medieval churches, generally with the lower part of the window unglazed, but fitted with shutters and barred. The purpose of such windows was to allow a person outside to communicate with the priest in the chancel. It used to be thought that they were provided for lepers, hence the alternative name—'leper window.'

Lozenge, a diamond-shaped figure; also used in heraldry. (*Illustrated* MOULDINGS, ENRICHED (ROMANESQUE).)

Lubetkin, Berthold (*b.* Caucasus, Russia, 1901), architect. He was trained in Moscow, then went to Warsaw, Vienna, and Paris, where he worked under Perret (q.v.) and studied at the École des Beaux Arts. He practised for a short time in Paris, where he built an apartment house at 25 Avenue de Versailles in 1927. He then moved to London about 1930, and established contacts there which resulted in forming the firm of Tecton, consisting of five young English architects and himself. Their striking designs soon became a famous landmark in the 'Modern Movement,' and included the Penguin Pool and other work at the London Zoo (1933–4); two huge blocks of flats at Highgate known as 'Highpoint I' (1934) and 'Highpoint II' (1937); buildings at the Dudley Zoo and the Whipsnade Zoo (1937); the Finsbury Health Centre (1938); and multistorey housing for the Borough of Finsbury (1951).

Lucarne (Fr.), a skylight, or attic window, or dormer.

Lunette (Fr., dim of *lune*, moon), a semicircular window, or occasionally a semicircular or crescent-shaped blank space in a vaulted or domed ceiling.

Lunghi, or **Longhi,** family of Italian architects (sixteenth to seventeenth centuries). The most important members of it were (1) MARTINO LUNGHI THE ELDER (b. Viggiù, Como; d. Rome, 11 June 1591), who went from Milan to Rome about 1573 and became architect to the Pope in 1575. His chief works in Rome were the completion of Michelangelo's Palazzo dei Conservatori (with G. della Porta, q.v.); the Borghese and Altemps palaces; and the churches of S. Girolamo dei Schiavoni (1588–90), S. Maria in Vallicella, and S. Maria della Consolazione. (2) ONORIO LUNGHI (b. Rome, c. 1569; d. there, 3 Dec. 1619), his son, who began the great church of S. Carlo al Corso in 1612, and designed other buildings in Rome. (3) MARTINO LUNGHI THE YOUNGER (b. Rome, 18 Mar. 1602; d. there, 1657), son of Onorio. He completed S. Carlo, and also designed S. Antonio dei Portoghesi (1652) and the façade of SS. Vinzenzo e Anastasio (1650)—all in Rome.

Lurago, Rocco (b. Pelsopra, Como; d. Genoa, Italy, 1590), Italian Baroque architect, came from a family of architects and sculptors. He designed the magnificent Doria-Tursi Palace, later the Municipio (1574–6), and possibly the Palazzo Rosso and the church of S. Pietro di Banchi (1580)—all in Genoa; also the Dominican monastery and church at Bosco Alessandrino, Piedmont.

Lutyens, Sir Edwin Landseer, O.M., R.A. (b. London, 29 Mar. 1869; d. there, 1 Jan. 1944), the most famous English architect of the first half of the twentieth century, was born from a family originating in Schleswig, and was the son of a painter whose admiration for Sir Edwin Landseer explains the names given to his distinguished son. Edwin Lutyens had a very meagre education, followed by a brief training in the office of Sir Ernest George (q.v.). There he met and became a close friend of one of the assistants, Herbert Baker (q.v.). At the age of eighteen he actually obtained his first commission: a country cottage for Miss Gertrude Jekyll, the landscape gardener, who encouraged, influenced, and inspired much of his earlier work. For many years this consisted almost exclusively of country houses, picturesque in design, and showing a sympathetic understanding of traditional English building materials. One of the most striking was Marsh Court, at Stockbridge (1901). His taste moved progressively towards a more formal neo-Georgian style, e.g. Gledstone Hall, Skipton (1923); but 'Heathcote,' on a suburban site at Ilkley (1906), was somewhat over-elaborate.

He designed the two churches, the Institute, and several houses at the Hampstead Garden Suburb in 1907–9. Although his Cenotaph in Whitehall had a primarily sentimental appeal for the public, it is in fact a masterly example of subtle architectural design. Among his other public buildings in London are Britannic House, Finsbury Circus (1926), and the headquarters of the Midland Bank (in partnership with J. A. Gotch, q.v.). At Oxford he designed Campion Hall (1934). His British Pavilion at the Rome Exhibition (1910) became the façade of the British School at Rome. Other important work abroad included the Art Gallery at Johannesburg (1911); the British Embassy at Washington; and the Viceroy's House at New Delhi (completed 1930). The immense Roman Catholic cathedral that he planned for Liverpool was started in 1929, but is far from finished (1959), and his original design has been much reduced in size. Lutyens was President of the Royal Academy from 1938 to 1944, and was awarded the R.I.B.A. Royal Gold Medal in 1921.

See monographs by R. Lutyens, 1942, and by C. Hussey and A. S. G. Butler, 1953.

Lych-gate, *see* LICH-GATE.

Lyminge, Robert (seventeenth century), English architect, carpenter, and builder. He designed Blickling Hall, Norfolk (1619–23), and some part at least of Hatfield House (1607–12).

M

Macartney, Sir Mervyn Edmund (*b.* 1853; *d.* London, 28 Oct. 1932), English architect and writer on architecture; one of the founders of the Art Workers Guild (q.v.) in 1884. From 1906 to 1931 he was surveyor of St Paul's Cathedral during a critical period in the history of the fabric, and from 1906 to 1920 he edited *The Architectural Review*. He graduated at Oxford, and then entered the office of Norman Shaw (q.v.). His private practice included many country houses and some public libraries. In 1901, jointly with John Belcher (q.v.), he published an important book on *Later Renaissance Architecture in England*.

Machicolation, in medieval military architecture, a series of openings in a stone parapet, through which missiles or boiling liquid could be dropped on to the heads of assailants beneath. It was introduced to western Europe from the East, after the Crusades.

Machuca, Pedro (*d.* Granada, 1550), Spanish architect, sculptor, and painter. He is said to have worked under Giuliano da Sangallo (q.v.) in 1516. He was 'master-mason' or architect of Charles V's palace at Granada, begun in 1526. His son Luis continued this work after his death.

McIntire, Samuel (*b.* Salem, Massachusetts, Jan. 1757; *d.* there, 6 Feb. 1811), American architect and wood carver. Though he was trained as a 'housewright,' his early work was quite academic, and he made free use of books on design by Batty Langley (q.v.) and others. His work consisted mainly of large houses in Salem and the neighbourhood, including the Pierce House (1779); the two Derby Houses (1780 onwards); and probably the Boardman House on Salem Common (1782 onwards). His later work, which was much influenced by Bulfinch (q.v.), included more large houses, and some churches which have mostly been destroyed or rebuilt. He died as a result of attempting to save a drowning child. Rooms from his houses are exhibited in the museums of Boston and Philadelphia, and specimens of his wood carving in the Metropolitan Museum at New York.

See F. Consius and P. M. Riley, *The Woodcarver of Salem*, 1916.

McKim, Charles Follen (*b.* Isabelle Furnace, U.S.A., 24 Aug. 1847; *d.* St James, Long Island, U.S.A., 14 Sept. 1909), American architect; R.I.B.A. Royal Gold Medallist, 1903. After leaving Harvard he attended the École des Beaux Arts, Paris, 1867–70. Returning to America, he became assistant to H. H. Richardson (q.v.) in 1872. He entered into partnership with W. R. Mead in 1877, and they were joined by Stanford White (q.v.) in 1879. The large number of public buildings erected by the firm are classical in type, and include the Boston Public Library (1887–95); the Agricultural Building at the

World's Fair, Chicago (1893); Herald Square Building, New York (1894); University Club, New York (1900); Columbia University Buildings (1893); Tiffany Building, New York (1906); restoration of the University of Virginia (1897); of the White House, Washington (1903); and of the New York Custom House, now National City Bank; Pierpont Morgan Library, New York; Pennsylvania Station, New York (1906–10); Madison Square Gardens, New York; Rhode Island State House; American Academy at Rome.

Mackintosh, Charles Rennie (*b.* Glasgow, 7 Jan. 1868; *d.* London, 10 Dec. 1928), architect and decorative designer. After serving his articles in Glasgow, he joined Messrs Honeyman & Keppie in that city as an assistant, and became their partner in 1904. Meanwhile a scholarship had taken him to Italy in 1891, and in 1896 he had won the competition for the Glasgow School of Art, a building which made him a pioneer of the 'Modern Movement.' In the same original style he decorated a series of tea-rooms in Glasgow. His other buildings were simple and unassuming, e.g. Hill House at Helensburgh (1902–3) and Windyhill at Kilmacolm (1900). By that time his School of Art had made him famous on the Continent; but in 1913 he relinquished his partnership and his practice, left Glasgow, and retired to Suffolk to paint pictures.

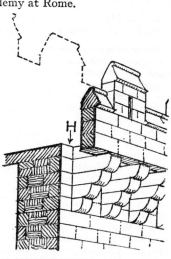

MACHICOLATION. Sectional view showing one of the holes or traps (H) behind the battlemented parapet

See monograph by T. Howarth, 1952.

Maderno, Carlo (*b.* Bissone, Italy, 1556; *d.* Rome, 30 Jan. 1629), Italian Baroque architect. He goes down to history as the designer of the bombastic façade of St Peter's, Rome (1612). He went to that city as a youth, working as modeller or decorator or assistant to D. Fontana (q.v.) and G. della Porta (q.v.) on the various buildings that they had in hand for Pope Sixtus V. Starting independent practice in 1592, he designed the façade of the church of S. Susanna (1596–1603); the Palazzo Mattei (1603–16); S. Maria della Vittoria (1608–20); and in 1624 began the Palazzo Barberini (completed by Borromini, q.v.). He also completed S. Andrea della Valle. All the above are in Rome.

See monograph by A. Muñoz, 1922.

Madrasah (Arabic), in Muslim architecture, a collegiate mosque; usually cruciform on plan (in Cairo).

Maeander (Lat.), or **Meander** (from Gk *maiandros*, the name of a winding river in Phrygia), an ornamental pattern of waving lines.

Mahometan Architecture, *see* MUSLIM ARCHITECTURE.

Majano, or **Maiano, Benedetto da** (*b.* Majano, Italy, 1442; *d.* Florence, 25 May 1497). Italian architect and sculptor. He is credited with the design of the great Strozzi Palace at Florence, but its immense cornice was added by Cronaca (q.v.). His chief sculptured works are the pulpit in S. Croce, Florence (1476), and the Strozzi tomb in S. Maria Novella, Florence (1491).

Malqaf (Arabic), a roof ventilator, conducting the cool north wind down into the rooms of an Egyptian house.

Malta, Architecture of. Like Cyprus, Malta was ruled by many races and dynasties before the British occupation in 1800. Apart from its remarkable prehistoric megaliths and a few medieval fragments, its architectural history begins in 1530, when it came into the possession of the Knights of St John, who reconstructed the magnificent natural harbour of Valletta, and laid out the new town before 1571. During the next two centuries a number of handsome stone buildings were erected in the Renaissance and Baroque styles, including the ornate church of St John (1573–8), the eight *auberges* of the various national branches of the Order, the Library (1786), and the Manoel Theatre (1731) in Valletta itself; also imposing Baroque churches at Floriana, Mdina, Luqa, etc. Among buildings of the nineteenth century are the extraordinary church at Musta (1864), with a stone dome 118 feet in diameter, and the large Opera House at Valletta (1861–6), which was among many casualties of the Second World War. The severe damage then suffered by the islands led to a report on post-war reconstruction by Messrs Harrison & Hubbard (1945). The largest modern building in Malta is the hospital, by Adams, Holden, and Pearson. The Hotel Phoenicia, by W. B. Binnie, harmonizes with the architectural tradition of the islands.

See J. Q. Hughes, *The Building of Malta, 1530–1795,* 1956.

Mandapam, or **Mantapam** (Sanskrit), an open pavilion or porch in front of an Indian temple.

Mandarah (Arabic), the reception-room of an Arab house in Cairo, etc.

Mannerist Architecture, a term invented about 1920 to describe Italian Renaissance architecture of the period between the 'High Renaissance' and the 'Baroque' (i.e. from *c.* 1530 to *c.* 1590), when strict canons of classical design **were** being relaxed or reversed. Among 'Mannerist' architects were Alessi, Michelangelo, Tibaldi, and Vignola (qq.v.).

Mansard Roof, a roof having two slopes on each face: the lower one very steep, the upper one of low pitch. This arrangement provides good attics with flat ceilings, and dormers can easily be contrived. Although used before the middle of the sixteenth century (e.g. in the Great Hall at Hampton Court in England, 1530–35; by Lescot in France, 1549; and also in Italy), this characteristically French type has been quite unjustifiably named after the architect F. Mansart

(1598–1666) (q.v.). A similar type used in America is called a 'gambrel' roof (q.v.). (*Illustrated* ROOF-TRUSS.)

Mansart, Francois (*b.* Paris, 1598; *d.* in same place, 23 Sept. 1666), architect. Although trained by the architect Gautier at Rennes, he was more influenced by De Brosse and Métézeau (qq.v.). There seems to be no evidence that he ever visited Italy, but he introduced scholarly design into France about 1630, a few years later than Inigo Jones (q.v.) brought the mature Italian Renaissance into England. Mansart's masterpiece is the beautiful château of Maisons, near Paris (1642–51). His other buildings include the châteaux of Balleroy (1626–36), Tilleroy (destroyed 1926), Bernis (1630), and Brécy in Normandy; the churches of the Feuillants or Reformed Christians (façade 1623–4), and of the Visitation of Ste Marie, now the Protestant Church (1632–4); the façade of the church of the Minimes (1636) now destroyed; and the noble church of Val-de-Grâce (1645–1665)—all these in Paris; the so-called Orléans wing of the château at Blois (1635–8); the Hôtel de la Vrillière, Paris (1635); the Galerie Mazarin, Paris (1644); and the remodelling of the Hôtel Argouge, now the Musée Carnavalet, Paris (1660–1). Mansart was appointed *architecte du Roi* in 1636.

See monograph by A. Blunt, 1941.

Mansart, Jules-Hardouin (*b.* Paris, 16 April 1646; *d.* Marly, 11 May 1708), architect; grand-nephew and pupil of François Mansart, whose surname he assumed in 1666. As the favourite architect of Louis XIV, a lavish patron, he amassed an enormous practice, and was ennobled as Baron de Jouy and Comte de Sagonne. His first royal commission was the château at Clagny (1674), followed in 1676 by responsibility for all work at the palace of Versailles, including the colonnade; the rebuilding of the Grand Trianon (1687–8), possibly the New Orangery (1686–8); the chapel—with his nephew Robert de Cotte—(1699); and the cathedral (1684–6). He also designed the royal château and pavilions at Marly (1679–86, since destroyed); numerous private châteaux, including Dampierre (1680); the Second Church of the Invalides, Paris, with its splendid dome (1693–1706); and the layout of the Place des Victoires (1684–7) and the Place Vendôme (1685)—both in Paris. He became director of the Academies of Painting, Sculpture, and Architecture.

Manse (from Med. Lat. *mansa*, a dwelling), originally the house and glebe land occupied by a priest; in modern usage, the house of a Presbyterian or Free Church minister.

Mansion (Old Fr. *mansion*; Lat. *mansionem*, from *manere*, to dwell). (1) Originally a place of abode. (2) A dwelling-place or apartment in a large house or enclosure (hence the reference in John xiv. 2: 'In my Father's house are many mansions'). (3) A manor-house. (4) In modern usage, a large house. (5) A block of residential flats. *See* HOUSE.

Mantelpiece, *see* CHIMNEY-PIECE.

Mantel-tree (now obsolete), either (i) a beam or bressummer (q.v.) or arch over a fire-place opening; or (ii) a mantelpiece (q.v.).

Manueline Architecture, *see* PORTUGUESE ARCHITECTURE.

Maqad (Arabic), an open loggia or belvedere in an Arab house.

Maqsurah (Arabic), in a mosque (q.v.), the sanctuary, enclosed by a screen of wooden lattice or pierced stonework.

Marble, a crystalline or granular limestone capable of taking a high polish. The term is, however, often loosely applied.

Marbling, the imitation in paint—on wood or stone or metal or plaster or even canvas—of the natural veining and colour of marble. The practice is very ancient.

Maristan (Arabic), a hospital for sick people.

Markelius, Sven Gottfrid (*b.* Stockholm, 25 Oct. 1889), Swedish architect; director of town-planning for Stockholm; member of the Advisory Committee for United Nations headquarters in New York, 1947, and for U.N.E.S.C.O. headquarters in Paris, 1952. After his training in Stockholm he was assistant to R. Östberg (q.v.). His own chief works have been the concert hall at Hälsingborg; Kollektiv-huis (flats) at Stockholm (1935); offices of the Stockholm Building Association (1936); Swedish pavilion at the World's Fair, New York (1939); interior decorations at United Nations Building, New York (1952); Trade Union Centre, Linköping; and several housing schemes.

Marot, Daniel (*b.* Paris, *c.* 1663; *d.* The Hague, 4 June 1752), architect, furniture designer, and engraver. He was the son of Jean Marot (*d.* 1679), also an architect. Daniel was trained by Le Pautre (q.v.); then settled in Holland, where he was employed by the Stadtholder, William of Orange (afterwards William III of England). He designed the audience hall of the States-General at The Hague (1686); then came to England about 1695, where he embellished the gardens and designed much of the furniture and decoration at Hampton Court. This work was described and illustrated in his book, *Œuvres du Sieur Marot, Architecte de Guillaume III*, 1712, and he also published a volume of other designs by himself and his father.

Marquetry, a development of 'intarsia' (q.v.). It consists of an inlay of ornamental woods, metals, bone, ivory, mother-of-pearl, tortoiseshell, etc., arranged to form decorative patterns.

Marquise (Fr.), a canopy, usually of metal and glass, sheltering the entrance doorway to an hotel, theatre, or public building.

Mars Group, abbreviation for the Modern Architectural Research Group, founded in 1933 by a number of young architects, engineers, and writers, including the following mentioned in this book: Casson, Fry, Gibberd, Gropius, Holford, Lubetkin, Martin, Sharp, Summerson, Tubbs, and Yorke. Its first exhibition was held in 1938.

Martin, Sir (John) Leslie (*b.* Manchester, 17 Aug. 1908), architect; Professor of Architecture at Cambridge University since 1956. He graduated from the Manchester University School of Architecture in 1930; taught there for a short time; and won the Soane Medallion of the R.I.B.A. in 1930. From 1934 to 1939 he was head of the School of Architecture at Hull; from 1939 to 1948 principal assistant architect to the L.M.S. Railway; from 1948 to 1953 deputy architect to the London County Council; and from 1953 to 1956 architect to the council. Jointly with R. H. Matthew (q.v.), whom he succeeded as architect, he designed the Royal Festival Hall, London, opened in 1951. His scheme of layout for the completion of London University was published early in 1959.

Martyrium (Lat., from Gk *marturion*), a chapel containing the relics of a martyr, or commemorating the site of a martyrdom.

Masjid (Arabic, literally 'a place of prostration'), transliterated into English, a mosque (q.v.).

Masons' Marks, distinctive symbols or monographs carved by medieval masons on their buildings to identify their work.

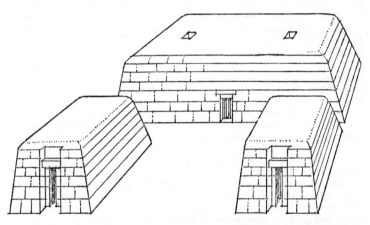

MASTABA. Three mastabas at Giza, Egypt (after Lepsius's 'Denkmäler,' 1849)

Mastaba (Arabic), either (i) a bench or seat for the guardian (*bawwab*) at the entrance to an Arab house; or (ii) a primitive Egyptian stone tomb with battered sides. From this type were evolved the Pyramids (q.v.).

Master-mason, *see* ARCHITECT.

Matroneum (Lat., from *matrona*, a mother), in early Christian churches, the part reserved for women. From the early days of worship in the catacombs, men and women were separated, and in the first cathedral of St Peter's at Rome the left side of the nave was occupied by the men, the right by the women. Traces of wooden screens round the women's side have been found in some Italian churches. In S. Agnese *fuori* and S. Lorenzo *fuori* at Rome there are arched galleries for women overlooking the presbytery, and known as *locus mulierum*. In the Roman churches of SS. Cosma e Damiano, S. Sebastiano, and S. Maria Maggiore, the *matroneum* consisted of a lower gallery surrounding and behind the apse, with windows looking into the presbytery.   There are also examples in S. Ambrogio at Milan and in St Mark's at Venice.   The women's gallery or *matroneum* at S. Sophia, Constantinople, was called *gynaekonitis* (from Gk *gunē*, woman) by the Greek historian Procopius.   In other Byzantine churches, an upper gallery for women is sometimes called a tribune (q.v.).

Matthew, Sir Robert Hogg (*b*. Edinburgh, 12 Dec. 1906), Professor of Architecture at Edinburgh University since 1953.   He was educated in Edinburgh; won the Soane Medallion of the R.I.B.A. in 1932 and the Bossom Medal in 1936; became chief architect and planning officer to the Department of Health for Scotland in 1945; and then architect to the London County Council from 1946 to 1953.   In that capacity, jointly with Dr J. L. Martin (q.v.), he designed the Royal Festival Hall, London, opened in 1951; with S. A. W. Johnson Marshall he designed the Commonwealth Building, Kensington, 1959.

Maufe, Sir Edward (*b*. Ilkley, 12 Dec. 1883), architect; R.I.B.A. Royal Gold Medallist, 1944.   He was articled to W. A. Pite in London, and then went up to St John's College, Oxford.   In 1936 he won the competition for the new cathedral at Guildford, still only partially erected, and after the Second World War was appointed one of the principal architects of the Imperial War Graves Commission.   Among his numerous works are Kelling Hall, Norfolk (1912); St Saviour's Church, Acton (1924); alterations at Trinity College, Cambridge (1927); Festival Theatre, Cambridge (1927); Yaffle Hill, Dorset (1929); chapel at Broadcasting House, London (1932); London Hospital Students' Hostel (1934); St Thomas, Hanwell (1935); work at St John's College, Cambridge (1938); the Playhouse, Oxford (1938); work at St John's College, Oxford (1949); rebuilding of St Columba's, Pont Street, London (1950); reconstruction of Gray's Inn (1947) and of the Middle Temple (1948); Whitla Hall, Queen's University, Belfast (1949); the Runnymede Memorial (1953); extensions of Bradford Cathedral.

Mausoleum (from Gk *mausōleion*), a stately place of burial for a royal or other important personage, so called after King Mausolus of Caria (fourth century B.C.) whose magnificent tomb at Halicarnassus was regarded in classical times as one of the 'Seven Wonders of the World.'

May, Hugh (*b*. Mid Lavant, 1622; *d*. 21 Feb. 1684), English architect, was chiefly concerned with financial affairs in the early part of his career.   He was appointed paymaster of the Royal Works in 1660 and controller in 1669; also as one of the commissioners for rebuilding London after the Great Fire of 1666.   Though little is known of his training as an architect, his abilities appear in his buildings, which included work at Cornbury Park, Oxfordshire (1663-8); Eltham Lodge, Kent (1664); Berkeley House, Piccadilly (1665, demolished 1733); extensive alterations at Windsor Castle (1675-83, mostly destroyed); and Cassiobury Park, Hertfordshire (*c*. 1677-80, rebuilt *c*. 1800).

Medallion, in architecture, a circular or oval plaque.

MAUSOLEUM. The famous mausoleum at Halicarnassus in Asia Minor, one of the 'Seven Wonders of the World,' built by King Mausolus (4th century B.C.). Based on the restoration by J. J. Stevenson in the British Museum, London

Meeting-house, the name given during the seventeenth and eighteenth centuries to dissenting places of worship, before the term 'chapel' (q.v.) came into use in the nineteenth century.   The Society of Friends ('Quakers') still use the word 'meeting-house.'   The old Congregational Church at Norwich (1693) is still called the 'Old Meeting,' and the Baptist Church at Bedford is still called 'Bunyan Meeting.'   *See* NONCONFORMIST CHURCH ARCHITECTURE.

Megaron (Gk), the principal or men's hall in a Mycenaean (q.v.) palace or house.

Mendelsohn, Erich (*b.* Allenstein, Prussia, 21 Mar. 1887; *d.* San Francisco, U.S.A., 16 Sept. 1953), architect, was trained in Munich and Vienna and started practice in 1911.   He was a designer of great originality.   He worked in England in 1933–4, in Palestine from 1934 to 1938, and then settled in the United States.   His principal

buildings in Germany were the Observatory or Einstein Tower at Potsdam (1921); a factory at Luckenwalde (1923); the Schocken Stores
at Chemnitz, Nuremberg, and Stuttgart; the Columbushaus, Berlin;
and the Universum Cinema, Berlin (1927). In partnership with S.
Chermayeff, he won the competition for the De la Warr Pavilion at
Bexhill, England, in 1934, and together they designed a remarkable
house at 64 Church Street, Chelsea. In Palestine he built the
hospital and power station at Haifa, and part of the Jewish University at Jerusalem.

See monograph by A. Whittick, 1940 (2nd ed., 1956).

Merlon (Fr.), one of the solid or tooth-like portions of a battlement,
between the 'embrasures' (openings). (*Illustrated* BATTLEMENT.)

Métézeau, family of French architects, included (1) CLÉMENT
MÉTÉZEAU I (*b.* Dreux, 1479; *d.* there, 1555), who built, with Jean
Desmoulins, the portal and towers of St Pierre, and, in part, the town
hall—both at Dreux; (2) his son THIBAUT MÉTÉZEAU (*b.* Dreux,
c. 1533; *d.* Paris), *architecte du Roi*, who reconstructed, with Jean
Bullant (q.v.), the Valois Chapel, St Denis, and, with two others,
rebuilt the Pont Neuf, Paris; (3) LOUIS MÉTÉZEAU, son of Thibaut
(*b.* Dreux, *c.* 1559; *d.* Paris, 1615), also *architecte du Roi*, who built
the upper part of the Great Gallery of the Louvre, Paris; (4) CLÉMENT
MÉTÉZEAU II (*b.* Dreux, 1581; *d.* Paris, 1652), also *architecte du Roi*,
who designed the breakwater at La Rochelle and the church of the
Oratoire, Paris.

Metope (Gk), a square panel between the triglyphs on the frieze
of the Greek Doric Order. (*Illustrated* ENTABLATURE.)

Mews, a row of stables with living quarters above, often built
behind large private houses in London during the seventeenth to
nineteenth centuries. The term is curiously derived from the royal
stables at Charing Cross, on a site where the royal hawks were formerly
kept at moulting time (Fr. *muer*, to moult, from Lat. *mutare*, to
change). During the present century, since the disuse of stables,
many London mews have been converted into small residences—
cramped but sought after.

Mexican Architecture. The former Aztec Empire of Mexico,
conquered by the Spaniards under Cortés in 1519–22, was administered as a vice-royalty under the name of 'New Spain' until 1810.
Since then, except for a brief interlude as an empire under Maxi-
milian, 1864–7, it has been a republic. Among its remarkable
monuments earlier than 1519, consisting mainly of temples and
stepped pyramids, are the large group of Chichén Itzá (*c.* 55 B.C.–
A.D. 340); others at Palenque and Mitla; the enormous Pyramid of the
Sun at San Juan Teotihuácan. These are relics of the Zapotec,
Toltec, and Maya periods; but the Aztec capital, Tenochtitlán, was
completely destroyed by the Spaniards, and modern Mexico City
stands on its site. Its cathedral was begun in 1573, Puebla Cathedral
in 1562; but nearly all the innumerable churches and monasteries of
the country are in the Baroque or Churriguesque style of the eighteenth century. The chief examples are the Sagrario in Mexico City;

the neighbouring collegiate church of Guadalupe; the cathedrals of Chihuahua and Morelia; and large churches at Ocotlan, Queretaro, San Cayetano, Taxco, and Tepozotlan. There was a phase of Greek and Gothic revivalism in the nineteenth century; but since about 1926 there has been a veritable 'Indian Renaissance,' in which Mexican architects have combined modern functionalism with their native Aztec tradition. Notable new buildings in Mexico City are the University Library, Medical School, and Arena for Water-Sports; the National Auditorium; the Ministries of Communications and Works; the Airport Building; and many large blocks of tall flats.

See S. Baxter, *Colonial Architecture in Mexico*, 1901; W. H. Kilham, *Mexican Architecture of the Vice-Regal Period*, 1927; Mexico, Department of Education: *Archaeological Monuments of Mexico*, 1933, and *Three Centuries of Mexican Colonial Architecture*, 1933; and monographs on recent architecture by E. Born, 1938, and I. E. Myers, 1952.

Mezzanine (Ital. *mezzanino*, dim. of *mezzano*, middle), a low storey between two higher ones. The French equivalent is *entresol*.

Michelangelo, properly **Michelangiolo Buonarroti** (*b.* Caprese, 6 Mar. 1475; *d.* Rome, 18 Feb. 1564), Italian sculptor, painter, and architect—the most famous and versatile of all Renaissance artists. Born of a family which was aristocratic though poor, he was apprenticed at the age of thirteen to Ghirlandaio, the leading painter of the day in Florence. With the powerful encouragement of Lorenzo dei Medici, he turned to sculpture, and in 1496 went to Rome. For the rest of his life he worked alternately in Rome and Florence. His first architectural commission was a monumental tomb for Pope Julius II, which he designed in 1513. This was followed by his fine statues and architecture in the New Sacristy at the church of S. Lorenzo in Florence (1523–9) and his design of the Laurentian Library, Florence (1524). From 1534 onwards he lived and worked in Rome, where he remodelled the group of buildings (the Palazzo dei Conservatori, the Museo Capitolino, and the grand flight of steps leading up to them) on the Capitol (1540 onwards); completed the half-finished Farnese Palace, with its noble cornice (1546); converted the ruined Baths of Diocletian into the church of S. Maria degli Angeli (1559–63); and succeeded Antonio Sangallo (q.v.) in 1546 as chief architect to St Peter's, one of his contributions being the magnificent dome. Although he turned from sculpture to architecture late in his career, his influence upon the subsequent emergence of the Baroque style was enormous, for he treated architecture from a sculpturesque and pictorial standpoint.

See monographs by A. Condivi, 1553 (English translation by H. P. Horne, 1904); C. B. Black, 1875; A. Gotti, 1875; C. Clément, 1880; C. H. Wilson, 1881; J. A. Symonds, 1893; C. Holroyd, 1903; D. Frey, 1923; L. Goldschieder, 1953.

Michelozzi, Michelozzo (*b.* Florence, 1396; *d.* there, 1472), architect and sculptor. He worked in Florence at engraving and other crafts under Ghiberti, Donatello, etc., and was about forty when he turned to architecture. His principal buildings in Florence were the reconstructed church, cloister, and library of S. Marco (c. 1437–71), and of SS. Annunziata (c. 1444–5); the façade of S. Felice (1457); the great Palazzo Medici-Riccardi (1444–59); the *cortili* of the Palazzo Vecchio (1454), and of the Palazzo Corsi; the Palazzi Caniagi and Strozzino. In the neighbourhood he rebuilt the castles of Carafaggiolo and Caraggi; and designed the church of S. Girolamo at Volterra (1447–1464). His other works included the Palazzo del Banco Mediceo at Milan (1462) and the picturesque reconstruction of the rector's palace at Ragusa (modern 'Dubrovnik') in Dalmatia, after a fire (1464).

See monograph by O. Morisani, 1951.

Mies Van der Rohe, L., *see* VAN DER ROHE.

Mihrab (Arabic), in Muslim architecture (q.v.), a niche in the wall of the sanctuary of a mosque, indicating the direction of Mecca, towards which a worshipper inclines in prayer.

Military Architecture, *see* CASTLE.

Mills, Robert (b. Charleston, South Carolina, 12 Aug. 1781; d. 3 Mar. 1855), American architect and engineer. Unlike many of the leading architects of his period in America, he had a proper professional training under James Hoban (q.v.), beginning in 1800. In 1803 he attracted the notice of Jefferson (q.v.) who took him into his house at Monticello. He was also advised by Bulfinch (q.v.), and then worked from 1803 to 1808 under Latrobe (q.v.). From 1802 onwards he was designing buildings on his own account, including the 'circular' Congregational Church at Charleston, 1804. He started independent practice at Philadelphia in 1808, remaining there till 1817, when he moved to Baltimore. He returned to Charleston in 1820, and finally moved in 1830 to Washington, becoming supervising architect of the Capitol there in 1836. He was one of the chief exponents of the Greek Revival (q.v.) in America. He retired in 1851. His long list of buildings includes the octagonal Unitarian Church at Philadelphia (1811–13); Dr Stoughton's Church (circular) at Philadelphia, seating 4,000 persons (1811–13); Upper Ferry Bridge, a single timber arch of 360-foot span (1812); the octagonal church at Richmond (1811); the Greek Doric monument to Washington at Baltimore (1814–29); the circular First Baptist Church at Baltimore; and, most important of all, the Washington Monument (won in competition) at Washington (1836 onwards); also a number of court houses and prisons, and an asylum.

Mimbar (Arabic), a pulpit in a mosque.

Minaret (from Arabic *manareh*), the tower of a mosque, with a gallery from which the muezzin (priest) chants the call to prayer. *See* MOSQUE and MUSLIM ARCHITECTURE.

Minoan Architecture, the primitive or pre-Hellenic architecture of Crete, c. 3000–1200 B.C., so called after a series of kings named 'Minos,' a title equivalent to 'Pharaoh' or 'Caesar' and not a personal name. *See* ARCHITECTURE, PERIODS OF, 1(c).

MINARET.   (A) *Primitive Mesopotamian type (Great Mosque, Samarra, 9th century*
A.D.); (B) *Turkish type (Sulimaniya, Istanbul, 1560–6); (C) Indo-Persian type (Taj*
Mahal, Agra, 1630–52); (D) Moroccan type (Kutubiya, Marrakesh (1146–96); (E)
Egyptian type (Mausoleum of Barquq, Cairo, 1400–10), (F) Rustic Egyptian example
(Kharga Oasis).   The top of (A) is a restoration

Minster (from Lat. *monasterium*), originally the church of a monastery, then any large church of monastic origin, e.g. York Minster, Beverley Minster, Minster church in Kent.

Minute, in classical architecture, one-sixtieth part of a module (q.v.).

Misericord (Lat. *misericordia*, compassion, pity), in the choir stalls of a medieval church, a hinged seat with a bracket beneath (often grotesquely or humorously carved) which, when the seat was tipped up, gave some support and relief to a person standing during a lengthy service.

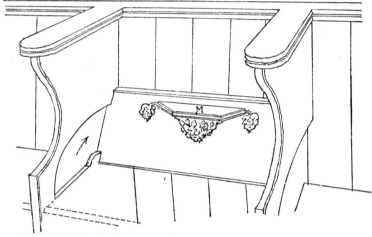

MISERICORD, showing one seat tipped back to expose misericord (M) *beneath*

Mitre, in joinery, a form of joint in which the line of junction bisects the angle (usually a right angle) of the two pieces joined, as at the corners of a picture frame.

Mnesicles (fifth century B.C.), Greek architect. He designed the Propylaea (436–432 B.C.), and probably the Erechtheum (*c.* 421–405 B.C.), both in Athens.

See monograph by J. A. Bundgaard, 1957.

Models, Architectural. In English architecture the term 'model' has, or has had, two meanings: (i) an architect's design for a building (now obsolete, but used in 1598 by Shakespeare: 'When we meane to build, We first survey the Plot, then draw the Modell'); (ii) in current usage, a three-dimensional representation of a building to a small scale, executed in wood or some other material. Models of buildings have been made since very remote times: e.g. the small model of an ancient Egyptian house found in the tomb of King Mentuhotep (*c.* 2000 B.C.) and the terra-cotta models of primitive Greek thatched houses found at Perachora. Following are more recent examples: (a) the model made by Brunelleschi in 1423 for completing the dome of the cathedral at Florence; now in the cathedral museum, made of somewhat worm-eaten wood to a scale of about 1 inch to 3 feet. There are other wooden models in the same museum, and several more in the Museo Petriano adjoining St Peter's at Rome. Occasionally Italian architects made rough models in clay to give their clients an idea of the ultimate appearance of a new building, or to help their own procedure in designing. (b) The papier mâché model of the church of St Maclou, in the Musée d'Art Normand at Rouen, dating from the early fifteenth century, coloured, and about 28 inches long; (c) the wonderful stone model showing the intended completion of the west front of St Pierre at Louvain, made in 1524. It is elaborately carved, and is 24 feet high; (d) the magnificent wooden model made under Wren's directions in 1673 for St Paul's Cathedral as he wished it to be. It cost £600, representing perhaps ten times as much to-day, and is beautifully finished, inside and out. The scale is 1 inch to 2 feet. The model is raised on a stand, in the 'trophy-room' of the cathedral, and is illuminated internally so that visitors can go inside it.

Models are used for most projected buildings of any importance.

Modillion, in Roman and Renaissance architecture, a small ornamental bracket, used in rows under the corona of a cornice.

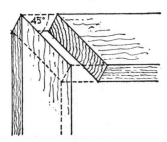
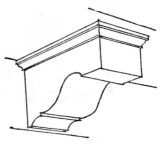

MITRE. A mitred joint, opened   *MODILLION. Plain Roman type*

Modular Society, The (offices: 22 Buckingham Street, Strand, London, W.C.2), founded by architects and others in 1953, is 'a non-profit-making company. . . . Its aim is to reduce the cost of building by promoting the development of modular co-ordination.' The society publishes *The Modular Quarterly.*

Module (from Lat. *modulus,* dim. of *modus,* a measure). (1) In classical architecture, a term used by Vitruvius in his manual *De Architectura* (IV. iii. 4) in framing his rules for the Orders of Architecture, his *modulus* being one-half the diameter of each column at its base. (2) In modern practice, a convenient unit (agreed as 4 inches or 10 centimetres) upon which all dimensions of buildings and components are to be based, with a consequent economy in time and efficiency of construction by facilitating standardization and pre-fabrication. For definitions of other terms used in 'modular design' see *B.S. 2900, Part 1 (1957)*; *Glossary*, obtainable from The British Standards Institution, 2 Park Street, London, W.1.

Mogul Architecture, *see* MUGHAL ARCHITECTURE.

Mohammedan Architecture, *see* MUSLIM ARCHITECTURE.

Monastery (from Gk *monastērion*, literally 'a place for living alone'). The word means not only (i) an organized and self-contained religious community bound by vows, but also (ii) the communal buildings. As the name 'monastery' implies, the first *coenobia*—predecessors of the monastery proper—were groups of

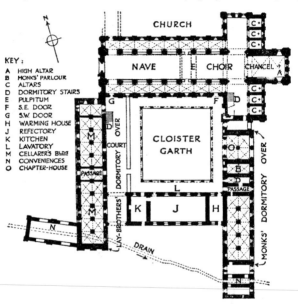

KEY:
A HIGH ALTAR
B MONKS' PARLOUR
C ALTARS
D DORMITORY STAIRS
E PULPITUM
F S.E. DOOR
G S.W. DOOR
H WARMING HOUSE
J REFECTORY
K KITCHEN
L LAVATORY
M CELLARER'S BLDG
N CONVENIENCES
O CHAPTER-HOUSE

Plan of a typical English monastery: Kirkstall Abbey (c. A.D. 1180)

isolated hermits who met together for worship in the Egyptian deserts during the fourth century A.D. The real origin of the monastic movement began, however, with St Benedict who, as a young man, retired from the busy life of Rome to a cave in the mountains near Subiaco, where he founded monasteries; and then, in A.D. 529, founded Monte Cassino, which became the mother-house and centre of innumerable Benedictine monasteries built during the following nine centuries in western Europe. Among these were several which eventually became English cathedrals—Ely, Chester, Exeter, Durham, Gloucester, Winchester, St Albans, Canterbury, Rochester, Norwich, Peterborough, Worcester; another was Westminster Abbey. After a time the Benedictine rule grew lax, and new Orders of Reformed Benedictines ('Cluniacs') and of Cistercians were founded in about 909 and 1098 respectively. The Cistercians founded many monasteries in England, especially in the Yorkshire Dales. Later Orders were the Augustinian or 'Austin' Canons, the Premonstratensians, and the Carthusians, whose monks (e.g. at Mount Grace Priory, Yorkshire) lived in separate cells.

When the English monasteries came to be dissolved in 1536–9, they numbered about 650 in all; but many of them were very small, with less than a dozen inhabitants, having shrunk greatly during the Middle Ages. Their buildings were then sold to laymen, who either converted them into dwelling-houses (e.g. Battle Abbey, Stoneleigh Abbey, Newstead Priory) or demolished them and sold the building materials, lead being especially valuable. Of all the monasteries, about one-third have completely disappeared, a similar number are represented by meagre fragments, several have become cathedrals (q.v.), and others have been converted into parish churches.

The buildings of a medieval monastery normally comprised a church, chapter-house (q.v.), cloister (q.v.), frater or monks' day-room with dormitory or 'dorter' over; refectory (q.v.); *cellarium*; and, detached from the main group, workshops, infirmary, and the house of the abbot, abbess, prior, or prioress. An abbey was governed by an abbot or abbess and was usually larger than a priory, governed by a prior or prioress. 'Nunnery' is an alternative name for a convent or monastery of nuns.

See A. H. Thompson, *English Monasteries*, 1913; M. R. James, *Abbeys*, 1925; D. H. S. Cranage, *The Home of the Monk*, 1926; F. H. Crossley, *The English Abbey*, 1935; and, for the destruction of the buildings, *see* M. S. Briggs, *Goths and Vandals*, 1952.

Monolith (Gk *monos*, one; *lithos*, a stone), a single block of stone fashioned into a pillar or an obelisk. *See* OBELISK and TRILITHON for notable examples.

Montereau, or **Montreuil, Pierre de** (*b.* Montreuil-sous-Paris, *c.* 1200; *d.* Paris, 17 Mar. 1266), architect. He has been credited with the design of the Sainte Chapelle at Paris (1242–8), but the evidence is inconclusive. He designed the nave and transepts of the Abbey Church at St Denis (1231 onwards); the refectory and Sainte Chapelle of the abbey of St Germain-des-Prés, since destroyed; also, probably, the refectory of the abbey of St Martin-des-Changes, the Court Chapel at St Germain-en-Laye; and the Sainte Chapelle at Vincennes (destroyed 1400).

Monument (from Lat. *monere*, to remind; hence, a reminder), a building erected either (i) over a sepulchre; or (ii) elsewhere as a memorial of some notable person or event. *See also* MAUSOLEUM.

Monuments, Ancient, *see* ANCIENT MONUMENTS.

Moorish Arch, usually known as a 'round horse-shoe arch,' having its centre struck from a point slightly above its springing. (*Illustrated* ARCH.)

Moorish Architecture, the Muslim architecture of Spain and North Africa. *See* MUSLIM and SPANISH ARCHITECTURE.

H

Mora, Francisco de (*b.* Cuenca, mid sixteenth century; *d.* Madrid, 3 Aug. 1610), Spanish architect. After being trained by Juan de Herrera (q.v.), he restored the royal palace of Alcazar at Seville, (1587), made designs for the Mint there, and in 1589 began additions to the Escorial, comprising the servants' quarters (*Casa de la Compaña*), the hospital, a fountain in the gardens, and plans for the lower palace (*Escorial de Abaijo*). In 1591 he was appointed 'master-mason' of the royal palaces of Madrid and El Pardo.

Morley-Horder, *see* HORDER, P. R. M.

Morris, Robert Schofield (*b.* Hamilton, Ontario, Canada, 1908), Canadian architect, president of the Royal Architectural Institute of Canada, 1952–4, was awarded the R.I.B.A. Royal Gold Medal in 1958. He was educated at Hamilton and in Ottawa, served in the First World War, and then began his training as an architect at McGill University. In 1929 he became a partner in the firm of Marani & Lawson, now Marani, Morris, & Allen. Their work, all in Canada, includes the Abitibi Building (1930) and Herbert House (1957)—both at Toronto; the Bank of Canada Head Office Building (1938) and War Savings Certificates Building (1943)—both at Ottawa; the grandstand at the Canadian National Exhibition at Toronto (1948); the Groves Memorial Hospital at Fergus (1956); the Guelph General Hospital (1950); and the large building of the Great West Life Assurance Co.

Morris, William (*b.* Walthamstow, 24 Mar. 1834; *d.* Kelmscott, Oxfordshire, 3 Oct. 1896), poet, sociologist, and decorative designer, never practised as an architect; but, after graduating at Oxford in 1856 and abandoning his intention of taking holy orders, he entered the office of the architect G. E. Street (q.v.) in order to qualify himself for that profession. Very soon, however, he turned to painting and poetry, but spent much of his time in superintending the building of a house to suit his very specific ideas, the actual architect being Philip Webb (q.v.). 'The Red House,' as it was called, near Bexley Heath in Kent, was finished in 1860, and then Morris concentrated on its furnishing. So dissatisfied was he with the furniture, fabrics, and other materials then on the market, that in 1862 he founded the firm of Morris & Co., with Webb as one of the partners. The others were Rossetti, Burne-Jones, Madox Brown, Faulkner, and Marshall. Morris himself designed much of the furniture, fabrics, and wall-papers manufactured by the firm. His influence upon architecture was immense, not only by reason of the example set by the Red House and the products of Morris & Co., but also through his constant plea for simplicity and honesty in craftsmanship as opposed to pedantic copying of antique styles; and above all because of his violent hatred of the 'restoration' of old churches by Sir G. G. Scott (q.v.) and others, which led Morris in 1877 to found the S.P.A.B. (q.v.) or, as he called it, 'the Anti-Scrape.' He also founded the Art Workers Guild (q.v.) in 1884.

See monographs by J. W. Mackail, 1899; H. Jackson, 1908; A. Clutton-Brock, 1914, etc.

Mosaic, a form of surface decoration of walls, vaults, domes, and pavements with small cubes (*tesserae*) of marble, opaque glass, or other hard materials; laid in fine mortar or cement plaster. The tesserae vary from $\frac{1}{4}$ inch to $\frac{1}{2}$ inch square, and are arranged in patterns incorporating human figures, animals, floral forms, and inscriptions. The art or craft of mosaic was practised to some extent in ancient Egypt, Assyria, and Greece; but was much more largely used in Roman, Byzantine, and medieval architecture. Roman mosaics, especially pavements, have been discovered in many countries; and notable examples can be seen in London at he Guildhall Museum, at Verulamium, York, Cirencester, Brading (Isle of Wight), and on the sites of many other Roman villas and owns in Britain. Vitruvius (q.v.), vii. 1, describes the process of manufacturing and laying the *tesserae*, which were normally of marble, the colours including red, yellow, black, and occasionally green. One of the finest examples in Rome itself is the vault of the circular church of S. Costanza, fourth century A.D.

In Byzantine architecture glass mosaic and gilding were largely used, especially in the apses and vaults of churches: e.g. in S. Vitale, S. Apollinare Nuovo, and S. Apollinare in Classe—all at Ravenna; the cathedrals at Parenzo, Monreale, Venice (St Mark's); S. Sophia at Constantinople; the church of the Nativity at Bethlehem; the church at Daphni in Greece, etc. Similar mosaics were also executed in the Great Mosque at Damascus and in the Muslim 'Dome of the Rock' at Jerusalem. A form of inlay, resembling mosaic, was largely used for decorating the pulpits, etc., of mosques in Cairo and elsewhere. Mosaic pavements of the type known as *opus alexandrinum* (q.v.) are common in Italy, and there are a few examples in England, e.g. in front of the high altar at Westminster Abbey (*c.* 1268). The family of the Cosmati in Italy did much mosaic work of great beauty during the thirteenth century. 'Cosmatesque' mosaic can be seen at Westminster Abbey in the tomb of Henry III (1291), and the shrine of the Confessor, 1269. The finest modern mosaics in England are at the Roman Catholic Cathedral at Westminster.

See E. Gerspach, *La Mosaïque*, 1881; C. H. Sherrill, *Mosaics in Italy, Greece, etc.*, 1933; E. A. Anthony, *A History of Mosaics*, 1935.

Moslem Architecture, *see* MUSLIM ARCHITECTURE.

Mosque (from Arabic *masjid*), a building for Muslim worship. The first mosque, built at Medina in Arabia by Muhammad, the founder of Islam, in A.D. 622, was merely a square enclosure surrounded by a wall. On the side of the enclosure where Muhammad led the prayers was a roughly built shed or shelter giving some protection from the sun. At first the worshippers knelt facing north, towards Jerusalem, but in 624 the direction was changed towards Mecca. So to-day, wherever a mosque may be, whether in London or Cape Town or Istanbul or Morocco or Singapore, the direction of Mecca (*qiblah*) is indicated by a niche (*mihrab*, q.v.) in the wall of the sanctuary. Before the end of the seventh century a minaret (q.v.) was added, from which the call to prayer was chanted by the muezzin, and another addition was the pulpit (*mimbar*, q.v.). In every large mosque (*gami* or *jami*) used for congregational worship, the open courtyard (*sahn*) was retained, usually with an arcaded *liwan* or covered aisle on each side, the *liwan* on the Mecca side being wider than the others and constituting the sanctuary, often enclosed by a carved screen (*maqsurah*). A *madrasah* is a mosque used for teaching purposes and is generally cruciform. A 'tomb mosque' is another type, unsuited for congregational worship.

For examples of mosques in various Islamic countries *see* MUSLIM ARCHITECTURE and the books there cited.

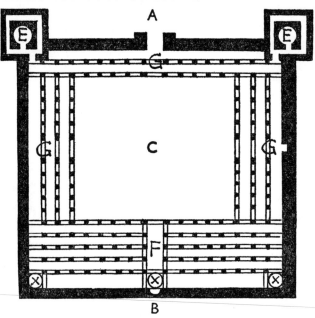

MOSQUE

Plan of the congregational mosque of Al Hakim at Cairo: A=*entrance;* B=*mihrab (prayer niche pointing to Mecca);* C=*sahn (open courtyard);* E=*minarets;* F= sanctuary;* G=*liwans (covered arcades);* X=*small domes*

Motel (American), a roadside inn providing transient and very simple accommodation for passing motorists.

    See G. Baker and B. Funaro, *Motels*, 1955, and J. S. Hornbeck (ed.), *Motels, Hotels, and Restaurants* (7th ed.), 1953.

Motif (Fr.), in architecture, the dominant or distinctive feature or element of a design.

Motif Palladio, *see* PALLADIAN MOTIF.

Motte (Fr.), an artificial mound of earth fortified as a castle, at first merely with a timber stockade around the top; later with a massive stone 'keep' (q.v.). There are examples at Canterbury (the 'Dane John'), at Oxford, and especially at Thetford in Norfolk. *See also* CASTLE.

Mouldings, ornamental and continuous lines of grooving or projections, worked respectively below or above a plane surface. They may be either simple or 'enriched.' Any individual part of a complex moulding is called a 'member' and any member which is carved is said to be 'enriched.' In each historical phase or period of architecture the mouldings were so distinctive in design, and so rigorously defined by practice and by rule, that it is possible to estimate the approximate date of a building from its mouldings alone. Greek mouldings, concave or convex, are formed from conic sections, whereas Roman mouldings are segments of a circle. The most characteristic enrichments of Greek and Roman mouldings are the 'leaf and dart' or 'egg and tongue,' and the 'bead and reel.'

Romanesque mouldings were based upon Roman prototypes, but were clumsier in design and execution. The doorways of 'Norman' churches of this period were often enriched with grotesque representations of animals' heads, chevrons (q.v.) or zigzags, and billets (q.v.). Gothic mouldings were much more varied and often deeply undercut. Gothic enrichments included the 'dog-tooth' (q.v.) in the thirteenth century, the 'ball-flower' (q.v.) in the fourteenth, and the 'Tudor flower' (q.v.) in the fifteenth.

CLASSICAL MOULDINGS
(Greek on left, Roman on right)

(A) *Fillet;* (B) *Astragal;* (C) *Cavetto;* (D) *Ovolo;* (E) *Cyma Recta;* (F) *Cyma Reversa;* (G) *Fascia;* (H) *Scotia;* (I) *Torus*

Renaissance mouldings, based on Roman models, are seen at their best in the work of Peruzzi (q.v.) and other Italian architects of the sixteenth century, and in the work of Wren and his craftsmen in England in the late seventeenth and early eighteenth centuries.

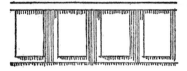

Dentils (Roman)

*Acanthus Ornament on Cyma Recta
(Roman)*

*Egg and Tongue (Roman) on Ovolo
Moulding*

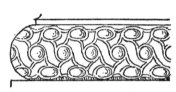

Guilloche (Greek) on Torus Moulding

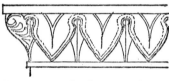

*Leaf and Dart (Greek) on Cyma Reversa
Moulding*

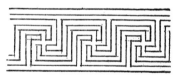

Fret or Key Pattern (Greek)

Bead and Reel (Roman)

Bead and Reel (Greek)

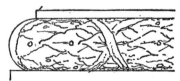

*Bay-leaf Garland Ornament (Roman) on
Torus Moulding*

MOULDINGS, ENRICHED (GREEK AND ROMAN)

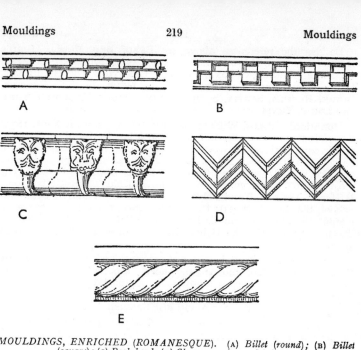

A   B

C   D

E

MOULDINGS, ENRICHED (ROMANESQUE). (A) *Billet (round);* (B) *Billet (square);* (C) *Beak-head;* (D) *Chevron or zigzag;* (E) *Cable*

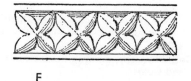

F

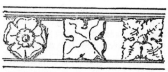

G   H

MOULDINGS, ENRICHED (GOTHIC). (F) *Dog-tooth;* (G) *Ball-flower;* (H) *Tudor flower, etc.*

Besides the references above *see* BEAD, BED MOULD, BIRD'S BEAK, BOLECTION MOULDING, BOWTELL, CABLE MOULDING, CAVETTO, CHAMFER, CORNICE, CORONA, CYMA (2), CYMATIUM, DENTIL, FILLET, FRET, GUILLOCHE, LABEL MOULDING, OGEE, OVOLO, PROFILE, QUIRK, REGULA, SCOTIA, SCRIBING, SIMA, STUCK MOULDING, SUNK MOULDING, TENIA.

Mountford, Edward William (*b.* Shipston-on-Stour, 22 Sept. 1855; *d.* London, 7 Feb. 1908), architect, had a long series of successes in public competitions, for which he adopted the 'Free Classic' style of design then in vogue. He was articled in London in 1872, and began practice in 1881, entering for competitions from the outset. His most notable achievements were the Sheffield Town Hall (1890); Battersea Town Hall and Polytechnic (1892–3); St Olave's Grammar School, Southwark (1893); the Northampton Institute, Clerkenwell (1896); the Museum and Technical School at Liverpool; Lancaster Town Hall; and the Old Bailey Sessions House, London, opened in 1907.

Mozarabic Architecture, Spanish church architecture built by Christian craftsmen who had fled north, especially to León, from Córdoba and the southern provinces occupied by the Muslim or Moorish invaders. The distinctive feature of these small churches is the horseshoe arch. *See* ARCH; *also* SPANISH ARCHITECTURE.

Mudejar Architecture, Spanish architecture (especially of churches in the north of Spain) executed by Muslim or Christian craftsmen trained in Moorish cities farther south. This phase is somewhat later than the Mozarabic phase (q.v.). *See* SPANISH ARCHITECTURE.

Mughal, or **Mogul Architecture,** Muslim architecture in India during Mughal rule, usually reckoned from the invasion of Babur, A.D. 1526, to the death of Aurungzeb, A.D. 1707. *See* INDIAN and MUSLIM ARCHITECTURE.

Muhammadan Architecture, *see* MUSLIM ARCHITECTURE.

Mullion, in medieval and early Renaissance architecture, a vertical bar of wood or stone dividing a window opening into 'lights.' (*Illustrated* TRACERY.)

Multifoil, in Gothic tracery, an arch having more than five cusps. *See* CINQUEFOIL and CUSP.

Mumford, Lewis (*b.* in U.S.A., 19 Oct. 1895), American writer on town-planning and sociological subjects; Professor of City Planning at the University of Pennsylvania since 1951. He was educated at Columbia University. Among his numerous books are *Technics and Civilization*, 1934; *The Culture of Cities*, 1938; *Art and Technics*, 1952. Awarded Royal Gold Medal of R.I.B.A., 1961.

Munnion (rare), a corruption of MULLION (q.v.).

Muntin, in a panelled wooden door, the vertical member between any two panels. (*Illustrated* DOOR.)

Museums, Architectural. The 'Royal Architectural Museum,' consisting mainly of casts of Gothic ornament in detail, was originally founded in 1851, at the instigation of Cottingham, Sir G. G. Scott, Sen. (qq.v.), and others. From 1869 to 1916 it was housed, in one of the most hideous buildings in London, at 18 Tufton Street, Westminster. The collection was then removed to the Victoria and Albert Museum, which still remains, in spite of sweeping and welcome recent changes, the nearest approach to a National Museum of Architecture in this country.

The 'trophy-room' at St Paul's Cathedral contains a fine collection of models (q.v.), drawings, prints, and objects connected with the design, erection, and repair of the fabric. There are similar exhibits in the *Opera del Duomo* at Florence and in that at Siena; also in the *Museo Petriano* adjoining St Peter's at Rome. Small buildings of historical interest have been re-erected in the national open-air museums or 'folk parks' at Aarhus in Denmark and at Arnhem in Holland, both well worth a visit.

Mushrabiyyah (Arabic), in Arab houses (in Cairo especially), wooden lattices formed of turned bobbins, attractively designed and used instead of glazed windows in order to admit shaded light and air without revealing or destroying the privacy of the interior. *See* HAREM.

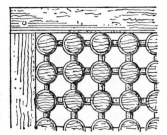 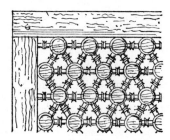

MUSHRABIYYAH. Two examples from Cairo

Muslim Architecture (otherwise known as Arab, Arabian, Islamic, Mahometan, Mohammedan, Moslem, Muhammadan, or Saracenic architecture). The Arabic word 'Muslim' is now generally adopted by scholars to describe the architecture produced by the Arab followers of the religion of Islam—i.e. Muslims—in many parts of the eastern hemisphere after the prophet Muhammad established Islam in Arabia in the year A.D. 622, which is the first year of the Muslim calendar.

This brief statement explains all the alternative names mentioned above, except 'Saracenic,' which is really a nickname, like 'Whig' or 'Tory' or 'Quaker,' and was introduced into English during the Middle Ages to describe the wild Arab warriors—'Saracens'—encountered by the Crusaders. 'Saracenic' was also applied by Sir C. Wren (q.v.) to Gothic architecture ('Gothic' itself being yet another nickname); and modern scholarship recognizes that his use of the term in that connection was not so absurd as it seemed to critics of a century ago, for many features of Gothic architecture

* H

(q.v.) are now attributed to the contacts made by the Crusaders with 'Saracenic' architecture, though that term is now discarded. Muslim architecture has, therefore, some significance in the history of European Gothic; but is even more important because it has been practised for thirteen centuries by a large part of the human race—as far north as Turkestan and Yugoslavia, as far west as Spain and Morocco, as far east as China and Indonesia, as far south as Nigeria and Zanzibar. There is a mosque for Malayan Muslims in Cape Town, and one for English Muslims at Woking.

When the Arab armies, composed of uncultured warriors, swept westwards from Arabia to Spain, and even into central France, within a century from the foundation of Islam, and eastwards as far as the frontiers of India and China, they had no domestic architecture of their own, for they were nomads, and their only dwellings were tents of black camel-hair such as the modern Bedouin still use. Their first mosques (*see* MOSQUE) were merely rough enclosures for prayer.

In each country that they conquered they utilized the services of local architects and craftsmen to build their mosques and, as they became settled and prosperous, their palaces and tombs. Thus, distinctive regional 'schools' or variants of Muslim architecture grew up, each influenced by the local tradition. Existing buildings —many of them Roman—were freely despoiled to provide material for mosques, and occasionally old buildings were incorporated into their structure (e.g. at Damascus).

The following were the five chief regions of Muslim architecture:

(1) *Syro-Egyptian*, including Syria and Egypt. The finest of all Muslim mosques, perhaps, are to be found in Cairo, where they are of stone. Many antique Roman columns and capitals were used in the earliest mosques there. At Jerusalem the famous 'Dome of the Rock' shows Byzantine influence. In 1517 the Turks (see below) conquered Egypt, and interrupted the magnificent sequence of building which had continued in Cairo since the ninth century.

(2) *Turkish*, in which the great Byzantine church of S. Sophia at Constantinople influenced the design of all the large mosques subsequently built there (*see* BYZANTINE and TURKISH ARCHITECTURE).

(3) *North African* or '*Moorish*,' comprising the modern countries of Tunis, Algeria, Morocco, and most of Spain (*see* SPANISH ARCHITECTURE).

(4) *Persian*, including modern Iraq as well as Iran, where the earlier brick-vaulted buildings of the Sassanids (*see* PERSIAN ARCHITECTURE) influenced mosque construction.

(5) *Indian* (*see* INDIAN ARCHITECTURE). India was invaded by Muslims from Persia in 1193, when the city of Delhi was founded. Some of the earliest Muslim mosques in India closely resemble Persian examples; but, as Hindu craftsmen were employed, a curious medley of design resulted, culminating in the splendid mosques, tombs, and palaces built by the Mogul emperors during the sixteenth and seventeenth centuries, and constituting the 'Mogul' or 'Mughal' style.

In all the five regions mentioned above the mosque plan (*see*

MOSQUE) remained fairly constant, with certain local variations, and minarets (q.v.) were provided everywhere. Domes too were largely used, and the 'horseshoe' arch (*see* ARCH, TYPES OF) became one of the hall-marks of Muslim architecture. The ordinary pointed arch was used in Iraq by the Arabs in the eighth century, 300 years or so before it was introduced into western Europe. Ornamental lattices of stone, marble, wood, and stucco (*see* MUSHRABIYYAH and QAMARIYYAH) were used in all the countries mentioned above, because the glare of the sun discouraged the use of ordinary glazed windows. Marble inlay, for lining walls and covering floors, was freely employed, and in Persia, where the brick walls were considered unsightly, the ancient craft of glazed tiling was revived, and spread thence into India, Syria, and Turkey. Because the representation of animal forms in architectural ornament, painting, or sculpture was prohibited, the decoration of Muslim buildings was confined to geometrical patterns, which reached a high degree of complexity, skill, and beauty. A large number of Arabic terms used in Muslim architecture, for which no equivalent exists in English, will be found in this book.

See H. Saladin and G. Migeon, *Manuel d'Art Musulman*, 1907; M. S. Briggs, *Muhammadan Architecture in Egypt and Palestine*, 1924; E. Diez and H. Gluck, *Die Kunst des Islams*, 1925; M. S. Dimand, *Handbook of Mohammedan Decorative Art*, 1930; K. A. C. Creswell, *Early Muslim Architecture* (2 vols.), 1932, 1940, *The Muslim Architecture of Egypt*, vol. i, 1952, and *A Short Account of Early Muslim Architecture*, 1958.

Mycenaean Architecture, the style of primitive and pre-Hellenic architecture found at Mycenae in southern Greece, *c.* 1500–1000 B.C. *See* ARCHITECTURE, PERIODS OF, 1(*c*).

Mylne, Robert, F.R.S. (*b.* Edinburgh, 4 Jan. 1734; *d.* Great Amwell, Hertfordshire, 5 May 1811), architect and civil engineer, was the son of Thomas Mylne, city surveyor of Edinburgh, who trained him. He studied in Paris and Rome from 1754 to 1758, when he won the coveted gold medal for architecture awarded by the Accademia di S. Luca, Rome. He then returned home, and in 1760 won the important competition for Blackfriars Bridge, London. This was duly built, but was demolished and rebuilt a century later. Other bridges designed by him were at Welbeck (1764); Jamaica Street, Glasgow (1767–72); Newcastle upon Tyne (1774, since demolished); Hexham (1784); and Edinburgh (North Bridge, 1765–72). His other engineering work included alterations to the New River (from Hertfordshire to London), and part of the drainage of the Fens. As an architect he had a considerable practice, besides his appointment as surveyor to St Paul's Cathedral, 1766–1811.

Among his buildings were St Cecilia's Hall, Edinburgh (1762–3); additions to Northumberland House, London (1765); Almack's Rooms, London (1770); Clumber Park, Nottinghamshire (1770); City of London Lying-in Hospital (1770–3); Addington Lodge, Croydon (1772–9); Hospital at Belfast (1792).

See monograph by Sir A. E. Richardson, 1955.

N

Nailhead (Ornament), in English Romanesque architecture, an ornament somewhat resembling the square head of a nail.

Naos (Gk), the sanctuary of a Greek temple.

Narthex (Gk), a large porch or vestibule across the entrance end of a basilican church (q.v., *illustrated*). Access to the narthex was permitted to women and non-communicants.

Nash, John (*b*. London, 1752; *d*. East Cowes, 13 May 1835), architect; the leading figure in 'Regency' architecture, and a most picturesque character. After brief training under Sir Robert Taylor (q.v.) in 1767–8, he started work on his own account as a speculative builder, not as an architect, but was declared a bankrupt in 1783. He then went to Wales to make a fresh start, still as a builder, in 1784, but about 1787 made his first appearance as an architect in designing a bath-room (then something of a novelty) for a mansion near Carmarthen. He then proceeded to remodel or rebuild three jails: Carmarthen in 1789–92, Cardigan in 1793, and Hereford in 1794–6. Next came his rebuilding of the west front of St David's Cathedral, and its chapter-house (demolished in 1829). In 1794–5 he designed the Market House at Abergavenny, and in 1795–7 a swing-bridge over the River Teme at Stanford (demolished 1905). He then moved to London where, in partnership with Humphrey Repton, the landscape gardener (q.v.), he started architectural practice about 1796. During the next few years Nash and Repton built or altered a number of important houses, including Southgate Grove, Middlesex (1797); the Casina at Dulwich (1797, demolished 1906); Sundridge Park, Kent (1799); Luscombe Castle, Dawlish (1800); West Grinstead Park (*c*. 1806); Killy Moon in Ireland (1803); Longner Hall, Shrewsbury (*c*. 1806); Cronkhill near Shrewsbury; Southborough Place, Surbiton (1808); Rockingham, Ireland; and a mock-medieval mansion for Nash himself—East Cowes Castle, Isle of Wight (1798). Thanks to the beautiful and complacent wife whom he married in that year, Nash became an intimate friend and protégé of the Prince of Wales, afterwards George IV, for whom he built the Royal Lodge in Windsor Park, remodelled Carlton House, and in 1815–23 erected the notorious and eccentric Pavilion at Brighton. In 1806, abreast of his private practice, he had been appointed to a minor post under the Commissioners of Woods and Forests, which led to his greatest works: the laying out of Marylebone Park (now Regent's Park), Regent Street, Carlton House Terrace, and the adjoining streets; All Souls, Langham Place (1822); Buckingham Palace (1825); and the United Services Club (1827).

See monograph by J. N. Summerson, 1935.

Natatorium (Lat.), a swimming-bath or covered swimming-pool.

National Buildings Record (offices: 31 Chester Terrace, London, N.W.1) was founded in 1941, following action taken in the previous autumn at the R.I.B.A., when a conference decided to make a comprehensive collection of photographs of important buildings in England, in view of their liability to damage or destruction during the war.   The response to a public appeal resulted in a far greater response than could be effectively dealt with by the R.I.B.A., and thus a separate organization, with its own premises and staff, was established.   By 12 April 1958 the collection had reached the enormous total of 490,757 measured drawings and photographs, all efficiently filed and available for reference.

National Trust for Places of Historic Interest or Natural Beauty (offices: 42 Queen Anne's Gate, London, S.W.1) was founded in 1905 by the combined efforts of Miss Octavia Hill, Sir Robert Hunter, and Canon Rawnsley.   At first these enthusiastic idealists were mainly concerned with the saving of beautiful scenery from destruction, notably in the Lake District, but as time elapsed famous country houses came into the picture, and Barrington Court, Somerset, was acquired in 1907.   More recent acquisitions include Blickling Hall, Bodiam Castle, Ham House, Hatchlands, Lacock Abbey, Little Moreton Hall, Montacute House, Osterley Park, and Petworth House.

Nave (from Lat. *navis*, a ship), the body of a church, often with aisles (excluding the chancel and the transepts—if any).   One authority ascribes the curious derivation to the fact that a ship was sometimes used as the symbol of the church.   (*Illustrated* CATHEDRAL.)

Necessaria (Lat., necessary, unavoidable things), the latrines of a medieval monastery.   Cf. the Victorian euphemisms: 'lavatory' (q.v.) and 'article.'

Necking, a small convex moulding near the top of the shaft of a column, and below the capital.

Necropolis (Gk *nekros*, a corpse; *polis*, a town), a town of the dead, hence, a cemetery.

Neo-Grec (Fr.), or **Neo-Greek,** terms occasionally applied to any revival of classical Greek architecture.

Nepveu, Eugène Charles Frédéric (*b.* Paris, 14 July 1777; *d.* Versailles, 23 Sept. 1862), architect, was trained by Percier and Fontaine (qq.v.).   In 1807 he was given charge of various palaces belonging to the state, including Fontainebleau and Rambouillet. In that capacity he carried extensive remodelling at Versailles and Trianon; he also built the theatre at Compiègne.

Nepveu, or **Trinqueau, Pierre** (*d.* Chambord, 26 Aug. 1538), French architect or master-mason, appears to have worked at Blois before being summoned to Amboise by Charles VIII in 1490 to build his new château there.   His name then occurs in connection with the château at Chenonceaux, and more definitely at Chambord, but his share in the design of these great mansions remains obscure.

Nervi, Pier Luigi (b. Sondrio, 21 June 1891), Italian engineer and architect, graduated from the School of Engineering at Bologna in 1913. Among his highly original buildings are the Memorial Stadium at Florence, holding 35,000 persons (1932); hangars for aircraft at Orvieto (1936) and Orbetello (1941); exhibition halls in reinforced concrete at Turin (1947–50); salt warehouse at Tortona (1950); the Gatti textile factory at Rome (1951); buildings at the Lido di Roma; baths at Chianciano; tobacco factory at Bologna (1952); Palazzo della Sport, Rome (1957); joint architect of UNESCO Conference Building, Paris (1958); also of Palazzetto della Sport (1957) and of Flaminio Stadium, Rome (1959). Awarded R.I.B.A. Royal Gold Medal, 1960.

See monographs by G. C. Argan, 1955; E. N. Rogers, 1957; and A. L. Huxtable, 1960.

Nesfield, William Eden (b. Bath, 2 April 1835; d. Brighton, 25 Mar. 1888, architect. He was articled to his uncle Anthony Salvin (q.v.) and travelled abroad, a volume of his sketches from France and Italy being published in 1862. In that year he started practice, sharing rooms with R. Norman Shaw (q.v.) till 1868. His principal works were Cloverley Hall, Shropshire (1864); additions to Kinmel Park (1866); Holy Trinity Church, Bingley (1867); Leys Wood (1868); Farnham Royal House; Loughton Hall; Westcombe Park; and the restoration of a few churches; but his share in the improvement of taste in English domestic architecture was more considerable than the amount of his building might suggest.

Neumann, Johann Balthasar (b. Eger, Bohemia, Jan. 1687; d. Würzburg, 18 Aug. 1753), architect; a brilliant exponent of the Baroque style. He was trained in Würzburg, but his work was influenced by subsequent visits to Paris in 1723 and to Vienna in 1750. His immense practice in South Germany consisted mainly of mansions, monasteries, and churches. In Würzburg itself the remodelling of the great Schloss which he began in 1720 continued until shortly after his death. His other notable works included the remarkable staircase in the Schloss at Bruchsal (1731); the Benedictine Abbey on the Michaelsberg near Bamberg (1742–6); the great church at Vierzehnheiligen (1743–62); additions to the monastery at Banz (1752–62); the Jesuit church at Mainz (1742); and the Schloss at Brühl near Cologne (1743).

See monograph by M. H. von Freeden, 1953.

Neutra, Richard Josef (b. Vienna, 8 April 1892), architect, was trained at the Institute of Technology in Vienna; served in the First World War, and then worked in the office of a landscape architect, 1919–20. He next became an assistant to Erich Mendelsohn (q.v.) in Berlin; but in 1923 left Germany for the United States, where he was naturalized in 1929. He had then already started private practice at Los Angeles in 1926. His principal works include 'The Lovell Health House' at Los Angeles (1927); the Military Academy at Los Angeles; numerous country houses, schools, and experimental dwellings in California; housing estates in Texas; schools, hospitals, and health centres in Puerto Rico.

See monographs by W. Boesiger, 1950, and by B. Zevi, 1954.

Newel, or **Newel-post,** a stout post fixed at the head and foot of each flight of a 'newel staircase,' at the point where the stairs intersect a floor or a landing. The handrail and strings of the stair-case are framed into the newel. In Elizabethan and Jacobean mansions newel-posts are often elaborately carved. *See also* STAIR-CASE, *illustrated.*

Newton, Ernest, R.A. (*b.* London, 12 Sept. 1856; *d.* there, 25 Jan. 1922), architect; President R.I.B.A., 1914–16; Royal Gold Medallist, 1918. He was articled in 1873 to R. Norman Shaw (q.v.) and then remained with him as an assistant until 1879, when he started independent practice. His work included Martin's Bank, Bromley (1898), and St Swithin's Church, Hither Green (1892); but consisted chiefly of country houses, among them Buller's Wood at Chislehurst (1889); Red Court, Haslemere (1889); Steep Hill, Haslemere (1899). He illustrated these and many others in two published volumes: *A Book of Houses,* 1890, and *A Book of Country Houses,* 1903. After his death his son W. G. Newton (*d.* 1949) continued to carry on his practice, and in 1925 published *The Work of Ernest Newton.*

'New Towns.' The New Towns Act of 1946 empowered the Minister of Town and Country Planning (after holding a public inquiry if any objections were raised) to 'designate' the areas of new towns, and to appoint, in each case, a development corporation to undertake necessary housing, roads, etc. Between 1946 and 1949 eight new towns were designated in the London region, including some which had been previously recommended in the London County Council's *Greater London Plan,* 1944. These eight—all outside the 'Green Belt'—were Stevenage, Hemel Hempstead, Hatfield, and Welwyn Garden City in Hertfordshire; Basildon and Harlow in Essex; Crawley in Sussex; and Bracknell in Berkshire. In each was an existing urban or village nucleus. (These eight do not include the so-called 'quasi-satellites' planted inside the precious 'Green Belt' by the London County Council immediately after the Second World War). Outside the London region six more new towns were designated: at Corby (Northamptonshire); Newton Aycliffe and Peterlee (County Durham); Cwmbran (Monmouthshire); Cumber-nauld, East Kilbride, and Glenrothes (Scotland). *See also* TOWN-PLANNING.

Niche, an ornamental recess in a wall, usually with an arched top; often but not invariably, intended to contain a statue. *See also* MIHRAB.

Niemeyer, Oscar (*b.* Rio de Janeiro, 15 Dec. 1907), Brazilian architect. After graduating from the School of Fine Art at Rio in 1934 he worked as assistant to L. Costa, in charge of historical monuments, and then with 'Le Corbusier' (q.v.) on designs for the university at Rio. His own buildings include a day nursery at Rio (1937); the Brazilian Pavilion at the New York World's Fair, in collaboration with Costa and Wiener (1938); hotel at Oura Preto (1940); Athletic Centre, Rio (1937–43); Education Offices, Rio (1937–1943); casino, church, yacht club, etc., at Pampulha (1943); Muni-cipal Theatre, Belo Horizonte (1943); offices of the *Tribuna Popular,*

Rio (1943); head offices of the Boavista Bank, Rio; Academy for Boys, Cataguazes; Hotel Regente Cavea, Rio (1949); exhibition halls for the São Paolo Centenary Exhibition (1951); Montreal Building (twenty storeys), São Paolo (1951); hospital at Rio (1952); television stations for Brazil (1952-4); flats for the International Reconstruction Fair at Berlin (1955-7), and for the Getulio Vargas Foundation (1955); numerous buildings—including the President's palace, houses of parliament, government offices, cathedral, and hotel—in the new capital, Brasilia (1958 onwards).

See monograph by S. Papadaki (3rd ed.), 1956.

'No-fines' Concrete, a mixture of concrete consisting of coarse aggregate and cement, without the normal admixture of sand.

Nonconformist Church Architecture, in Britain, has a history of nearly four centuries. Although the predecessors of modern Presbyterians, Congregationalists, and Baptists had become numerous by the end of the reign of Elizabeth I, their only surviving place of worship that can be attributed to the sixteenth century is the quaint little thatched chapel at Horningsham in Wiltshire, built about 1566 for the use of Scottish masons then working at the neighbouring mansion of Longleat. During the first half of the next century, in spite of much persecution, a few more small buildings were erected, including the Congregational chapel at Halesworth, Suffolk (1647, but somewhat altered internally). There was a temporary halt at the Restoration; but from 1688 onwards, when toleration came into force, great activity followed, and many hundreds of Congregational, Baptist, and Presbyterian (afterwards Unitarian) chapels were built. Some of these have architectural pretensions, and are more or less in the style of Wren's City churches. Examples are Norwich 'Old Meeting' (1693); Friar Street Chapel, Ipswich (1700); Churchgate Street Chapel, Bury St Edmunds (1711); Mary Street Chapel, Taunton (1721); Underbank Chapel, Stannington, Yorkshire (1742); Lyme Regis Congregational Chapel (1750-5); and the Octagon Chapel, Norwich (1754-6). Wesley's Chapel, City Road, London (1777), marks the advent of Methodism.

Most of these buildings were oblong on plan, with a high pulpit in the centre of one of the longer sides, and the communion table below it. Galleries were usual, but organs were seldom provided (*see* ORGAN). This type of meeting-house or 'chapel' (q.v.) continued in vogue up to the Gothic Revival (q.v.) in the nineteenth century, after which the various Free Churches (except the Quakers) tended to abandon their architectural tradition and to imitate Gothic models, sometimes with deplorable results; but during the twentieth century their taste, like that of Anglicans and Roman Catholics, has followed more original lines. Among the Quaker meeting-houses, that at Jordans in Buckinghamshire is one of the oldest (1688) and most picturesque.

See R. P. Jones, *Nonconformist Church Architecture*, 1914; A. L. Drummond, *The Church Architecture of Protestantism*, 1934; M. S. Briggs, *Puritan Architecture*, 1946; E. B. Perkins and A. Hearn, *The Methodist Church Builds Again*, 1946.

Norman Architecture, *see* ENGLISH and ROMANESQUE ARCHITECTURE.

Norwegian Architecture, *see* SCANDINAVIAN ARCHITECTURE.

Nosing, the rounded or moulded projecting edge of a step in a staircase.

Nymphaeum (Lat., from Gk *numphaion*, literally 'a temple of the nymphs,' or the Muses), a Roman pleasure-house, usually adorned with fountains, flowers, and statues.

O

Oast, or **Oast-house** (from Lat. *aestus*, heat, fire), a kiln for drying hops. Most surviving examples are in Kent and Sussex, some of them still serving their original purpose, but others have been recently converted with great ingenuity into picturesque but inconvenient week-end residences.

Obelisk, a tall tapering shaft, square on plan, generally monolithic (q.v.) and of granite, which was often used in pairs at the entrance to ancient Egyptian temples. The tallest examples in Egypt are about 100 feet high. Many have been brought to Europe and re-erected. Of these the most famous are in St Peter's Piazza, Rome (83 feet high); on the Thames Embankment in London (Cleopatra's Needle, 68 feet high); and (its twin) in Central Park, New York. There is another in Paris; and, among several more in Rome, a miniature example, set by Bernini (q.v.) on the back of an elephant, outside the church of S. Maria sopra Minerva.

See monograph by H. H. Gorringe, 1882.

Oblique Arch, *see* SKEW ARCH.

Oblique Projection, a method of pictorial projection, not much used by architects, in which the elevation, section, or plan is first drawn; and then parallel projectors, generally at 30 degrees or 45 degrees, represent the other sides of the solid. (*Illustrated* DRAWING.)

Octastyle, in classical architecture, a portico which has eight columns in a row. (*Illustrated* TEMPLE.)

Oculus (Lat., an eye), either (i) a round or 'bull's-eye' window; or (ii) in classical architecture, the eye or disk at the centre of the spiral volute (q.v.) of the Ionic capital.

Odeion (Gk), **Odeum** (Lat.), or **Odéon** (Fr.), in Greek or Roman architecture, a building for musical performances.

Œil-de-Bœuf (Fr., a bull's eye), a circular window. *See* BULL'S-EYE WINDOW.

Ogee Arch, a pointed arch of double curvature, the lower curve being convex and the upper curve concave, used in late Gothic and Muslim architecture. (*Illustrated* ARCH, TYPES OF.)

Ogee Moulding, a moulding of double curvature. If the convex curve is below and the concave above, it is sometimes called a Cyma Recta (q.v.); if concave below and convex above, a Cyma Reversa (q.v.).

Ogival Arch, strictly speaking, the same as an ogee arch (q.v.), but the term is often loosely applied to any pointed arch. (*Illustrated* ARCH, TYPES OF.)

Ogive (rare), strictly, an arch having a double or ogee curve; but the term is sometimes loosely applied to any pointed arch.

Okel (Arabic), *see* WAKALAH.

Open Well Stairs, a staircase constructed around a rectangular open well. (*Illustrated* STAIRCASE.)

Opisthodomos (Gk), or **Opisthodomus** (Lat.), an open porch at the rear of a Greek temple; usually a duplicate of the *pronaos* or front porch. (*Illustrated* TEMPLE.)

Optical Refinements. In Hellenic Greek architecture, especially at the Parthenon, subtle and imperceptible curves were introduced in the tapering of columns (entasis, q.v.), and in apparently level surfaces such as the platforms of temples, to correct optical illusions. These refinements were described in detail by F. C. Penrose (q.v.) in 1851. Sir E. Lutyens introduced similar subtleties into his Cenotaph (q.v.) in Whitehall, London. On the other hand, optical illusions were deliberately contrived by Borromini (q.v.) in the Palazzo Spada, Rome (1631–6), and by Bernini (q.v.) in his Scala Regia at the Vatican, Rome (1663).

Opus Alexandrinum (Lat., Alexandrine work), paving of variously coloured marbles, used especially in Italy.

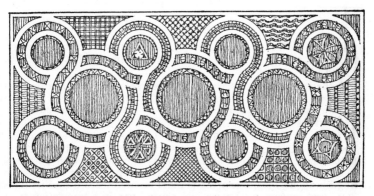

OPUS ALEXANDRINUM: from church of S. Prassede, Rome (13th century)

Opus Incertum (Lat.), in Roman architecture, concrete walling faced with irregularly shaped and sized stones. (*Illustrated* p. 232).

Opus Quadratum (Lat.), in Roman architecture, walling of squared stones.

Opus Reticulatum (literally 'net work,' from Lat. *rete*, a net), Roman concrete walling faced with squared stones arranged diagonally like the meshes of a net. (*Illustrated* p. 232).

Orangery, a building having large windows on the south side, used in northern climates for growing oranges, e.g. in the palaces of Hampton Court, Kensington, and Versailles—all built between *c.* 1680 and *c.* 1710.

OPUS INCERTUM   *OPUS RETICULATUM*

Oratory (Lat. *orare*, to pray).   (1) A small chapel for private prayer.
(2) A larger church of 'the Congregation of the Fathers of the
Oratory.'

Orchestra.   (1) In a classical theatre, a circular space in front of
the stage, where the chorus sang and danced.   (2) In a modern
theatre, a narrow space in front of the stage and the footlights,
reserved for an orchestra or band.

Orders of Architecture, The (from Lat. *ordo*, rank, row, series).
The term 'Orders,' which looms so large in Greek, Roman, and
Renaissance architecture, and which has reference to some buildings
in every modern town, appears to have been first introduced into
English about 1563, when the manual on architecture by Vitruvius
(q.v., first century B.C.) came into general use, in a translation from
the Latin.   He himself uses the words '*dorico genere*' (not '*dorico
ordine*') to describe the Doric Order.

In brief, his system provides rules for architectural design based
upon the proportions of three standard types of columns, together
with their bases, their capitals, and the entablature (horizontal
beams) which they support.   His three types of columns are the
Doric, Ionic, and Corinthian Orders, named respectively after the
three regions of Greece—Doris, Ionia, Corinthos—in which they
originated.

The Doric Order is the oldest and sturdiest of the three.   Its
fluted column has a capital consisting of a flat abacus resting
upon an echinus moulding.   Below the latter are a series of
fillets or annulets; then a space (*trachelion*); and, below that,
a groove (*hypotrachelion*).   The entablature (q.v.) consists of three

members: architrave, frieze, and cornice. Of these the plain architrave is the lowest. The frieze is divided into square panels ('metopes') by grooved 'triglyphs,' representing, in stone, the ends of beams in primitive timber construction. Beneath each triglyph is a row of 'drops' (*guttae*).

The Ionic Order has a slenderer column, and a curious capital with spiral 'volutes' (q.v.) beneath its abacus. The Corinthian capital, slenderer still, has a capital decorated with carved leaves of acanthus (q.v.). It was seldom used by the Greeks.

The Romans borrowed all three Orders, making certain modifications in their design, and specially favouring the Corinthian. They also introduced two additional types—the Tuscan Order, a simplified version of the Doric, and the Composite Order, a rather clumsy combination of Ionic and Corinthian. When all these Roman types were revived at the Renaissance (q.v.), pattern-books of the Orders were produced in quantities in western Europe. They greatly influenced architecture in England and elsewhere up to the Gothic Revival (q.v.) in the nineteenth century, and even to-day architectural students are required to possess a sound knowledge of the Orders.

Organ (from Gk *organon*), a musical instrument; more specifically, a musical instrument which has pipes supplied with wind through bellows operated manually or by mechanical means, and sounded by means of keys, pressed down to operate trackers and pallets. Organs

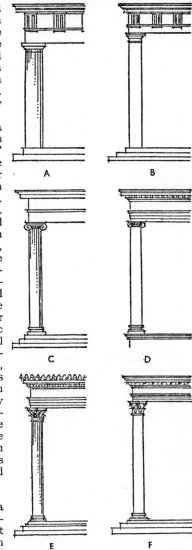

ORDERS: THE CLASSICAL (GREEK AND ROMAN) ORDERS OF ARCHITECTURE

(A) *Greek Doric;* (B) *Roman Doric;* (C) *Greek Ionic;* (D) *Roman Ionic;* (E) *Greek Corinthian;* (F) *Roman Corinthian*

of a sort were used as early as the second century B.C., but were banned by the early Christians on account of pagan associations. They slowly came into use in churches during the eighth to eleventh centuries A.D. Under an Order of Queen Elizabeth I (1563), they were condemned as 'superstitious'; but a proposal to remove them from all parish churches was defeated by one vote in the Lower House of Convocation. Nevertheless many were removed, and in one Yorkshire village, in 1572, the parishioners hid the 120 pipes of their organ when its destruction seemed imminent. Organs came into more general use during the age of Wren (q.v.), when some of his churches had instruments designed by Renatus Harris and 'Father' Smith, and organ cases richly carved. Yet even so late as 1708, in London itself, only twelve organs are known to have been installed in some fifty new churches, while most churches elsewhere had nothing more than a fiddle, a string band, or a tuning-fork. Wren favoured the placing of the organ in a western gallery. Oliver Cromwell maintained an organist in his own house. Though Isaac Watts was one of our greatest hymnologists, organs were hardly ever provided in Nonconformist 'chapels' of the seventeenth and eighteenth centuries.

ORIEL WINDOW. Sherborne (15th century)

Oriel Window, a window projecting from the wall face of the upper storey of a building, and supported on brackets or corbelling. Oriels were much used in late Gothic and Tudor civil architecture.

Orientation of buildings (from Lat. *oriens, orientem,* the rising sun), either (i) the position or 'aspect' of a building in relation to the points of the compass; or (ii) the siting of a church with its main axis east–west, and its chancel and high altar at the east end. This latter practice is not, however, universal. The earliest Christian churches were 'oriented' westwards, as the most famous of them, St Peter's, Rome, still is. In rebuilding the London City churches after the Great Fire of 1666, Wren ignored the eastward orientation when a cramped site or other practical considerations made it inconvenient. Among Muslims, the orientation of their mosques is always in the direction of Mecca, e.g. in Morocco it is eastwards, in Singapore westwards, in Istanbul southwards, in Zanzibar northwards, at Woking south-east. *See* MIHRAB.

Orme, Philibert de L', *see* DE L'ORME, P.

Orthographic Projection (Gk *orthos,* straight, correct; *graphos,* writing; drawing), the method of projection used by all architects

for working drawings. Objects are represented by plans and elevations, points being projected at right angles to the planes of projection. (*Illustrated* DRAWING.)

Östberg, Ragnar (*b.* Stockholm, 14 July 1866; *d.* there, 6 Feb.
1945), Swedish architect; R.I.B.A. Royal Gold Medallist, 1926. He
was trained in Stockholm at the academy and the technical school,
travelled and studied abroad, 1896–9, and returned to Stockholm in
1900. He became Professor of Architecture in 1921, and a member of
the academy in 1922. He was one of the Advisory Committee for the
completion of the League of Nations Building at Geneva. He is
chiefly known for his masterpiece, the Stockholm City Hall, 1911–23.
Among his other buildings were the Stockholm High School for
Boys; the Maritime Museum (Sjöhistoriker Museet) at Stockholm,
1938; the theatre at Umea; and a college at Uppsala University.

Oubliette (Fr., from *oublier*, to forget), in medieval castles, a
secret dungeon, entered only through a trap-door from above, into
which prisoners were thrown and then 'forgotten.'

Oud, Jacobus Johannes Pieter (*b.* Purmerend, Holland, 9 Feb.
1890), Dutch architect. He was trained in Amsterdam and Munich,
then travelled in Italy, and started independent practice in Leyden.
His first commission was a cinema at Purmerend. From 1918 to
1933 he was city architect of Rotterdam, where he carried out
several housing schemes and
designed some public buildings.
Other work included houses
at Hook of Holland (1925–7)
and at the Stuttgart Exhibition (1927); also the Apostolic
Church at Rotterdam (1929).
See monograph by G.
Veronesi, 1953.

Overdoor, a small pediment
(q.v.) over a doorway.

Overhang, in old timber-
framed houses, the projecting
upper storeys, usually supported
by cantilevers or brackets. The
same method has recently been
adopted in many buildings of
steel and concrete framing.

*OVERDOOR. Clifford's Inn, London
(c. 1687)*

Oversailing Course, a course of brickwork or masonry projecting
over the main face of a wall.

Overspill, in modern town-planning, a term recently invented to
describe the number of persons in any specific area who are surplus
to an ideal density of population in that area.

Ovolo Moulding (Med. It. *ovolo*, dim. of *ovo*, an egg; from Lat.
ovum, an egg), a convex moulding used in all periods of architecture.
The Greek ovolo or *echinus* (q.v.) was elliptical in section; the Roman
was a quarter-circle. (*Illustrated* MOULDINGS, CLASSICAL.)

P

Pagoda (Port. *pagode*, apparently a corruption of an Indian word), a temple or sacred tower, usually Buddhist and of pyramidal form, built in a series of diminishing stages with boldly projecting roofs. Most of them are richly carved, and sometimes decorated with colour and gilding. They are found especially in China, Japan, and Burma. (*See* CHINESE and JAPANESE ARCHITECTURE.) In Kew Gardens, near London, is the famous 'Chinese Pagoda' designed in 1761 by Sir William Chambers (q.v.) who had travelled and studied in China as a youth, and published in 1757 a book entitled *Designs of Chinese Buildings*, etc.

Pain, family of English architects (to be distinguished from the PAINE family—see next item). The most notable member was WILLIAM PAIN (*c.* 1730–*c.* 1790), who styled himself 'architect and joiner' or 'architect and carpenter,' and published, between 1763 and 1786, a whole series of manuals, the first entitled *The Builder's Pocket Treasure; or, Palladio delineated and explained*, while the last was *The British Palladio; or Builder's General Assistant: all the Rules of Architecture, Designs for Houses, etc., with Prices*. (A selection from his designs was reprinted and published in 1946.)

Of his sons, JAMES, GEORGE, and HENRY became pupils of John Nash (q.v.), who enabled them to settle in Ireland, where they practised as architects or builders indiscriminately, building several bridges, jails, churches, and mansions, including Mitchelstown Castle, near Cork, 1823.

Paine, James (*b. c.* 1716; *d.* in France, autumn 1789), architect. Little is known of his early life, studies, or training, but he himself stated that at the age of nineteen he 'was entrusted to conduct a building of consequence in the West Riding of the County of York.' This was Nostell Priory, an enormous mansion begun in 1735. It was quickly followed by a stream of other lucrative commissions, so that, by the middle of the eighteenth century, Paine and Sir R. Taylor were rival practitioners on the grand scale, until they made way for Adam and Chambers and James Wyatt (qq.v.). Many of Paine's lengthy list of mansions have been demolished, but the following are a few specially interesting survivals of his work: Richmond Bridge, Surrey (1774–7, since widened); Heath House, Wakefield (1744–5); Belford, Northumberland (1754–6); stables and bridge at Chatsworth (1758–62); Stockeld Park, Yorkshire (1758–63); Brocket Hall, Hertfordshire (1760–70); central block of Kedleston Hall, Derby (1757–61).

His only son JAMES (1745–1829) was trained as an architect and studied in Rome, but seems to have been content to live on his father's considerable fortune.

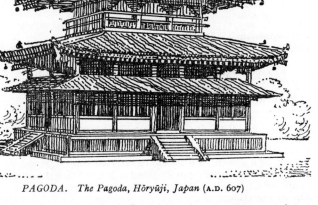

*PAGODA. The Pagoda, Hōryūji, Japan (*A.D.* 607)*

Palace (from Lat. *palatium*, derived from the proper name of one of the 'Seven Hills of Rome,' the *Mons Palatinus* on which stood the houses of the Caesars: hence, an imperial dwelling), in modern speech, the official residence of a sovereign or other ruler of a nation, or of an archbishop or bishop.   Because such a building was often lavishly decorated, the irony of applying the term to a 'gin-palace' is obvious.   (Cf. also the 'People's Palace' in the East End of London, 1885.)   In Italy the name *palazzo* is applied to the fine old town houses belonging to the heads of noble families, many of whom bear the title of 'Prince.'

Palaestra (Lat., from Gk *palaiein*, to wrestle), a gymnasium or school of wrestling.

Palladian Architecture, English architecture of the late Renaissance, designed according to the principles of the Italian architect Palladio (q.v.).   *See* ENGLISH ARCHITECTURE, 5(*a*).

Palladian Motif (from the French term *Motif Palladio*), the use in design of a central arched opening between two flanking rectangular openings spanned by an entablature.   This combination of architectural elements was, however, practised by the Romans and by early Renaissance architects in Italy long before the time of Palladio (q.v.).

Palladio, Andrea (*b.* Vicenza, 30 Nov. 1518; *d.* there, 19 Aug. 1580), Italian architect and writer on architecture.   He had a great influence on the course of architecture in England and other European countries for two centuries after his death, i.e. from the early work of Inigo Jones (q.v.) to the last buildings of Sir William Chambers (q.v.).   From 1540 to 1550 he made an intensive study of the ancient buildings of Rome; and it was his book, *I Quattro Libri dell' Architettura*, published in 1570, and translated into many languages, that was the cause of his influence abroad.   His own buildings, however, were of great importance in themselves.   In his native town of Vicenza he built the Palazzi della Ragione (1549 onwards), Porto (1556), Thiene (1556–65), Valmarana (1556), Chierigati (1560), Barbaran (1570), Prefettizio (1571), and Giulio Porto—the 'Casa del Diavolo' (1570); in the neighbourhood, the villas of Foscari ('Malcontenta'), Rotonda (1567), and Repetta; in Venice, the churches of S. Giorgio Maggiore (1560–75) and Il Redentore (1576).
    See monographs by B. F. Fletcher, 1902; F. Burger, 1909; C. Gurlitt (2nd ed.), 1920; G. K. Loukomski, 1927; A. Melani, 1928; R. Pane, 1948.

Pane, a single sheet of window glass.

Panelling (from Old Fr. *panel*, a piece of cloth, parchment, or wood), in architecture, from medieval times onwards, a series of thin sheets of wood ('panels') framed together by means of stouter strips of wood—vertical ('styles') and horizontal ('rails')—to form either a door, or a screen, or a lining for internal walls.   Panelling was first used as a wall covering in England in the thirteenth century, when a chamber at Windsor Castle was lined with imported Norway pine. Up to the sixteenth century the framing was almost as massive as in half-timber construction; then it was progressively lightened until, by the middle of the century, the thickness of the framing was reduced to an inch, and the thin oak panels were also reduced in size. During the seventeenth to eighteenth centuries there was a complete

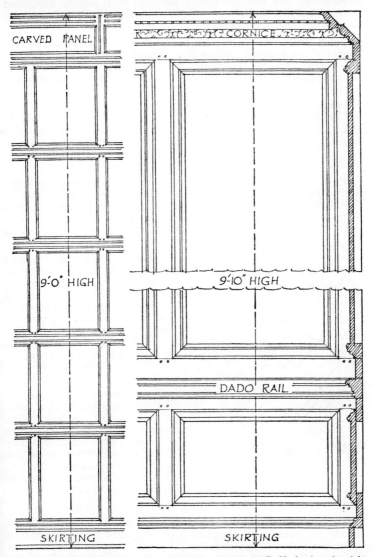

CARVED PANEL

9'-0" HIGH

SKIRTING

CORNICE

9'-10" HIGH

DADO RAIL

SKIRTING

PANELLING, ENGLISH OAK. Left, from Swinsty Hall, Yorks. (1579); right, from Clifford's Inn, London (1686–8), now in the Victoria and Albert Museum. In both examples the framing is secured at the joints by oak pegs, as shown above

reversal of this process: panels became much larger, mouldings became heavier, and pine gradually replaced oak. *See* BOLECTION MOULDING, DOOR, FIELDED PANELS, LINENFOLD PANELLING.

Panel Walls, in very modern buildings, 'walls' consisting of thin sheets of any material capable of resisting the entry of rain or excessive thermal changes, but incapable of affording structural support, which is provided by a framework of concrete or steel stanchions and girders. *See also* CLADDING.

Pantheon (Lat., from Gk *pan*, all; *theos*, a god), a temple dedicated to all the gods; more specifically, the famous temple in Rome so dedicated, and built about 25 B.C. The name was inappropriately applied to a place of amusement in Oxford Street, London, built in 1772 by James Wyatt (q.v.), destroyed by fire in 1792, rebuilt, and finally demolished in 1937.

Panthéon (Fr. form of Lat. *Pantheon*, q.v.), the name given to the church of Ste Geneviève in Paris, built in 1757–90 from designs by Soufflot (q.v.), and secularized in 1791, when the Revolutionary Convention decided to dedicate it to the memory of the illustrious dead of the revolution. It is still secularized.

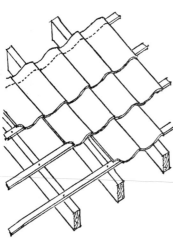

Pan-tile, a clay roofing tile of curved section, resembling a flattened S. Pan-tiles were the traditional form of roofing in East Anglia up to the nineteenth century, but are now seldom used except for farm buildings, etc., although many modern patterns are weather proof and of pleasing appearance. Glazed pan-tiles are obtainable.

Pantry (from Old Fr. *paneterie*, a bread-room), originally a room for storing bread, but now a room furnished with a sink, where table silver, glass, and china may be washed; sometimes called 'the butler's pantry,' whereas the store for food in a modern house is called the 'larder' (q.v.).

PAN-TILES: also showing rafters and battens

Papier Mâché (Fr., chewed paper), *see* CARTON PIERRE.

Papworth, family of English architects, etc. (eighteenth to nineteenth centuries). Of this numerous clan four members attained some distinction in architecture: (1) JOHN BUONARROTI PAPWORTH (1775–1847) designed several mansions near London; the Rotunda, St James's Church, and the layout of the Montpellier Estate—all at Cheltenham; carried out much landscape gardening; became architect to the king in 1820, director of the Government School of

Design in 1836, and one of the founders of the R.I.B.A. in 1834. (2) GEORGE PAPWORTH (1781–1855), his younger brother and pupil, settled in Dublin and created a large practice there. (3) JOHN WOODY PAPWORTH (1820–70) and (4) WYATT PAPWORTH (1822–94), sons of John Buonarroti, jointly founded in 1848 the Architectural Publication Society, which published during the years 1853–92 the massive eleven folio volumes of *The Dictionary of Architecture*, and jointly acted as editors.

Paradisus (Lat.), *see* PARVISE.

Parapet (from It. *parare*, to protect; *petto*, the breast), originally a breastwork in fortifications; later, as in modern usage, a low wall around a roof or platform, to prevent people falling over the edge.

Paraskenion (Gk), in an ancient Greek theatre, one of the wings of the *scena* (q.v.) projecting into the orchestra.

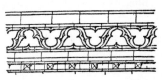

PARAPET. Above, from Heckington Church, Lincs. (1345–80); *below, from Castle Ashby, Northants.* (1572)

Parclose Screen, in medieval architecture, a screen dividing a chantry chapel or a tomb from the body of a church.

Pargetting, or **Parging** (probably from Old Fr. *parjeter*, or *pargeter*, to throw or cast, over a surface). (1) In traditional English building, and especially in the eastern counties, the covering of the exterior (including the timbers) with a tough plaster of lime mixed with ox-hair; sometimes decorated in patterns made with a comb. (2) In modern building the lining of flues with mortar, giving a smooth surface to facilitate sweeping and also reducing risks of fire reaching any adjoining timbers.

Parlour (from Fr. *parler*, to talk), a room for talking in, first applied to such a room in a monastery or an inn; then to a family sitting-room in a dwelling-house; also used for the 'mayor's parlour' in a modern town hall. (*Illustrated* HOUSE.)

Parquet Flooring, a thin layer of small hardwood blocks, about ¼ inch thick, laid in glue on an ordinary boarded floor. The term is sometimes applied, quite wrongly, to wood-block flooring laid on concrete.

Part, in formal classical architecture, one-thirtieth part of a module (q.v.).

Parthenon (from Gk *parthenos*, a virgin), the name of a famous temple at Athens, dedicated to the goddess Athena Parthenos, and built about 490 B.C. from the designs of the architects Ictinus and Callicrates (qq.v.). It measures about 100 feet by about 230 feet, and is regarded as the finest temple of the Greek Doric Order. It is notable not only for the excellence of its general design, but also for its optical refinements (q.v.), the subtlety of which has never been surpassed in architectural history, and which were first described accurately by John Pennethorne (q.v.) in 1844, and later by F. C. Penrose (q.v.) in 1878. (*See* TEMPLE for plan.)

Party Wall, a wall, jointly owned, which separates two adjacent buildings. An elaborate mass of legislation and procedure exists for dealing with any proposal by either of the adjoining owners to raise, underpin, or thicken the wall. One purpose of these regulations is to ensure that the risk of fire passing from one property to the other is reduced to a minimum.

Parvise (from Lat. *paradisus*, an enclosed garden), an enclosed space in front of a church; as formerly existed in front of St Paul's Cathedral, London. To describe a room over a church porch as a 'parvise' is incorrect.

PATERA

Patera (Lat.), a circular ornamental sinking (resembling a dish) in any plane surface. (The other meaning of the word is 'dish.')

Patina (Lat., possibly with same derivation as *patera*, q.v.), originally a greenish film or incrustation that appears on very old bronze vessels; later the term has been loosely applied to the various changes of colour and texture produced on the surface of materials by weathering.

Patio (Sp.), in a Spanish or Latin-American house, an inner court-yard, corresponding to the Italian *cortile*.

Pattern, a term occasionally used in the sixteenth and seventeenth centuries as a synonym for an architect's plan. In the eighteenth century 'pattern-books' of designs for details of mantelpieces, balusters, cornices, etc., all based on the principles of revived Roman architecture, were in common use by building craftsmen in Britain and America. For some of their compilers *see* HALFPENNY, LANGLEY, PAIN.

Pavilion (from Fr. *pavillon*, a tent). (1) Originally a large tent or marquee used for important occasions. (2) A lightly constructed and often ornamental building on a sports ground, e.g. a cricket pavilion. (3) An ornamental summer-house in a nobleman's park. (4) A projecting feature at the end of a classical façade. (5) A detached block or unit of a modern hospital or sanatorium, isolated for medical reasons.

Paxton, Sir Joseph, M.P. (*b.* Milton Bryan, Bedfordshire, 3 Aug. 1801; *d.* Sydenham, London, 8 June 1865), landscape gardener, engineer, and architect, began his career as a gardener's apprentice. In 1826 he became foreman gardener at Chatsworth to the Duke of Devonshire, for whom he designed several greenhouses, including a conservatory 300 feet long. He also constructed some fountains in the park, and remodelled the villages of Chatsworth and Edensor in

1839–41. This work led to a personal friendship with the duke, and they travelled abroad together. Paxton, against 233 competitors, won the competition for the great building of the 1851 Exhibition, and then superintended the demolition of that gigantic greenhouse and its re-erection in 1853–4 at Sydenham as the 'Crystal Palace.' He designed several other buildings.

See monograph by V. R. Markham, 1935.

Pearce, Sir Edward (*d.* Stillorgan, County Dublin, 16 Nov. 1733), military engineer and architect, served in the Army as a captain of dragoons, and was elected a member of the Irish Parliament in 1727. Three years later he succeeded Thomas Burgh as director-general of buildings and fortifications in Ireland. In that capacity he completed Burgh's designs for the Parliament House, now Bank of Ireland, in Dublin (1729), but was unable to finish the building before his death. He also designed the theatre in Aungier Street, Dublin (1732).

Pearson, John Loughborough, R.A. (*b.* Brussels, 5 July 1817; *d.* London, 11 Dec. 1897), architect, a prominent figure of the Gothic Revival; awarded the R.I.B.A. Royal Gold Medal in 1880. After being articled in Durham in 1831, he worked as assistant in the offices of A. Salvin (q.v.) and P. Hardwick (q.v.), and started independent practice in 1843. His first commissions were for small churches in Yorkshire: Ellerker (1843); Elloughton and Wouldby (1844); Ellerton and North Ferriby (1846). He then developed a large London practice, mainly ecclesiastical. This included several London churches: Holy Trinity, Bessborough Gardens (1850); St Peter, Vauxhall (*c.* 1859); St Augustine, Kilburn (*c.* 1870); St John, Red Lion Square (1874, gutted in the Second World War). His greatest buildings were Truro Cathedral (1879–87) and Brisbane Cathedral, opened 1901. He restored Westminster Abbey, Westminster Hall, and the cathedrals of Bristol, Canterbury, Chichester, Exeter, Lincoln, and Rochester. Other work included the Astor Estate Office on the Victoria Embankment, London; and extensions of Emmanuel and Sidney Sussex Colleges—both at Cambridge.

Pebble-dash, an alternative name for ROUGH-CAST (q.v.).

Pedestal, in classical architecture, the base supporting a column, statue, or obelisk.

Pediment, in classical architecture, the triangular end or gable of a building with a low-pitched roof; sometimes filled with sculpture, e.g. at the Parthenon, Athens. (*Illustrated* ACROTERION.)

Pele, or **Peel-tower,** one of the massive towers or keeps built in the border counties of England and Scotland, especially during the sixteenth century, as a defence against border raids.

Pendant (Fr., from *pendre,* to hang). (1) In late Gothic architecture, an ornamental terminal suspended from a fan-vault (q.v.) or from an open timber roof. (2) In Jacobean architecture, an ornamental terminal on the foot of a newel-post in a staircase, or beneath the ends of an overhanging gable in a timber-framed house.

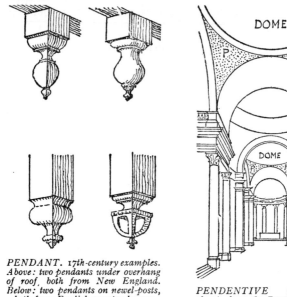

PENDANT. 17th-century examples.
Above: two pendants under overhang
of roof, both from New England.
Below: two pendants on newel-posts,
both from English country houses

PENDENTIVE   (marked   P
above), from the Panthéon at Paris

Pendentive, in the construction of a dome resting upon a square base, the spherical triangle formed between each pair of supporting arches.

Pennethorne, Sir James (*b.* Worcester, 4 June 1801; *d.* Malden, Surrey, 1 Sept. 1871), architect; awarded the R.I.B.A. Royal Gold Medal in 1865.   He was remotely related, it is believed, to the wife of John Nash (q.v.); and Nash certainly brought him up in childhood as an adopted son, and trained him in his office between 1820 and 1822.   Pennethorne then worked for two years under Augustus Pugin (q.v.), travelled in Italy, etc., 1824–6, and returned to Nash in 1826 as chief assistant.   When Nash retired in 1832, Pennethorne was appointed by the Commissioners of Woods and Forests to continue various schemes for improving London.   His work comprised New Oxford Street, Endell Street, Cranbourn Street, Garrick Street, and Commercial Street (Stepney); also the laying out of Battersea Park, Victoria Park, Kennington Park, Finsbury Park, and the Chelsea Embankment.   His numerous buildings included the west wing of Somerset House, the Geological Museum in Piccadilly (since demolished), and the Civil Service Commissioners' offices in Burlington Gardens.

Pennethorne, John (*b.* Worcester, 4 Jan. 1808; *d.* Isle of Wight, 20 Jan. 1888), architect, younger brother of Sir James (q.v.), was likewise trained by John Nash (q.v.).   He travelled abroad in 1830–5, and made a significant contribution to architectural scholarship by his study of optical refinements in the Parthenon at Athens and also in certain Egyptian temples. He made a second visit to Greece in 1837, to verify his conclusions, which he published in 1844 as a pamphlet, *Elements and Mathematical Principles of the Greek Architects*. His work was followed up in Athens by F. C. Penrose (q.v.); and in 1878 Pennethorne published an important folio on *The Geometry and Optics of Ancient Architecture*, embodying all the information then available.

Penrose, Francis Cranmer, F.R.S. (*b.* Bracebridge, Lincolnshire, 29 Oct. 1817; *d.* London, 15 Dec. 1903), architect, archaeologist, and astronomer; President R.I.B.A., 1894–6; R.I.B.A. Royal Gold Medallist, 1883. After his training from 1835 to 1839 in the office of Edward Blore (q.v.), he entered Magdalene College, Cambridge, and in 1842 was appointed 'travelling bachelor' of the university. While he was still engaged in study under that award, the Society of Dilettanti invited him, in 1844, to test on the spot, in Athens, the accuracy of the remarkable theories then recently advanced by John Pennethorne (q.v.) in his pamphlet. Penrose's response took the form of a folio entitled *Investigation of the Principles of Athenian Architecture: Optical Refinements in the Construction of Ancient Buildings at Athens*, published in 1851 and twice reprinted. From 1852 to 1897 he was surveyor to St Paul's Cathedral, London, and in 1882 he designed the premises of the British School of Archaeology at Athens, of which he was director in 1886–7, and again in 1890–1.

Pentastyle (Gk *penta*, five; *stulos*, a column), a Greek temple with a portico having five columns in a row.

Pent-house (occasionally **Pentice**), a building which is an appendage, e.g. a lean-to or other subsidiary building; in tall modern residential flats, a small apartment on the flat roof, often commanding a very high rent for its view.

Pentice, *see* PENT-HOUSE.

Percier, Charles (*b.* Paris, 22 Aug. 1764; *d.* there, 5 Sept. 1838), architect and writer on architecture. After his pupilage under Peyre, he was an assistant to Chalgrin in Paris. Having won the Prix de Rome, he made an exhaustive study of Trajan's Column in Rome, and returned to Paris in 1790. With Fontaine (q.v.), a friend of this student period in Paris and Rome, he helped to start a school of architecture shortly afterwards, and later it became famous as the École des Beaux Arts. They also collaborated as designers of theatrical scenery in a severe classical style, were introduced by the painter David to Napoleon, and soon became his architects and the pioneers of the 'Empire' style. They remodelled Malmaison and the Palais Bourbon in 1805; built the magnificent Arc du Carrousel in 1806; decorated several of the royal palaces in the new fashion; added a new wing to the Louvre; and designed the north side of the Rue de Rivoli with its fine arcades.

Pergola (from Ital. and Lat.), an arbour or shaded walk, formed either of trellis (q.v.) or of brick piers or stone pillars or wooden posts, on which rest beams or joists, with creepers trained over them.

I

Peribolus (Lat.), or **Peribolos** (Gk), an enclosure, or the wall around an enclosure.

Peripteral (from Gk *peri*, around; *pteron*, a wing), having a single row of surrounding columns. (*Illustrated* TEMPLE.)

Peristyle (from Gk *peri*, around; *stulos*, a column), a row of columns around a building or a courtyard.

Perpend, any vertical joint recurring in alternate courses of brickwork. The term is used (only in the plural) by bricklayers who speak of 'keeping the perpends,' i.e. keeping the joints vertical above each other.

Perpendicular or Rectilinear Style, the last phase of Gothic architecture in England (and in England only) from *c.* 1360 to *c.* 1550; so called because vertical and horizontal lines predominated in the design of its tracery. Horizontal transomes (q.v.) were introduced to stiffen the vertical mullions (q.v.) of large windows, and thus formed, with the mullions, convenient frames for the stained-glass 'pictures' then becoming popular. *See* ENGLISH ARCHITECTURE, 4(iii).

Perrault, Claude (*b.* Paris, 25 Sept. 1613; *d.* there, 9 Oct. 1688), physician, naturalist, poet, archaeologist, and (from middle age onwards) architect, was a versatile person whom his brother Charles, a courtier, persuaded to submit designs for the completion of the Louvre in Paris, in 1664. He seems to have had no more professional training than Wren (q.v.) when, at almost exactly the same date and the same age, he suddenly plunged into architecture. Unfortunately his designs perished in a fire in 1871, so that little is known of his actual competence; but if he was responsible for introducing the colonnade into the design, it certainly marked an important change in French architecture. At any rate, he supervised the erection of the building; designed the Observatory in Paris (*c.* 1667); and published a translation of Vitruvius (q.v.); also, in 1683, a treatise on the Orders of architecture.

See monograph by A. Hallays, 1926.

Perret, Auguste (*b.* Brussels, 1874; *d.* Paris, 4 Mar. 1954), architect; one of the pioneers of reinforced concrete construction; awarded the R.I.B.A. Royal Gold Medal in 1948. After studying under Guadet at the École des Beaux Arts in Paris, he started practice about 1897 in partnership with his younger brother Gustav (*b.* 1876). The principal buildings designed by the brothers were the casino at St Malo (1899); a garage in the Rue Ponthieu, Paris (1905); the Champs-Élysées Theatre, Paris (1911); the church of Notre-Dame at Raincy, near Paris (1922–3); the church of Sainte-Thérèse at Montmagny, near Paris (1925); the Marinoni engineering works, Montataire (1927); the Museum of Public Works, Paris (1936); the École Nationale de Musique, Paris (1939); and the Marignane Airport (1947). Perret also conducted an *atelier* for 160 pupils at the École des Beaux Arts.

See monograph by P. Jamot, 1927.

Perron (Fr.), a platform or landing outside the entrance doorway of a mansion or large public building, usually approached by a double flight of steps.

Persian Architecture is a vague and variable term. The Persian Empire at its maximum extent under the Achaemenid dynasty (559–331 B.C.) included not only modern Iran (Persia), but also Egypt, Libya, Asia Minor, Iraq (Mesopotamia), Afghanistan, and part of Turkestan. From this period date the ruined palaces at Pasagardae, Persepolis, and Susa, with flat roofs carried on tall slender stone pillars. After an interval under Parthian and Seleucid rule, the Sassanian or Sassanid kings governed Persia from A.D. 226 to A.D. 641. Their palaces at Firuzabad and Sarvistan are great vaulted buildings with domes, and are important in the general history of architecture. In 641 Persia was conquered by the Arabs, and became a Muslim province. The long succession of fine mosques and other buildings produced during the next thousand years, and decorated with magnificent glazed tiling, form one of the most attractive and significant branches of Muslim architecture (q.v.).

See A. Upham Pope, *An Introduction to Persian Art*, 1930, and vol. ii of his great *Survey of Persian Art*, 1939.

Persiennes (Fr., plural of a feminine adjective, Persian), external window blinds made of thin laths in a fixed frame, like Venetian blinds (q.v.).

Perspective Drawing, a system of drawing which represents buildings or other objects upon a plane surface, in such a way as to produce the same visual effect as seen by the eye or in photographs. (*Illustrated* DRAWING.)

Peruzzi, Baldassare (*b.* Accajano, near Siena, 1481; *d.* Rome, 6 Jan. 1536), architect and painter. He began his career as a painter, and decorated a chapel in Siena Cathedral in 1501. He then went to Rome and continued painting, but also studied architecture. In 1509–11 he built the beautiful Villa Farnesina there. He became chief architect to St Peter's, Rome, in 1520; but fled to Siena when Rome was sacked in 1527 and remained there till 1532. He then returned to Rome and built the remarkable Palazzo Massimi alle Colonne (1532–6). The Orsini, Lante, and Ossoli palaces in Rome are also attributed to him, as are the Palazzo Albergati at Bologna and the cathedral at Carpi. It seems certain that he built the portal of the church of S. Michele in Bosco at Bologna (*c.* 1523), and planned the fortifications of Siena. His son Giovanni designed the façade of S. Maria in Trastevere, Rome (1566).

See monograph by W. W. Kent, 1925.

Pevsner, Nikolaus (*b.* 30 Jan. 1902), writer on art and architecture; educated at the universities of Leipzig, Munich, Berlin, and Frankfurt. He was assistant keeper in the Dresden Gallery, 1924–8, and lecturer at Göttingen University, 1929–33. Since settling in England he has been Slade Professor of Fine Arts at Cambridge, 1949–55, and is head of the Department of the History of Art at Birkbeck College, London. He is also art editor of Penguin Books

PEW.   Harmondsworth, Middx.
(c. 1500)

PEW.   St John's Church, Leeds
(1634)

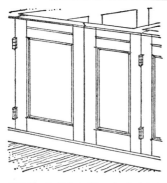

PEW.   St John's Church, St John's
Wood, London (1813)

and a member of the editorial board of *The Architectural Review*. His books have included *Pioneers of the Modern Movement*, 1936; *An Outline of European Architecture*, 1942; and the series, under publication since 1951, entitled 'The Buildings of England.'

Pew, originally a platform or desk in a church, for the use of the priest or reader; then a platform with enclosed seats for an important person's family; finally, from the seventeenth century onwards, applied to all enclosed seats in a church. At that period pews came into general use for the whole congregation, and rents were charged for them, to meet church expenses; but in recent years there has been a movement for their abolition in favour of open seating—partly to remove the impression of exclusiveness that the pews suggested. Probably the best surviving example of eighteenth-century exclusiveness of this kind is in the old parish church at Whitby, Yorkshire.

Pharos (Gk, a lighthouse). Although this word has passed into other languages (e.g. It. *faro*; Fr. *phare*) to denote a lighthouse, it is originally derived from the name of the island of Pharos, outside the harbour of Alexandria in Egypt, where formerly stood that famous lighthouse or beacon tower which was one of the 'Seven Wonders of the World.' There is another lighthouse known as the 'Pharos,' at Dover Castle in England, built in Roman times and perhaps the oldest Roman building in Britain.

Piano Nobile (Ital., noble floor), in a large Italian town house (*palazzo*), the principal floor, raised one storey above ground level, and containing the main reception-rooms, which were arranged *en suite*.

Piazza (Ital.), a formal open space

surrounded by buildings, in a town (cf. Fr. *place*; Sp. *plaza*; Ger. *platz*). The nearest equivalent term in English is 'square'; but a *piazza* need not be square or even rectangular, and perhaps the finest in the world is the elliptical Piazza di San Pietro at Rome (1656–67), designed by Bernini (q.v.).

'Picturesque, The,' a phase of taste, especially in the decoration of parks and gardens, prevailing in England during the late eighteenth century, and stimulated by the publication in 1794 of Sir Uvedale Price's *An Essay on the Picturesque.*

> *See* C. Hussey, *The Picturesque,* 1927.

Pier, in architecture, an independent solid mass of stone, brick, or concrete which supports a vertical load or the thrust of an arch.

Pietra Dura (Ital., hard stone), or **Florentine Mosaic,** an ornamental mosaic of lapis lazuli, marble, etc., highly polished.

Pigeon-cote, or **Pigeon-house,** *see* COLUMBARIUM.

Pilaster, a flat column against the face of a wall, usually 'engaged' (i.e. built into it), and projecting there from a distance not exceeding one-third of its surface breadth. A Greek pilaster is called an 'anta' (q.v.). The

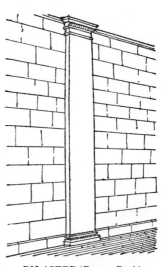

PILASTER (Roman Doric)

pilaster gradually tended to become a decorative rather than a structural feature.

Piling, a form of construction consisting of long piles (of timber, concrete, steel, or reinforced concrete) driven under great pressure into loose or unreliable soil as a rigid basis upon which the foundations of a building may be laid. Whatever the material, the foot or lower end of the pile is usually pointed and shod with metal. The cities of Amsterdam and Venice are largely built upon piles, and at Amsterdam the town hall (now the Royal Palace), erected in 1648–1655, stands on a foundation of 13,659 piles.

Pillar (from Lat. *pila*), a slender vertical structural member bearing a load. A wooden pillar is generally called a post (q.v.). Whereas a pillar may be square, oblong, polygonal, or circular in section, a 'column' is always circular.

Pilotis (Fr., stilts), a term recently introduced into architecture to describe a building, often of many storeys, which stands upon rows of widely spaced reinforced concrete columns, thus leaving the whole of the ground-floor space available for car-parking and other purposes. (*Illustrated* p. 250.)

PILOTIS. Part of the Lake Shore Drive apartment blocks at Chicago (1945–51), standing on pilotis, and designed by Mies Van der Rohe (q.v.)

Pinnacle (from Lat. *pinnaculum*, dim. of *pinna*, a wing), a small quasi-ornamental feature, terminating either in pyramidal or conic form, on the top of a Gothic buttress, but also serving a structural purpose by counteracting the outward thrust of a vault or roof-truss. Pinnacles were largely used elsewhere, however, as purely ornamental features, e.g. on wooden traceried screens.

Pisani, or **Pisano, Andrea,** otherwise **Andrea da Pontedera** (*b.* near

Pisa, 1270; *d*. Orvieto, 1348), sculptor and architect. He made the bronze doors of the Baptistery at Florence in 1330–7; and became *capomaestro* (architect) of Florence Cathedral in 1336 and of Orvieto Cathedral in 1347. He was not related to Giovanni or Niccola Pisani (*see* below).

Pisani, Giovanni (*c.* 1245–1314), Italian architect and sculptor, son of Niccola (q.v.), assisted his father, and was *capomaestro* of Pisa Cathedral from about 1299 to about 1308. He probably designed the choir of Arezzo Cathedral, the west front of Siena Cathedral, and the Castel Nuovo at Naples; also, possibly, the arcades of the Campo Santo at Pisa.

Pisani, Niccola, or **Niccolò,** otherwise **Niccola da Apulia** (*c.* 1225–*c.* 1287), Italian architect and sculptor, carved the fine pulpits in the Baptistery at Pisa and in Siena Cathedral, also a fountain at Perugia, and completed the Castel dell' Uovo at Naples. Arnolfo del Cambio (q.v.) was among his pupils.

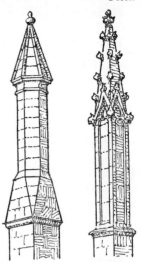

PINNACLE. Left, early Gothic; right, late Gothic

Piscina (from Lat. *piscis*, a fish), originally a pond or basin for fish; later, in Christian churches, a perforated stone basin for disposal of the water after the priest had washed his hands and the sacred vessels. It was normally placed in a niche, often richly carved, on the south side of the altar.

In earlier times, however, the Romans used the term *piscina* to describe any basin or tank containing water, e.g. a fish pond or aquarium, a fountain basin. In modern Italian the word is similarly used, but is also applied to a swimming-bath or swimming-pool, e.g. in the modern Foro Italico at Rome.

PISCINA: from Cumnor Church, Berks. (c. 1350)

Pisé, or **Pisé de Terre** (Fr., from *piser*, to beat or pound), otherwise known as cob (q.v.); stiff clay, well kneaded, used for building the walls of cottages, etc. Owing to the shortage of bricks after the First World War, it was seriously tested as a possible walling material.

See *Special Report No. 5 of the Building Research Board,* 1922.

Pitch (of a roof), the inclination of a sloping roof, reckoned as an angle with the horizontal, either in degrees (e.g. '30 degrees pitch') or as a ratio of rise to span (e.g. 'a pitch of 1 : 4').

Pitched Roof, any type of sloping roof, as opposed to a flat roof. (*Illustrated* ROOF.)

Plain Tiles, ordinary roofing tiles of burnt clay, measuring 10½ inches by 6½ inches, slightly cambered (curved), and provided with two nibs for fixing. (See *British Standard Specification No. 402*.)

Plan (from Lat. *planus*, flat), strictly speaking, a drawing of the various parts of any floor or storey of a building, projected upon a horizontal plane. A plan was once called a plot (q.v.), or occasionally a model or a pattern (qq.v.).

Planetarium (Lat.). (1) A working model showing the movements of the planetary system. (2) A building containing such a model. A planetarium was opened in 1958 as an annexe of Madame Tussaud's Exhibition in Marylebone Road, London.

Planted Moulding, a separate strip of moulded wood which is glued or nailed around panels, as opposed to a stuck moulding (q.v.), which is worked on the framing itself.

Plaque (Fr.), an ornamental or commemorative tablet affixed to a wall.

Plasterwork. Apart from its normal function of providing a smooth external or internal surface for walls and ceilings, plaster-work has often reached a high level of artistic excellence—in England, from the sixteenth century onwards. *See* STUCCO.

> *See also* G. P. Bankart, *The Art of the Plasterer*, 1908; W. Millar and G. P. Bankart, *Plastering: Plain and Decorative* (4th ed.), 1927; M. Jourdain, *English Decorative Plasterwork of the Renaissance*, 1926.

Platband (obsolete), a flat rectangular moulding or fillet.

Plateresque Architecture (Sp. *plateresco*, from *platero*, a silver-smith), a phase of Spanish architecture lasting from the late fifteenth to the early sixteenth centuries, in which decoration was so profuse and so delicate that it resembled silversmith's work. *See* SPANISH ARCHITECTURE.

Plate Tracery, a rudimentary or embryonic form of Gothic tracery, in which geometrical shapes were pierced through a solid slab or 'plate' of stone, as opposed to later tracery formed of moulded stone bars. (*Illustrated* TRACERY.)

Playfair, William Henry (*b.* London, 7 or 8 July 1789, *d.* Edinburgh, 19 Mar. 1857), architect, was the son of James Playfair, also an architect. After being trained in Glasgow by Starkie, he began independent practice in Edinburgh; and in 1815, at a very early age, he was commissioned to lay out part of what had come to be called the 'New Town' of Edinburgh, originally planned by Craig (q.v.). The numerous buildings that he designed in Edinburgh included the new gateway and lodge of Heriot's Hospital (1819); Royal and Regent Terraces (1820); the remodelling and extension of the University (1817–24); the new Observatory (1818); the unfinished National

Memorial on Calton Hill (begun 1822); the Advocates' Library (1819); the Royal Institution (1822–36); the College of Surgeons (1830); St Stephen's Church (1826–8); and the National Gallery of Scotland (1850). Most of these buildings were in neo-Greek style, so that Edinburgh has been called the 'Modern Athens'; but for Donaldson's Hospital (1842–8), and for the Free Kirk Training College (1846–50), he adopted a neo-Tudor style. He also designed Dollar Academy (1818).

Plinth (from Lat. *plinthus*; Gk *plinthos*), the square or moulded projecting member at the base of a wall or column.

Plot, an obsolete name for the plan of a building.

Plumbery (obsolete), the plumbers' workshop or yard attached to a cathedral. There is an example on the south side of Salisbury Cathedral.

Plumbing (from Fr. *plomb*; Lat. *plumbum*, lead), leadwork connected with building. Besides its obvious external uses for roofs, gutters, etc., and its internal utility for water services, leadwork has often attained high artistic merit, e.g. in rainwater-heads and cisterns, and also, occasionally, in ornamental gutters and downpipes.

> *See* W. R. Lethaby, *Leadwork*, 1893, and L. Weaver, *English Leadwork*, 1909.

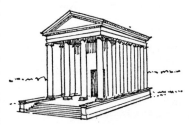

Podium (Lat.), in classical architecture: (1) The square member forming the lowest stage of a column pedestal; or (2) a continuous base or platform under a building.

PODIUM. Temple of Fortuna Virilis, Rome

Poelzig, Hans. (*b* Berlin, 30 April 1869; *d.* there, 14 June 1936), architect; a pioneer of reinforced concrete construction, was trained in Berlin. Among his buildings were the water tower at Posen (1910); a chemical factory at Luban (1911); shops and offices at Breslau (1912); the Grosses Schauspielhaus at Berlin (1919); and the Capitol Cinema at Berlin (1925).

Pointed Architecture, *see* GOTHIC ARCHITECTURE.

Pointing, in brickwork, the finishing of rough mortar joints with a specially fine and strong mortar after the walling is otherwise complete.

Polish Architecture. Poland, although under Russian rule from 1815 to 1918, has always been a predominantly Roman Catholic nation, and her architecture has followed the western rather than the Byzantine or eastern tradition. Thus her chief medieval buildings are Roman Catholic cathedrals and churches, e.g. in Warsaw, Cracow, Lemberg (Lwow), etc., though unfortunately many of them were seriously damaged during the world wars. The

* I

Renaissance movement in architecture came to Poland direct from Italy during the sixteenth century. Examples are the Royal Palace, Cracow (1502–16); the town hall, Poznan (1550–60); and the lay-out and buildings of the new town of Zamosc (1579–1622). Baroque buildings of note include the churches of SS. Peter and Paul, Cracow (1597–1619); the Summer Palace of Wilanow, near Warsaw (1667–94); and numerous picturesque mansions. A Classical Revival followed the Baroque period in the late eighteenth century, producing the Lazienski Summer Palace (1773); the Opera House (1825); and the Ministry of Finance—all in Warsaw. The most distinctive buildings in Poland, however, are the timber-built synagogues (q.v.), mainly of the eighteenth century. Poland has made a commendable recovery from the brutal damage done to her architecture during the Second World War, and the rebuilding of Warsaw and Gdynia is a notable achievement. In Warsaw, though the fine old houses in the market-place and elsewhere in the old city have been reconstructed in their former attractive style, the newer parts of the city have been re-planned on stately modern lines; but the colossal 'Stalin Palace of Science and Culture,' a pompous post-war product, dominates the whole of Warsaw. New buildings include the Post Office Savings Bank and the headquarters of the United Party.

See Z. Dmochowski, *The Architecture of Poland*, 1957.

Polychromy (from Gk *poluchrōmos*, many-coloured), the use of many colours in one building. In modern English architecture, William Butterfield (q.v.) was specially addicted to this practice.

Polygonal Masonry was much used in Mycenaean and Minoan architecture (*see* CYCLOPEAN MASONRY), and also by the Romans (*see* OPUS INCERTUM).

Pompeian Architecture, *see* ITALIAN ARCHITECTURE, I.

Pontelli, or **Pintelli, Baccio** (*b.* Florence, *c.* 1450; *d.* Urbino, 1492), architect. He was trained in drawing by Francesco di Giovanni at Pisa, 1471–8, and in architecture by Francesco di Giorgio Martini. With the latter he built the Castello at Ostia and restored the fortress of Civitavecchia for Pope Sixtus IV; and, after 1488, remodelled the fortresses of Jesi, Osimo, and Offida for Innocent VIII. According to Vasari, he also designed the churches of SS. Apostoli, S. Pietro in Vincoli, and S. Maria del Popolo; the hospital of S. Spirito in Sassia; the Ponte Sisto; and the Old Vatican Library—all in Rome.

Ponzio, Flaminio (*b.* Milan, *c.* 1560; *d.* Rome, 3 April 1613), architect. As a youth he went to Rome, where he later designed the following buildings: the Palazzo Rospigliosi (1603); the façade of the Palazzo Sciarra-Colonna; the completion of the façade of the Palazzo Borghese(1608–9); the Capella Paolina and the New Sacristy in S. Maria Maggiore (1605–11); and the Casino Borghese. At Frascati he built the Villa Grazioli (1612).

Pope, John Russell (*b.* New York City, 24 April 1874; *d.* there, 27 Aug. 1937), American architect. He studied at the American Academy in Rome, 1895–8, and at the École des Beaux Arts in Paris,

1898–1900. He then started practice in New York. His work, which was highly academic in character, included additions to the Metropolitan Museum and to the Henry Frick Art Gallery in New York City; the Nassau County Hospital on Long Island, the First Presbyterian Church at New Rochelle, the Memorial Hospital at Syracuse, and the City Hall at Plattsburgh—all in New York State; the Temple of the Scottish Rite, the National Archives Building, the National Gallery of Art, the Pharmaceutical Institute, the Constitution Hall, and the Jefferson Hall—all in Washington; the Museum of Art at Baltimore; the American Battle Memorial at Montfaucon, France; and the sculpture halls at the Tate Gallery, London.

Pöppelmann, Mattheus Daniel (*b.* Herford, Germany, 3 May 1662; *d.* there, 17 Jan. 1736), German architect. After studying in Italy and France, he became one of the leaders of the Baroque movement in Germany. Among the numerous churches and palaces which he designed for the court and nobility of Saxony, the most important was the florid Zwinger Pavilion at Dresden (1711–22), which was destroyed in 1945, during the Second World War.

See monographs by B. A. Doering and H. G. Ermisch, 1930.

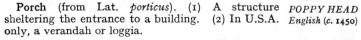

Poppy-head, an ornament often carved on the wooden ends of benches in English late Gothic churches.

Porch (from Lat. *porticus*). (1) A structure sheltering the entrance to a building. (2) In U.S.A. only, a verandah or loggia.

POPPY HEAD
English (c. 1450)

Porta, Giacomo della (*b.* 1539; *d.* Rome, 1602), architect. He seems to have been a Lombard by birth, but worked in Rome, except from 1565 to 1570 when he was in Genoa. He was trained by Vignola (q.v.) whom he succeeded as architect to St Peter's, the Gesù church, and the Palazzo Farnese. At St Peter's his chief work was the completion, with D. Fontana (q.v.), of Michelangelo's great dome. Among his many buildings in Rome were the churches of the Madonna dei Monti and S. Giuseppe dei Falegnami (1588); the façade of S. Luigi dei Francesi (1589) and the completion of S. Giovanni dei Fiorentini; the Maffei, Crescenzi, and Capizucchi palaces; most of the Muti and Aldobrandini (later Chigi) palaces and the Collegio Clementino; several fountains and tombs. In the neighbourhood of Rome he designed the Villa Aldobrandini at Frascati (1598–1603); the church of S. Sinforosa at Tivoli; and the Palazzo Communale at Velletri.

Portail (Fr.), the whole entrance front of a church: not merely the entrance portal itself or a porch.

Portal (from Lat. *porta*, a door or gate). (1) The doorway, often richly carved, of any large or important building. (2) In poetical language, any doorway.

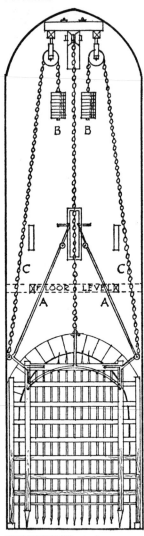

PORTCULLIS at Carcassonne (1285), after Viollet-le-Duc, 'Dictionnaire Raisonné' (1864), showing portcullis lowered. A=iron rods; B=counterweights; C=chains

Portcullis (Fr. *porte*, a door or gate; *coulisse*, a groove), in military architecture, a heavy frame or grid of timber or iron, constructed to slide vertically in grooves cut in the stone sides of a gateway tower, in order to repel assault. Used from Roman times onwards.

Porte-Cochère (Fr., a gateway for coaches), a large porch to shelter persons alighting from a carriage, outside the entrance doorway of a mansion or public building.

Portico (Ital., from Lat.), a roofed space, open on one side at least, and enclosed by a range of columns which also support the roof. A portico may stand free, but usually forms part of a building.

Porticus (Lat., plural *porticŭs*), a small porch; a term specifically applied to porches built on the north and south sides of certain English pre-Conquest ('Saxon') churches, and thus forming rudimentary transepts.

Portuguese Architecture is akin to Spanish (q.v.), and Portugal was under Spanish dominion from 1580 to 1640; otherwise it has been independent since 1114. Previously it had been successively ruled by Romans, Visigoths, and Moors, but there are only scanty remains from those periods. Many Portuguese castles date from the Romanesque period; also the Old Cathedral at Coïmbra, and the much restored cathedrals of Evora, Lisbon, and Oporto. The abbeys of Alcobaça and Batalha are Gothic. The Manueline style, a florid and unique form of late Gothic, named after King Manuel I (1495–1521), appears in the abbeys of Tomar, Batalha (in the 'unfinished chapels'), and especially Belem. The chief examples of Renaissance architecture are the cathedrals of Leiria and Portalegre, the Jesuit church and college at Evora, and S. Roque at Lisbon (1566). Baroque architecture flourished exuberantly in Portugal, notably in the royal palaces of Mafra (1717–30) and Queluz (c. 1785), and in the Basilica of Estrella at Lisbon (1779–96). Portuguese architecture then experienced the Classical Revival, and lost most of its individuality.

> See W. C. Watson, *Portuguese Architecture*, 1908, and S. Sitwell, *Portugal*, 1954.

Post (from Lat. *postis*), a stout and long piece of timber, usually square or cylindrical in section, erected in a vertical position to support some part of the substructure of a building.

Post, Pieter (*b.* Haarlem, 1608; *d.* The Hague, 1669), architect. He and Van Kampen (q.v.) were mainly responsible for introducing the Palladian style into Holland. Their buildings included the Mauritshuis (1643–4) and the Huis ten Bosch (1644–6)—both at The Hague. Post also designed the Stadhuis at Maastricht (1659–1664); the Weigh-house and Butter-market at Leyden (1659–64); the Weigh-house at Gouda (1668–9); the Gemeenlandshuis at Rotterdam (1662–5); and probably the Prinzenhof at Cleve (1664).

Postern (from Lat. *posterula*, a small back entrance): especially in medieval castles, a private gateway, doorway, or tunnel serving as entrance or exit from the keep to the moat or outworks. *See* CASTLE.

Pozzo, Andrea del (*b.* Trent, 30 Nov. 1642; *d.* Vienna, 31 Aug. 1709), priest, painter, architect, and perspective artist, was admitted to the Jesuit Order in 1665. For a time he practised painting, continuing to do so after he was summoned to Rome in 1681. There he designed and actually painted many altar-pieces, and also the ceiling of S. Ignazio, a remarkable achievement, picturing 'the entry of St Ignatius into Paradise.' This work occupied six years. He made plans for a new cathedral at Laibach (Ljubljana) in 1700. He was then invited by the Emperor Leopold (to whom he had dedicated his book on perspective) to visit Vienna, where he decorated the Jesuit church, and painted ceilings in the Liechtenstein palace. The book which made him famous was soon translated into English by John James (q.v.), and published about 1700 as *Rules and Examples of Perspective Proper for Painters and Architects*.

Pozzolana, a volcanic ash found near Rome, possessing special qualities which largely accounted for the excellence of Roman mortar and concrete.

Prakara, in Indian architecture, a wide passage between a temple and the surrounding wall.

Pratt, Sir Roger (*b.* 1620; *d.* Ryston, Norfolk, 20 Feb. 1685), architect, matriculated at Magdalen College, Oxford, in 1637, and began training for the law; but having inherited a fortune from his father in 1640, escaped the civil war by travelling abroad in 1643–9 to study architecture. Soon after returning home, he took some part in designing for his cousin, Sir George Pratt, the beautiful house at Coleshill, Berkshire, in 1650–2. Inigo Jones (q.v.), then an old man, advised him, and it is uncertain whether Jones or John Webb (q.v.) prepared the actual plans. Pratt was a commissioner for rebuilding St Paul's Cathedral just before the Great Fire, and also for rebuilding the City of London after the fire.   This work, for which he was knighted, brought him into contact with Wren (q.v.).   He himself designed four other mansions: Kingston Lacy, Dorset (1663–9, afterwards altered); Horseheath, Cambridgeshire (1663–5, demolished 1777); Clarendon House, Piccadilly, London (1664–7, demolished 1683); and his own house, Ryston Hall, Norfolk (1669–1672, altered 1784).

See R. T. Gunther, *The Architecture of Sir Roger Pratt,* 1928.

Predella (Ital.).   (1) A kneeling-stool.   (2) The step or platform upon which an altar stands.

Prefabrication, the manufacture of components of a building before erection, so that only the assembly of such components is necessary on the site, with a consequent saving of the time and money lost in bad weather.   Prefabrication was rapidly developed during and after the Second World War.   It is greatly facilitated by standardization.

Presbytery (Late Lat. *presbyterium,* from *presbyter,* a priest or elder). (1) The portion of a church reserved for the clergy; normally the eastern part of the chancel.   (2) A dwelling-house for the clergy.

Pre-stressed Concrete Construction, a method of building in which pre-cast reinforced concrete members are subjected to artificial stress before actual use, so that they may more effectively resist the tensile stresses that will be put upon them.

Principal Rafter, in any timber roof-truss (q.v.), the main sloping beams between wall plate and ridge, supporting the purlins (q.v.). (*Illustrated* ROOF.)

Priory.   (1) A monastery or nunnery governed by a prior or prioress respectively, usually attached to an abbey.   (2) A house of Canons Regular.   In either case the term is used of the building as well as of the monastic community.

Profile, the section of a moulding.

Pronaos (Gk), in a Greek or Roman temple, a vestibule in front of the doorway to the sanctuary (*naos*), enclosed by side walls and with columns in front.

Proportion in architecture means the due relation of the various parts or portions of a building to one another.   The rules of proportion followed by Greek and Roman architects were published and used during the sixteenth to eighteenth centuries; also for all 'classical' buildings during the nineteenth century.   No rigid formulae for the proportions of Gothic buildings have ever been evolved, though one or two architectural writers in the eighteenth century made attempts to do so.   Contemporary architecture does not follow any precise rules of proportion, its design depending upon the judgment of the designer.   *See* ARCHITECTURE, PERIODS OF.

See also P. H. Scholfield, *The Theory of Proportion in Architecture,* 1958.

Propylon, Propylaeum, plural **Propylaea** (Gk *propulon; propulaion;* from *pro,* before; *pulē,* a gateway).   (1) A structure erected in front of an entrance gateway. (2) The specific name of such a structure on the Acropolis (q.v.) at Athens, built 437–432 B.C.

Proscenium (Gk *proskēnion*). (1) In an ancient theatre, the space between the *skēnē* (fixed background) and the orchestra; hence, the stage. (2) In a modern theatre, the architectural frontispiece of the stage, facing the auditorium. *See* THEATRE.

Prostyle (Gk *pro*, in front; *stulos*, a column), literally 'having columns in front'; used of a temple (q.v.) having a portico with columns.

Prytaneum (Gk, from *prutanis*, a prince), the public hall of a Greek state or city; occasionally used, as in Athens, for the entertainment of distinguished visitors.

Pseudo-Dipteral (from Gk, literally 'with false double wings'), used of a temple (q.v.) which has its columns spaced as in a dipteral (q.v.) manner—i.e. with two ranges of columns; but with the inner range omitted. (*Illustrated* TEMPLE.)

Pseudo-Peripteral (from Gk, literally 'false peripteral'), a temple (q.v.) which appears to have a double range of columns all round the building, but in which the inner range does not stand free but has its columns 'engaged' (i.e. built into the walls of the temple itself).

Pteroma (from Gk *pteron*, a wing), in a Greek temple (q.v.), the space between the walls of the temple itself and the surrounding colonnade.

Pugin, Augustus Charles (*b*. in France, 1762; *d*. London, 19 Dec. 1832), architectural draughtsman. Although he never practised as an architect, he exerted a great influence upon the Gothic Revival in England, through his published volumes of drawings and through his son, A. W. N. Pugin (q.v.), whom he trained. Augustus himself came of an aristocratic family, and fled to England as a political refugee during the French Revolution. He obtained employment as a draughtsman in the busy London office of John Nash (q.v.), who made full use of his great artistic ability, and especially of his knowledge of Gothic architecture and ornament—Nash being quite ignorant in that field. He assisted Nash in the remodelling of Windsor Castle in 1824, and their association lasted many years. Abreast of this work, Pugin conducted an *atelier* or academy of architecture in his house at Islington, where his numerous pupils lived and worked in Spartan austerity. Among his numerous publications were several volumes of drawings of Gothic architecture, ornament, and furniture in England and France; and *Illustrations of the Public Buildings of London* (jointly with John Britton), 2 vols., 1825–8.
    See monographs cited at end of next item.

Pugin, Augustus Welby Northmore (*b*. London, 1 Mar. 1812; *d*. Ramsgate, 14 Sept. 1852), architect, draughtsman, writer on architecture, and pamphleteer. He was one of the most brilliant, fanatical, eccentric, and picturesque characters in English architecture, and the most forceful figure of the English Gothic Revival. He was the son of A. C. Pugin (q.v.). After his schooling at Christ's

Hospital, he entered his father's *atelier* at Islington. His tempestuous career ultimately led to the loss of his reason, and, soon afterwards, to his premature death in 1852. He burned himself out by the fierceness with which he entered into the contemporary violent controversies on religion, ritual, and art, abreast of the exacting demands of a large practice. His chief title to fame rests on his share in the design of the new Houses of Parliament.

The great competition for this building was won in 1835 by Charles Barry (q.v.), the nominal designer. The masterly plan was certainly his; but the elevations were largely, and the detail entirely, the work of A. W. N. Pugin, who afterwards designed all the profuse decoration and much of the furniture. At that period no craftsmen were capable of carrying out this elaborate Gothic work, so Pugin had to train them himself in the niceties of the Gothic tradition. His own buildings included the Roman Catholic cathedrals of St George, Southwark (1840–8, gutted in 1941 and since restored), and of Kilkenny (1846); collegiate and conventual buildings at Downside, Maynooth (Ireland), Leicester, Birmingham, Liverpool, Redcliffe, Rugby, Nottingham, Oscott, Bermondsey, Waterford and Gorey (in Jersey), etc.; a great many Roman Catholic Churches; the restoration of St Mary's, Beverley; the gateway of Magdalen College, Oxford; Scarisbrick Hall (begun 1837); and two houses for his own occupation—St Marie's Grange at Laverstock, near Salisbury (1835); and St Augustine's, Ramsgate, with the adjoining church (1846). His most important published books were *The True Principles of Pointed or Christian Architecture*, 1841; *A Glossary of Ecclesiastical Ornament*, 1844; and *A Treatise on Chancel Screens and Rood Lofts*, 1851.

See monographs by B. Ferrey, 1861, and M. Trappes-Lomax, 1932.

Pulpit (from Lat. *pulpitum*, a raised platform or stage from which actors recited), in Christian churches, from the earliest times onwards, a raised structure, approached by steps, from which a sermon is preached. In England pulpits are first mentioned in twelfth-century records, but the earliest known surviving example in a parish church is dated 1330. There are also early monastic examples in the refectories at Beaulieu Abbey and Chester Cathedral. Even up to the fifteenth century not more than one parish church in four contained a pulpit. It having been ordained in 1603 that every parish church must have one, there are some fine Jacobean examples surviving, though unfortunately many more were replaced by gaudy neo-Gothic substitutes during the Gothic Revival. In Wren's City churches the pulpit was generally prominent, and was furnished with a 'tester' or sounding-board. Tall 'three-decker' pulpits were often used in galleried churches of the eighteenth century, and in the Nonconformist meeting-houses or chapels of the seventeenth to nineteenth centuries the pulpit was the focus of interest. The use of twin pulpits (*see* AMBO) has been revived in some recent Anglican churches.

See monograph by J. C. Cox, 1915.

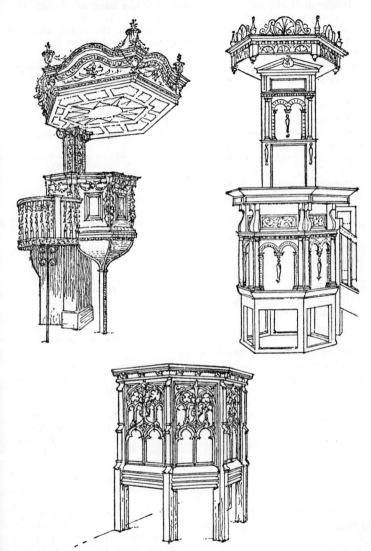

PULPIT. Below, Worstead, Norfolk (late Gothic); top right, Abbey Dore, Herefordshire (c. 1620); top left, St Mary Abchurch, London (1681–7), by Wren, woodwork
probably by Grinling Gibbons.

Pulpitum (Lat., *see* PULPIT above). When used in English this Latin word is applied specifically to the massive stone gallery or rood-screen (q.v.) separating the nave from the ritual choir in certain large cathedrals and formerly monastic churches (e.g. York Minster, St Albans Abbey). *See also* JUBÉ.

Pulvin (from Lat. *pulvinus*, a cushion), an alternative term for Dosseret (q.v., *illustrated*).

Pulvinated (from Lat. *pulvinatus*, cushion-shaped), a term applied to a classical frieze (q.v.) which has a convex or bulging section.

PULVINATED. A Roman pulvinated frieze (marked P above)

Puncheon, in timber construction, a short post or strut.

Purlin, in a timber roof, one of the transverse horizontal beams carrying the common rafters upon which rest the battens for the slates or tiles. The purlins may be supported (i) by partition walls, if these occur at sufficiently close intervals; or (ii) by upright posts rising from walls below; or (iii) by roof-trusses spaced at appropriate intervals. (*Illustrated* ROOF.)

Putlog, in timber scaffolding, a short horizontal member, built at one end into the wall under construction or repair, and secured to the scaffold poles at the other end. Putlogs support temporary platforms of boarding.

Pycnostyle (from Gk *puknos*, dense; *stulos*, a column), literally 'closely spaced columns'; more specifically, in Greek temples (q.v.), columns spaced $1\frac{1}{2}$ diameters apart.

Pylon (from Gk *pulōn*, a gateway), originally, a gate tower; then, more specifically, one of the tall tapered towers flanking the entrance to an ancient Egyptian temple, e.g. at Edfu and Karnak; more recently (twentieth century), one of the tall tapered towers of steel lattice used to carry cables for the transmission of electric power.

PYLON: from the Egyptian temple of Edfu (237 B.C.)

Pyramid (from Gk *puramis*, plural *puramides*), a structure having a square base and sloping sides meeting at an apex. This type of structure originated in Egypt, was erected there from the fourth to the twelfth dynasties (i.e. before 3000 B.C.), and after that date occurs only in small pyramidal tombs imitated from the ancient Egyptian prototypes. The pyramid is derived from the *mastaba* (q.v.), a tomb of rectangular plan with 'battered' (slightly sloping) sides and a flat top. The next stage was the compound *mastaba* or 'stepped pyramid,' as at Sakkara and Meidum. Then came the true pyramid with sides faced with dressed stone, sloping at about 50 degrees, as in the famous trio at Giza, across the Nile opposite Cairo. These three were erected between *c.* 4700 B.C. and *c.* 4550 B.C. There are, however, many others north and south of Giza, extending, in all, for about fifty miles along the west bank of the Nile, because the west, the direction of the setting sun, was favoured for religious reasons (hence, presumably, the modern saying that the souls of the dead have 'gone west'). The erection of these vast masses of masonry, with their elaborate internal tombs, corridors, and barriers, entailed an appalling waste of human energies and lives but also represents great technical skill and accuracy.

See I. E. S. Edwards, *The Pyramids of Egypt*, 1947.

Q

Qaʻah (Arabic), the great hall or saloon of old Arab houses in Cairo.

Qalʻah (Arabic), a fortress or citadel.

Qamariyyah, or Shamshiyyah (Arabic), a pierced window, or lattice, of stone or stucco.

Qasr (Arabic), a castle or palace.

Qastal (Arabic), a wall fountain in a street, e.g. at Jerusalem.

Qiblah (Arabic), in a mosque, the direction of Mecca, marked by a prayer niche, the *mihrab* (q.v.).

Quadra, in classical architecture, the plinth of a *podium* (q.v.).

Quadrangle, in architecture, a square or oblong courtyard enclosed on all sides by buildings; or, occasionally, with one side left open.

QAMARIYYAH: from Cairo
(c. A.D 1340)

Quadriga (Lat.), a chariot drawn by four horses abreast, as on the triumphal arch at the top of Constitution Hill, London.

Quadripartite (literally 'in four parts'), a term applied to Romanesque vaulting, at first with groins only, later with ribs. *See* VAULTING.

Quarenghi, Giacomo (*b.* near Bergamo, 20 Sept. 1744; *d.* St Petersburg, 18 Feb. 1817), architect, was trained as a painter, but was attracted to architecture after reading the treatise by Palladio (q.v.). He spent several years in studying the work of Palladio and other architects, among them Inigo Jones (q.v.), and in 1771 he rebuilt the church of S. Scolastica at Subiaco, near Rome. A few years later he became known to Catherine the Great, Empress of Russia, and in 1779 he journeyed to St Petersburg, where he spent the remainder of his life. His chief buildings were the English Palace of Peterhof (1781–9); the Hermitage (1782–5); the Alexander Palace at Tsarskoe Selo (1792–6); the Stock Exchange (1784–1801); the Marinski Hospital (1803); the Narva Triumphal Arch (1804); the Smolny Institute (1806–8)—all these in St Petersburg; the Old Gostiny Dvor and the monument of the Napoleonic war (1812)—both in Moscow.

See monograph by G. Colombo, 1879.

Quarry, or **Quarrel** (from Old Fr. *quarel,* derived from Lat. *quadrellus,* dim. of *quadrus,* a square), a small pane of glass, square or diamond-shaped, but usually the latter.

Quarry, or **Quarry Tile** (derivation same as last item), a square clay paving-tile, usually red in colour.

Quarter Landing, a square landing at the turn of direction between two flights of stairs. (*Illustrated* STAIRCASE.)

Quarter Round Moulding, an ovolo (q.v.) moulding which is one-quarter of a circle in section, as used in Roman architecture. *See* MOULDING.

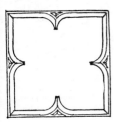  

QUATREFOIL. English late Gothic examples

Quatrefoil (literally 'four-leaved'). (1) A conventionalized leaf or flower having four leaflets or petals. (2) In Gothic tracery, a circular or square opening having four 'foils' (q.v.) separated by 'cusps' (q.v.).

Quattrocento (Ital.), literally 'the fourteen-hundreds'; i.e. the years 1400–1499 inclusive: hence, the *fifteenth* century, not the fourteenth.

Qubbah (Arabic), a dome; hence, a domed tomb.

Queen Anne Style, strictly speaking, English Renaissance domestic architecture of Queen Anne's reign, 1702–14, when the Palladian style (q.v.) was becoming popular in England; a revival of this style took place in the latter part of the nineteenth century under Norman Shaw (q.v.). The term is not, however, precise: some critics equate it with the style of Wren; others make it the first phase of the Georgian period.

Queen-post Roof-truss, a form of timber truss in which two vertical queen-posts are framed at their heads into the principal rafters, and at their feet into the tie-beam. One advantage of this roof, as compared with the single king-post type, is that an attic can be contrived between the queen-posts; but the main purpose is to provide support for one more purlin (q.v.) on each side of the roof than the king-post type can support; so that the queen-post truss is suitable for spans of 30 to 40 feet, whereas the king-post type only covers about 25 feet. Neither type is much used to-day. (*Illustrated* ROOF-TRUSS.)

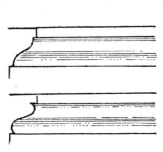

QUIRK. Above, a simple cyma reversa moulding; below, a quirked cyma reversa—both Roman

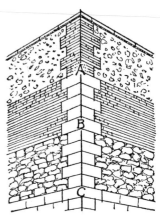

QUOIN. A=brick quoins in flint walling; B=stone quoins in brick walling; C=ashlar quoins in rubble stone walling (see also 'Rustication')

Quirk, a sharp-edged groove or hollow moulding between two other mouldings, chiefly used in Gothic architecture.

Quoin (cf. Fr. *coin*, a corner). (1) The external angle of a building or of a boundary wall. (2) The large corner stones, used at the angle, often of dressed stone when the rest of the wall is of rubble masonry. (3) In brick walls, to produce the same effect of strength at the angle, quoins are imitated in brickwork; or even (4), as at Eastbury Manor House, Barking (built in 1572), in brickwork covered with plaster.

R

R.A., abbreviation for Royal Academician or Royal Academy. *See* ACADEMY.

Rab (Arabic), a block of tenement houses in an eastern town.

Rail, in panelled doors or in wall-panelling, any one of the horizontal members of the framing. *See also* CHAIR RAIL and DADO RAIL.

Rainaldi, Carlo (*b*. Rome, 4 May 1611; *d*. there, 8 Feb. 1691), architect, prominent in the Baroque (q.v.) movement, was the son and grandson of architects practising in Rome. He helped his father, Girolamo (1570–1655), with the drawings for S. Agnese in Rome, and then himself designed the following churches in that city: the façade of S. Andrea della Valle (1665); the twin churches of S. Maria in Montesanto and S. Maria dei Miracoli in the Piazza del Popolo (1662), afterwards finished by Bernini and Carlo Fontana (qq.v.); S. Maria del Suffragio (1669); alterations to S. Maria Maggiore (1673); S. Sudario (1687). In Rome he also designed the Palazzo Salviati (formerly Aldobrandini) in the Corso, and the *loggetta* of the Palazzo Borghese. Outside Rome he designed the façades of three churches in the Marches.
See monograph by E. Hempel (n.d.).

Rainwater-head, the metal box or receptacle, at the top of a rainwater pipe or 'down pipe,' which collects the water from the gutters. Many English examples of the sixteenth to eighteenth centuries are of ornamental leadwork, admirably designed.

Ramp. (1) A slope or inclined plane, connecting two levels. (2) In a staircase, the part of the handrail which curves upward at a landing, etc.

Rampart (Fr. *rempart* or *rampart*), in fortifications, a defensive bank of earth, with or without a stone parapet.

Rampart Walk, a footway on the inner or sheltered side of a rampart (q.v.).

Raphael Sanzio, or **Santi** (*b*. Urbino, 6 April 1483; *d*. Rome, 6 April 1520), painter and architect, was the son of an artist and had himself made a reputation as a painter before he was twenty. He was trained by Perugino. He visited Florence in 1504, and returned from 1506 to 1508, when he moved to Rome. His first commission in Rome was the famous series of paintings in the *Stanze* (Apartments) of the Vatican. In 1514, apparently when he had had no training whatever in architecture, he was appointed chief architect of St Peter's, in succession to Bramante (q.v.). During the six years which remained before his death, he prepared an entirely new plan, but it was never carried out, so that his share in the designing of the existing building is slight. The principal architectural works which he did actually accomplish were, in Rome, the completion of the Cortile of S. Damaso and of the Loggie—both in the Vatican (1513–18); the Palazzo dell' Aquila (since demolished); the small domed Oratory of S. Eligio degli Orefici; the Villa Madama (1516); and the Palazzo Vidoni (1520). His designs for the Pandolfini Palace at Florence (1520) were carried out after his death.

See monograph by H. Geymüller, 1884.

Rasmussen, Steen Eiler (*b.* Copenhagen, 9 Feb. 1898), architect, and writer on architecture and town-planning; Professor at the Royal Academy of Arts, Copenhagen, since 1938; Lethaby Professor of Architecture at the Royal College of Art, London, for 1958; president of the Danish Town-planning Institute, 1942–8; president of the Copenhagen Regional Town-planning Committee, 1944. In 1941 he published *London: the Unique City*, and in 1949 his admirable book which later appeared in an English translation in 1951 as *Towns and Buildings described in Drawings and Words*.

Rastrelli, Bartolomeo Francesco (*b.* ? Florence, *c.* 1700; *d.* St Petersburg, 1770), architect, was the son of an Italian sculptor who brought him to St Petersburg in 1716. There the young architect soon made himself a name, and was given charge of several buildings in the city. In 1730 the Empress Anne commissioned him to build a wooden palace, the 'Annenhof,' at Lefortovo. Two years later he began remodelling and redecorating the Second Winter Palace at St Petersburg; but before it was finished he started to design a palace for the empress's favourite, Count Biron; and in 1741 yet another wooden building at St Petersburg—the 'Summer Palace' (since destroyed). His other work included the Vorontsov Palace (1745); the Stroganov Palace (1750); the Winter Palace (1754–61)—all in St Petersburg; the Great Palace of Tsarskoe Selo (1749–56); St Andrew's Church at Kiev (1744–67); and the huge cathedral and convent of Smolny, begun in 1748. Rastrelli's work lies on the border-line between the Baroque and Rococo styles.

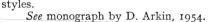

See monograph by D. Arkin, 1954.

Rauza, or **Roza** (Arabic), a tomb in an enclosure.

Rectilinear Style, *see* PERPENDICULAR STYLE.

Reeding, the decoration of a surface by a series of parallel convex mouldings of equal width; the opposite of fluting (q.v.).

Reel and Bead, *see* BEAD AND REEL.

Refectory (from Med. Lat. *refectorium*), the communal dining-hall of a monastery or college; furnished with long 'refectory tables' and benches; and, in the case of monasteries, sometimes provided with a pulpit, of which examples exist at Beaulieu Abbey and at Chester Cathedral (formerly a monastery).

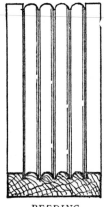

REEDING

Regency Style, strictly speaking, the style of architecture prevailing in England during the period of the regency of George III (1811–20); but usually the term is extended to cover the reign of George IV (1820–30), formerly Prince Regent, whose favourite architect was John Nash (q.v.). It was essentially an age of stucco (q.v.).

Regula. (1) In the Greek Doric Order, a short band or moulding with *guttae* (q.v.) beneath. (2) Any small fillet-moulding. *See* ORDERS OF ARCHITECTURE and MOULDINGS.

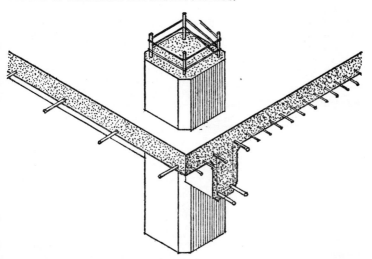

REINFORCED CONCRETE. Diagram showing construction of a column, a girder, and a floor slab

Reilly, Sir Charles Herbert (*b.* London, Mar. 1874); *d.* there, 2 Feb. 1948), architect, teacher, and writer on architecture; R.I.B.A. Royal Gold Medallist, 1943. He is best known as professor and director of the School of Architecture at Liverpool University from 1904 to 1933. He raised the school to a position of great influence. In 1904 it contained only twenty students, taking a two-year course; in 1933 there were over two hundred working on a five-year course. He was the son of Charles Reilly, a London architect, in whose office he worked after his education at Merchant Taylors' School and at Queen's College, Cambridge, where he took a good degree in the Mechanical Sciences Tripos. He then entered the office of John Belcher (q.v.), and began lecturing in the School of Architecture at King's College, London. He made seven visits to the United States, where he established many contacts. One result was his association with T. Hastings (q.v.) for the rebuilding of Devonshire House, London. His other buildings, few in number, included St Barnabas Church, Dalston; the Students' Union and Gilmour Hall at Liverpool University; and the Accrington War Memorial. He also acted as consultant architect for the building of the Peter Jones Store in Sloane Square and the John Lewis Store in Oxford Street—both in London. He was a brilliant architectural journalist; and also published in 1938 his own autobiography, with the curious title: *Scaffolding in the Sky.*

'Reilly Plan, The,' in modern town-planning, a system of small self-contained units within a larger community; advocated by the late C. H. Reilly (q.v.), and now adopted for most recent housing schemes.

Reinforced Concrete, or Ferro-Concrete (in Fr., *béton armé*), a form of construction in which steel rods and mesh are embedded in the concrete, thus greatly increasing the tensile strength which concrete lacks, while utilizing its strength in compression. The steel reinforcement is so disposed as to exert its maximum strength, and

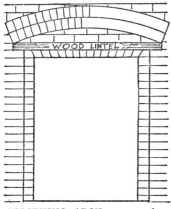

is protected by the concrete from the risks of failure under fire, to which naked steel is liable. Reinforced concrete first appeared in England towards the end of the nineteenth century, having been developed in France a few years earlier. (*Illustrated* p. 269.)

Reja (Sp.), a richly decorated iron grille or screen, much used in Spanish churches.

Relieving Arch, a brick or stone arch, usually concealed, built over a lintel (q.v.) across an opening, in order to relieve it of some of the superincumbent weight of brick or stone walling above it.

RELIEVING ARCH: as seen from inside of window opening

Renaissance Architecture, *see* ARCHITECTURE, PERIODS OF, 7. 'Renaissance' (Fr.) means re-birth, i.e. the revival of classical learning and art, in the fifteenth to seventeenth centuries.

Rendering. (1) In external plastering, a coat of mortar or stucco applied to a wall, in order to produce a smooth surface and also to prevent the penetration of damp. (2) In internal plastering, the first coat of plaster on a wall. (3) In architectural draughtsmanship, the accurate projection of shadows on an elevational drawing.

Renwick, James (*b.* New York City, 1 Nov. 1818; *d.* there, 23 June 1895), American architect. He graduated precociously at Columbia University in 1836, before his eighteenth birthday, and then joined the engineering staff of a railway company. In 1843, apparently without any architectural training whatever, he won a competition for the new Grace Church, New York's wealthiest and most fashionable congregation. This building, consecrated in 1846, was followed by many other churches in the city during the next quarter-century.

The most important of them was St Patrick's (Roman Catholic) Cathedral, commissioned in 1853 and dedicated in 1879, the spires being added in 1887. It is in Decorated Gothic style and built of white marble. In 1846 Renwick had built the new Smithsonian Institution at Washington in 'Norman' style, and in many of his other buildings he adopted either Romanesque or some form of Gothic. His work in New York City included the Clarendon, Albemarle, and St Denis Hotels; Booth's Theatre (1869) and many commercial buildings and banks; also buildings at Vassar College (1865); the Corcoran Gallery at Washington; and several hospitals. One of his pupils was B. G. Goodhue (q.v.).

Repoussé (Fr., from *pousser*, to push or hammer), metalwork raised or beaten in relief by hammering from the reverse side, usually for ornamental purposes.

Repton, Humphry (*b.* Bury St Edmunds, 2 May 1752; *d.* near Romford, 14 Mar. 1818), landscape gardener and architect, had a curious career. From 1764 to 1768 he was at school in Holland, and was then apprenticed to a draper in Norwich. In 1773 he started business on his own account as a general merchant in Norwich, failed, and then turned to farming and gardening near Aylsham in Norfolk. In 1783 he went to Ireland as private secretary to the Lord Lieutenant, but soon returned to England, settled near Romford in Essex, and embarked on another venture connected with mail coaches. This too failed, so at the age of thirty-nine he decided to become a 'landscape gardener'—a new profession created by 'Capability Brown' (q.v.), who had just died. Repton had considerable ability as an artist in water-colour, which now stood him in good stead, and soon he had a large and fashionable practice. He figures in Jane Austen's *Mansfield Park*. Finding the need of an architect's services to carry out his schemes, he made a partnership agreement with John Nash (q.v.), just as Brown had done with Holland (q.v.). His first commission, in 1790, was the laying out of a large garden at Cobham, and his later work included the laying out of the gardens in Russell Square (1800) and Bloomsbury Square (*c.* 1800). His son, JOHN ADEY REPTON (1775–1860). became an architect.

Reredos (literally 'behind the back,' from Fr. *dos*, back), an ornamental structure covering the wall behind and above an altar in a church.

Respond (from Old Fr. *respondre*, to answer), a half-pillar or corbel, attached to a wall, and supporting one side of an arch at the end of an arcade, thus balancing or 'responding to' a pillar on the other side of that arch.

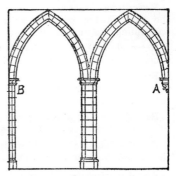

RESPOND. Two types: (A) *Corbel;* (B) *Half-column*

Restoration, in architecture, means the restoration of any decayed or ruined building to its original condition. The interpretation, or misinterpretation, of this term led to heated controversy during the second half of the nineteenth century. Long before that time the drastic repair of English cathedrals by James Wyatt, 'the Destroyer' (q.v.), had been bitterly attacked by A. W. N. Pugin (q.v.); but it was not until 1875 that the much more skilful and scholarly restoration of Tewkesbury Abbey by Sir George Gilbert Scott (q.v.) aroused the fierce indignation of William Morris (q.v.), resulting in his formation in 1877 of the Society for the Protection of Ancient Buildings (q.v.), nicknamed by Morris himself as 'the Anti-Scrape.' The policy of that society has always been to preserve every possible scrap of old material, and to design all replacements and insertions in such a manner that it is obvious that they are modern. The alternative (which may be described as 'invisible mending') is to make all new work as inconspicuous as possible, thus producing a harmonious general effect. Scott wanted to go further, and too often destroyed old work which was not really ruinous in order to 'restore' the building to what he conceived to have been its appearance during 'the best period,' which, for him, meant the fourteenth century. Another very able architect, with a profound knowledge of Gothic, was Viollet-le-Duc (q.v.), whose restorations at Carcassonne and elsewhere in France have been severely criticized.

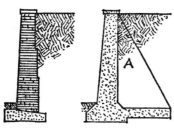

RETAINING WALL. Left, in brick; right, in reinforced concrete with counterforts (A) at intervals

See M. S. Briggs, *Goths and Vandals*, 1952.

Retaining Wall, a wall which supports a mass of earth. It is often increased in thickness ('battered') towards its spreading base or foundation, known as its 'foot.'

Reticulated Tracery (Lat. *reticulum*, a small net), stone tracery of the mid Gothic periods, with openings repeated in rows, thus resembling the meshes of a net. *See* TRACERY.

Retro-choir (Lat. *retro*, back), in a large church, the portion of the choir which lies at the back of the high altar.

Return, a change of direction—usually at right angles—in the line of any architectural feature, such as a cornice, an architrave, or a row of choir stalls.

Reveal, the side of a doorway or window opening, in so far as it is revealed (i.e. not covered by the door frame or window frame).

Rez-de-Chaussée (Fr., literally 'level with the ground'), hence, the ground floor or ground storey of a building.

Rhenish Architecture, *see* GERMAN ARCHITECTURE.

Riaño, Diego de (*d.* Valladolid, 27 Nov. 1534), Spanish architect, was *maestro mayor* (architect) of Seville Cathedral (1526–34), and designed the new sacristy and chapter-house there; also the Ayuntamiento or town hall, and the Casas Capitulares—both at Seville; and several parish churches. His style was midway between Gothic and Renaissance.

Rib. (1) In medieval vaulting (q.v., *illustrated*), the stone, or occasionally brick, arches on the groins (q.v.) or surface of a vault, which carry the thin web of the vault, as the ribs of an umbrella support the thin fabric when stretched. (2) In Tudor or Jacobean ceilings, the narrow wood or plaster mouldings which divide the ceiling into ornamental panels and patterns.

RETICULATED TRACERY
Madley, Herefordshire (c. 1330)

REVEAL in brickwork:
marked R above

R.I.B.A., abbreviation for Royal Institute of British Architects (q.v.).

Ribbon Development, a term invented by town-planners to describe the natural tendency of a town to grow outwards along the existing main roads, thus causing 'urban sprawl' over the countryside, and increased cost in providing municipal services, e.g. sewers, lighting, etc.

Ribera, Pedro de (*d.* Madrid, 1742), Spanish Baroque architect. He was trained by Churriguera (q.v.), and became *maestro mayor* (chief architect) of Madrid, in or near which are his chief buildings: the Hospicio Provincial (1722), the Puente de Toledo (1718–21); the Hermitage of La Virgen del Puerto (1718); the churches of Nuestra Señora de Montserrat (*c.* 1720), and S. Gaetano (in part) (1722–37); also several theatres and fountains.

Ricchini, Francesco Maria (*b.* Milan, 1584; *d.* there, 1652 or 1658), architect. The influential Cardinal Federico Borromeo took him to Rome to be trained in architecture, and he returned to Milan in 1603. Having submitted to his patron a scheme for completing the west front of Milan Cathedral, he was appointed as *capomaestro* (architect) in 1605. His principal buildings, all in Milan, were the churches of S. Giuseppe (1607), S. Vito al Carobbio, and S. Giorgio al Palazzo; the Durini and Bartolomeo Arese palaces; the façades of the Annoni Palace and of the Collegio Elvetico; the church, gateway, and *cortile* of the Ospedale Maggiore; and his masterpiece—the magnificent Palazzo Brera (formerly a Jesuit college), begun in 1615, and finished by his son Domenico (1618–1701).

Richardson, Sir Albert Edward, R.A. (*b.* London, 19 May 1880; *d.* Ampthill, Beds., 3 Feb. 1964), architect and writer on architecture; R.I.B.A. Royal Gold Medallist, 1947; Professor of Architecture at University College, London, 1919–46, and at the Royal Academy from 1947; president of the Royal Academy, 1954–6. He worked in the offices of Leonard Stokes and of F. T. Verity before he started practice in London in partnership with C. L. Gill in 1908. Their work included several large blocks of offices in London; the Opera House at Manchester; and many buildings for the Duchy of Cornwall Estate. Work designed by Professor Richardson alone includes the Jockey Club, Newmarket; the Royal Pavilion, Ascot; Ripon Hall, Oxford; the Great Hall of University College, London; the Battle of Britain Chapel in Westminster Abbey; also many churches in Bedfordshire and elsewhere, and the restoration of York Minster. More recent work, in partnership with his son-in-law, E. A. S. Houfe, includes rebuilding or restoration, after bombing, at Somerset House; Trinity House; St Alfege's Church, Greenwich; St James, Piccadilly; the Carlton Club; University College; and the Safe Deposit Company's premises in Chancery Lane—all these in London; also the rebuilding of St Mary's College, Twickenham; a new court at Christ's College, Cambridge; work at Jesus College and at St Hilda's College —both in Oxford; housing estates in Greenwich, Lewisham, Bedfordshire, and Suffolk. Among his published books are *Monumental Classical Architecture in Great Britain*, 1914, and (with H. O. Corfiato, q.v.), *The Art of Architecture*, 1939.

Richardson, Henry Hobson (*b.* St James, Louisiana, U.S.A., 28 Oct. 1838; *d.* Boston, 27 April 1886), American architect. After graduating at Harvard, he studied at the École des Beaux Arts at Paris, and continued to work there in architects' offices until he started independent practice in New York in 1865, moving in 1878 to Boston where he worked until his death. In his relatively short career he designed a number of important buildings which had a great influence upon American architecture, and he also evolved a new fashion of revived Romanesque. His chief buildings were Brattle Square Church, Boston (1870); Trinity Church, Boston (1872); alterations to the State Capitol, Albany (1876); several public libraries (1877–83); Austin Hall, Harvard University (1881);

the Chamber of Commerce, Cincinnati (1885); the Marshall Field Wholesale Store, Chicago (1885); several railway stations (1881–5), and the Alleghany Court House and Jail, Pittsburgh (1884–6).

See monographs by M. G. Van Rensselaer, 1888, and H. R. Hitchcock, 1936.

Rickards, Edwin Alfred (*b*. 1872; *d*. Bournemouth, 28 Aug. 1920), English architect, brilliant draughtsman, caricaturist, and a close friend of Arnold Bennett. He worked in several London architects' offices before joining H. V. Lanchester (q.v.) and James Stewart in partnership in 1897. Stewart died in 1904, and his surviving partners enjoyed a phenomenal run of successes in competitions up to the outbreak of war in 1914. These included the City Hall and Law Courts at Cardiff (1897); Deptford Town Hall (1902); Hull Art School (1902); and the Wesleyan Hall, Westminster (1905). Rickards's early death in a sanatorium was the result of his military service. Arnold Bennett wrote, after Rickards's death: 'The two most interesting, provocative, and stimulating men I have yet encountered are H. G. Wells and E. A. Rickards.'

See monograph compiled jointly by A. Bennett, H. V. Lanchester, and A. Fenn, 1920.

Rickman, Thomas (*b*. Maidenhead, 8 June 1776; *d*. Birmingham, 4 Jan. 1841), architect and writer on architecture, had an extraordinarily chequered career. Starting as a druggist's assistant, he then qualified as a doctor, actually practised medicine from 1801 to 1803, and then became a clerk. In 1809 he began to sketch old churches, eventually amassing a collection of 3,000 drawings. In 1812–15 he delivered a course of lectures on Gothic architecture at Liverpool. These led to his important book, published in 1817, *An Attempt to Discriminate the Styles of Architecture from the Conquest to the Reformation.* This work went into several editions during his own lifetime. In 1818 he won an open competition for the design of a church, and soon created a very large practice, chiefly ecclesiastical; but his work (in partnership with Henry Hutchinson, *d*. 1831) also included Clitheroe Town Hall (1820); the New Court of St John's College, Cambridge (1826–31); and many country houses.

See monograph by his son T. M. Rickman, 1901.

Ridge, of a roof; either (i) the line of intersection produced by the two sides of a sloping or 'pitched' roof; or (ii) the piece of timber (strictly known as the 'ridge-piece') along the line of the ridge, against which rest the upper ends of the sloping rafters. (*Illustrated* ROOF.)

Ripley, Thomas (*b*. in Yorkshire, *c*. 1683; *d*. Hampton, Middlesex, 10 Dec. 1758), architect and builder. He started work as a carpenter, and is said to have tramped to London seeking his fortune. He was admitted to the freedom of the Carpenters' Company of London in 1705. His marriage to a maidservant of the all-powerful Sir Robert Walpole furthered his career, so that in 1718, while he was acting as clerk of the works on the Royal Mews, he was commissioned to design a new Custom House to replace the building which had just been destroyed by fire; but his own Custom House suffered a similar fate in 1814. He succeeded Grinling Gibbons, the carver, as chief carpenter to the Office of Works in 1721; from 1722 to 1730 he was also acting as clerk of the works at Houghton, designed by Colin Campbell for Sir Robert Walpole; in 1726 he succeeded Vanbrugh as Controller of the Works; in 1729 became surveyor to Greenwich Hospital; in 1742, now a widower, he married an heiress, and became Master of the Carpenters' Company. Pope wrote some scathing verses about him. His work as an architect, apart from the Custom House, was limited mainly to the Admiralty in Whitehall, except the screen (1723–6), and Wolterton Hall, Norfolk (1724–30).

Rise. (1) Of a staircase, the height from one landing to the next, or from one step to the next. (2) Of an arch, the height from the springing-line to the crown. *See* ARCH.

Riser, the vertical front of a step in a wooden staircase (q.v., *illustrated*).

Robertson, Sir Howard Morley, R.A. (*b.* Salt Lake City, U.S.A., 16 Aug. 1888; *d.* London, 5 May 1963), architect and writer on architecture; R.I.B.A. Royal Gold Medallist, 1949; President R.I.B.A., 1952–4; member of the Advisory Committee for United Nations Headquarters, New York. He was trained at the Architectural Association's School, London, 1905–7, and at the École des Beaux Arts, Paris, 1908–12. After his war service he started independent practice in London in 1919 with J. M. Easton (q.v.), and from 1920 to 1935 he was also principal of the Architectural Association's School. For a list of the most important buildings designed by Easton and Robertson *see* EASTON.

Sir Howard Robertson's published books include *Principles of Architectural Composition*, 1924; *Architecture Explained*, 1926; *Modern Architectural Design*, 1932 (revised edition 1952); and *Architecture Arising*, 1944.

Robertson, Sir William (*d.* 3 Nov. 1712), surveyor-general in Ireland from 1679 to 1712, was the designer of Kilmainham Hospital, Dublin (1680–6), founded by Charles II for disabled soldiers. This work has often been wrongly attributed to Wren. Hardly anything is known of Robinson's early life or career, and the only other surviving building that can be ascribed to him is Marsh's Library, Dublin (1702–7).

Rococo Style (apparently from Fr. *rocaille*, rockwork, as used in artificial grottoes, etc), a style of architecture and decoration prevailing especially in France, Germany, and Switzerland during the late eighteenth century, after the Baroque phase (*see* ARCHITECTURE, PERIODS OF, 7). The term is sometimes misapplied to any over-decorated building of the nineteenth century.

Rogers, Ernesto Nathan (*b.* Trieste, 1909), Italian architect. He graduated in architecture at Milan in 1932, and has been Professor of the Theory of Architecture at the Milan Polytechnic since 1952. He has also delivered courses of lectures in the universities of Lausanne, 1944–5; Tucuman (Argentina), 1948; Harvard, 1954 and 1955; and at the Architectural Association School of Architecture in London,

1949. He has edited the review *Domus*, and since 1954 the review *Casabella*. He is a member of the C.I.A.M. (q.v.) and a partner in the firm of Banfi, Belgiojoso, Peressuti & Rogers. (For their buildings *see* BELGIOJOSO.)

Roman Architecture, *see* ARCHITECTURE, PERIODS OF, 3; *also* references in separate articles on the various modern countries formerly included in the Roman Empire, e.g. England, France, Germany, Spain, etc., as well as Italy.

Romanesque Architecture, *see* ARCHITECTURE, PERIODS OF, 5, as well as the separate articles on the European countries in which Romanesque architecture is found: e.g. England, France, Germany, Italy, Spain, Scandinavia, etc.

Romano, Giulio, or **Giulio Pippi de' Giannuzzi** (*b*. Rome, 1499; *d*. Mantua, 1 Nov. 1546), painter and architect. He was a pupil of Raphael (q.v.), whom he helped in the Loggie and Stanze at the Vatican, and at the Villa Madama on Monte Mario, Rome; and whom he succeeded as leader of the Roman painters. In 1524, at the invitation of Federico Gonzaga, Duke of Mantua, he went to Mantua to work in the duke's service. There he drained the marshes, restored the medieval cathedral, embellished the medieval castle, and in 1524 began building his masterpiece, the Palazzo del Te. As an architect he was a follower of Bramante (q.v.).

See lives by C. d'Arco, 1842, G. K. Loukomski, 1932, and F. Hartt, 1959.

Rood-loft, a gallery across the entrance to the chancel of a church, carried on a 'rood-beam' and supporting the 'rood' (crucifix), generally flanked by statues of St John and the Blessed Virgin. Along the top of the rood-loft were placed candles which were lit for festivals. Rood-lofts were uncommon in England before the fourteenth century. During the early years of the Reformation no attempt was made to remove them, but an order of 1561, in the reign of Elizabeth I, condemned them as 'superstitious,' and enacted that they should be removed down to the level of the rood-beam,

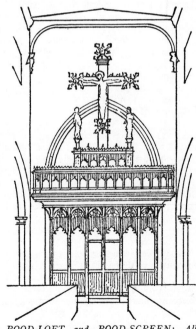

ROOD-LOFT and ROOD-SCREEN: All Hallows, Wellingborough (1917)

K

which was allowed to remain.   In the remote little village church of Hubberholme in the Yorkshire Dales is a quaint and rustic example still intact.

Rood-screen, an open screen, often richly carved and painted, across the entrance to the chancel of a church, extending from floor level to the underside of the rood-beam (*see* ROOD-LOFT).   An order of 1561 permitted such screens to remain undisturbed, as they were not regarded as 'superstitious,' but later iconoclasts damaged and defaced many of them because of the 'images' of saints, etc., depicted upon their panels.   The finest surviving English examples are in East Anglia, Devon, and Somerset.

See monographs by F. Bond, 1908, and A. Vallance, 1936.

Roof (from Old Eng. *hrof*), a protective cover over a building. This may take any one of the following forms: (1) Curved, as a vault (q.v.) or dome (q.v.) of concrete, reinforced concrete, brick, stone, or metal—notably aluminium in recent years—and derived from the primitive beehive hut or wigwam.   (2) Flat—theoretically, but in fact always laid to a slight fall, so that rain-water may drain off— and covered with lead, zinc, asphalt, or other waterproof material. (3) Sloping or 'pitched' roofs, having either a single slope (a 'lean-to roof'), a slope in two directions (a 'span roof'), or a double slope in each direction (a 'mansard' (q.v.) or 'gambrel roof').

The 'pitch' (angle or slope) is determined partly by climate and partly by the nature of the roof-covering.   The pitch is steepest in countries liable to heavy snow (e.g. Germany) and slightest in warm countries (e.g. Italy), while flat roofs have always been popular in very dry climates (e.g. North Africa and many eastern countries) and they are now largely used everywhere.   Thatch entails a very steep pitch, plain tiles 45 degrees to 50 degrees, slates about 30 degrees or from $\frac{1}{4}$ to $\frac{1}{3}$ the 'span,' i.e. the distance between the supports of the roof.

In any form of timber sloping roof, the covering material, if of tiles or slates, rests upon wooden battens; if of lead or zinc, upon boarding.   The battens (which often have boarding beneath them) rest, in turn, upon wooden rafters spaced 12 inches to 18 inches apart, carried upon purlins 4 to 6 feet apart.   (These figures apply to ordinary English traditional construction in timber.)   If the purlins cannot be supported by cross-walls every 10 feet or so of their length, roof-trusses are required (*see* ROOF-TRUSS).   It must be noted, however, that they are never required for small dwelling-houses, where the purlins are carried by cross-walls, and the span is less than 20 feet.

A simple timber span roof formed of common rafters only is called a 'couple roof' (q.v.); if a tie-beam is added, as in all roofs exceeding about 10 feet span, it becomes a 'couple close roof'; but if the tie-beam is fixed some distance above the level of the wall-plates to give more internal head-room, the tie-beam becomes a 'collar-beam,' and the roof a 'collar-beam roof' (q.v.).   Between this type and the trussed roof (*see* ROOF-TRUSS) there are many intermediate types, much used for small houses.

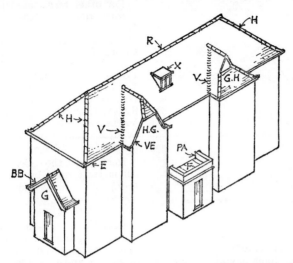

ROOF: THE PARTS OF A ROOF DRAWN IN ISOMETRIC PROJECTION
BB=*barge-board*; E=*eaves*; F=*flat*; G=*gable*; GH=*gabled hip*; H=*hip*;
HG=*hipped gable*; PA=*parapet*; R=*ridge*; V=*valley*; VE=*verge*, X=*dormer*

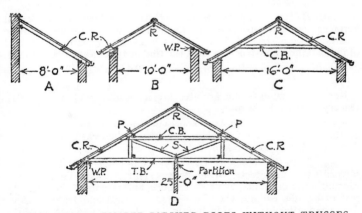

ROOF: SIMPLE TIMBER PITCHED ROOFS WITHOUT TRUSSES
(A) *Lean-to*; (B) *Couple roof*; (C) *Collar-beam roof*; (D) *Purlin roof.* CR=
common rafter; BC=*collar-beam*; P=*purlin*; R=*ridge*; S=*strut*; TB=*tie-beam*;
WP=*wall-plate*

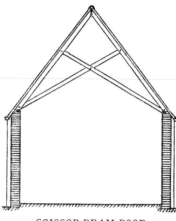

SCISSOR-BEAM ROOF

For other terms used in roof construction *see* BARGE-BOARD, BATTEN, BONNET TILE, COMMON RAFTER, DORMER, EAVES, FLAT, GABLE, GABLED HIP, HELM, HIP, HIPPED GABLE, LANTERN LIGHT, LOUVRE, PAN-TILE, PRINCIPAL RAFTER, PURLIN, RIDGE, SHINGLES, SKYLIGHT, SPAN, SPROCKET, STRUT, THATCH, TIE-BEAM, TILE, VALLEY, VERGE, VERGE-BOARD, WAGON ROOF. *See also illustration.*

Roof-line, the sky-line or silhouette formed by the ridges (q.v.) of a roof, and by any spires, chimneys, pinnacles, etc., projecting therefrom.

Roof-truss, a triangulated frame of timber or steel, usually placed at intervals of 8 to 12 feet apart, to carry the purlins and rafters; used for roofs having a clear span of 20 feet and upwards without any intermediate support by cross-walls or columns. The normal traditional timber types are: (1) The king-post truss, for spans of 20–30 feet, which has a vertical 'king-post' between the ridge and the tie-beam, to prevent sagging. (2) The queen-post truss, which has two 'queen-posts,' and allows of better accommodation in the attic, if any; used for spans of 30–45 feet. (3) The mansard truss (q.v.), with a double slope on each side; used for roofs over 20 feet span. (4) The Belfast (q.v.) or 'bowstring' truss, which has a curved surface. (5) The obsolete and inefficient but picturesque Gothic 'hammer-beam' truss (q.v.). Steel trusses are of many types, and of much lighter construction than the timber types above mentioned.

Rosette, any conventional ornament carved or modelled to resemble a rose.

Rose Window, in Gothic architecture, a circular window filled with tracery to resemble a rose.

Roshan (Arabic), in old Arab houses in Cairo, etc., a niche contrived in the wooden window lattices (*see* MUSHRABIYYAH), in which a porous water-jar can be kept cool.

Rossi, Carlo (*b.* Naples, 18 Dec. 1775; *d.* of cholera, St Petersburg, 6 April 1849), architect. When he was eight years old he went with his mother, a ballerina, to St Petersburg, and remained there for the rest of his life, except when he visited England and Italy in 1802. Two years after his arrival in Russia, he entered the household of the architect-decorator Brenna, who taught him to design and draw (Brenna himself had been a pupil of the architect Charles Cameron, q.v.). By the time he was eighteen Rossi had become Brenna's assistant, and accompanied him to Florence in 1802. From 1805 to 1809

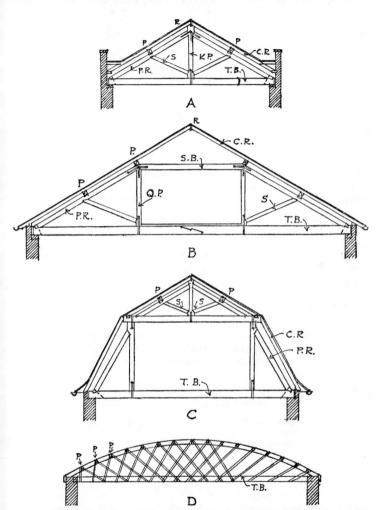

ROOF-TRUSS, VARIOUS TYPES OF. (A) *King-post truss, for 20–30-ft span;* (B) *Queen-post truss, for 30–45-ft span;* (C) *Mansard truss, for over 20-ft span;* (D) *Belfast or bowstring truss.* KP=*king-post;* QP=*queen-post;* R=*ridge;* P=*purlin;* PR=*principal rafter;* CR=*common rafter;* S=*strut;* TB=*tie-beam;* SB=*straining-beam*

there was an interruption in Rossi's career, when he worked for four years in a factory; but in 1809 he was selected as one of a panel of architects charged with the restoration of historical buildings in Moscow. Next came an appointment as architect to the Czar's brother, the governor-general of Tver, where Rossi modernized the palace and did much other work in the town; but in 1815 he was back in St Petersburg. All his chief new buildings were in that city. They included the layout of the Elagin Island and the remodelling of the palace there for the Czar's mother (1818–22); the Michael Palace (begun 1819); the hemicycle at the Winter Palace (1820); the theatre in the Nevski Prospekt (1825–7); and the twin buildings of the Senate and the Synod (1827–35).

See monograph by V. G. Suboff, 1914.

Rossi, Giovanni Antonio de' (*b.* Rome, 1616; *d.* there, 9 Oct. 1695), architect, is usually credited with the design of the Palazzo Altieri in Rome; but various other buildings vaguely ascribed to him seem to have been designed by his contemporary, Mattia de' Rossi (1637–95).

Rostrum (from Lat. *rostrum*, beak, or prow of a ship). (1) In ancient Rome an actors' stage near the Forum, decorated with prows of ships captured at Antium in 338 B.C. (2) In modern speech a raised and railed platform used for public speeches and preaching.

Rotunda (from Lat. *rotundus*, round). (1) A circular building, generally with a domed roof. (2) A dome over part of a large building, in the sense that Wren used the term at St Paul's Cathedral. (3) The name given specifically to the Pantheon (q.v.) at Rome, which is a circular domed building. *See also* THOLUS.

Rough-cast, sometimes called **Pebble-dash,** or **Harling,** a form of external plastering (normally consisting of two coats of mixed cement and sand), in which a coating of pebbles or gravel is thrown on to the second coat before it has set.

Roundel (from Old Fr. *rondel*), a disk or circular decorative panel; may be applied to stained glass.

Round Window, *see* BULL'S-EYE WINDOW, ROSE WINDOW, WHEEL WINDOW.

Royal Academy, *see* ACADEMY.

Royal Commission on Historical Monuments: England (offices at 34 Chester Terrace, London, N.W.1) was first appointed on 27 Oct. 1908 'to make an inventory of the Ancient and Historical Monuments and Constructions connected with or illustrative of the contemporary culture, civilizations, and conditions of life of the people in England, excluding Monmouthshire, from the earliest times to the year 1700, and to specify those which seem most worthy of preservation.' (The limiting date has since been extended to 1714.) A long series of handsome volumes has now been issued, completely covering London, Middlesex, Essex, Hertfordshire, the cities of Oxford and Cambridge, etc., and partially covering several other counties.

Similar schemes are now in operation for Wales (including Monmouthshire) and Scotland.

Royal Fine Art Commission (offices at 5 Old Palace Yard, Westminster, London, S.W.1.) was appointed in May 1924 'to inquire into such questions of public amenity or of artistic importance as may be referred to them from time to time by any . . . Departments of State; and furthermore to give advice on similar questions when so requested by public or quasi-public bodies.' In August 1933 the terms of reference were extended to allow the Commission to call the attention of Departments of State or public bodies to 'any project or development' likely to 'affect amenities of a public or national character'; and again in May 1946 to permit the Commission to call such witnesses, examine such documents, and enter such premises as might assist them in their work. A similar Royal Fine Art Commission for Scotland was appointed in 1927.

Royal Institute of British Architects (66 Portland Place, London, W.1) was founded in 1834, and was granted a royal charter by King William IV in 1837 'for the general advancement of Civil Architecture, and for promoting and facilitating the acquirement of the knowledge of the various Arts and Sciences connected therewith.' The Institute has conducted examinations since 1863, but provides no teaching, though it 'recognizes,' for exemption from certain of its examinations, a number of schools in Britain and overseas. The number of corporate members (Fellows, Associates, and Licentiates) in 1958 was 18,170, many of them in the Dominions overseas; and, of about 19,000 members on the National Register (United Kingdom), over 15,000 were members of the R.I.B.A. The Institute publishes a monthly journal.

Royal Society of Arts (offices at 6–8 John Adam Street, Adelphi, London, W.C.2), founded in 1754, concerns itself with many matters of interest to architects.

R.S.A., abbreviation for Royal Society of Arts (q.v.).

Rubbed Brickwork, or **Gauged Brickwork,** a form of brickwork utilizing relatively soft bricks—'rubbers'—which can be cut with a saw to exact shapes for the voussoirs (q.v.) of arches, etc., and then rubbed on a stone to produce very smooth surfaces for fine jointing, which is executed in special white mortar. Rubbed brickwork was favoured by Wren, who used it freely at Hampton Court Palace and elsewhere.

Rubble Masonry, walling composed of rough stones which have not been 'dressed' with hammer or chisel. It is classified as (i) random rubble, built without courses; and (ii) coursed rubble, in which the stones are built in regular courses (layers) of a uniform height. *See* p. 284.

Rubens, Peter Paul (*b.* Siegen, Westphalia, 28 June 1577; *d.* Antwerp, 30 May 1640), painter. He made drawings of the palaces of Genoa which were published in two volumes of engravings at Antwerp in 1663, most of the original drawings being now in the library of the R.I.B.A. in London. He has also been credited with the design of his own house at Antwerp (1611), and of the Jesuit church of S. Carlo Borromeo at Antwerp (1614–20). He finished painting the magnificent ceiling of the Banqueting House in Whitehall, London, in 1635.

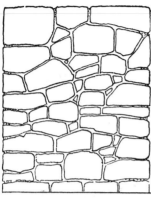

RUBBLE MASONRY. Random rubble

RUBBLE MASONRY. Coursed rubble

Ruskin, John (*b.* London, 8 Feb. 1819; *d.* Coniston, 20 Jan. 1900), writer and lecturer on sociology and art, including architecture. The only son of a wealthy wine merchant, he was foolishly cosseted by his parents, and never went to school. He entered Christ Church, Oxford, in 1837, won the Newdigate Prize in 1839, and graduated in 1842. As early as 1837–8 he wrote a series of articles entitled *The Poetry of Architecture* (published in book form in 1893); and, among his more famous works, *The Seven Lamps of Architecture* appeared in 1849, and *The Stones of Venice* in 1851–2. In his later years he was more concerned with sociological subjects, and in the end his mind gave way. While his writings on architecture were magnificent prose, and did some service in popularizing the subject among the Victorians, his outlook was prejudiced, unduly determined by his early love of Venetian Gothic, and quite out of touch with the conditions of modern life, of which he knew little, thanks to his upbringing, his health, and his temperament. His influence upon William Morris (q.v.) was considerable. His interest in the so-called ' Ruskin Museum ' at Oxford (1855–60; *see* DEANE, SIR T.) has done little to enhance his reputation, but recalls the fact that he was Slade Professor of Fine Art at Oxford in 1870–9 and 1883–4.

See monographs by E. T. Cook, 1890; W. G. Collingwood, 1900; A. Williams-Ellis, 1928.

Russian Architecture. The story of Russian architecture begins in 988, when Vladimir I, Grand Duke of Kiev, was converted to Christianity. Until 1462 Kiev and Novgorod were the chief cities. Owing to lack of skilled talent architects and craftsmen had to be sent to Constantinople to be trained, and naturally they brought back the Byzantine style (*see* ARCHITECTURE, PERIODS OF, 4) to Russia. Of the enormous number of churches erected in Kiev within a few years of their return, three-quarters were destroyed by fire in 1124, many others by the Mongols in 1240, and most of the remainder in the Second World War. The finest were the cathedral of St Sophia at Kiev (1036, now much altered in appearance); the Lavra (1073) and St Michael (1070), both at Kiev; the Monastery of the Caves at Kiev; and the Vydubetski Monastery. The chief examples from the next century were the cathedral of the Mizhorski Monastery at Pskov; and the churches of the Intercession at Nerl, of the Saviour at Nereditsa, and of St Nicholas the Wonderworker at Novgorod. Domes were largely used, often from five to twenty on a single church, and were of the characteristic Russian onion shape.

There was no architecture of note in Moscow until 1477, when Italian architects and craftsmen, directed by Aristotile Fioravanti of Bologna, were imported to rebuild the cathedral of the Dormition. He decided to follow the Russian fashion, though utilizing Italian methods of building. Other Italians designed the Palace of Facets in Moscow, and rebuilt or remodelled the Kremlin in 1485–92, producing a picturesque medley. In the cathedral of St Basil the Beatified (1555), and in most other churches of the sixteenth century, the Russian plan, with numerous domes, continued to be followed.

When the new city of St Petersburg (later Leningrad) was founded by Peter the Great in 1703, the architects chiefly employed were the Russian Zemtsov, the Italians Trezzini (who designed the cathedral of St Peter and St Paul) and Michetti, the German Schädel, and the Frenchman Le Blond. The style of the layout and of the buildings followed Renaissance rather than Byzantine tradition; and under Elizabeth (1714–62) the leading architects in St Petersburg were Italians: Rastrelli (designer of the Winter Palace) and Rinaldi (qq.v.; *see also* SCHÄDEL). Her successor, Catherine the Great, likewise employed an Italian, Quarenghi, as well as the Russians Bazhenov, Kazakof, and Starov; but also a Scot, Charles Cameron (*c*. 1740–1812), from 1779 onwards (qq.v.). His work for her included royal palaces and public buildings, many of which were destroyed in the Second World War. (*See also* VORONYKHIN and ZAKHAROV.) As in western Europe, there was a 'Greek Revival' during the first quarter of the nineteenth century, and revived classicism persisted up to the middle of that century. The leading Russian architect of the period, Thomon (q.v.), designed the church of the Annunciation at St Petersburg and the huge cathedral of St Saviour at Moscow (1838–83, in Lombard-Byzantine style), both since destroyed. Most of the architecture of the period about 1850–1917 was undistinguished, often shoddy in execution, and a medley of all styles.

Notable buildings erected since the 1917 Revolution include the Palace of the Soviets by Yofan, the Red Army Theatre by Alabyan, the Meyerhold Theatre by Schusev, the Lenin Library by Shuko, the Military Academy, the Dynamo Aquatic Station by Morchan,

* K

and the University—all in Moscow; the flats for war veterans by Simonov—in Leningrad; the Lenin Dam by Vesnin; and the State Theatre at Novobisirsk by Greenberg.

Recent buildings vary in style from the stark and advanced 'functional' architecture so popular in western Europe, to a vague striving after a new and distinctive national style. Thus the new offices of *Pravda*, by Golossov, have an excess of glass surface most unsuitable to the severe Russian climate; while the enormous Hotel Moscow, the State Theatre at Batum, and the Metro stations suffer from over-ornamentation, gaudy colouring, and various forms of decoration too lavishly applied. Other recent examples of Soviet architecture are the Nizami Museum at Baku and the sanatoria at Sochi.

See D. R. Buxton, *Medieval Russian Architecture*, 1934; L. Réau, *L'Architecture russe*, 1945; A. Voyce, *Russian Architecture*, 1947; T. Talbot Rice, *Russian Art*, 1948; G. H. Hamilton, *The Art and Architecture of Russia*, 1954.

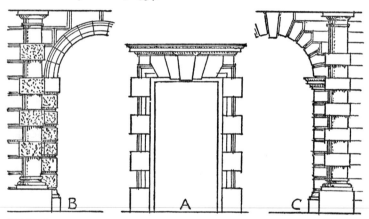

RUSTICATION. (A) *Rusticated doorway by Gibbs (q.v.),* 1732; (B, C) *Rusticated columns and arches by Chambers (q.v.),* 1759

Rustication, a term used since 1715 or earlier, in books on Roman and Renaissance architecture, to describe a method of working external blocks of stone to give an impression of great strength, especially at the base of buildings. Normally this was done with a hammer, producing a rough surface, though the margins of each block were often chiselled smooth; but the term afterwards came to be applied absurdly to smooth blocks which had carefully recessed margins accentuating the joints.

S

Saarinen, Eliel (*b.* Rantasalmi, Finland, 20 Aug. 1873; *d.* Detroit, U.S.A., 1950), Finnish architect; Gold Medallist of the American Institute of Architects, 1947, and of the R.I.B.A., 1950. He was trained as an architect in Helsinki, and started practice there in 1896 with H. Gesellius and A. Lindgren. His first notable work was the Finnish Pavilion at the Paris Exhibition, 1900. After making an intensive study of railway stations in Germany and Britain, he won the important competition for Helsinki station in 1904. This building, finished in 1914, was generally regarded as a masterpiece. Meanwhile he had severed his connection with his partners in 1907, and had won another competition—for the new Finnish Parliament Buildings—in 1908; but these were not erected. He made town plans for Helsinki, Budapest, and Reval; built the city hall at Lahti, Finland, in 1911; and obtained the second place in the competition for Canberra in 1912. He visited Chicago in 1923, in connection with a competition for the *Chicago Tribune* building; designed a scheme for the Lake Front; and settled there permanently. Abreast of his practice he started teaching. His principal buildings in America were the Cranbrook Academy of Art (near) Detroit (1926–43), of which he was also appointed director; the Kleinhaus Music Hall, Buffalo (1938–40); the Tabernacle Church of Christ Scientist, Columbus, Indiana (1942–3); Crow Island School, Winnetka, Illinois (1939–40); Music Center at Tanglewood, Stockbridge, Massachusetts (1938–40); High School at Birmingham, Michigan (1944); Museum at Des Moines, Iowa (1944). His son Eero (*b.* 1910) also became an architect, and designed the remarkable auditorium at the Massachusetts Institute of Technology (1935); the G. M. Technical Center at Warren, Mich. (1944), and the U.S. Embassy, London (1959).

See monograph by A. Christ-Janer, 1948.

Sabil, or **Sebil** (Arabic), a small and usually ornamental type of building in Cairo, etc., containing a public fountain.

Sacconi, Count Giuseppe (*b.* Montalto, Italy, 4 July 1853; *d.* Pistoia, 24 Sept. 1905), architect, entered the Istituto di Belle Arti, Rome, in 1874, after previous professional training at Fermo. He then spent several years on a project for restoring the baths of Caracalla, Rome. In 1884, against 293 competitors, he won the great competition for the monument to King Vittorio Emanuele II, commonly called the 'Vittoriano,' in Rome. Building on this vast and ostentatious pile of white marble began in 1885; but it was not completed till 1911, after his death. Modern critics regard the whole monument—its general design, its siting, and its details—as a colossal error of taste; for the building dominates the centre of Rome by its mere size and colour. The kindest thing that can be said of Sacconi's masterpiece is that it shows a great knowledge of Roman architecture, and faithfully typifies the grandiloquence of imperial Rome at its worst. Sacconi was a deputy in the Italian Parliament from 1886 to 1904.

See monograph by P. Acciaresi, 1911.

Sacristy, a room attached to any large church for the storage of sacred vessels and vestments; often used as a robing-room for the clergy.

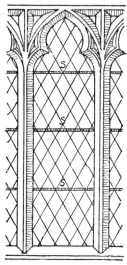

SADDLE-BAR (marked S above)

Saddle-bar, an iron bar fixed horizontally across the lights of a mullioned window, serving to stiffen the leaded glazing against wind pressure.

S.A.D.G. (Fr.), abbreviation for *Société des Architectes Diplomés par le Gouvernement*; a qualification held by some English architects.

Sahn (Arabic), the central open court of a mosque (q.v.).

Sally Port (from Fr. *saillir,* to rush out), a gateway in a medieval fortress, through which the garrison could 'sally forth' to make a sortie.

Salvi, Nicola, or **Niccolò** (*b.* Rome, 6 Aug. 1697; *d.* there, 8 Feb. 1751), architect. He was trained by the painters Ricciolini and Canevari, and was admitted to the course in architecture at the Accademia di S. Luca, Rome, in 1733. His first designs were for firework displays, and then came a series of small buildings—some of which he won in competition, and others which he carried out in collaboration with Vanvitelli (q.v.). He is best known for his masterpiece, the Fontana di Trevi, which all visitors to Rome see. Of all the numerous Roman fountains, it is the most imposing, and it is also a notable example of the Baroque style (q.v.).

Salvin, Anthony (*b.* Worthing, 17 Oct. 1799; *d.* Hawksfold, near Haslemere, 17 Dec. 1881), architect; R.I.B.A. Royal Gold Medallist, 1863. He was trained by John Nash (q.v.), started practice very early, and became an authority on medieval military architecture. Among many old castles which he restored were Windsor, the Tower of London, Alnwick, Bangor, Brancepeth, Carisbrooke, Carnarvon, Dunster, Durham, Greystoke, Naworth, Newark, Petworth, Rockingham, Warkworth, Warwick, and West Cowes. He also built a new castle 'in the strictest Plantagenet manner' at Peckforton. He built or restored many country mansions, including Keele Hall; Mamhead (1828); Methley Hall (1830); and Morby Hall (1828). He restored numerous ecclesiastical buildings, and designed at least nine new churches and several parsonage houses.

Sanctuary (Lat. *sanctuarium,* a holy place), either (i) any sacred building; or (ii) more specifically, the holiest part of a church, i.e.

the presbytery or portion of the chancel reserved for the clergy; or (iii) a church or its precincts in which, by medieval ecclesiastical law, a fugitive from justice could take refuge and be immune from arrest.

Sanctuary Knocker, an ornamental knocker on the door of a church, which a fugitive had to touch when claiming 'sanctuary' (*see* last item).   There is a splendid example, of Norman date, at Durham Cathedral.

Sanctus Bell, in medieval and Roman Catholic churches, a bell rung at the Sanctus and Elevation at Mass.   Although it was often only a small handbell, there are examples of a larger bell hung in a stone turret over the chancel arch and rung by a rope within the church.

Sandby, Thomas, R.A. (*b.* Nottingham, 1721; *d.* Windsor, 25 June 1798), architect and draughtsman, a brother of Paul Sandby, the painter.   Together they journeyed to London in 1742 to take up employment in the military drawing-office at the Tower.   Within a year Thomas was attached to the Duke of Cumberland, commander-in-chief, with whom he

SANCTUARY KNOCKER (*Romanesque*), *Durham Cathedral*

saw active service in Flanders, Scotland, and probably Holland, up to about 1748, when he became successively draughtsman, steward, clerk of the stables at Windsor, and finally deputy ranger of Windsor Great Park, a post which he held up to his death. The work which he carried out in that capacity included the formation of the large artificial lake of Virginia Water, the design of a stone bridge there, and some formal gardening.   His most important building was the Freemasons' Hall in Queen Street, London (1775, demolished in 1932).   Most of his drawings, which are of high excellence and mainly topographical, are preserved at Windsor Castle, at Sir John Soane's Museum, and in the Victoria and Albert Museum.
See monograph by W. Sandby, 1902.

Sangallo, Antonio, the Elder (*b.* Florence, *c.* 1455; *d.* there, 27 Dec. 1534), sculptor and architect; worked in collaboration with his brother Giuliano.   Most of his work consisted of military architecture, including the fortifications of Civita Castellana, Livorno, Montefiascone, Poggio Imperiale, and Castel S. Angelo at Rome (1492–5).   His masterpiece is the church of S. Biagio at Montepulciano (1518–37).

See monographs on the Sangallo family by Clausse, 1900, and G. K. Loukomski, 1934.

Sangallo, Antonio, the Younger (*b.* Florence, 1483; *d.* Terni, 3 Aug. 1546), architect, was the nephew of Antonio the Elder (q.v.) and of Giuliano (q.v.). Starting his career as a woodworker, he went while a youth from Florence to Rome, where he proceeded to make an intensive study of the ancient monuments. This work attracted the attention of Bramante (q.v.), whose service Sangallo entered, and he was set to work on the plans for St Peter's. His earliest work on his own account appears to have been the church of S. Maria di Loreto in Rome (1507); and in 1513 he began his masterpiece, the great Farnese Palace in Rome. He died before this was finished, and Michelangelo (q.v.) added the magnificent cornice. Sangallo also completed the Villa Madama, Rome, left unfinished by Raphael (q.v.) and Giulio Romano (q.v.). He designed the fortifications of Civitavecchia (1515), Ancona, and other places. After Raphael died in 1520 and was succeeded by Peruzzi (q.v.) as chief architect of St Peter's, Sangallo became Peruzzi's deputy, and finally chief architect up to his death.

See monographs by Clausse and Loukomski, as last item.

Sangallo, Giuliano (*b.* Florence, 1445; *d.* there, 20 Oct. 1516), sculptor and architect; brother of Antonio the Elder (q.v.) and uncle of Antonio the Younger (q.v.). Beginning as a woodworker in Florence, he then turned to architecture. His first commissions were two convents in Florence and the Villa Poggio at Cajano (1483–5). These were followed by the church of the Madonna delle Carceri at Prato (*c.* 1485); the large Gondi and Strozzi palaces in Florence (*c.* 1490 and 1489 respectively); the Palazzo della Rovere at Savona (1496); and the completion of the great basilican church at Loreto (1499). He carried out the fortifications of Ostia and Arezzo; and from 1514 to 1516 collaborated with Fra Giocondo and Raphael (qq.v.) on the building of St Peter's at Rome.

See monographs by Clausse and Loukomski, cited under the name of SANGALLO, ANTONIO, THE ELDER.

Sanmicheli, Michele (*b.* Verona, *c.* 1484; *d.* there, 1559), was the most distinguished member of a family of architects, and was trained in Verona by his father Giovanni and his uncle Bartolommeo. He went to study in Rome about 1500, and was sent on papal missions to several Italian cities. From 1520 onwards he was engaged in remodelling the fortifications of Verona, including the fine Porta Nuova (1535) and Porta Palio. For the Venetian Republic he designed fortresses at Legnago, Peschiera, Brescia, Bergamo, the Lido (outside Venice), Zara, Sebenico, and Candia. His other buildings included the Corner-Mocenigo and Grimani palaces and some churches in Venice, and the Bevilacqua, Canossa, Della Torre, Malfatti, Pompei, and Verzi palaces in Verona.

See monographs by Ronzani and Luciolli, 1832, and Selva, 1814.

Sansovino, Andrea, called **Contucci** (*b.* Monte Sansavino, near Arezzo, *c.* 1460; *d.* there, 1529), sculptor and architect, was trained in sculpture by Pollaiulo and in architecture by Antonio Sangallo the Elder (q.v.). In the early part of his career he worked as a sculptor, including a period spent in Portugal from 1491 onwards in the service of the king. He then returned to Rome, where he designed and carved a number of fine monumental tombs, notably those of two cardinals, commissioned by Pope Julius II in 1505, for the church of S. Maria del Popolo. Other examples of his work may be seen in churches in Rome, Florence, Loreto, and Genoa in Italy, and in Lisbon and Coimbra in Portugal. His only purely architectural work of any size was the casing of the Casa Santa at Loreto with white marble, including many niches and statuettes, executed in 1512–1520.

See monograph by L. Pittoni, 1909.

Sansovino, Jacopo (*b.* Florence, 1486; *d.* Venice, 27 Nov. 1570), architect, received his surname from his master, Andrea Sansovino (q.v.), his real surname being Tatti. He accompanied Andrea to Rome in 1505, and there built the church of S. Marcello (1519) and the Palazzo Gaddi (*c.* 1520). When the sack of Rome occurred in 1527 he fled to Venice, where he remained until his death; and in 1529 he became chief architect to the Venetian Republic. In Venice he built the Loggetta adjoining St Mark's (1537–40); the Zecca (1535–45); the Libreria Vecchia (1536 onwards); the Palazzo Cornero della Ca' Grande (1537–56); the churches of S. Martino (1514), the Incurabili, S. Francesco della Vigna (1534), S. Spirito (1542, since destroyed), S. Geminiano (1557, since destroyed), and S. Fantino (1564); and the School of the Brotherhood of the Misericordia (1532).

See monograph by L. Pittoni, 1909.

Sanzio, Raphael, *see* RAPHAEL SANZIO.

Saracenic Architecture, *see* MUSLIM ARCHITECTURE.

Sash (corruption of Fr. *chassis*, a frame). The term seems to have been first used in England about 1686, soon after sash-windows were introduced; and Wren, in a letter of 21 Sept. 1693, refers to 'shasshes.' A sash is one of the two vertically sliding frames forming a sash-window.

Sash-window, *see* SASH.

Sassanian Architecture comprises the buildings erected in Persia

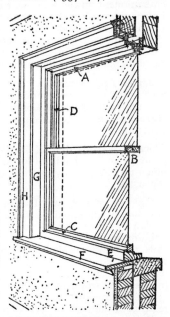

SASH-WINDOW. A=*top rail;* B=*meeting-rails;* C=*bottom rail;* D=*pulley stile;* E=*sill;* F=*window board;* G=*lining;* H=*architrave*

under the Sassanid or Sassanian kings, A.D. 226–641. *See* PERSIAN ARCHITECTURE.

Satellite Town, a term first used in 1919 as an alternative description of Welwyn Garden City. The term 'garden city' (q.v.) had then come to be wrongly applied to any well-planned industrial suburb. A satellite town, strictly speaking, is self-contained for most of the purposes of communal life, and is surrounded by a green belt (q.v.); but depends upon a much larger parent city (to which it stands in the relation of a satellite to a planet) for higher education, cultural opportunities above a certain level, and other amenities which a town with a population under 50,000 cannot provide. *See also* NEW TOWNS and TOWN-PLANNING.

Savage, James (*b.* London, 10 April 1779; *d.* there, 7 May 1852), architect, one of the pioneers of the Gothic Revival in England. He was articled to D. A. Alexander, with whom he stayed for many years, simultaneously attending the Royal Academy Schools. In 1805 he won a competition for rebuilding Ormonde Bridge, Dublin (not carried out), and in 1808 another for Richmond Bridge, Dublin, which was duly erected. He obtained second place for his design of London Bridge in 1823; and in 1825 published a plan for a new embankment on the south side of the Thames in London. His most important work was the church of St Luke, Chelsea, won by competition in 1819, and erected in 1820–4. Although its Perpendicular Gothic appears meagre to modern eyes, it heralded the coming Gothic Revival. In 1840 he began restoring the Temple Church, London, and he also built several other new churches.

Saxon Architecture, a term formerly used to describe English architecture of the centuries after the Roman evacuation of Britain and before the Norman Conquest. It is now generally described as '(Pre-conquest) Romanesque Architecture.' *See* ENGLISH ARCHITECTURE, 2.

Scagliola (Ital., dim. of *scaglia*, a scale or chip of marble), plaster painted and stained, often very skilfully, to represent marble; much used, especially in Italy, during the seventeenth to eighteenth centuries.

Scale (from Lat. and Ital. *scala*, a ladder). (1) In architectural drawing, a graduated instrument. Hence (2) the representation in a plan or model, by means of using such an instrument, of some building in its proper proportions but in a convenient smaller size: thus, the scales normally used by architects in England are ⅛ inch = 1 foot (or 1 : 96) for working drawings; ½ inch = 1 foot (or 1 : 24) for detail drawings. In other countries, where the metric system is in operation, approximately similar scales are used, e.g. 1 : 100. (3) In architectural design, 'scale' means the visually satisfactory relation of the various parts of a building to the whole, to each other, to the surroundings, and to the human figure; but exact definition of the term is difficult if not impossible, and its meaning is only intuitively apprehended by a highly trained critic.

Scallop, a carved ornament resembling a scallop shell, and used in Renaissance architecture.

Scalloped Capital, a Romanesque cushion capital which has its four sides cut into segmental convex projections like a scallop shell. (*Illustrated* CAPITAL ('E').)

Scamozzi, Vincenzo (*b*. Vicenza, 1552; *d*. Venice, 7 Aug. 1616), architect and writer on architecture, was trained by his father, an architect, and then by Jacopo Sansovino (q.v.). His principal buildings were the Palazzo Verlato, Villaverla (1576); Villa Pisani, Lonigo (1576); Palazzo Trissino (1577–9); church of S. Gaetano, Padua (1581–6); Procuratie Nuove, Venice (1584–1611); cathedral at Palmanuova (1603–5); Palazzo Contarini degli Scrigni, Venice (1609). He spent several years of study and travel in preparing his important book *L'Idea dell' Architettura Universale*, which appeared in Italian in 1615, in English in 1669, and also in other languages.

See monographs by T. Temanza, 1770; F. Scolari, 1837; F. Barbieri (n.d.); R. K. Donin, 1948.

Scandinavian Architecture. The three kingdoms constituting Scandinavia—Denmark, Norway, and Sweden—although now separate, have at various periods in history been combined one with another; and in any case there has always been a measure of family resemblance in their architecture, which has generally drawn its inspiration from countries farther south and west. In the present century, however, Sweden in particular has been a leader in some branches of architecture. The conversion of the three countries to Christianity occurred somewhat late; it was not fully achieved in Denmark till the tenth century and in Sweden till the twelfth. Because the Roman Empire never included any part of Scandinavia, the earliest surviving buildings are churches in the Romanesque style of western Europe, not the Byzantine style of south-eastern Europe. In Denmark they include the cathedrals of Viborg (much restored), Ribe, and Roskilde, also the remarkable church at Kalundborg; in Sweden the heavily restored cathedral at Lund; and in Norway the quaint but diminutive timber church at Borgund (twelfth century), which recalls a Japanese pagoda in the bold picturesqueness of its design. Of Gothic buildings, the chief examples are the cathedral of Odense in Denmark; the cathedrals of Uppsala and Linköping, and the monastic churches of Varnhem and Vadstena in Sweden; the cathedrals of Trondheim and Stavanger in Norway.

The Renaissance reached Scandinavia in the sixteenth century, mainly via Holland, and produced a crop of picturesque and imposing royal palaces during the periods corresponding to the English 'Elizabethan' and 'Jacobean.' They included the so-called castles of Rosenborg (1620–4), Kronborg (1577–85), and Frederiksborg (1602–20) in Denmark; of Gripsholm (1537) and Vadstena (1545) in Sweden; and Akershus Castle (1624) at Oslo in Norway.

Dutch influence also prevailed in the next period, when the Baroque style, which had spread from Italy to other parts of Europe, reached Scandinavia. In Denmark it produced the palaces of Charlottenborg and Frederiksborg, as well as the curious twisted spire of St Saviour's church at Copenhagen (1682–96); in Sweden the Riddarhuset at Stockholm (1656–72), the Karlberg Palace (1670), the huge palace of Drottningholm (begun 1662, by Nicodemus Tessin the Elder), and the royal palace at Stockholm (1656–1670, by Tessin the Younger).

Next came the Rococo style, seen at its best in the Amalienborg Palace (1760), the Prince's Palace, and the small Eremitagen Palace —all in Copenhagen; in the China Palace at Drottningholm, Sweden; and also in many charming Danish and Swedish country houses.

During the present century, in addition to a large number of admirably designed houses and public buildings, the most important architectural works in Scandinavia have been the remarkable Grundtvig Memorial Church, near Copenhagen (1921), by J. Klint, and the city hall at Stockholm (1911–22) by R. Östberg (q.v.).

See ASPLUND, JACOBSEN, MARKELIUS, RASMUSSEN, TENGBOM.

See also A. Lindblom, Sveriges Konsthistorie, 1944; E. Hiort, Contemporary Danish Architecture, 1949; B. Hultén, Building Modern Sweden, 1951; E. de Maré, Scandinavia, 1952; G. E. K. Smith, Sweden Builds, 1957; T. Paulsson, Scandinavian Architecture, 1958; G. Kavli, Norwegian Architecture, 1958.

Scena (Lat., from Gk skēnē, a tent), at first, a players' booth; then the architectural background of the stage in a Greek or Roman theatre.

Schädel, Gottfried (b. near Hamburg, 1680; d. Kiev, Russia, 21 Feb. 1752), architect, known in Russia as Ivan Ivanovich. In 1713 he went to Russia; between 1713 and 1725 designed the palaces of Oranienbaum and Vassili Ostrov; moved to Moscow where he built the small Annenhof Palace in the Kremlin; and finally retired to Kiev, where he remodelled several churches and added new towers to the cathedrals of St Sophia and St Andrew.

Schinkel, Karl Friedrich (b. Neuruppin, Germany, 13 Mar. 1781; d. Berlin, 9 Oct. 1841), architect, who became prominent in the 'Greek Revival' in Germany, was trained by David and Gilly, then studied in Italy, returning to Berlin in 1805. For a time he worked as a painter, but soon turned to architecture, and in 1811 was elected to the Academy of Architecture in Berlin. Within a few years he had become the leading architect in that city, where all his chief buildings were erected. They included the Königswache in Unter den Linden (1816–18); the theatre (1818–21); and the Old Museum (1823–30)—all in the classical or neo-Greek style; the Wordersche Kirche (1825–8), in English Gothic; and the School of Architecture (1831–5), a brick building in a more functional and non-traditional style. Among several fanciful schemes which were never realized was his design for a great royal palace on the Acropolis at Athens. He published his various projects in several volumes which appeared between 1820 and 1846.

See also monographs by F. Kugler, 1842; J. I. Hittorff, 1857; A. Grisebach, 1924; H. V. Pommern, 1942; P. O. Rave, 1948; and many others.

Schloss (Ger.), a castle or palace.

Scotia (Lat.), or **Trochilus,** a concave moulding used in Greek architecture, so called because it throws a sharp shadow (Gk *skotos,* darkness). (*Illustrated* MOULDINGS, CLASSICAL.)

Scott, Geoffrey (*d.* New York, 14 Aug. 1929, aged forty-six), architect and writer on architecture, was educated at Rugby, and at New College, Oxford. He then became librarian and secretary to Bernhard Berenson, the American writer on Italian art, in Florence, and subsequently practised there for some years in partnership with Cecil Pinsent. It was during this period that he wrote and published his admirable book, *The Architecture of Humanism* (1914), described by a competent critic as 'perhaps the most important contribution to the literature of aesthetics since the writings of Ruskin,' with whose opinions Scott so profoundly disagreed. He also published in 1925 a volume of poems and a biography, and was engaged at the time of his death in editing Boswell's letters, in America. During the First World War he was honorary attaché and then press secretary at the British Embassy in Rome.

Scott, Sir George Gilbert, R.A. (*b.* Gawcott, Buckinghamshire, 1811; *d.* London, 27 Mar. 1878), architect, the most prominent figure in English mid-Victorian architecture; R.I.B.A. Royal Gold Medallist, 1859; President R.I.B.A., 1873–6. The son of a poor village clergyman, he was articled in 1827 to James Edmeston. He next acted as assistant or clerk of the works to various architects from 1831 to 1834, and then embarked into practice with W. H. Moffatt, the two young men obtaining their work by vigorous canvassing of local guardians who were beginning to build the new-fangled 'workhouses.' Before 1845, when he severed his connection with Moffatt, the firm had secured some fifty such commissions. Meanwhile, in 1840, he had won the competition for the Martyrs' Memorial at Oxford, and at about that time he began his long, notable, and notorious career as a church restorer, with work at Chesterfield and Stafford. In 1844 he had a sensational success in the great international competition for St Nicholas's Church at Hamburg. This fairly launched him upon his enormous practice, which ultimately included many hundreds of new or restored churches and thirty-nine cathedrals or 'minsters.' His work as a restorer, beginning with Ely Cathedral in 1847, aroused some criticism, becoming bitter when William Morris (q.v.) attacked his restoration of Tewkesbury Abbey, and founded the S.P.A.B. (q.v.), just before Scott's death. This agitation clouded his last years. In his favour it must be admitted that he saved far more than he destroyed; and much of his restoration (e.g. the Chapter-house at Westminster Abbey) bears witness to his profound knowledge of Gothic architecture. Conversely, he was prone to make the restored cathedrals look too mechanical and shiny within. His preference for Decorated Gothic of the fourteenth century sometimes led him to destroy old features not in keeping with that period, and his treatment of St Michael's, Cornhill, London (by Wren), approached vandalism. His chapels at Exeter College, Oxford (1856), and St John's College, Cambridge (1862), show no sympathy with the *genius loci*. Among his many new churches were St Giles, Camberwell (1844); St Mary Abbots, Kensington (1869–72); and Christ Church, Ealing (1852). His other new buildings included the Albert Memorial (1864); Glasgow University (1864); Leeds Infirmary (1863); St Pancras Station (1865); St Mary's Cathedral, Edinburgh (1874–9); the Great Hall of Bombay University (1874); and the Foreign Office and India Office in Whitehall—the result of a very dubious competition in 1856, followed by acrimonious debates in Parliament, led by Sir William Tite (q.v.). Of his books, *Gleanings from Westminster Abbey*, 1861, and his reprinted *Lectures on Medieval Architecture*, 1879, delivered as Professor of Architecture at the Royal Academy, are excellent; but his *Recollections*, 1879, is mainly a defensive apologia, and is far too complacent.

Scott, George Gilbert, the Younger (*b.* 8 Oct. 1839; *d.* 6 May 1897), architect, was the son of Sir George Gilbert Scott (q.v.) and the father of Sir Giles Gilbert Scott (q.v.). Among many new churches designed by him, the most imposing is the fine Roman Catholic church of St John the Baptist at Norwich (1882–1910), and another good building was St Agnes, Kennington, London (1877, destroyed by bombing, 1941). He also designed St Mark, Leamington (1879), and at Pembroke College, Cambridge, he added a new block (1883).

Scott, Sir Giles Gilbert, O.M., R.A. (*b.* London, 9 Nov. 1880; *d.* there, 8 February 1960), architect; R.I.B.A. Royal Gold Medallist, 1925; President R.I.B.A., 1933–5; son of George Gilbert Scott the Younger (q.v.), and grandson of Sir George Gilbert Scott, R.A. (q.v.). He was educated at Beaumont College, and then articled to Temple Moore (1856–1920), who in his turn had been articled to Scott's father. He was still an articled pupil when in 1903, at the amazingly early age of twenty-two, he won the great public competition for the new (Anglican) cathedral at Liverpool against 103 rivals, among them his own chief. In view of the extreme youth of the winner, the Cathedral Committee appointed G. F. Bodley, R.A. (q.v.), one of the two assessors of the competition, as joint architect. The foundation-stone was laid in 1904, and work has continued ever since, but the work is still (1961) incomplete. Among Sir Giles Scott's other important buildings are the new Waterloo Bridge, London (completed 1940); the two huge power stations at Battersea and Bankside, London (completed in 1934 and 1954 respectively); Cambridge University Library (1935); the new Bodleian Library, Oxford (1941); Whitelands College, Putney (1930); Park Royal Brewery (1936); additions to Clare College, Cambridge (1934); Charterhouse School Chapel (1927); St Alban's Church, Golders Green (1933); rebuilding of the House of Commons (1950), and the Guildhall, London.

Scottish Architecture differs in many respects from that of England. Ignoring prehistoric remains, primitive round towers, and early Christian stone crosses as not constituting architecture proper, its story really begins with several monastic churches built in the twelfth century, including the cathedral of St Magnus, Kirkwall (1137); the abbeys of Dunfermline (1128–50), Jedburgh (1147), and Kelso

(1128); also the small parish churches of Leuchars (1183–7) and Dalmeny (c. 1160). The transition from Romanesque to Gothic reached Scotland later than England; examples: the ruined nave of Holyrood Abbey; the abbeys of Dundrennan, Glenluce, and Dryburgh; Elgin Cathedral (as remodelled, 1124); and, especially, the cathedrals of Glasgow and Dunblane. Early in the thirteenth century Scottish architecture, owing to strong French influence, began to drift away from the English tradition and to develop a distinctive national style, particularly in the design of window tracery and carved ornament, e.g. at Melrose Abbey, Sweetheart Abbey, Lincluden Abbey (properly Lincluden 'College'), and the unfinished choir of the church at Roslin, commonly called 'Roslin Chapel' (1457). The last phase of Gothic in Scotland also produced King's College Chapel, Aberdeen; St Giles's Cathedral, Edinburgh (both of which had 'crown' steeples); Paisley Abbey (c. 1450); and the church of the Holy Rude, Stirling (begun c. 1414). Further French influence in design appears in the first buildings of the Renaissance period, as a wish arose for more elegant and civilized places for living in than the rude but picturesque castles and 'peel-towers' (see PELE) of the Middle Ages. Examples are the courtyards of Caerlaverock Castle (c. 1638) and Crichton Castle, but the tendency may best be studied in the 'palace' added to Stirling Castle, and at Falkland Palace (1502–42). Other picturesque and even beautiful semi-medieval Scottish houses, bristling with turrets and adorned with 'corbie steps' (q.v.), are Craigievar (1610–24), Fyvie Castle, Glamis Castle, Midmar, Pinkie House (1613), Tolquon Castle (1584–1589), and Traquair. The Canongate Tolbooth, and Heriot's Hospital, both in Edinburgh, date from 1591 and 1628 respectively.

The full-blown or 'Palladian' Renaissance reached Scotland from England rather late, its leading Scottish architect being Sir William Bruce (q.v.) (d. 1710), who reconstructed Holyrood Palace, Edinburgh, in 1671–9, and then erected the huge Hopetoun House, which was completed after his death by his pupil William Adam, father of a still more famous son, Robert (q.v.), who in turn became the leading Scottish architect and designed some buildings in the magnificent 'New Town' of Edinburgh, as well as part of Edinburgh University. The planning of the 'New Town' was begun in 1767 by James Craig (q.v.), and continued by W. H. Playfair (q.v., 1789–1857), who also designed the Advocates' Library, the College of Surgeons, the National Gallery of Scotland, and Dollar Academy—mostly in revived Greek style (see ARCHITECTURE, PERIODS OF, 8; also THOMSON, A.). Many of the principal buildings in Scotland since c. 1850 are mentioned here under their architects' names (see BURNET, SIR J., LORIMER, SIR R., MACKINTOSH, C. R., SCOTT, SIR GEORGE GILBERT).

See also G. Scott-Moncrieff, *The Stones of Scotland*, 1938, and J. Fleming, *Scottish Country Houses*, 1954.

Scottish Baronial Style, a term used to describe the semi-fortified houses of the Scottish nobility during the medieval and Stuart periods, specially characterized by turrets with conical roofs. This style was revived by the architect William Smith of Aberdeen in his design of Balmoral Castle (1850–4).

Screen (Mid. Eng. *skrene*). (1) In any building, a partition to exclude draughts or to give privacy between two parts of a room. (2) In a church, either a rood-screen (q.v.) at the entrance to the chancel, or a parclose screen (q.v.) elsewhere. (3) In a college hall, or in the great hall of a medieval house, a panelled screen between the hall itself and the entrance to the kitchen-quarters. In such cases the space between the screen and the doors to the kitchen, pantry, etc., was called the 'screens' (plural.)

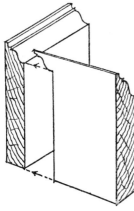

SCRIBING at angle of a moulded wooden skirting

Scribing, the cutting of two pieces of moulded woodwork (e.g. skirtings) where they meet at an angle, so that one fits over the mouldings of the other, this forming a 'scribed joint,' as opposed to a 'mitred joint' (*see* MITRE).

Scriptorium (Lat.), a writing-room, especially in a medieval monastery, where manuscripts were copied.

Scroll Moulding, in early Gothic architecture, a moulding resembling a scroll.

Sedding, John Dando (*b.* Eton, 13 April 1838; *d.* Winsford, Somerset, 7 April 1891), architect, younger brother of another architect, Edmund Sedding (1836–68). He entered the office of G. E. Street (q.v.) in 1858. His practice consisted mainly of churches, one of the first being St Clement, Bournemouth (1872). Others were Holy Trinity, Sloane Street (1888–90), showing great originality of design; the Holy Redeemer, Clerkenwell (1887–8); St Augustine, Highgate (1885)—all these in London; St Edward, Netley; All Saints, Falmouth; Salcombe; and St Dyfrig, Cardiff. For many years he was architect to the Diocese of Bath and Wells, in which he restored several churches. He was keenly interested in the Arts and Crafts movement. His *Garden-Craft: Old and New* was published in 1891, and *Art and Handicraft* in 1893.

See monograph by H. Wilson, 1892.

Sedilia (Lat., plural of *sedile*, a seat), in a church, a range of seats (generally three) on the south side of the chancel, for the use of the clergy. They are mainly of late Gothic date and are recessed in niches crowned with carved canopies and pinnacles.

Segmental Arch, an arch of which the contour is a segment of a circle, but less than a semicircle. (*Illustrated* ARCH, TYPES OF.)

Seicento (Ital., literally 'the sixteen-hundreds'), applied to Italian architecture of the seventeenth century, 1600–1699.

Semper, Gottfried (*b.* Hamburg, 29 Nov. 1803; *d.* Rome, 15 May 1879), architect and writer on architecture. He was trained as a

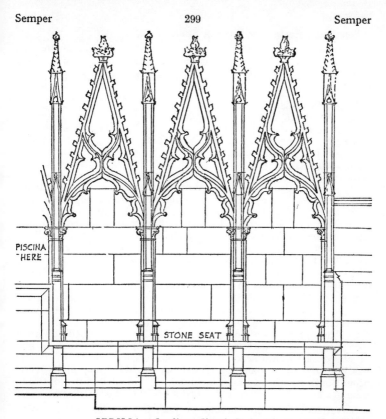

SEDILIA at Sandiacre Church, Derby. (1342)

lawyer, but became interested in classical architecture, and travelled extensively in Italy and Greece, 1830–5.   On returning to Germany, he became Professor of Architecture at Dresden in 1834, simultaneously practising as an architect, building the synagogue (1838–1840), the museum adjoining the Zwinger (1847–54), and the theatre (1838–41).   He became embroiled in the revolution of 1848, and eventually fled to London, where he was befriended by the Prince Consort, and was given work to do at the museums as well as lectures on art.   In 1853 he became Professor of Architecture at Zürich, where he also built the Polytechnic (1858–64), the Observatory, the railway station, and a hospital, besides the town hall at Winterthur (1865–71).   He then moved to Vienna where, in partnership with Hasenauer, he built the large Burgtheater (1873–88) and the two great museums (1872–81).   After a second brief spell in Dresden he spent the last years of his life in Italy.   He wrote several books on art and architecture.

See monograph by C. Lipsius, 1880.

Sepulchre, Easter, *see* EASTER SEPULCHRE.

Seraglio (Ital.), literally 'a place of confinement'; specifically, the women's apartments in a Turkish house. *See also* HAREM.

Serai (Turkish), either (i) a caravanserai (q.v.); or (ii) a Turkish palace.

Serlio, Sebastiano (*b.* Bologna, 6 Sept. 1475; *d.* Fontainebleau, 1554), architect and writer on architecture. He was originally trained by his father as a painter, and actually painted perspectives at Pesaro, but went to Rome in 1514, worked for Peruzzi (q.v.), and fled with him to Venice at the sack of Rome in 1527. After much preliminary travel and study he started writing his famous work *Architettura*, first published in Italian in 1537, and in English (in part) in 1611, also in French. While in Venice he assisted Jacopo Sansovino (q.v.) in designing the church of S. Francesco della Vigna, and himself designed the ceiling of St Mark's Library. In 1541, at the invitation of François I, he went to France and worked for many years at Fontainebleau. There he certainly designed the Hôtel d'Este (1546), and perhaps the Hôtel Montpensier, but of these only the gateways now remain; and his authorship of the Aile de la Belle Cheminée and the Grotte des Pins is doubtful. Thus no whole authenticated building by him survives in France.

Sert, José Luis (*b.* in Spain, 1902), architect and town-planner; succeeded Gropius (q.v.) as Professor of Architecture at Harvard University, U.S.A., in 1953, having been previously Professor of City Planning at Yale University, 1945. He was trained at Barcelona; then worked with 'Le Corbusier' (q.v.) in Paris, 1928–9; and practised on his own account in Barcelona from 1929 to 1939. He has prepared town plans for Barcelona, Bogotá, Lima, and several other South American cities, including the industrial town of Chimbote in Peru. In 1942 he published a book: *Can our Cities Survive?*

Servandoni, Giovanni Niccolò, or **Jean Gerome** (*b.* Lyons, 2 May 1695; *d.* Paris, 19 Jan. 1766), architect and designer of stage scenery. Although he studied both architecture and painting in Italy at the beginning of his career, he was exclusively concerned in designing stage *décor* in Paris for several years up to 1732, when he won a competition for completing the west front of the church of St Sulpice in Paris, which the architect Oppenord had left unfinished. This work, completed in 1754, was his only building of note in Paris, but he designed a theatre for the château of Chambord. Otherwise his work consisted of theatrical scenery and sundry pyrotechnic displays, of which the two most striking commemorate the Peace of Aix-la-Chapelle in 1749—one in Paris and one in London.

Settecento (Ital., literally 'the seventeen-hundreds'), applied to Italian architecture of the eighteenth century, 1700–1799.

Severy, in vaulting, a bay (q.v.).

Sexpartite Vault, a vault in which there are six intersections. (*Illustrated* VAULTING.)

Sgraffito (Ital., literally 'scratched off'), a form of decorative plasterwork, by which portions of the top coat of one colour are scratched off in order to expose an undercoat of another colour, thus producing the desired pattern.

Shaft. (1) Of a column, the body of the column between base and capital. (2) Of a chimney, the portion above a roof, from the base or plinth up to the capping.

Shaft Ring, an annulet or moulded ring around a shaft (q.v.) or circular pillar.

Shamsiyyah (Arabic), *see* QAMARIYYAH.

Sharawadgi, or **Sharawaggi,** a curious term, of unknown etymology, said by lexicographers not to be Chinese; but see quotations below. It was used in 1685 by Sir William Temple: 'The Chinese have a particular word to express it [sc. the beauty of studied irregularity], and where they find it hit their Eye at first sight, they say the *Sharawadgi* is fine or is admirable.' Horace Walpole, in a letter to Mann dated 25 February 1750, writes: 'I am almost as fond of the *Sharawaggi*, or Chinese want of symmetry, in buildings, as in grounds or gardens.' *See also* CHINOISERIE.

Sharpe, Edmund (*b.* Knutsford, 31 Oct. 1809; *d.* Milan, 8 May 1877), architect and writer on architecture. R.I.B.A. Royal Gold Medallist, 1875. He graduated at St John's College, Cambridge; spent three years studying in France and Germany as a 'travelling bachelor' of the university, was articled to Thomas Rickman (q.v.) and then began independent practice at Lancaster in 1836. During the next fifteen years he designed about forty churches, favouring the Romanesque rather than the Gothic style; and simultaneously wrote the first of a number of books, of which *The Seven Periods of English Architecture*, published in 1851, became a classic. In that year, however, he suddenly and surprisingly abandoned architecture for railway engineering.

Shaw, Richard Norman, R.A. (*b.* Edinburgh, 7 May 1831; *d.* London, 17 Nov. 1912), architect, who became the outstanding figure in English domestic architecture of the last third of the nineteenth century. When his family moved in 1845 from Edinburgh to London, he was articled to a London architect; later entered the busy office of William Burn, and in 1858 that of G. E. Street (q.v.), as head assistant. Meanwhile he had won the Gold Medal and Travelling Scholarship of the Royal Academy in 1854. The results of his subsequent and previous travels, elaborated after his return, were published in 1858 as *Architectural Sketches from the Continent*. In 1862 he started independent practice in London with W. E. Nesfield (q.v.) who had influential connections. The partnership lasted six years. (For their joint work *see* NESFIELD.) Thereafter Shaw's own immense practice included Cragside, Northumberland (1870); Preen Manor, Shropshire (1870); Grim's Dyke, Harrow Weald (1872); New Zealand Chambers, London (1872); Lowther Lodge, Kensington (1873); St Michael's Church, Bournemouth (1875); 196 Queen's Gate, London (1875); Swan House and Cheyne House, Chelsea (1876); 8 Melbury Road, Kensington (1876); Bedford Park, including St Michael's Church (1878); St Margaret's Church, Ilkley (1878); Flete, Devonshire (1878); Albert Hall Mansions, London (1879); The Clock House, and Nos 9, 10, 11 Chelsea Embankment (1879); Dawpool, near Birkenhead (1882); Alliance Assurance Company's offices, Pall Mall, London (1882); 180 Queen's Gate, London (1885); New Scotland Yard, London (1888); 170 Queen's Gate (1890); the enormous mansion of Bryanston, Dorset (1890); the Gaiety Theatre, London (1902); the Piccadilly Hotel, London (1905). This last work formed part of the rebuilding of the Quadrant of Nash's Regent Street; but the massiveness of its arches on the ground floor produced shop windows too restricted for commercial display, and the remainder of the Quadrant was rebuilt in a modified style by Sir Reginald Blomfield (q.v.) after Shaw's death.

See monograph by Sir R. Blomfield, 1940.

Shingles, thin pieces of wood used instead of tiles for roofing; once common in England, and still much used in America, where cedar is the normal material for them.

Shippon, a north-country name for a cow-house.

Shish (Arabic), light wooden fretted lattice, used in parts of Egypt.

Shoring, temporary timber framing to support the walls or floors of a building during alterations or because a wall is cracked or leaning. There are three principal types: (1) a 'dead shore' is a vertical timber post to support a floor or beam temporarily; (2) a 'raking shore' is a heavy timber beam fixed in a steeply sloping position against a wall, to prop it up; (3) a 'flying shore' (q.v.).

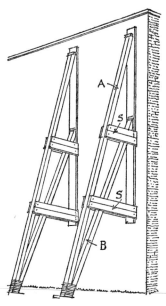

SHORING. A pair of raking shores against a wall. A=upper raker; B=lower raker; S=strutting

Shute, John, who lived between *c.* 1500 and *c.* 1570, was an English writer on architecture who is known to have studied in Italy, and was the first Englishman to describe himself as 'architect.' In 1563 he published *The First and Chief Groundes of Architecture,* the earliest manual on the subject in English. Nothing more seems to be known about him.

Shutter, a movable wooden or iron or steel screen, hung on hinges or pins inside or outside a window; in modern times, mainly for purposes of security. *See also* PERSIENNES.

Silo, a weatherproof chamber, or underground pit, for the storage of fodder, etc.

Sima, American spelling of Cyma (q.v.).

Simons, Ralph, *see* SYMONS.

Simpson, Sir John William (*b.* Brighton, 9 Oct. 1858; *d.* Highgate, 30 Sept. 1933), architect; President R.I.B.A., 1919–21. He was the son of an architect. Much of his work was carried out in partnership with Maxwell Ayrton, notably the layout of the British Empire Exhibition at Wembley, 1924, including the Stadium and the Palace of Industry. Among other buildings designed by the firm or by Simpson alone were the Cartwright Memorial Hall, Bradford; the offices of the Crown Agents for the Colonies, Millbank, London; Roedean School, Brighton; Gresham's School, Holt; school buildings at Lancing and Haileybury; and the National Hospital for the Paralysed, Queen Square, London. In 1923 he published *Essays and Memorials.*

Sinan (sixteenth century), a Turkish architect of Albanian origin who, according to Montani Effendi in *L'Architecture ottomane* (1873), lived to the age of 110, and claimed to have designed 73 mosques, 45 oratories, 52 madrasahs and schools, 7 aqueducts, 7 bridges, 27 palaces, 3 hospitals, 18 caravanserais, 31 baths, 18 tombs, and several other buildings. He certainly designed the two great mosques known as the Suleymaniye (1550–7) at Istanbul, and the Selimiye (1570–4) at Adrianople, now Edirne.
    See monograph by E. Egli, 1954.

Sitwell, Sacheverell (*b.* Scarborough, 1897), writer on architecture, etc.; son of Sir George Sitwell, Baronet, and brother of Sir Osbert and Edith Sitwell. He was educated at Eton. Of his many published books, which include fifteen volumes of poems, the following are concerned directly with architecture: *Southern Baroque Art,* 1924; *German Baroque Art,* 1927; *Spanish Baroque Art,* 1931; *Mauretania,* 1939; *British Architects and Craftsmen,* 1945; *Arabesque and Honeycomb,* 1957; and several of his travel books contain much penetrating architectural criticism, i.e. *The Netherlands,* 1948; *Spain,* 1950; *Portugal and Madeira,* 1954; *Denmark,* 1956.

Skene, *see* SCENA.

Skew Arch, an arch with its axis oblique with its faces.

Skidmore, Louis (*b.* Lawrenceburg, Indiana, U.S.A., 8 April 1897), architect. He was trained in Boston at the Massachusetts Institute of Technology; worked for Maginnis and Walsh in that city, 1924–6; travelled and studied in Europe, 1926–8. In 1936 he founded the firm of Skidmore, Owings, & Merrill, who were appointed Associated Architects for the great new United Nations Building in New York (1950). Other work by the firm includes the Terrace Plaza Hotel, Cincinnati, the Bellevue Medical Center, New York; and the Lever Building (1952).

Skylight, a glazed frame fitting over an opening in a sloping roof, to admit light. (*See also* LANTERN LIGHT.)

Skyscraper, a term apparently first used in America about 1891 to describe an unusually tall building. Such buildings are especially characteristic of New York, as the combined result of exceptionally high site values and of a subsoil of rock. Among them the most familiar are the Empire State Building, the Chrysler Building, and the Woolworth Building.

Slum (etymology unknown), a dwelling or group of dwellings unfit for healthy human habitation according to modern standards.

Slype, in a medieval monastery, a covered passage between the transept and the chapter-house, leading to the cloisters.

Smirke, Sir Robert, R.A. (*b.* London, 1 Oct. 1781; *d.* Cheltenham, 18 April 1867), architect; R.I.B.A. Royal Gold Medallist, 1853; has been described as 'probably the most successful architect of the early nineteenth century, though not the most gifted.' Son of an architect, he was fortunate to be admitted to the office of Sir John Soane (q.v.) at the age of fifteen, but wasted this opportunity and only stayed there a few months. In 1799, however, he won the Gold Medal of the Royal Academy, and travelled in Italy and Greece from 1801 to 1805. In 1806 he published some of his drawings as *Specimens of Continental Architecture*. Soon after his return to England, work began to pour into his hands: Lowther Castle, a huge Gothic mansion for the Earl of Lonsdale, in 1806; an appointment as architect to the Board of Trade in 1807; and one of three coveted posts as 'official architect' to the Board of Works in 1813—Soane and Nash (q.v.) being the other two. With the exception of Lowther and Eastnor Castles, a few small secular buildings in the provinces, and some restorations of Gothic churches, including York Minster, most of his work was in his favourite neo-Greek style. Selected from a very lengthy list, the following were his most important buildings—all in London: Covent Garden Theatre (1809, rebuilt 1857); the General Penitentiary, Millbank (1816, demolished); United Service Club, Lower Regent Street (demolished); Royal College of Physicians (1824–5); Union Club, Trafalgar Square (1924–7, now Canada House); General Post Office (1824–9, demolished); British Museum, excluding the domed Reading Room (1823–47); King's College, Strand (1831); Carlton Club (1835–6, since rebuilt); Oxford and Cambridge Club (1836–7); extensive work in the Inner Temple (1819–38); and the façades of buildings (now mostly demolished) in Lancaster Place, Moorgate Street, and King William Street.

Smirke, Sydney, R.A. (*b.* London, 1798 or 1799; *d.* Tunbridge Wells, 8 Dec. 1877), architect; R.I.B.A. Royal Gold Medallist, 1860; younger brother of Sir Robert Smirke (q.v.), to whom he was articled. He travelled in Italy and Sicily in 1820, and served as a clerk of the works from 1828 to 1832. His principal buildings were: the mansion in Gunnersbury Park, Middlesex (*c.* 1834); and the following in London: the reconstruction of the Pantheon, Oxford Street (1834, since demolished); the restoration of the Temple Church, 1841 (with D. Burton, q.v.); extensions of the British Museum, including the Reading Room (1847–55); rebuilding of the Carlton Club (1857, since gutted); extensions of Bethlehem Hospital, including the dome (1838–40); the Inner Temple Hall (1868–70, gutted by bombing); exhibition galleries of the Royal Academy at Burlington House (1866–70). He was Professor of Architecture at the Royal Academy from 1861 to 1865.

Smithson, or Smythson, Family of Architects, etc. (seventeenth century), included at least three members who may be regarded as architects. The oldest of them, father of the other two, was ROBERT (*b. c.* 1535; *d.* at Wollaton, near Nottingham, 1614, where a tablet in the church describes him as 'gent, architector, and survayor unto the most worthy house of Wollaton with divers others of great account'). It is generally assumed, though it is not certain, that he designed the florid and bombastic Wollaton Hall (1580). Of the two sons who followed in his footsteps, HUNTINGDON SMITHSON (*d.* Bolsover, 1648) is usually credited with the design of the fine terrace of Bolsover Castle, and with the chief share in making the remarkable 'Smithson Drawings' now in the library of the R.I.B.A. It is believed that he was sent to Italy to study by a 'noble patron,' but the crude details of Bolsover may well have been derived from Italian, German, or Flemish pattern-books. JOHN SMITHSON (*d.* Bolsover, 1634), another son of Robert, worked as a mason at Bolsover, but has been credited with the design of a glasshouse at Wollaton, and of the riding-school (1623) and stables at Welbeck.

Smythson, *see* SMITHSON.

Soane, Sir John, R.A. (*b.* Goring-on-Thames, 10 Sept. 1753; *d.* London, 20 Jan. 1837), architect, was the son of a bricklayer. In 1768 he entered the office of George Dance the Younger (q.v.), the city surveyor, and in 1771 was admitted to the Royal Academy Schools. In 1772 he was awarded the Silver Medal for a measured drawing of Inigo Jones's Banqueting House, and in 1776 the Gold Medal for a drawing of 'a triumphal bridge.' By that time he was working as an assistant for Henry Holland (q.v.), with whom he remained till 1778, when he was awarded the king's Travelling Studentship. After travelling in Italy for two years he set up private practice in London, and in 1784 married the daughter of a wealthy builder, whose property she inherited in 1790. In October 1788, through the influence of William Pitt, Soane was appointed architect to the Bank of England, a most important and lucrative post. Soon afterwards a series of government appointments followed, culminating in 1814 in one of the three posts as 'attached architects' of the Board of Works, with personal responsibility for Whitehall, Westminster, and Hampton Court Palaces, etc. In addition to all these he conducted a considerable private practice, and was also Professor of Architecture at the Royal Academy from 1806 until his death. His busy and sometimes harassing career is one of the most interesting in our architectural history, and his designs were original as well as classical and scholarly. Apart from his rebuilding of the Bank of England (1788–1833), his enormous list of work includes the Mausoleum and Art Gallery at Dulwich College (1811–14); the Infirmary at Chelsea Hospital (destroyed by bombing);

churches at Walworth (1822), Holy Trinity, Marylebone (1825), and Bethnal Green (1824–5); Nos. 12, 13, 14 Lincoln's Inn Fields; Bentley Priory, Stanmore (1798); his own house, Pitzhanger Manor, Ealing—now the public library—(1800–2); Freemasons' Hall, London (1826); and a number of country houses.   Before his death he left a handsome sum to the R.I.B.A. which provided a valuable travelling studentship; another for distressed architects and their families; and in 1833 bequeathed his fine town house in Lincoln's Inn Fields and his art collections, with an endowment for upkeep, to the nation.   It remains exactly as he inhabited it, and among its treasures are Hogarth's *The Rake's Progress* and *The Election*.   It is known as 'Sir John Soane's Museum.'   He himself published a description of it in 1832, and several larger books.

See monographs by A. T. Bolton, 1924 and 1927, and by J. N. Summerson, 1952.

Society for the Protection of Ancient Buildings (offices at 55 Great Ormond Street, London, W.C.1) was founded in 1877 by William Morris (q.v.), who himself originated its familiar nickname of 'the Anti-Scrape.'   For its objects, etc., *see* RESTORATION.

Society of Architects, founded in 1884, was amalgamated with the R.I.B.A. (q.v.) in 1925.

Soffit (from Fr. *soffite*), the underside of a lintel, arch, or cornice. (*Illustrated* ARCH, PARTS OF AN.)

Solar, in a large late medieval or Tudor house, a parlour or private sitting-room for the owner's family, away from the turmoil of communal life in the 'Great Hall.'   (*Illustrated* HOUSE.)

Solarium (Lat., from *sol*, the sun), a terrace or room exposed to the sun; especially a verandah in a sanatorium.

Soufflot, Jacques Germain (*b.* Irancy, France, 22 July 1713; *d.* Paris, 29 July 1780), architect.   He studied from 1734 to 1737 at the French Academy in Rome, travelled extensively in Italy and Asia Minor, and finally settled in Paris.   He was admitted to the French Academy of Architecture in 1749, worked for some time in official employment, and in 1755 won the important competition for the church of St Geneviève (afterwards called the Panthéon), of which the building began in 1764, but was not finished before his death.   He was appointed *architecte du Roi* in 1757, and was given charge of work at the Louvre.   His other buildings included the École de Droit (1756–71) and the sacristy of the cathedral of Notre-Dame—both in Paris; the Hôtel-Dieu, etc., at Lyons; the church of the Visitation at Le Mans; the hospital at Maçon (1770); additions to the cathedral at Rennes (1754–60); and to the town hall at Bordeaux (1755).

See monograph by J. Mondain-Monval, 1918.

Sounding-board, a board or screen, fixed behind or above a pulpit, in order the reflect the preacher's voice towards the congregation; much used in England during the seventeenth to eighteenth centuries and, in many of Wren's City churches, richly decorated.   The panelled canopy or board above the pulpit is also sometimes called a 'tester' (q.v.).

South African Architecture. When the Dutch established a trading station on the site of modern Cape Town in 1652, it was intended merely as a convenient fortified halfway house on the shipping route to their valuable East Indian colonies. Five years later the first batch of nine married burghers arrived as colonists, and by 1672 the total adult male population, including the garrison, was 370. The present castle, begun in 1665, was enlarged by the first governor, Simon van der Stel, in 1679. At Rondebosch is his fine old farm and barn, bearing the name of Groote Schuur (*see* below). The population grew rapidly, and by 1793, when the British captured the colony (to prevent it falling into French hands), numbered 13,830 Dutch burghers and 17,767 slaves. There was no native architecture in South Africa. The first church in Cape Town was built in 1700–4; and surviving secular buildings of this early period include the 'Old Town House' (1755) and the Koopmans-de Wet House: both are now art galleries. The latter may have been designed by the French architect, L. M. Thibault (*c.* 1750–1815). Many French Huguenot refugees came to the Cape, from 1686 onwards, to escape persecution, and Thibault may well have contributed French Rococo ideas to the design of the numerous charming farmsteads erected during the eighteenth century near Cape Town, at French Hoek and The Paarl, many of which bear French names (*see* below). Examples of Cape country houses include Groot Constantia, the governor's own house (1691, altered later by Thibault); Morgenster, Somerset West (1786); 'Picardy,' 'Dauphiné,' 'Provence,' and 'Burgundy'—all at French Hoek. They have picturesque curved 'Cape gables,' neither quite French nor quite Dutch. Cape architecture experienced the normal sequence of European architectural fashions during the nineteenth century, and the chief public buildings then erected were in the 'Free Classic' style. In 1892, when Herbert Baker (q.v.) arrived in South Africa to seek his fortune as an architect, he was befriended by Cecil Rhodes, then all powerful in the colony, and proceeded to revive the charming old Dutch architecture, then out of fashion. He restored Groote Schuur for Rhodes, and then established a very large practice, including the great block of Parliament Buildings at Pretoria, started soon after the Union Government made Pretoria the capital in 1910, and the Rhodes Memorial (1912). Since about 1925 the architectural centre of gravity has moved to the great city of Johannesburg; and the prevailing style, influenced from France, Germany, and America, has become cosmopolitan rather than regional.

See D. Fairbridge, *Historic Houses of South Africa*, 1922; G. E. Pearse, *Eighteenth Century Architecture in South Africa*, 1933; J. Walton, *Homesteads and Villages of South Africa*, 1952.

South American Architecture, *see* Brazilian Architecture.

S.P.A.B., abbreviation for Society for the Protection of Ancient Buildings (q.v.).

Spalling, the breaking away of chips or fragments (spalls) of the facing of dressed stonework in a building, due either to insufficient bedding of the blocks in mortar, or to the pressure of superincumbent masonry.

Span, the distance between the supporting abutments of an arch, the supports of a beam, or the walls carrying a roof. (*Illustrated* ARCH, PARTS OF AN.)

Spandrel, the quasi-triangular space between the outer curve ('extrados') of an arch and its enclosing rectangular moulded frame (if any); or between two adjacent arches and the horizontal moulding or string-course above them. The spandrel is sometimes richly carved, e.g. at Stone Church, Kent.

SPANDREL at Stone Church, Kent (c. 1260)

Spanish Architecture, chiefly because of the Muslim invasion and occupation of much of the land, is more difficult to describe briefly than that of any other European country. Spain possesses many well-preserved remains of Roman buildings, notably in the town of Mérida; but the finest surviving monuments are the great bridge over the Tagus at Alcántara, which has been continuously in use since it was built in A.D. 105, and the colossal aqueduct at Segovia, half a mile long, with its central arches 95 feet high. The Visigoths, who invaded Spain in A.D. 415, were converted to Christianity, and erected a number of small churches; but only a few of these, commonly called 'Visigothic,' are certainly original. Five remain fairly intact, and are ascribed to the seventh century or thereabouts: among them is S. Juan de Baños near Palencia. When the Muslim Arabs invaded Spain from Africa in 711 the rudimentary architecture of their mosques was based upon Muhammad's original mosque in Arabia (*see* MOSQUE). In 786 the construction of the famous mosque at Córdoba was begun, and its building continued for more than two centuries. (In 1236 it became a Christian cathedral and underwent some alteration.) It is very large, intricately designed, and richly decorated. The Puerto del Sol at Toledo is almost the only other example in Spain of early Muslim, or—as it is sometimes called— 'Moorish' architecture.

Meanwhile the Christian Visigoths had taken refuge in the mountains of Asturias in the north of Spain, where they built a number of small churches. Of ten still surviving from the period, *c.* 715–*c.* 915, five are situated near Oviedo, including S. Miguel in that town and S. Julian de los Prados at Santullano. Three more—S. María de Naranco, S. Cristina de Lena, and S. Miguel de Lino—apparently by one architect, were built 842–50. They had apses, round arches, and stone barrel-vaulting. In the province of León, refugee Christian craftsmen from the south built several 'Mozarabic' (i.e. Christian-Moorish) churches in the tenth century, all small and rather inaccessible; but in these we find the 'round horseshoe' arch (*see* ARCH), which is a characteristic feature of Muslim architecture. The campaigns of the eleventh century drove back the Moors to the south, and then a great boom in church-building began in North Spain. The finest Romanesque example is the cathedral of Santiago de Compostela (1078 onwards); others are S. Isidoro at León and the Old Cathedral at Salamanca. Abreast of these, but over a long period, the Moors in the south built the Alcázar at Seville, the Alhambra at Granada, and the beautiful Giralda tower or minaret at Seville (1184–96). (*See* MOZARABIC and MUDEJAR.)

Gothic churches in Spain are derived from French and German sources. They include the cathedrals of Toledo (1227); Burgos (1221); León (*c.* 1240); Barcelona (1298); Gerona (1312); Pamplona (1317); then, in a florid style showing Moorish influence, Salamanca (New Cathedral) (1512), Segovia (1522), and Seville (1402).

The impact of the Renaissance on Spain during the sixteenth century produced the 'Plateresque' style, so called because its intricate decorations suggested the work of a goldsmith (*platero*). There are many examples in Valladolid, Salamanca, and Zaragoza. The larger houses of this period included a beautiful internal courtyard (*patio*). The fully developed Italian Renaissance appears in the cathedrals of Granada (1520), Málaga (1538), and Jaén (1532); but most of all in Charles V's immense palace, monastery, and church known briefly as 'the Escorial,' begun in 1559. (*See* HERRERA, MACHUCA, MORA, RIAÑO, TOLEDO.)

The Baroque style was welcomed with enthusiasm in Spain, where some of its most remarkable and picturesque buildings are to be seen, several of them by the Spanish architect Churriguera, others by Italian architects. They include the façades of the cathedrals of Santiago, Jaén, Granada, Murcia, and Valladolid; the royal palaces at Madrid, La Granja, and Aranjuez; and the great Jesuit college at Loyola. (*See* RIBERA and CHURRIGUERA.)

After about 1750 Spanish architecture experienced the succession of architectural revivals that occurred in other countries. During the past hundred years its most striking buildings have been the huge and bizarre church of the Holy Family at Barcelona, begun 1881, and the university city of Madrid, half destroyed in the civil war of 1936–9. Since that date modern buildings have tended to follow the 'functional' fashions of other parts of Europe.

See S. Sitwell, *Spanish Baroque Art*, 1931, and *Spain*, 1950; B. Bevan, *History of Spanish Architecture*, 1938.

Speculative Builder, *see* BUILDER.

L

Speer, Albert (*b.* Mannheim, 19 Mar. 1905), architect; son of an architect of the same name, practising at Heidelberg. He was trained at the Technical High School at Karlsruhe and elsewhere. He attracted the interest of Hitler, who himself had always wished to become an architect, but who had failed to pass the entrance examination for the profession and had therefore been compelled to work as a house painter. In Speer he found an able architect capable of carrying out his ambitious schemes, and content to develop a new distinctively German style in contrast to the internationalist modernism practised by Gropius (q.v.) and his disciples, many of whom were Jews. This style was solid, and somewhat classical, unlike the glass and concrete designs of the modernists. Speer's immense commissions began with the Congress Hall in Nuremberg (holding 20,000 persons), which he won in competition. He also designed the huge stadium and the grandstands on the Zeppelin Field at Nuremberg, and in Berlin the New Chancellery (Reichskanzlei) and the Sports Centre. Hitler appointed him Generalbauinspektor for the Reichshauptstadt in 1937, and after the Second World War began, made him Minister of Armaments. At the Nuremberg trials of 1945–6, Speer was sentenced to twenty years' imprisonment for 'war crimes' and 'crimes against humanity.' For illustrations and descriptions of his work, see his *Neue Deutsche Baukunst*, 1943.

Spence, Sir Basil Urwin, R.A. (*b.* Bombay, 13 Aug. 1907), architect; President R.I.B.A., 1958–9; was trained in Edinburgh; then worked for some years in the offices of Sir G. Washington Browne and of Sir E. L. Lutyens (q.v.). He started private practice in 1932, and in the following year was awarded the Pugin Studentship of the R.I.B.A. In 1951 he won the important competition for Coventry Cathedral, now under construction. His other work has included the Scottish Pavilion at the Empire Exhibition (1938); the Sea and Ships Building at the South Bank Exhibition (1951); the rebuilding of the fishing village at Dunbar (1951); the Nuclear Physics Building at Glasgow University (1952); Secondary School at East Kilbride (1952); Edinburgh University Library and Chapel (1954); Southampton University Engineering Block and Women's Hall of Residence (1954); buildings for chemistry and agricultural sciences, Nottingham University; physics buildings at Durham and Liverpool Universities; Hampstead Town Hall (1958); Church of St Francis, Wythenshawe, Manchester (1958); new buildings for Queen's College, Cambridge; layout of new University College of Sussex, 1959; British Embassy at Rome, 1961. He was appointed first Hoffmann-Wood Professor of Architecture at Leeds University, 1958–9.

Spindle and Bead, an enriched moulding consisting of alternate spindles (cylinders) and beads.

Spire (Old Eng. *spīr*), an elongated pyramidal structure erected upon the top of a tower. Though often regarded as an ornamental feature, it was originally a normal plain pyramidal roof (as at Southwell Cathedral); but in Gothic times its height came to be greatly increased, either for visual effect or to rival other churches or to

SPIRE. (A) *Southwell Cathedral (Romanesque style)*; (B) *Godalming—timber and lead, with broaches* (X); (C) *Ewerby, Lincs., with broaches* (X); (D) *Kettering;* (E) *Newcastle Cathedral, c.* 1470 *(crown-steeple type)*; (F) *St Mary-the-Virgin, Oxford (early 14th century)*

express medieval religious aspiration—'a finger pointing heaven-wards.' Sometimes an octagonal spire rises direct from a square tower, the transition being contrived by 'broaches' (*see* BROACH); this type is characteristic of Northamptonshire. Otherwise the tower has a parapet. In England there are notable stone spires at Salisbury, Chichester, Norwich, and Lichfield cathedrals, and at the parish churches of Louth, Newark, and Patrington. The tall spires of the parish churches of Chesterfield and Harrow are of timber covered with lead. The famous spire of Old St Paul's, London, was destroyed by fire in 1567. *See also* HELM, STEEPLE, and *illustration*.

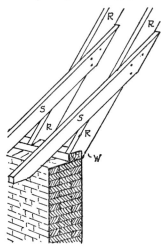

SPROCKET (S) *on a roof.* R=*rafter;* W=*wall-plate*

Spirelet, a small spire. *See* FLÈCHE.

Splay, a slope or bevel; more especially the slope of the sides of a window where the external opening is narrower than the internal, the sides or 'jambs' being then described as 'splayed.' (Cf. BEVEL, CHAMFER.)

Springer, the lowest voussoir (q.v.) of a masonry arch, with its under-side level with the springing-line (q.v.).

Springing-line, the level from which an arch begins to 'spring,' i.e. to curve inwards and upwards. (*Illustrated* ARCH, PARTS OF AN.)

Sprinklers, an elaborate arrange-ment of small pipes and 'heads' (or 'sprinkler heads') fixed under a ceiling, and coming into operation automatically whenever the temper-ature of the room beneath exceeds 150 degrees F. At that point the solder in each 'head' begins to melt, thus opening a valve, and then each 'head' sprays water downwards as a fire-extinguisher.

Sprocket, in a timber roof, a piece of wood nailed to each rafter near its foot, and having a gentler slope than the rafter itself, thus forming projecting eaves.

Spur-stone, a cylindrical piece of stone, built into the salient angle of a building on a street, in order to prevent damage to the angle.

Squinch, or **Squinch Arch,** a small arch built obliquely across each internal angle of a square tower or other structure in order to carry a circular dome or octagonal spire. This form is of very ancient eastern origin. (*Illustrated* p. 313.)

Squint, or **Hagioscope** (Gk *hagios,* holy; *skopein,* to look at), a small aperture cut through a wall or pier of a church to enable a worshipper to see the elevation of the Host in the chancel.

Stack, Chimney, *see* CHIMNEY-STACK.

SQUINCH arches (S) *at the Great Mosque, Quairawan, Tunisia* (862)

STADDLE-STONES under a granary at Cowdray, Sussex

Staddle-stones, short stone posts used to support a granary or a haystack.

Stadium (Lat., from Gk *stadion*), a place for athletic exercises, so called because the original Roman stadium was one-eighth of a Roman mile (or approximately one furlong) in length, this measure of length being called a *stadium*. The original stadium at Athens, laid out about 330 B.C., was restored at vast expense in 1895, and used for the first Olympic Games in 1896. It accommodates 70,000 spectators. Mussolini's Olympic Stadium in Rome holds 65,000 and that at Wembley in England about 100,000.

Stained Glass. All coloured glass used in windows is 'stained,' in the sense that it derives its colour from some metallic oxide added during its manufacture; but most medieval and modern 'stained glass' is also painted by hand, after manufacture, to give additional detail, e.g. the faces of the saints and delicate floral ornament. Thus the term 'stained' is more appropriate than 'painted' as a general description. In early Byzantine churches (e.g. S. Sophia at Constantinople) and in many early Muslim mosques, from the sixth century onwards, small pieces of coloured glass were set in a framework or lattice of plaster or marble. These were 'stained,' not 'painted.' The introduction of didactic pictures or 'stories' into windows (hence Milton's description of 'storied windows richly dight') began in the churches of northern Europe during the eleventh century, and the fashion became so popular that in 1134 the austere Cistercian Order insisted on plain glass in their churches. Notable windows of this early period can be seen at Canterbury Cathedral in England and at Chartres in France, the glass being boldly coloured and set in heavy leadwork. In the thirteenth century there was a move in the opposite direction, and *grisaille* (Fr., greyish) glass was favoured, with very little strong colour and much clear glass, details being painted in brown. A fine example is the famous 'Five Sisters' in York Minster, but there are many others in England, France, and Germany. As Gothic tracery became more complicated, and didactic pictures or 'stories' increasingly popular, the glass painters demanded more suitably shaped frames for their pictures than the irregular shapes produced by curvilinear tracery. This demand led to the rectilinear openings of the English Perpendicular Gothic style in the fifteenth to sixteenth centuries, and made possible the magnificent windows at Henry VII's Chapel, Westminster, and at King's College Chapel, Cambridge. Colours now became richer and more varied. At the Reformation much of the best English glass was destroyed by iconoclasts who attacked indiscriminately, but often with official support, all 'idolatrous images' of saints, etc., whether carved in stone or painted on wood or glass. There was a brief and feeble attempt to revive the craft in the eighteenth century (e.g. the window by Sir Joshua Reynolds in New College Chapel, Oxford, 1782); but in the Gothic Revival under A. W. N. Pugin (q.v.) and others, in the second quarter of the nineteenth century, a great deal of modern stained glass was produced in England; and towards the close of the nineteenth century, largely as a result of the artistic skill of W. Morris (q.v.) and E. Burne-Jones, a real revival of the art took place, and some recent stained glass compares favourably with the best work of the past.

 See monographs by H. Holiday, 1896; L. F. Day, 1903 and 1909; W. R. Lethaby, 1905; F. S. Eden, 1913; L. B. Saint and H. Arnold, 1913; C. W. Whall, 1920; E. W. Twining, 1928. *See also* R. Sowers, *The Lost Art*, 1954.

Staircase, originally the enclosure of a flight of stairs; in modern usage, the actual flight or flights of stairs. See *illustration.*

Stairs (generally used in plural), a series of steps ascending from one level to another; nowadays synonymous with STAIRCASE (q.v.).

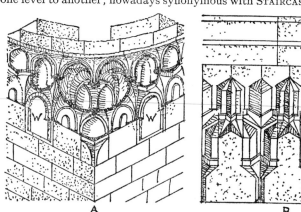

STALACTITE ORNAMENT. (A) *Beneath and inside a dome* (W=*windows*); (B) *In a stone cornice. Both from Cairo. (Based on Gayet's 'L'Art arabe,'* 1893)

Stalactite Ornament (from the Gk adj. *stalactos*, a dripping [stone]). Applied in geology to a formation of calcium carbonate resembling an icicle and hanging from the roof or walls of a cavern. In architecture, applied to a type of ornament supposed to resemble such a feature,

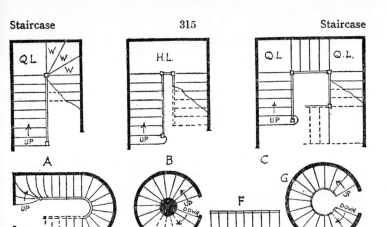

STAIRCASE: PLANS OF VARIOUS TYPES. (A) *Dog-legged;* (B, C) *Open newel;* (D) *Geometrical;* (E) *Circular newel;* (F) *Straight;* (G) *Circular geometrical.* W=*winder;* HL=*half-landing;* QL=*quarter-landing*

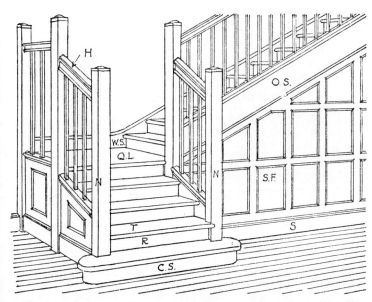

STAIRCASE: PARTS OF A WOODEN (NEWEL). CS=*curtail step;* H=*hand-rail;* N=*Newel-post;* OS=*outer string;* QL=*quarter-landing;* R=*riser;* S=*skirting;* SF=*spandrel framing;* T=*tread;* WS=*wall string*

and peculiar to Muslim architecture (q.v.). It appears to have originated in the multiplication of small squinch arches (*see* SQUINCH) on a pendentive, as illustrated at A; then came to be used in the heads of doorways, in rows along a cornice as at B; and finally in all parts of Muslim buildings—even on wooden pulpits and minor furniture—from Morocco and Spain to the Far East. It thus became one of the hall-marks of Muslim architecture, and its complicated arrangement of prisms appealed to the Arab love of geometrical decoration, stimulated by the Islamic prohibition of the use of natural forms in ornament.

Stall. (1) In a cow-house or stable, a division providing standing-room for one beast. (2) In a church, one of a row of seats separated by arms, and provided for the clergy and choir. The term is applied especially to richly decorated and canopied seats in cathedrals, or monastic or collegiate churches. *See also* MISERICORD.

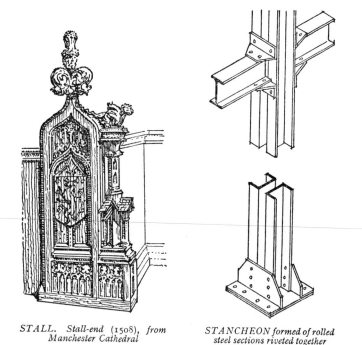

STALL.   Stall-end (1508), *from Manchester Cathedral*

STANCHEON formed of rolled steel sections riveted together

Stancheon (from Old Fr. *estanchon*), in steel-frame construction, a vertical member supporting a girder.

Stand. (1) In a meeting-house of the Society of Friends ('Quakers'), a rostrum for the elders. (2) In the U.S.A., a witness-box in a court of law.

Starov, Ivan Jegorowich (*b.* Moscow, 1743; *d.* St Petersburg, 1808), architect. After studying at the university of Moscow, at the academy at St Petersburg, in Paris, and in Rome, he was articled to the architect Prince D. V. Ukhtomski, a follower of Rastrelli (q.v.). His first important commissions were a palace and church at Bobriki (1773–9), for the Empress Catherine; and later she employed him to design the Tauride Palace at St Petersburg (1783–8), with its vast 'Catherine Hall' and its winter garden, for her favourite, the Prince of Tauride. Starov's other buildings included a mansion at Nikolskoe, near Moscow, for Prince Gagarin, and the Alexander or 'Trinity' Cathedral at St Petersburg (1776–90).

Steeple, a term sometimes applied to a tall tower with a spire; but more specifically to the curious lanterns or spires in the form of a crown at Newcastle Cathedral, St Giles's Cathedral at Edinburgh, King's College Chapel at Aberdeen, and St Dunstan-in-the-East, London (by Wren) which is derived from them. It is also applied loosely to Wren's other spired church towers in London. (*Illustrated* p. 318.)

Stela (Lat., from Gk *stēlē*), in classical Greece, an upright block of marble or stone used as a tombstone; usually about 5 feet high, $2\frac{1}{2}$ feet wide, and 9 inches thick, its upper part carved in low relief with commemorative figures, etc.

Stellar Vaulting (Lat., *stella*, a star), a type of Gothic vaulting in which the lierne ribs and intermediate ribs converge at regular intervals to form a star.

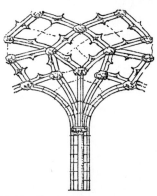

STELLAR VAULTING: from St Mary Redcliffe, Bristol

Stephenson, Şir Arthur George (*b.* 7 April 1890; *d.* Melbourne, Australia, 18 Nov. 1967), R.I.B.A. Royal Gold Medalist, 1954; first Australian architect to receive that award. He was educated in Melbourne, worked in various offices in Sydney, took part in an expedition to New Guinea, and spent some time in Western Australia before the First World War, when he served in France. After a short spell at the Architectural Association School (q.v.) in London, he returned to Australia and founded the firm of Stephenson & Meldrum at Melbourne in 1921. He specialized in hospital design and built the very large Royal Melbourne Hospital (1945); the Royal Children's Home and Health Centre, also at Melbourne (1954); the Ballarat Hospital (1935); the General Military Hospital at Yaralla, Sydney (1941); the Dental Hospital, Sydney (1941); the Children's Hospital, Frankston (1927); and St Vincent's Hospital, Sydney (1942). His other buildings include several large office blocks in Sydney; the Australia Hotel, Sydney (1953); and the Darwin Hotel (1939).

Stereotomy (from Gk), literally 'the cutting of solids'; hence the

* L

STEEPLE. *Left, St Mary-le-Bow; centre, above, St Martin, Ludgate; centre, below, St Dunstan-in-the-West; right, St Bride, Fleet Street. All in London and all designed by Wren*

art or science of cutting stones into regular forms, involving a considerable knowledge of solid geometry.

Stile, in joinery, one of the upright members of a panelled door. (*Illustrated* DOOR.)

Still-room, in old farmhouses, etc., a room in which stood the 'still,' for the distillation of cordials and perfumes.

Stilted Arch, a form of arch in which the springing-line (q.v.) is above the impost instead of (as normally) at impost level; used in Romanesque and Muslim architecture. (*Illustrated* ARCH, TYPES OF.)

Stoa (Gk), a portico or roofed colonnade. The finest example is the great Stoa of Attalos (second century B.C.) on the Agora at Athens, recently restored as a museum.

Stoep (Dutch), in South Africa, the verandah of a Dutch house.

Stokes, Leonard Aloysius Scott (*b.* Southport, 1858; *d.* London, 25 Dec. 1925), architect; President R.I.B.A., 1910–12; R.I.B.A. Royal Gold Medallist, 1919. His family moved to London in 1871, and Stokes entered the office of S. J. Nicholl in 1874. He subsequently worked for G. E. Street (q.v.), first as clerk of the works and then as draughtsman to T. E. Collcutt and G. F. Bodley (qq.v.). In 1880 he won the Pugin Studentship of the R.I.B.A., travelled in Germany and Italy, 1881–2, and started private practice in 1883. From that date until 1915, when his health gave way, his work consisted mainly of Roman Catholic churches and convents, schools, private houses, and telephone exchanges. The last item is not surprising, as he married the daughter of the manager of the National Telephone Company (then operating the telephone service) in 1898. Of the nineteen exchanges which he designed, the best was in Gerrard Street, London (1904), but it was rebuilt about 1930. His only civic building was the extension of Chelsea Town Hall (King's Road frontage) in 1904–8. His most important domestic building was Minterne House, Cerne Abbas, Dorset, for Lord Digby (*c.* 1905). Among his numerous ecclesiastical commissions, All Saints Convent, at London Colney (1899), is outstanding. In 1914 he began the Roman Catholic Cathedral at Georgetown, British Guiana, but it was unfinished at his death. He made additions to Downside Abbey, Bath (1907), and to Emmanuel College, Cambridge (1909–11). His work is marked by great originality, and his treatment of Gothic was both fresh and scholarly. His fine presidential portrait at the R.I.B.A., by Orpen, depicts him in a beige dressing-gown.

Stone, Edward Durrell (*b.* Fayetteville, Arkansas, U.S.A., 9 Mar. 1902), architect, was trained at Harvard and the Massachusetts Institute of Technology. He began independent practice in 1936. With P. L. Goodwin, he designed the Metropolitan Museum of Modern Art, New York (1939). His other work includes the U.S. Embassy at New Delhi (1957) and the American Pavilion at the Brussels Exhibition (1958).

Storey, plural **Storeys,** one of the horizontal stages of a building. (Although often spelt STORY, with plural STORIES, this latter spelling is apt to cause confusion; and, even in architecture, is applied to the didactic pictures in stained-glass windows—*see* STAINED GLASS.)

Storey-post, one of the stout posts carrying the upper part of a timber-framed building.

Stoup, a vessel to contain holy water, in a church: usually taking the form of a small stone basin in a niche, placed in or near the porch, but occasionally fixed on a pedestal or stand.

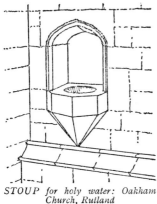

STOUP for holy water: Oakham Church, Rutland

Straight Arch, synonymous with flat arch (q.v.). (*Illustrated* ARCH, TYPES OF.)

Straight Stair, a single flight of steps, without winders (q.v.). (*Illustrated* STAIRCASE.)

Strapwork, in Elizabethan architecture, a form of ornament composed of interlacing bands, resembling straps, with 'rivets' at their intersections.

Street, George Edmund, R.A. (*b.* Woodford, Essex, 26 June 1824; *d.* London, 18 Dec. 1881), architect; President R.I.B.A., 1881; R.I.B.A. Royal Gold Medallist, 1874; a distinguished leader of the Gothic Revival. He was articled from 1841 to 1844 to O. B. Carter of Winchester; then worked for Sir George Gilbert Scott (q.v.) until 1849, when he started independent practice. He was appointed honorary architect to the diocese of Oxford, and soon moved to Oxford. Among his pupils were Edmund Sedding and Philip Webb (q.v.). His work at this period included Cuddesdon College, the Sisterhood Building at East Grinstead, and St Peter's, Bournemouth. In 1855 he moved to London, and for the remainder of his life enjoyed an enormous practice. This was due partly to his success in competitions, notably for the Law Courts in London; but though that competition took place in 1866, the award was not made till 1868, and the great building was unfinished at his death. His other work included the new nave and western towers of Bristol Cathedral, 1868–88; a large number of Anglican churches in England, and several more abroad: for the British communities in Rome, Genoa, Vevey, Lausanne, and Mürren, and for the American communities in Paris and Rome. He also restored five cathedrals—York, Salisbury, Carlisle, Christ Church at Dublin, and St Bridgid's at Kildare, Ireland. Abreast of this prodigious activity, he found time to write and illustrate two admirable books—*Brick and Marble in North Italy*, 1855, and *Gothic Architecture in Spain*, 1865; and, just before his death, he was appointed Professor of Architecture at the Royal Academy.

See memoir by his son, A. E. Street, 1888.

STRAPWORK: from a house in Houndsditch, London (c. 1650)

Strickland, William (*b.* Philadelphia, *c.* 1787; *d.* Nashville, 6 April 1854), American architect, engineer, and engraver. He was the son of a carpenter who had worked for Latrobe (q.v.) and he had very little professional training, but eventually became a leader of the 'Greek Revival' (q.v.) in America. His first building, however—the Masonic Temple at Philadelphia (1810)—was Gothic of a sort, and contrasts with the severity of his later Custom House, built for a branch of the Bank of the U.S.A. in 1824, and modelled upon the Parthenon at Athens. His Merchants' Exchange at Philadelphia shows more confidence in the use of Greek elements, and is crowned by a replica of the Choragic Monument of Lysikrates at Athens. His other buildings include the New Chestnut Street Theatre (1822), St Stephen's Church, a synagogue, the Friends' Lunatic Asylum, the United States Naval Asylum (1827), the United States Mint (1829)—all in Philadelphia; and the marble sarcophagus of Washington at Mount Vernon. His last and most important work was the Capitol or State House at Nashville, Kentucky (1845 onwards).

Striges (Lat.), the channels of a fluted classical column.

String (of a wooden staircase), one of the sloping members carrying the ends of the horizontal treads (q.v.), which are housed into the 'wall string' (fixed to the wall) at one end, and at the other end are housed into the 'outer string,' which is let into 'newel-posts' (q.v.). (*Illustrated* STAIRCASE.)

String-course, a moulding or a projecting course of stone or brick, running horizontally across the face of a building.

Structure (Lat. *structura*). (1) A building. (2) The framework or fabric of a building, as opposed to its ornamental features.

Strut, in any framed structure (e.g. a roof-truss or a lattice girder), an inclined member which is in compression.

Stucco (Ital.). (1) In its original meaning, a slow-setting hydraulic lime plaster, much used in Roman and in Renaissance architecture on walls and vaults as a ground for modelling in low relief or for fresco painting. Vitruvius (q.v.), in his manual on architecture (VII. ii–vi), treats of the slaking of lime for stucco, of its composition and its uses, of precautions to be taken in damp places, and of painting on stucco. The brothers Adam (q.v.) experimented with stucco in London for external walls, and it was largely used by architects of the Regency, especially Nash and Burton (qq.v.). (2) In modern terminology, though the word is sometimes applied loosely to any external cement or plastering, it should be confined to such as are finished with a plasterer's float.

Stuck Moulding, any moulding worked on the actual frame of wood panelling, as opposed to a 'planted' moulding, which is separate and is screwed or nailed to the framing.

Stupa (Sanskrit), or **Tope,** a commemorative or sepulchral Buddhist monument in India.   The finest example is at Sanchi (third to first centuries B.C.).

Style, in architecture, a manner or mode or fashion of building practised at any one period (e.g. the Gothic style), or in any particular region in that period (e.g. the German Gothic style); and distinguished by certain characteristics of general design, construction, and ornament.   (The term seems to have been applied to literary 'style' long before it was applied to architecture, and to have been derived from Lat. *stilus*, a pen).   *See* ARCHITECTURE, PERIODS OF.

STYLOBATE (marked S) *of the temple on the Ilissus, Athens (c.* 450 B.C)

See also J. Leathart, *Style in Architecture*, 1940.

Stylobate (Lat. *stylobata*; Gk *stulobatēs*, from *stulos*, a column), a continuous basement or platform beneath a row of columns.   Usually it is composed of three steps, in which case, strictly speaking, only the top step is the stylobate, and the three together constitute a crepidoma (q.v.).

Subtopia (presumably a hybrid: suburbia + utopia; the latter word a graceful tribute to the welfare state), a derisive term coined in 1957 by an architectural journalist to comprise the less attractive artificial features to be seen in the outskirts of our modern cities: e.g. badly designed hoardings, posters, pylons, lamp standards, filling stations, bus shelters, and other street furniture; as well as suburban architecture.

Sullivan, Louis Henry (*b.* Boston, U.S.A., 3 Sept. 1856; *d.* Chicago, 14 April 1924), architect.   He was trained at the Massachusetts Institute of Technology, went to Paris in 1874, returned to America, and started practice in 1880 at Chicago in partnership with Dankmar Adler.   He is chiefly notable for his attempt to break away from the current revivals of obsolete styles—Gothic or Classic or Romanesque —by designing buildings which should be expressive of their function and structure, and also distinctively American.   He achieved the former object in his Wainwright Building, St Louis (1891), and the latter in his remarkable Transportation Building at the Chicago World's Fair (1893).   His other work included many banks, warehouses, and commercial buildings in Chicago and St Louis; the Guaranty Building, Buffalo (1894–5), and the Auditorium Building, Chicago (1887–9.   He was followed by a brilliant pupil, Frank Lloyd

Wright (q.**v.**). Sullivan formulated his architectural theories in *The Autobiography of an Idea*, 1926, and *Kindergarten Chats*, 1934.
  See monograph by H. Morrison, 1934; 2nd ed., 1952.

Summerson, Sir John Newenham (*b*. Darlington, 25 Nov. 1904), architect and writer on architecture. He was educated at Harrow, and, after graduating in architecture from University College, London, worked for some time in the office of Sir Giles Gilbert Scott (q.v.). He then became successively a lecturer at the Edinburgh College of Art; assistant editor of *The Architect and Building News*, 1934–41; and deputy director of the National Buildings Record, 1941–5. Since 1945 he has been curator of Sir John Soane's Museum, and in 1958 was elected Slade Professor of Fine Art at Oxford. His numerous scholarly books include: *John Nash*, 1935; *The Bombed Buildings of Britain* (with J. M. Richards), 1942 and 1945; *Georgian London*, 1946; *The Architectural Association Centenary History*, 1947; *Heavenly Mansions* (essays), 1949; *Sir John Soane*, 1952; *Sir Christopher Wren*, 1953; *Architecture in Britain, 1530–1800* ('Pelican History of Art'), 1953; *A New Description of Sir John Soane's Museum*, 1955.

Sunk Moulding, in panelling, any moulding which is below the face of the framing.

SWAG with heraldry: from overdoor in chapel at Farnham Castle, Surrey
(late 17th century)

Swag, an ornamental festoon of flowers, fruit, and foliage, often tied with 'ribbons,' carved in wood or modelled in plaster, suspended at each end and hanging down in the middle: much used in late Renaissance architecture.

Swedish Architecture, *see* SCANDINAVIAN ARCHITECTURE.

Swiss Architecture, for historical and geographical reasons, has only developed distinctively national characteristics in recent times.

The Confederation of 1291, when the nation first became virtually independent, only included three of the cantons; and the great Alpine barriers that still divide it into French-speaking, German-speaking, and Italian-speaking cantons have similarly encouraged the French, German, and Italian architectural traditions in the three sectors. The oldest buildings in Switzerland are the scanty Roman remains at Basel (*Augusta Rauracorum*) and the Carolingian choir of the church at Münster (ninth century). The Romanesque period is represented by the abbeys of Payerne, Romainmôtier, Grandson, St Imier, St Ursanne, St Pierre de Clages, and Hauterive; churches at Spiez and Schaffhausen; the castle at Neuchâtel; and parts of the cathedrals of Basel and Zürich. The chief Gothic buildings are the cathedrals of Basel (in part), Berne, Coire, Fribourg, Lausanne, and Sion, and the castles of Champvent, Chillon, Habsburg, Kyburg, Tourbillon, and Vufflens. Several picturesque town halls and town gates survive from the Renaissance period, but in the subsequent Baroque and Rococo period (seventeenth to eighteenth centuries) there was a positive boom in the building of great monasteries with their attached churches. They included the enormous rebuilt abbeys of Einsiedeln and St Gall—both very ancient foundations. Among other interesting works of the same period are the abbey at Arlesheim, the cathedral at Solothurn, the Jesuit church at Lucerne, the collegiate church at Bellinzona, notable parish churches at Sarren and Schwyz, the hospital at Porrentruy, and the town hall of Bischofszell. In the early years of the present century the huge League of Nations building near Geneva was erected, and the second quarter of the century saw a brilliant flowering of Swiss national architecture. This was heralded in 1926 by the striking concrete church of St Antonius at Basel, the work of Professor K. Moser. Other excellent buildings since erected include the City Hospital, University, and Museum at Basel; the Technical College at Berne; the Infantry Barracks and the Conference Hall at Lucerne; the Conference Hall at Geneva; the Protestant Church, the First Church of Christ Scientist, the Public Baths, the Conference Hall, and many fine schools and office buildings at Zürich.

See G. Pillement, *La Suisse architecturale*, 1948, and G. E. K. Smith, *Switzerland Builds*, 1950.

Symons, or **Simons, Ralph** (*fl. c.* 1580–1604), an architect and master-builder who was working at Whitehall Palace in 1580, but is chiefly remembered for his work at Cambridge, viz.: the remodelling of Emmanuel College (1584 onwards); the Great Court of Trinity College (1593); Sidney Sussex College (1596–8); the Hall (1604) and Nevile's Court (1601 onwards) at Trinity College; and the Second Court of St John's College (1598–1602) with Gabriel Wigge.

Synagogue (Late Lat. *synagoga*, from Gk *sunagōgē*, an assembly), a building for Jewish worship and religious instruction. The date when synagogues were first built is uncertain: it is known that some were erected during the Babylonian captivity (sixth century B.C.), but they have been destroyed. At Jerusalem an inscription records the existence of a synagogue in the first century B.C. The best

Synagogue of timber at Wolpa, Poland (1650). *Destroyed by the Germans in the Second World War*

preserved among a few ruined examples is at Capernaum (late second century A.D.). It is orientated southwards, and its architecture is rustic. Persecution during the Middle Ages accounts for scarcity of medieval synagogues, but at Worms there is a Romanesque example, at Prague another which is Gothic, and in Spain at least two which have been converted into Christian churches. Only in Poland has a distinctive type of synagogue architecture emerged, the construction being in timber, and very picturesque. Elsewhere the regional type of architecture has usually been adopted, but at the recently demolished synagogue in Great Portland Street, London (nineteenth century), a Moorish style was employed. There are important late Renaissance examples at Amsterdam (1675), and in Bevis Marks, London (1700–1), but the Great Synagogue in Duke Street, Aldgate, London (rebuilt 1790), was entirely destroyed by bombing in the Second World War. The oldest example in the United States is at Newport, Rhode Island (1763). The plan of a synagogue is normally oblong, with seats downstairs for men and upstairs for women. There is a niche for the ark opposite the entrance, with a rostrum or pulpit (*almenar*, from Arabic *mimbar*, q.v.) in front of it.

See E. L. Sukenik, *Ancient Synagogues in Palestine*, 1934, and G. Loukomski, *European Synagogues from the Middle Ages to the Eighteenth Century*, 1947; *also* monographs on modern American examples by P. Blake, 1954, and R. Wischnitzer, 1955.

Systyle (Gk *stulos*, a column), in Greek architecture, an arrangement of columns spaced two diameters apart, i.e. rather widely spaced.

T

Tabernacle (Lat. *tabernaculum*, dim. of *taberna*, a hut or booth).
(1) Originally any temporary or movable dwelling or tent; hence
(2) the tabernacle or 'portable sanctuary' used by the Israelites in
their wanderings. (3) A place of worship not dignified by the name
of 'church,' hence applied to the temporary churches erected in
London after the Great Fire of 1666 before permanent buildings could
be provided. (4) In the eighteenth century a term of contempt
applied to Nonconformist chapels, even to Whitefield's enormous
'tabernacle' in Tottenham Court Road, London, and later to
Spurgeon's 'tabernacle,' holding 5,000 persons, in South London
(1860)—both very substantial buildings. (5) In the nineteenth
century applied to temporary churches of galvanized iron ('tin
tabernacles') erected by all denominations.

Tabernacle-work, in Gothic architecture, comprises the canopies,
crockets (q.v.), and tracery over niches, etc.

Table, or **Tabling,** in medieval architecture, a projecting horizontal
string-course.

TABERNACLE-WORK: from Church of Walpole St Peter, Norfolk

Tabling, *see* TABLE.

Tablinum (Lat.), in ancient Greek and Roman
houses, a room having one side open to the
atrium (q.v.) or central courtyard.

Tabularium (Lat.), a building or room for
the storage of public records (*tabulae*). There
is a ruined example (78 B.C.) near the Capitol
at Rome.

Taenia, or **Tenia** (Lat.), a fillet above the
architrave in the Doric Order. (*Illustrated*
ENTABLATURE.)

Tait, Thomas Smith (*b.* Paisley, 18 June
1882; *d.* Aberfeldy, 20 July 1954), architect,
son of a builder. He was trained at the Paisley
Technical College and the Glasgow School of
Art, articled to James Donald (a disciple
of 'Greek' Thomson, q.v.), and then became
an assistant in the office of Sir (then Mr)
John Burnet (q.v.). He rose to be partner,
then senior partner after Burnet's retirement.
His influence, which was definitely towards
modernism, had shown itself already in many
works of the firm: e.g. Adelaide House
(1922–4), Unilever House (1930–2), the *Daily
Telegraph* building, the Second Church of

326

Christ Scientist (1922–6), Lloyds Bank head office (1926–30), Selfridge's Store extension, and Mount Royal flats—all in London; and he alone designed the Paisley Infectious Hospital (1934–6), the Royal Masonic Hospital at Ravenscourt Park (1931–3), the Burlington School at Hammersmith (1934–6), Dingle's Store at Plymouth (1950–2), the new Colonial Office in London, and the pylons of Sydney Harbour Bridge.

Taj (Persian, a crown). A term applied to the Taj Mahal at Agra, the magnificent marble mausoleum erected in A.D. 1630–51 by the Emperor Shah Jahan in memory of his queen. *See* INDIAN ARCHITECTURE.

Takhtabosh (Arabic), in old Cairo dwelling-houses, a room or alcove with one side opening on to the *hosh* or inner courtyard.

Takiyyah (Arabic), a convent of dervishes.

Talman, William (*b*. West Lavington, Wiltshire, 1650; *d*. Felmingham, Norfolk, 22 Nov. 1719), architect. Nothing is known of his early life till he appears as alleged designer (at the incredibly early age of twenty-one) of Thoresby House, Nottinghamshire, for the Marquis of Dorchester, in 1671. He certainly built other mansions: the south and east fronts of Chatsworth (1687–96); Swallowfield, Berkshire (1689–91); Dyrham Park, Gloucestershire (1698–1700); Kiveton Park, near Sheffield (*c*. 1689, demolished 1811); Herriard Park, Hampshire (1704); Fetcham Park, Surrey (*c*. 1718); and perhaps Stanstead Park, Sussex (1686, burnt down 1900), and Uppark, Sussex (*c*. 1690). From 1689 to 1702 he was Controller of Works, and in that capacity had frequent altercations with Wren (q.v.), then employed in rebuilding Hampton Court Palace.

Tapper, Sir Walter John, R.A. (*b*. Bovey Tracey, 20 April 1861; *d*. London, 21 Sept. 1935), architect; President R.I.B.A., 1927–9. After being articled to an architect at Newton Abbot, he became assistant to Messrs Bodley (q.v.) & Garner, and started independent practice in London in 1900. He did some domestic work (including the important restoration of Penshurst Place in Kent), but is chiefly known as a designer of churches. These included the church of the Annunciation in Quebec Street, London (1913); the church of the Ascension, Malvern Link; St Erkenwald, Southend (1905); St Stephen, Grimsby; and St Mary, Harrogate. He was consulting architect to York Minster, Manchester Cathedral, and, from 1928 onwards, to Westminster Abbey, where he altered the library; but a project to build an elaborate new sacristy was—fortunately, in the opinion of many critics—not carried out.

Tas-de-charge (Fr.), the lowest courses of Gothic vaulting-ribs. (*Illustrated* p. 328.)

Taut, Bruno (*b*. Königsberg, Prussia, 4 May 1880; *d*. Istanbul, 1938), architect and writer on architecture. He was trained as a bricklayer, then in architecture by Theodor Fischer at Stuttgart. He designed notable pavilions for the Leipzig Exhibition, 1913, and the Cologne Exhibition, 1914. In 1924 he was appointed chief

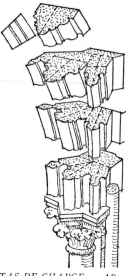

TAS-DE-CHARGE.   After Viollet-le-Duc, '*Dictionnaire raisonné*' (1854–68)

architect to a group of Berlin building societies, for whom he erected 12,000 houses and flats. He became professor at the Technische Hochschule at Berlin, and in 1937 at Istanbul. His book, *Modern Architecture*, appeared (in English) in 1929.

Taylor, Sir Robert (*b.* Woodford, 1714; *d.* London, 27 Sept. 1788), architect, has been described as 'the most successful architect of his time.' He began his career by apprenticeship in his father's own craft, that of a mason-sculptor; but, at the conclusion of his apprenticeship, was sent by his father to study in Rome. This tour was cut short by his father's bankruptcy and death; but, in 1744, a year later, Robert was already obtaining important work as a sculptor. Turning to architecture, he worked furiously, starting his days at 4 a.m., and soon he and James Paine (q.v.), as rivals, were dividing the plums of the profession between them, till Robert Adam (q.v.) appeared on the scene. In 1765 Taylor became surveyor to the Bank of England, in 1769 'Architect of the King's Works,' then surveyor to Greenwich Hospital, H.M. Customs, Lincoln's Inn, the Foundling Hospital, and the great Grafton and Pulteney estates. He left his (then) immense fortune of £180,000 to found the 'Taylorian Institution' at Oxford. C. R. Cockerell (q.v.) was one of his pupils, and John Nash (q.v.) worked in his office. His new buildings included Maidenhead Bridge (1772–7); Stone Buildings, Lincoln's Inn, London (1774–80); Salisbury Council House (1788–95); a number of country mansions; and some London houses, among them Ely House, 37 Dover Street.

Tecton, *see* LUBETKIN.

Telamones (Gk, plural of *Telamōn*, the proper name of a hero in mythology). *See* ATLANTES.

Temenos (Gk), a sacred enclosure or precinct, surrounding a temple.

Tempietto (Ital., dim. of *tempio*, a temple), a small temple. The term is usually applied to Bramante's beautiful little circular detached chapel (1503) adjoining the church of S. Pietro in Montorio, Rome.

Template, Templet. Although these two words are apt to be confused, and used indiscriminately, the former correctly means a block of hard stone set in a wall of rubble-stone or brickwork to bear the concentrated weight of a roof-truss or a girder, and to distribute the pressure; whereas a 'templet' is a thin piece of zinc or other metal cut to the shape of some moulding or other geometrical form, and used by masons to mark that form on to stone preparatory to cutting.

Temple (from Lat. *templum*), a building used for religious worship of diverse cults throughout history, and in most parts of the world, but excluding the Christian church (q.v.), the Muslim mosque (q.v.), and the Jewish synagogue (q.v.). There are, however, certain exceptions to this general usage, viz. (1) The famous Jewish Temple at Jerusalem. (2) The buildings of the Knights Templars in London, Paris, and elsewhere, erected by their Order, founded about 1118 and suppressed 1312. In London the 'Temple Church' is still standing, though bombed in the Second World War. (3) Various Protestant churches in France, including several in Paris and the large example at Charenton (1623). (4) The large Congregational church in London known as the 'City Temple' (1874, bombed in 1941). (5) The 'temples' of the Mormon sect in Utah, U.S.A., late nineteenth century.

Temple Architecture, Greek and Roman. The pre-classical temples of Egypt and western Asia are briefly described under ARCHITECTURE, PERIODS OF, 1. Those of Greece and Rome are important in the history of architectural development. Occasionally they are circular in plan (*see* PANTHEON and THOLUS); but are usually oblong and contain a sanctuary—Naos (q.v.) in Greek, Cella (q.v.) in Latin. Sometimes there is a compartment (Pronaos, q.v.) in front of the sanctuary, and another (Opisthodomos, q.v.) behind it. The Roman writer Vitruvius (q.v.) made a classification of temples which has been followed ever since. They are treated, firstly, according to the 'Order' or type of column used—Doric, Ionic, or Corinthian (*see* ORDERS). The next classification is based upon the arrangement of the columns: whether they stood between Antae (q.v.) or not; whether there was a single Peristyle (q.v.) or colonnade all round the building (Peripteral, q.v.) or a double row (Dipteral, q.v.); or whether the columns were 'engaged'—i.e. half built into the walls (Pseudo-Peripteral, q.v.). According to the number of columns in the portico—two, four, six, eight, or ten—the temple was described as Distyle, Tetrastyle, Hexastyle, Octastyle or Decastyle (qq.v.). The spacing apart of the columns was similarly classified, in terms of their diameters—*see* PYCNOSTYLE, SYSTYLE, EUSTYLE, DIASTYLE, ARAEOSTYLE. If there was a portico at each end, the temple was Amphiprostyle (q.v.); if at one end only, Prostyle (q.v.). A temple usually stood on a platform (Podium, Crepidoma or Stylobate, qq.v.), and was surrounded by an enclosure (Temenos, q.v.).

Tengbom, Ivar (*b.* Vireda, Sweden, 7 April 1878; *d.* 6 Aug. 1968), architect; R.I.B.A. Royal Gold Medallist, 1938. After his training at the Technical Institute at Gothenburg and the Academy at Stockholm, he travelled abroad, then worked as assistant in architects' offices, and started independent practice in 1912. His principal buildings in Stockholm are the Enskilda Bank (1912–15); Högalid Church (1917–23); the Concert Hall (1923–6); the Commercial High

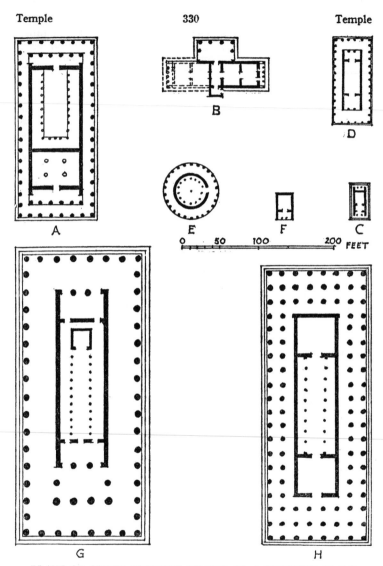

Temple 330 Temple

PLANS OF GREEK TEMPLES DRAWN TO A UNIFORM SCALE

(A) *The Parthenon, Athens (peripteral octastyle);* (B) *The Erechtheion, Athens;* (C) *Temple of Artemis at Eleusis (distyle in antis, both ends);* (D) *The Theseion, Athens (peripteral hexastyle);* (E) *The Tholos at Epidauros;* (F) *Temple at Rhamnus (distyle in antis);* (G) *Great temple at Selinus (pseudipteral octastyle);* (H) *The Olympieion, Athens (dipteral octastyle)*

School (1926); Esselte Building (1934); Bonnier Building (1945). Elsewhere he designed banks at Boras, Vanersborg, and Örebro; Churches at Arvika and Höganäs; the Swedish Academy at Rome (1940). From 1922 he was in charge of the royal palaces at Stockholm and Drottningholm; and he became Professor of Architecture at Stockholm.

Tenia, *see* TAENIA.

Tennis-court, a walled and roofed enclosure, 110 feet by 38 feet 8 inches, having a playing area 96 feet by 31 feet 8 inches, surrounded on its two ends and one side by a pent-house. The game, which is quite distinct from lawn tennis, was played in England and France during the Middle Ages. The famous tennis-court at Hampton Court Palace was built in 1529 by Henry VIII.

Teocalli (Mexican, literally 'god-house'), in Mexico and Central America, a pyramid built in steps or stages, and surmounted by a temple.

Term, more correctly, **Terminal Figure,** in classical architecture, a half-statue or bust, representing the upper half of a human figure, springing from a pedestal or pillar.

Terrace, either (i) a raised level promenade, paved or covered with turf or gravel, and usually with a balustrade or dwarf wall on one side; or (ii) a continuous row of houses in a uniform style (e.g. the 'Nash Terraces' round Regent's Park, London).

TERM. Two examples

Terra-cotta (Ital., 'burnt earth'), a hard burnt-clay product used for wall-facings and architectural details. If glazed it is described as faience (q.v.). Terra-cotta was largely used by the Etruscans (q.v.) in the remote past, and its use was revived in the nineteenth century in England, especially by the architect Waterhouse (q.v.).

Terrazzo (Ital.), a flooring material composed of marble chips in plain or coloured cement.

Tessellated Pavement, a flooring of MOSAIC (q.v.).

Tessera, one of the small cubes of marble or glass used in mosaic (q.v.).

Tessin, Nicodemus, the Elder (*b.* Stralsund, 7 Dec. 1615; *d.* Stockholm, 25 May 1681), architect. He settled in Stockholm as a young man, eventually becoming architect to the king in 1646, and to the city of Stockholm in 1661. He was ennobled in 1674. His principal buildings were the Baroque cathedral at Kalmar (1660–9); Drottningholm Castle, near Stockholm (1662 onwards); the Old State Bank in Järntorget, Stockholm (1676 onwards); several mansions in Stockholm; and his own country house at Sjöö on Lake Malar.

Tessin, Nicodemus, the Younger (*b.* Nyköping, 23 May 1654; *d.* Stockholm, 10 May 1728), architect, son of Nicodemus the Elder (q.v.), was the chief exponent of Baroque in Sweden, and has been called 'Sweden's Christopher Wren.' He did, in fact, study in Rome under the great Baroque architect Bernini (q.v.), during his extensive travels in Italy, France, and England (1673–80). He succeeded his father as architect to the king, was ennobled in due course, and became successively a state counsellor, chancellor of the university, and Lord High Chamberlain. His principal works were the completion of the royal palace at Stockholm (1688 onwards) and the Södra Town Hall, Stockholm.

Tester (from Old Fr. *teste*, the head), first a canopy over a bedstead; in later years, a sounding-board (q.v.) over a pulpit.

Tetrastyle (from Gk *tetra*, four; *stulos*, a column), in classical architecture, a portico having four columns in a row.

Thatch (from Old Eng. *thack*), a roof-covering composed of straw or reeds. In England the most efficient type is of Norfolk reeds, but the craft is dying, and few competent thatchers remain. To obviate fire risks the thatch may be sprayed with a solution.

Theatre (from Lat. *theatrum*; Gk *theatron*). (1) A place for viewing dramatic performances; at first in the open air, later a roofed building. (2) In modern universities, etc., a lecture-room with tiers of seats. Early Greek theatres (e.g. at Epidaurus, fourth century B.C.) were excavated in a hillside, and their plan was rather more than a semicircle. The tiers of seats rose from a level circular enclosure, the *orchestra* (q.v.). Behind it rose the rectangular *scena* (q.v.), generally two storeys high. Some Roman theatres, e.g. at Orange, followed the same arrangement; but, more often, the tiers of seats (*auditorium* (q.v.) or *cavea*) were artificially raised upon a substructure of arches and radial walls, e.g. at the theatre of Marcellus, Rome, 11 B.C. This substructure was connected with the *scena*, and from the *scena* projected the *pulpitum* or stage, which reduced the *orchestra* to a a semicircle. There are famous Roman theatres at Pompeii, Syracuse, and Fiesole in Italy; Timgad in North Africa; and Verulamium in England. English theatres in Shakespeare's day were timber-framed, e.g. the 'Globe' in Southwark, London. Other notable theatres are the Teatro Olimpico at Vicenza (1584), by Palladio (q.v.); several in Italy designed by the Bibiena family (q.v.) during the seventeenth to eighteenth centuries; the Sheldonian Theatre at Oxford (1663–9) by Wren (q.v.), with a roof having the enormous span of 68 feet; and the modern Shakespeare Memorial Theatre at Stratford-on-Avon (1932).

Thermae (Lat.), public bathing establishments erected by the later Roman emperors, especially in the city of Rome itself. The provision for actual bathing was varied and elaborate; but the additional amenities provided—recreational, social, and even cultural—corresponded roughly to those of a modern social club. The actual baths occupied a large vaulted building, with the heating plant beneath it. They usually included a *tepidarium* (warm bath), *caldarium* (hot

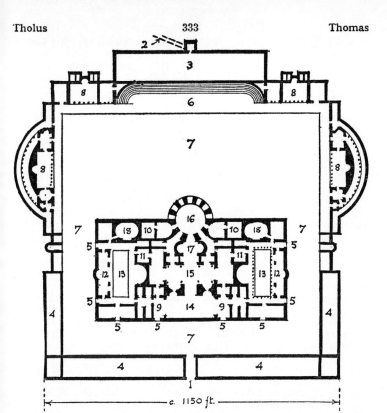

THERMAE. Plan of the baths of Caracalla, Rome (A.D. 211 *onwards*). 1, *Entrance to enclosure;* 2, *aqueduct* (*Aqua Marcia*); 3, *reservoirs* (*two storeys*); 4, *porticus and small chambers;* 5, *entrances to central block of baths, etc.;* 6, *stadium;* 7, *xystus* (*open space planted with avenues of trees*); 8, *lecture-halls and libraries;* 9, *anterooms;* 10, *warm baths;* 11, *hot baths;* 12, *ephebia;* 13, *open peristyle;* 14, *frigidarium;* 15, *trepidarium* (*or possibly the apodyterium or 'changing-room'*); 16, *calidarium;* 17, *ante-room, or secondary tepidarium;* 18, *rooms for games.*

room with hot bath), *sudatorium* ('sweating-room'—the hottest room), *frigidarium* (cooling-room), *unctoria* (anointing-rooms), *piscina* (swimming-bath), and *apodyteria* (dressing-rooms). All these, as well as rooms for indoor games, colonnades, shops, lecture-rooms, and libraries, were grouped around the *xystus*, an open space laid out partly as a garden and partly as playing fields. In Rome the finest *thermae* are those of Caracalla (*c.* A.D. 215) and of Diocletian (A.D. 306); in England the smaller examples at *Uriconium* (Wroxeter) and at *Aquae Sulis* (Bath).

Tholus (Lat., from Gk *tholos*), originally the dome of a circular building; then the building itself, e.g. at Epidaurus in Greece.

Thomas, Sir Alfred Brumwell (*b.* 1868; *d.* Virginia Water, 22 Jan. 1948), architect, chiefly known as the designer of the imposing and very Edwardian city hall at Belfast, the result of a competition in 1906. He won other competitions for the Woolwich (1908) and Stockport (1908) town halls, the Eye Infirmary at Exeter, and the Addey and Stanhope schools; and also designed the Skefco Works at Luton (1919) and the war memorial at Dunkirk (1923). He was knighted in 1906.

Thomas, Sir Percy Edward (b. South Shields, 13 Sept. 1883), architect; President R.I.B.A., 1935-7 and 1943-6; R.I.B.A. Royal Gold Medallist, 1939. He was articled to E. H. Bruton, and obtained much of his large practice from competitions. His work includes Cardiff Technical College (1915); Bristol Police and Fire Station (1926); Accrington Police and Fire Station (1932); Swansea Civic Centre (1936); Temple of Peace and Health, Cardiff (1938); Tunbridge Wells Civic Centre (1938); Worcester Police and Fire Station (1940); Carmarthen County Offices (1952); buildings at Aberystwyth University College (1938 and 1953), and at Bangor University College (1952-4); Cardiff New Grammar School (1953); huge steelworks at Abbey, Margam, and Trostre; industrial buildings for British Nylon Industries and for Imperial Chemical Industries; research laboratories at Avonmouth and Banbury; power station on Cardigan Bay (1954).

Thomon, Thomas de (b. Nancy, France, 21 Dec. 1754; d. St Petersburg, 22 Aug. 1813), architect. He studied at the Academy of Architecture in Paris, travelled abroad, worked in Vienna and Hungary, then settled in Russia about 1798. He began teaching there in 1802, and became Professor at the Academy of Fine Arts in St Petersburg in 1810. His principal buildings in that city were his additions to the Great Theatre (1802-5); his continuation (1805-10) of the Bourse, begun by Quarenghi (q.v.) in 1784; and the Laval Palace. In Odessa he built the theatre (1803, since rebuilt) and the hospital (1806 onwards).

Thomson, Alexander (b. Balfron, near Glasgow, 1817; d. Glasgow, 22 Mar. 1875), architect; commonly called 'Greek Thomson' because he was the foremost exponent in Scotland of the 'Greek Revival' (q.v.), though he never visited Greece. He was articled in Glasgow, where he afterwards practised. His early work consisted of houses in 'Scottish Baronial' (q.v.) or neo-Gothic styles; but his original adaptation of Greek architecture was exemplified in his three Presbyterian churches in Glasgow—St Vincent Street, Caledonia Road, and Queenspark—also in Great Western Terrace. His competition designs for the Albert Memorial and the Natural History Museum, both in London, were unsuccessful.

Thornely, Sir Arnold (b. Godley, Cheshire, 1870; d. Cobham, Surrey, 1 Oct. 1953), architect, was articled in Liverpool and practised there from 1898 onwards. He won competitions for the Mersey Docks and Harbour Board Offices, and for the Liverpool Bluecoat Hospital—both in 1900; joined the firm of Briggs & Wolstenholme in 1906; and won the competition for Wallasey Town Hall in 1914. In 1928-32 he designed and completed the handsome Parliament Buildings for Northern Ireland at Stormont, near Belfast.

Thornton, Dr William (*b.* Tortola, British West Indies, 20 May 1759; *d.* Washington, 28 Mar. 1828), a doctor who became an engineer and then a most successful architect. He was educated in England, graduated in medicine at Edinburgh University in 1784, journeyed to America, and became an American citizen in 1788. After winning a competition in 1789 for the Philadelphia Library Company's building (demolished 1880), he tried his hand at inventing paddle-steamers; then reverted to architecture, and competed unsuccessfully with a design for the Capitol at Washington in 1792, but won the second competition in 1793. The north wing of the present building, containing the Senate, is his work; but the twin south wing was carried out by Latrobe (q.v.) after the British burned down the Capitol in 1814. Thornton also built the Octagon in Washington (the fine premises now occupied as headquarters by the American Institute of Architects, who seem to have no professional objection to inhabiting a building designed by an amateur architect). From 1802 he found time to serve as a Commissioner of Pensions.

Thorpe, John (*b.* in Northamptonshire, *c.* 1563; *d.* 1655), land surveyor and reputedly architect, employed in the Office of Works, 1583–*c.* 1601. He left a book containing 280 pages of drawings, in plan, elevation, and section, of Elizabethan and Jacobean buildings, mostly domestic; but there is no conclusive evidence that he designed any of them.

Threshold, a stone or timber sill across an external doorway.

Thrust, the downward and outward pressure or force exerted by a dome, vault, arch, roof-truss, or other structural member upon its supporting walls or piers; counteracted, especially in medieval buildings, by buttresses.

Tibaldi, Pellegrino (*b.* Puria di Valsolda, 1527; *d.* Milan, 27 May 1596), architect, sculptor, and painter; a prominent figure in the 'Mannerist' (q.v.) or late Renaissance period. He became a follower of Michelangelo (q.v.). After working in Rome (1547–50), Ancona, and Ferrara, he became architect to the city of Milan in 1562, and there built the churches of S. Fedele (1569) and S. Sebastiano (1576). Elsewhere in Italy his buildings included the Collegio at Pavia (1546–8), and the churches of S. Gaudenzio at Novara (1577), S. Ambrogio at Genoa, the Chiesa dei Martiri at Turin (1577), and some sanctuary churches. From 1587 to 1596 he worked on the building of the Escorial in Spain (*see* HERRERA).
See monograph by W. Hiersche, 1913.

Tie-beam, in a timber pitched roof (i.e. with two slopes) the horizontal beam tying together the feet of the sloping rafters to prevent them from spreading and thus overturning the supporting walls. (*Illustrated* ROOF; ROOF-TRUSS.)

Tier (from Fr. *tire*), one of a series of rows of seats on a slope, e.g. in a theatre.

Tierceron, in Gothic vaulting, an intermediate arched rib.

Tile (from Lat. *tegula*), *see* BONNET TILE, ENCAUSTIC TILES, PANTILE, PLAIN TILES, QUARRY, TILE HANGING.

Tile Hanging, or **Vertical Tiling,** consists of tiles hung on battens nailed to a wall-face or to timber-framing. They are used as a protection against damp, and may be either plain tiles (q.v.) or 'imbricated,' i.e. with a rounded lower edge, producing a scalloped effect.

Timber-framing, *see* HALF-TIMBER CONSTRUCTION.

Tite, Sir William, M.P., F.R.S. (*b.* London, Feb. 1798; *d.* Torquay, 20 April 1873), architect; President R.I.B.A., 1861–3 and 1867–70; R.I.B.A. Royal Gold Medallist, 1856. He was articled to David Laing (q.v.), 1812–18, and attended Soane's lectures at the Royal Academy. He began entering for competitions in 1819, and actually started independent practice before 1824, when he had his first competition successes, with designs for a new Presbyterian church in Regent Square, London, and for the new buildings of Mill Hill School. The former is a meagre neo-Gothic galleried building, with an ambitious stone façade echoing the west front of York Minster. The Mill Hill school-house is an austere classical building. In 1840, after carrying out other work, he contrived to be placed first in the 'competition' for the new Royal Exchange in London; but the story of that award is squalid, and some of his brother architects never forgave him for his share in it. However, the Exchange was duly built, a knighthood followed, and thereafter he enjoyed a most lucrative practice, consisting largely of railway stations, but also including the extraordinary church of St James, Gerrards Cross (1858). He was Liberal M.P. for Bath from 1855 to 1872; and was tireless in advocating 'Classic' rather than 'Gothic' for the new government offices in Whitehall, during the long-drawn 'Battle of the Styles' in Parliament. He amassed a large fortune, and in his will left a sum to the R.I.B.A. to provide the 'Tite Prize' for the study of architecture in Italy.

Toledo, Juan Bautista de (*b.* near Madrid; *d.* 19 May 1567), architect. He studied under Michelangelo in Rome; then went to Naples, where he built the church of S. Giacomo degli Spagnuoli. In 1559 King Philip II summoned him to Spain to design the enormous monastery and palace of the Escorial, the erection of which began in 1563 and was completed by Herrera (q.v.). It is not certain whether de Toledo designed the church there, but he certainly designed the royal palace at Aranjuez, the façade of the conventual church of Descalzas Reales at Madrid, and perhaps the palace at Martin Muñoz de Posadas, near Arévalo (1566–72).

Tooling, the dressing of a stone face with a broad chisel.

Tope, *see* STUPA.

Torching, the plastering of the underside of slates or tiles on a roof with mortar, in order to exclude driving rain and wind; not to be recommended, as it is liable to cause decay in the timber rafters and battens.

Torus (Lat.), a large convex moulding. (*Illustrated* MOULDINGS, CLASSICAL.)

Tower (from Lat. *turris*; cf. Fr. *tour*; Ger. *turm*; Ital. *torre*). Any lofty structure (other than a dome) rising above the general roof level of a building, for purposes of defence, observation, or effect; or, a tall isolated structure serving for defence or observation, or as a landmark (*see* PHAROS). For Christian bell-towers *see* CAMPANILE; for Muslim towers attached to mosques *see* MINARET. The earliest English church towers are of pre-Conquest date, placed centrally or at the west end. In later churches western towers are normal and central towers are mainly reserved for large churches, where a central and two western towers are often found. Picturesque defensive towers adorn the medieval towns of S. Gimignano in Italy, and Rothenburg in Germany. *See also* HELM and STEEPLE.

Town and Country Planning Association (offices at 28 King Street, Covent Garden, London, W.C.2), founded in 1899. The association, which has always supported the garden city movement, publishes a monthly journal, *Town and Country Planning*.

Town, Ithiel (*b.* Thompson, Connecticut, 3 Oct. 1784; *d.* New Haven, Connecticut, 6 Dec. 1844), American architect. As a youth he worked as a carpenter, and then did a little teaching. Moving to Boston, he picked up some knowledge of architecture in the school run by A. Benjamin (q.v.). He soon appears as the architect of the ingeniously designed and constructed Center Church on New Haven Green. It was quickly followed by the neighbouring Trinity Church (1814), of stone and 'in the Gothic taste.' His other work included State Capitols at New Haven, Indianapolis, and Raleigh, North Carolina; a hospital at New Haven; the Custom House in Wall Street, New York City; Christ Church at Hartford, Connecticut; and an asylum, in Greek Revival style, close to the present cathedral of St John the Divine in New York City. From 1829 onwards he worked in partnership with A. J. Davis.

Town-planning (Fr. *L'urbanisme*; Ger. *Der Städtebau*), a term introduced into English about 1904. According to the Oxford English Dictionary, it should be spelt with a hyphen, as above; but the omission of the hyphen is common, and appears inevitable when the term is extended, as often nowadays to 'town and country planning.' When used, however, as an adjective (e.g. 'town-planning' powers), or when one refers to 'town-planners,' the use of the hyphen seems preferable. The first book in English on town-planning (*see* Bibliography) was published in 1909; the first School of Town-planning was established at Liverpool University in the same year; and the Town-planning Institute (q.v.) was founded in 1914.

Modern town-planning may be defined as the preparation of plans to regulate the growth or extension of a town so as to make the most of the natural advantages of the site, and to secure the best possible conditions for housing, traffic, industry, educational facilities, social and cultural amenities, and recreation. In England powers to carry out such planning were first given to the larger local authorities, subject to ministerial approval, by the Housing and Town-planning Act of 1909.

Yet examples of systematic planning of towns can be found at

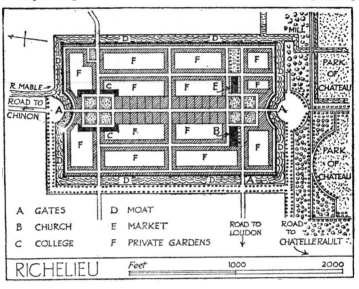

A	GATES	D	MOAT
B	CHURCH	E	MARKET
C	COLLEGE	F	PRIVATE GARDENS

RICHELIEU

Feet   1000   2000

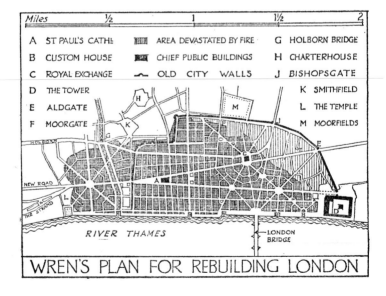

A	ST PAUL'S CATHL	▦	AREA DEVASTATED BY FIRE	G	HOLBORN BRIDGE
B	CUSTOM HOUSE	▨	CHIEF PUBLIC BUILDINGS	H	CHARTERHOUSE
C	ROYAL EXCHANGE	⌐	OLD CITY WALLS	J	BISHOPSGATE
D	THE TOWER			K	SMITHFIELD
E	ALDGATE			L	THE TEMPLE
F	MOORGATE			M	MOORFIELDS

RIVER THAMES

WREN'S PLAN FOR REBUILDING LONDON

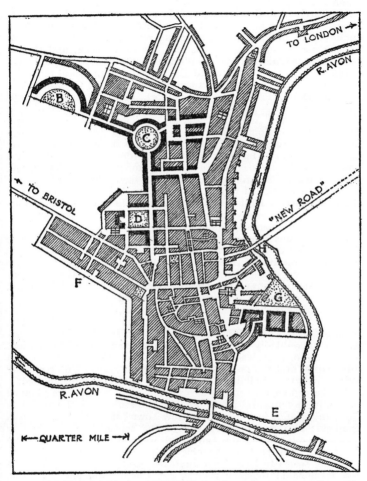

BATH IN THE LATE 18th *CENTURY, based on a contemporary plan. The work of the Woods, father and son (qq.v.), is indicated in solid black.* (A) *Bath Abbey;* (B) *Royal Crescent;* (C) *The Circus;* (D) *Queen's Square;* (E, F) *Site of modern railway stations;* (G) *The Bowling Green;* (H) *Pulteney Bridge*

intervals through 4,500 years of history, interrupted by lapses into squalor, muddle, and indiscriminate building. The oldest known of planned towns are the great city of Babylon (*c.* 2500 B.C. onwards), now entirely ruined, and the small 'model village' of Kahun in Egypt (*c.* 2500 B.C.), laid out on a rectilinear plan for workmen employed in building a neighbouring pyramid. Neither Hellenic Athens nor imperial Rome was laid out as a whole; and though each had a magnificent nucleus of monumentally designed and sited public buildings, each contained also a good deal of sordid property. The best examples of Greek town-planning are at Olynthus, The Piraeus, Delos, Priene (in Asia Minor), Pompeii (in Italy), and Alexandria (in Egypt). Roman town-planning may be studied at Ostia, Turin, and Aosta in Italy, and at Timgad in North Africa. The layout of Roman London, Verulamium (near St Albans), Colchester, Wroxeter, and Silchester is also interesting, Silchester being a remarkable instance of a small 'garden city,' with detached houses. Medieval towns were seldom planned systematically, and were often huddled around the skirts of a feudal fortress; but there are a few examples of formal planning, e.g. Winchelsea (1282) and the older part of Hull (1296) in England; the *Ville Basse* at Carcassonne (1247) and several *bastides* (q.v.) in France; Neu-Brandenburg (1248) and some others in Prussia.

Italy contains a number of Renaissance examples. Rome itself was improved by a succession of popes between 1471 and 1566, but especially by Sixtus V (1585–90), employing the architect Domenico Fontana (q.v.), whose ideas have contributed largely to the splendour of the modern city; and the work was continued by Bernini (q.v.) in the Baroque period. French towns planned in the sixteenth to seventeenth centuries include Vitry-le-François, Charleville, Henrichemont, and, above all, Richelieu, a remarkable little town in Touraine, built in 1631–8 as an appendage to the cardinal's great château. This is undoubtedly the most interesting town plan of the period. The layout of Paris was improved under Henri IV (1589–1610), and afterwards under Louis XIII and Louis XIV. Unfortunately Wren's plan for rebuilding London (1666) was never implemented.

In the eighteenth century several European towns were planned on really monumental lines: notably Karlsruhe and Mannheim in Germany, Nancy in France, the 'New Town' of Edinburgh, Bath in England; also, at the very end of the century, Washington in America. Meanwhile the Industrial Revolution had begun, and for the greater part of the nineteenth century the art of town-planning seems to have been forgotten, except in the layout of a few fashionable Regency resorts, e.g. Cheltenham and Brighton, and, of course, the splendid schemes by Nash (q.v.) for Regent Street, Regent's Park, and their surroundings, in London. The first model industrial town was Saltaire in Yorkshire (1851), but it was somewhat grim. Much more attractive were Port Sunlight (1888) and Bournville (1895), with their pleasant avenues and gardens. All these were due to enlightened industrial employers; but the First Garden City at Letchworth (1903), and its successor at Welwyn (1919), had a wider purpose. The Hampstead Garden

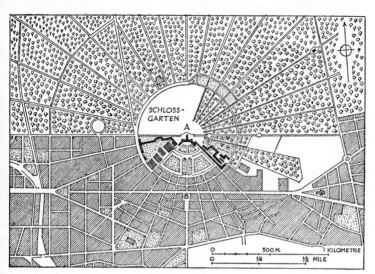

PLAN OF CENTRAL KARLSRUHE. (A) *Schloss;* (B) *Market-place;* (C) *Grand Ducal Stables*

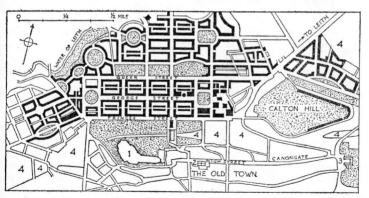

CENTRAL EDINBURGH. Showing Craig's (18th-century) 'New Town' in solid black, early 19th-century additions cross-hatched, open spaces dotted. 1, *Edinburgh Castle;* 2, *St Giles's Cathedral;* 3, *Holyrood House;* 4, *modern railway stations and sidings*

M

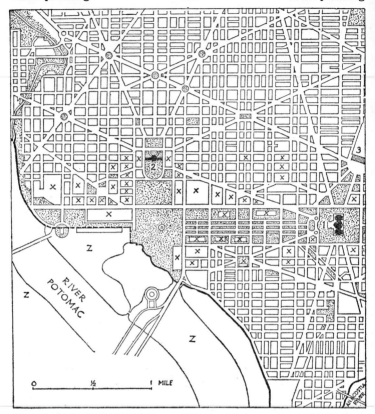

CENTRAL WASHINGTON IN 1951, laid out mainly in accordance with L'Enfant's revised scheme of 1791, the Capitol (1) and the White House (2) forming focal points. The approximate line of the waterfront in the 1791 scheme is shown with a thick black line, subsequent areas reclaimed and laid out as parks and gardens being marked Z. Blocks now wholly or partially occupied by public buildings marked X, railway buildings marked 3

Suburb (1907) was not a garden city, but followed the same type of open and imaginative planning. More recent developments have been satellite towns, new towns, and all the problems of urban expansion, revealed by a series of massive planning reports covering many of the chief areas of Britain, London among them. Town-planning Acts since 1909 have been supplemented and inspired by the issue of three government reports: the 'Barlow Report' (1937) on *The Distribution of Population*; the 'Scott Report' (1942) on *Land Utilization*; and the 'Uthwatt Report' (1942) on *Compensation and Betterment*.

See BASTIDE, BOULEVARD, CONURBATION, GARDEN CITIES, GREEN

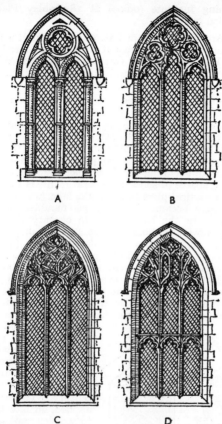

TRACERY: DEVELOPMENT OF ENGLISH
(A) *Plate tracery;* (B) *Geometrical tracery;* (C)
Curvilinear or flowing tracery; (D) *Perpendicular
or rectilinear tracery, with transome*

BELT, NEW TOWNS, OVERSPILL, REILLY PLAN, RIBBON DEVELOP-
MENT, SATELLITE TOWNS, SUBTOPIA, TOWN AND COUNTRY PLAN-
NING ASSOCIATION, TOWN-PLANNING INSTITUTE; *also* ABERCROMBIE,
HOLDEN, HOLFORD, LANCHESTER, UNWIN.

  See also R. Unwin, *Town-planning in Practice* (1st ed., 1909;
2nd ed., 1932); H. V. Lanchester, *The Art of Town-planning*
(1st ed., 1925; 2nd ed., 1932); P. Abercrombie, *Town and
Country Planning* (1st ed., 1931; 2nd ed., 1943); T. Sharp,
Town-planning (1st ed., 1940; 3rd ed., 1945); M. S. Briggs, *Town
and Country Planning*, 1948.

Town-planning Institute (offices at 18 Ashley Place, London, S.W.1), founded in 1914.

Trabeated Architecture (from Lat. *trabs*, a beam), a term applied to Greek architecture to contrast it with the arcuated (q.v.) styles (e.g. Roman, Romanesque, and Gothic), in which the main openings are spanned by arches rather than by beams. Egyptian architecture is likewise 'trabeated.'

Tracery, in Gothic architecture, an arrangement of intersecting stone moulded bars forming a geometrical or flowing pattern in the curved heads of pointed windows. Tracery was used in England from the thirteenth to the sixteenth century, and was occasionally constructed in brickwork, especially in East Anglia. The first stage in its development consisted in grouping two or more lancet (q.v.) windows under an enclosing arch, and piercing circular openings in the intervening spaces of solid stonework. This is known as 'plate tracery.' The vertical piers between the lancets were then reduced in size until they became slender stone moulded bars known as mullions (q.v.). In the late thirteenth century the various geometrical shapes were elaborated into flowing shapes, and where these shapes occurred in rows reticulated tracery (q.v., from Lat. *rete*, a net) was produced; but in France their supposed resemblance to flames (Fr. *flambeau*, a torch) resulted in flamboyant tracery (q.v.). The last phase in the evolution of English tracery, not matched abroad, was due to the widespread demand for stained glass (q.v.), which encouraged rectilinear panels rather than complicated ornamental shapes, so that horizontal transomes (q.v.) were introduced to provide these, and also to stiffen the increasing large windows laterally. Thus flowing tracery gradually gave place to gridiron patterns in the sixteenth century. Tracery was also applied, in late Gothic work, to wooden screens and blank walls for purely ornamental purposes. (*Illustrated* p. 343.)

Trachelion, in a Greek Doric column, the space between the annulets and the hypotrachelion (q.v.). (*Illustrated* ENTABLATURE.)

Tracing-house, or **Trasour**, a medieval master-mason's drawing-office.

Transenna, in early Christian churches, an open-work screen or lattice, generally of marble.

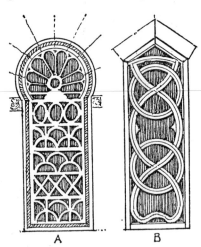

TRANSENNA: (A) *From S. Juan de Baños, Spain* (661); (B) *From Barnack Church, Northants.* (10th century). *See also* 'Qamariyyah'

Transept (from Med. Lat. *transeptum*), in a cruciform church, the whole transverse arm, normally aligned north and south; but the two projections are commonly called the 'north transept' and 'south transept.' Canterbury, Lincoln, Salisbury, and Worcester cathedrals, among other large churches, have an additional 'eastern transept,' but transepts are uncommon in English parish churches. (*Illustrated* CATHEDRAL.)

Transitional Architecture, the name given by Sharpe (q.v.) to the period in England about 1145–90, when the transition from 'Norman' (or Romanesque) to 'Early English Gothic' was taking place.

Transome, a horizontal bar of stone or wood across a mullioned window, introduced in the late Gothic period. *See* TRACERY.

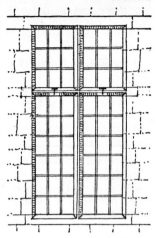

TRANSOME (marked T) in stone, English, 16th-century style

Trasour, *see* TRACING-HOUSE.

Travertine, a fine cream-coloured limestone quarried in Italy and much used since ancient Roman times, partly because it polishes well.

Tread (of a staircase), the horizontal upper part of each step, between the vertical risers (q.v.). The normal width is 9 to 12 inches. (*Illustrated* STAIRCASE.)

Trefoil (from Lat. *trifolium*, 'three-leaved'), in Gothic architecture, either (i) a three-lobed panel or opening in tracery; or (ii) a three-lobed carved leaf.

Treillage, *see* TRELLIS.

Trellis, or **Treillage,** a lattice, or light structure of interlacing bars of wood or metal, crossing each other at right angles or diagonally, and fastened at the intersections; used for climbing plants.

TREFOIL in English late Gothic masonry

Trezzini, Domenico (*b.* Lugano, 1679; *d.* Moscow or St Petersburg, 1734), architect and engineer; the leading exponent of Baroque (q.v.) in Russia during the reign of Peter the Great. He worked as an engineer in Copenhagen before settling in St Petersburg about 1703, where he later became city architect. His principal buildings in St Petersburg were the university (1723); the fortress and cathedral of

SS. Peter and Paul (1714–33, destroyed by fire, 1753, and then rebuilt); the conventual church in the Alexandro-Nevskaya Laya (*c.* 1716); and the Summer Palace (*c.* 1716); also some buildings in Moscow.

Triapsidal, [a building] having three apses, usually abreast. *See* APSE.

Tribune (from Med. Lat. *tribuna*), either (i) the semicircular or polygonal apse of a basilican church; or (ii) a rostrum or pulpit in a church; or (iii) a gallery in a church. *See also* MATRONEUM.

Triclinium (Lat., from Gk *triklinion*, three couches), a dining-room, normally having couches on three of its four sides.

Triforium, *see* BLIND STOREY.

Triglyph (Lat. *triglyphus*, from Gk *trigluphos*, thrice-grooved), in the frieze of the Greek Doric Order (*see* ORDERS), a slightly projecting block having three grooves or channels on its face. (*Illustrated* ENTABLATURE.)

Trilithon (Gk, three stones). (1) Any prehistoric monument having one stone lintel resting on two upright stones, e.g. at Stonehenge. (2) A famous group of three gigantic stone blocks at Baalbek, Syria.

Trim, in American usage, the finishings of a room, including skirtings, architraves, etc.

Trochilus, *see* SCOTIA.

Trophy (from Gk *tropē*, a putting to flight), originally, in classical times, a monument celebrating a military victory and displaying captured arms or spoils; later, a carved festoon or swag (qq.v.) incorporating martial or triumphal symbols or tokens.

Trulli (Ital.), primitive beehive-shaped stone huts found in groups in northern Apulia, Italy; peculiar to that area, believed to be ultimately of Mycenaean (q.v.) origin, and still inhabited.

Truss. Either (i) a framed structure, usually triangulated, and so designed as to bear a superincumbent weight, e.g. a 'roof-truss' (q.v., *illustrated*); or (ii) a term seldom used to-day: an ornamental bracket or console or modillion (qq.v.).

Tubbs, Ralph (*b.* Hadley Wood, 9 Jan. 1912), architect. Educated at Mill Hill and at the Architectural Association School, came into prominence as the designer of the aluminium 'Dome of Discovery' (365 feet diameter, the largest dome in the world), at the 1951 Exhibition in London. Among his other works are the Indian Students' Hostel, Fitzroy Square, London, and a residential area at Harlow New Town, Essex.

Tudor Arch, a depressed four-centred arch, used in Tudor architecture (q.v.). (*Illustrated* ARCH, TYPES OF.)

Tudor Architecture, a term covering the period *c.* 1500–*c* 1600 in England, and thus including Elizabethan architecture (q.v.). *See also* ENGLISH ARCHITECTURE.

Tudor Flower, a conventional leaf form, much used as an ornament, especially in rows as a cresting (q.v.) to screens (q.v.) in churches.

Tudor Rose, a conventionalized rose much used in Tudor architecture (q.v.), not to be confused with the Tudor flower (q.v.).

Tufa, a generic name for porous stones; more precisely, a volcanic conglomerate found in Italy, and much used in Roman buildings.

Tunnel Vault, *see* BARREL VAULT.

Turkish Architecture includes only two significant phases. The first comprises the buildings of the Seljuk Turks, who invaded Asia Minor from Central Asia in the eleventh century and established the 'Kingdom of Roum,' embracing most of Syria, Asia Minor, and Mesopotamia. Making their capital at Konia, they employed Persian craftsmen on their buildings, which include several important mosques in Konia—all of the thirteenth century. The next wave of invaders consisted of the Ottoman Turks, another warlike race from Central Asia, who superseded the Seljuks about 1300, and established their capital at Brusa—nearly opposite Constantinople (now Istanbul), the capital of the Byzantine Empire, which contained many fine Christian churches. At Brusa the Ottoman Turks erected a number of handsome mosques between 1379 and 1402; then, in 1453, they besieged and captured Constantinople itself. They proceeded to convert S. Sophia into a mosque; and during the next 200 years built six more large mosques in the city—all in the Byzantine rather than in the 'Muslim' style, but furnished with minarets. The chief architect of the sixteenth century was Sinan (q.v.). After about 1650 Turkish architecture progressively deteriorated, but at the new capital, Ankara, excellent modern buildings, designed on western lines, are rising rapidly. *See* MUSLIM ARCHITECTURE and SINAN.

> *See also* Montani, *L'Architecture ottomane,* 1873; C. Gurlitt, *Die Baukunst Konstantinopels,* 1907–12; E. Diez and H. Glück, *Alt-Konstantinopel,* 1920; R. Saffet, *Les Caractérisques de l'architecture turque,* 1938; B. Ünsal, *Turkish Islamic Architecture,* 1959.

Turret (from Old Fr. *tourette,* dim. of *tour*), a small tower.

Tuscan Order, *see* ORDERS OF ARCHITECTURE.

Tympanum (Lat., from Gk *tumpanon,* originally, a drum), in classical architecture, either (i) the die (q.v.) of a pedestal; or (ii) the vertical triangular space between

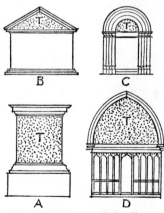

TYMPANUM (*marked* T *and shaded*): (A) *On a classical pedestal;* (B) *On a pediment;* (C) *Over a Romanesque doorway;* (D) *Over a rood-screen and below a chancel arch*

the horizontal and raking courses of a pediment (q.v.). In medieval architecture, either (i) the vertical triangular or segmental space over a doorway between the lintel (q.v.) and the enclosing arch; or (ii) in churches, a light screen of lath and plaster or of wood boarding, filling the space between the rood-screen (q.v.) and the chancel arch, and usually painted with a representation of the Last Judgment.

U

Undercroft, in a medieval monastery, a range of vaulted store-rooms, etc., beneath the dormitories and principal rooms.

Underpinning, the strengthening of an existing wall by removing and renewing its lower portions in short lengths at a time: always a difficult operation.

United States, Architecture of the. There were Spanish settlements on the coast of Florida, etc., before the end of the sixteenth century, but for all practical purposes the story begins in the British colonies of Virginia (founded in 1607) and New England (founded by the Pilgrim Fathers in 1620). In each case the colonists erected no permanent buildings during their first years, being preoccupied with defending themselves against the Indians and contenting themselves with temporary wooden buildings protected by stockades. Within a generation a small brick Gothic church (still standing) was erected at Jamestown in Virginia in 1632, and other brick buildings followed. In New England, where no brick was available, all the houses were timber-framed, covered with 'clapboards' (weather-boarding), and roofed with shingles. This type of building became very popular in New England, and still continues to be repeated. The beautiful parsonage at Topsfield, Massachusetts (1683), is a fine surviving example; another is the 'House of the Seven Gables' at Salem, Massachusetts. In 1623 the Dutch founded New Amsterdam, which was captured by the British in 1664 and rechristened 'New York'; but not a trace remains there of the picturesque Dutch gabled houses which, in old engravings, recall European Amsterdam. Towards the end of the seventeenth century, when the British occupation of all the north-eastern states was securely established, a more formal and ambitious type of architecture was introduced from England. A splendid example exists in Williamsburg, founded 1691 as the new capital of Virginia, and restored to its original appearance from 1925 onwards, regardless of cost. Here is the handsome William and Mary College (1693–7), vaguely reputed to have been designed by Wren (q.v.), and certainly characteristic of his style. Other fine buildings are the country mansion of Westover in Virginia (*c.* 1726) and George Washington's home at Mount Vernon (1743, enlarged 1785). From about 1720 onwards the influence of the English Palladian style, and later that of Robert Adam (q.v.), is very apparent. The White House at Washington was built in 1792–9, and the Capitol at Washington was begun in 1793. Thomas Jefferson (q.v.), whose name is familiar as the third President of the U.S.A., but who also practised architecture, built himself a charming house called Monticello in Virginia (1796–1809), and designed, among other things, the Capitol at Richmond, Virginia (1785–9). *See also* BULFINCH, HARRISON (P.), HAVILAND, HOBAN, LATROBE, L'ENFANT,

McIntire, Thornton, Town, Walter, Warren.   America, now independent of Britain, continued to follow British architectural fashions, so in due course the 'Greek Revival,' the 'Gothic Revival,' and the 'Free Classic Revival' appeared (*see* Upjohn). In the third quarter of the nineteenth century, however, H. H. Richardson (q.v.) introduced a ' Romanesque Revival' which showed some originality; and his pupil, L. H. Sullivan (q.v.)—notably in the Transportation Building at the World's Fair, Chicago (1894)—led the 'Chicago School' of architects in a movement to create a modern style for commercial buildings.   (*See* Burnham and Jenney.)   His mantle fell, in turn, upon his brilliant pupil, Frank Lloyd Wright (q.v.), who became the leading architect in America by the middle of the twentieth century; but from about 1900 to about 1940 most of the important buildings in the U.S.A. were designed by architects trained in the classical tradition at the École des Beaux Arts, Paris, though some of them favoured Gothic, especially for churches and collegiate buildings.   Their names and principal buildings are dealt with separately (*see* Carrère, Corbett, Cram, Gilbert, Goodhue, Hastings, McKim, Pope, Renwick, S. White).   The invention of the skyscraper (q.v.) in the late nineteenth century was due partly to the tremendously high cost of land in the centre of New York and other American cities, partly to the rock subsoil of New York, capable of sustaining immense loads.   (*See* Harrison, W. K., and Skidmore.)

Political and racial persecution in Germany and central Europe during the second quarter of the twentieth century led to the settlement in America of many distinguished architects.   Many became professors in American universities: all created large practices and became dominating forces in the trend of architectural design (*see* Breuer; Gropius; Neutra; Saarinen; Van der Rohe).   The powerful influence of Frank Lloyd Wright, however, still persisted, and gave American architecture a distinctive character.

> See T. F. Hamlin, *The American Spirit in Architecture*, 1926;
> T. E. Tallmadge, *The Story of Architecture in America*, 1928;
> F. Kimball, *Domestic Architecture of the American Colonies and the Early Republic*, 1928; M. S. Briggs, *Homes of the Pilgrim Fathers*, 1932; H. Morrison, *Early American Architecture*, 1952;
> F. Gutheim, *Architecture in America, 1857–1957*, 1957; I. MacCallum, *Architecture U.S.A.*, 1959.

Unwin, Sir Raymond (*b.* Rotherham, 2 Nov. 1863; *d.* Lyme, Connecticut, U.S.A., 28 June 1940), architect and town-planner; President R.I.B.A., 1931–3; R.I.B.A. Royal Gold Medallist, 1937. These high honours were awarded to him by his professional brethren for his town-planning rather than for his architecture, of which he produced very little, and he has rightly been called 'the father of English town-planning.'   He started as an engineer, and his interest in social questions led him to study this comparatively new subject. He and his partner, Barry Parker, who was a trained architect, were in practice at Buxton when they won the competition for the plan of the First Garden City, at Letchworth, in 1903, and later they laid out the Earswick model village near York. In 1906 he was invited to design the Hampstead Garden Suburb, and produced a most admirable plan. From 1914 to 1928 he was in government service—at the Local Government Board, the Ministry of Munitions, and, finally, as chief architect and town-planner, at the Ministry of Health. His book, *Town-planning in Practice*, 1909, became a standard work, and was translated into French and German.

Upjohn, Richard (*b.* Shaftesbury, Dorset, England, 1802; *d.* Garrison, New York, U.S.A., 1878), architect, became a leader of the Gothic Revival (q.v.) in America. He was apprenticed to a cabinet-maker at Shaftesbury, and actually started a business of his own there in that craft. Going to America in 1829, he worked first at New Bedford, Massachusetts, and in 1834 became assistant to the architect Bulfinch (q.v.). In 1837 he started independent practice in New York, and began rebuilding the old 'Colonial style' Trinity Church in Gothic—then an innovation. He adopted the same style for the church of St Thomas, New York. He was a founder and the first president of the American Institute of Architects. His son, Richard Michell Upjohn (1827–1903), designed the Connecticut State Capitol at Hartford, Connecticut (1885).

See monograph by Everard Upjohn, 1939.

Urbanisme (Fr.), town-planning (q.v.).

Utility Room (American), a room, usually in the basement of an American house, where are installed the heating plant, the washing-machine, and other utilities.

V

Vallée, Jean de la (*b*. in France, 1620; *d*. Stockholm, 9 Mar. 1696), architect, who practised in the Baroque (q.v.) style, accompanied his father, Simon de la Vallée (q.v.), from Holland to Sweden in 1637, was trained by his father, and after his death entered municipal service in Stockholm. The city granted him a sum for travel abroad, and from 1646 to 1649 he studied in France and Italy. He became royal architect in 1649, and lord mayor of Stockholm in 1671. His principal works were the completion of the Riddarhuset at Stockholm, begun by his father; the extension of the royal palace at Stockholm (1654); several other palaces; a town plan for Stockholm; and the church of Queen Hedvig Eleanora at Stockholm.

Vallée, Simon de la (*b*. in France; killed in a duel at Stockholm, 21 Nov. 1642), father of Jean (q.v.), was son and pupil of a French architect. After studying in Italy he became architect to Prince Henry of Orange, and worked in Holland, 1633–7. He then went to Sweden, where he designed the Riddarhuset at Stockholm (unfinished at his death), and several mansions.

Valley, the internal intersection of two roof slopes. *See* ROOF.

Vanbrugh, Sir John (*b*. London, Jan. 1664; *d*. there, 26 Mar. 1726), architect and dramatist; the most picturesque character in English architectural history. His father was a Flemish Protestant merchant, who fled to England from Catholic persecution. John, fourth of his nineteen children, was born in London, but the family moved to Chester before he was three years old, probably to escape the Great Plague of 1665. The first known fact of his career is that he obtained an infantry commission in January 1686. He resigned it soon afterwards, was arrested in Calais for being there without a passport, spent eighteen months in French prisons, obtained a commission in the Marines on being released, and served till 1698. By that time he had started writing plays, *The Relapse* and *The Provok'd Wife* both being successes in 1697, but in 1699, apparently without any technical or artistic training, he was commissioned by the Earl of Carlisle (a fellow member of the famous Kit-Cat Club) to design the vast mansion of Castle Howard, Yorkshire (completed 1726). This was followed in 1705 by the colossal Blenheim Palace (completed 1720); extensive additions to Greenwich Hospital, of which he became surveyor in 1716; the remodelling of Kimbolton Castle (1707–9); King's Weston, Bristol (1711–14); Claremont House, Esher (*c*. 1715–20); Eastbury Park, Dorset (*c*. 1718 onwards); Seaton Delaval, Northumberland (*c*. 1720–8); and many other buildings. He is commonly regarded as a Baroque (q.v.) architect; but his theatrical style of design was entirely his own. His protracted and bitter correspondence with the Duchess of Marlborough about Blenheim is easily the most amusing thing in architectural literature.

See monographs by C. Barman, 1924; L. Whistler, 1938; G. F. Webb, 1928.

Van der Rohe, Ludwig Mies (*b.* Aachen, 27 Mar. 1886), architect; the son of a master-mason. His original surname was Mies, but he adopted his mother's name of Van der Rohe. He was articled to Bruno Paul from 1905 to 1907, studied under Behrens (q.v.) in Berlin, 1908–12, and then spent a year at The Hague. After the First World War he returned to Berlin, where he built some large blocks of municipal flats, and produced some remarkable designs for skyscrapers. In 1930 he became Director of the Bauhaus at Dessau, on the recommendation of Gropius (q.v.); but went to America in 1937, settled there, and became director of the Illinois Institute of Technology at Chicago in 1938. He carried out a number of educational buildings there from 1939 onwards; also two tall blocks of flats on the Lakeside front in 1940 and 1951 (*illustrated* PILOTIS); also the celebrated Seagram Building, New York (1956–8).

See monographs by P. J. Johnson, 1952; M. Bill, 1955; A. Drexler, 1960.

Van de Velde, Henry (*b.* Antwerp, 1863; *d.* Zürich, 25 Oct. 1957), architect. He was one of the apostles of the 'Modern Movement' in architecture during the early years of the twentieth century. He was trained in Antwerp, but went to Germany in 1900 and founded the famous Bauhaus at Weimar. He remained its director till 1914, when he returned to Belgium at the outbreak of war. He subsequently became a professor in the University of Ghent, and Director of the Institut Supérieur des Arts Decoratifs at Brussels. His chief buildings were the Folkwang Museum at Hagen, Germany (1902); the remarkable theatre at the Cologne Exhibition (1914); and the Belgian Pavilion at the New York World's Fair (1939). His lectures in Germany were published in 1903.

Van Kampen, Jacob, *see* KAMPEN.

Vanvitelli, Luigi (*b.* Naples, 12 May 1700; *d.* Caserta, 1 Mar. 1773), a prominent architect in the Italian Baroque style. He was the son of a Dutch painter named Kaspar van Witel, and he too started as a painter, but then turned to architecture and studied under Juvara (q.v.). Although he was unsuccessful in the competition for the new façade of S. Giovanni in Laterano, Rome (1734), his design led to his appointment as architect to St Peter's in 1735. He also designed the large convent of S. Agostino in Rome, and successfully converted the hall of Diocletian's *thermae* (q.v.) into the splendid church of S. Maria degli Angeli. His masterpiece was the immense royal palace at Caserta (1751–3) for the King of Naples. Among his other works were the Lazzaretto (1733), Arco Clementino (1735), and Jesuit Church—all at Ancona; the churches of the Olivetani at Perugia (1740) and of the Misericordia at Macerata; the campanile of the Basilica at Loreto; and bridges at Eboli and Benevento.

See monograph by F. Fichera, 1937.

Vardy, John (*d.* 17 May 1765), architect, and an accomplished draughtsman, was closely associated with William Kent (q.v.), and helped to publish some of that architect's designs. He spent most of his career in the royal service as clerk of the works at Greenwich, Hampton Court, Whitehall, St James's, and Kensington, until 1756 when he became clerk of the works at Greenwich Hospital. The most important building designed by him was Spencer House, London (1756–65), for Lord Spencer.

Vasari, Giorgio (*b*. Arezzo, 30 July 1511; *d*. Florence, 27 July 1574), architect, painter, and writer, is chiefly remembered as a writer. He worked in Florence and Arezzo as a student of painting till 1531, when Cardinal Ippolito dei Medici took him to Rome to continue his studies there. He was advised by Michelangelo to turn to architecture, but continued painting until, in 1546, the influential Cardinal Faruese suggested that he should compile a series of lives of famous painters. He soon decided to accept that advice, and started his task in Florence, with the result that in 1550 the first edition appeared of his *Lives of the Painters, Sculptors, and Architects*—to give it its English title—which has since been reprinted many times, and translated into several languages. As an architect or a painter his work is unimportant: it comprises the Palazzo degli Uffizi, Florence (1560); the mediocre tomb of Michelangelo in S. Croce, Florence (1564); the Loggie in his native town of Arezzo (1573); and the enormous but feeble wall-paintings in the Palazzo Vecchio, Florence (1554), and in the Sala Regia of the Vatican, Rome (1570).

See monograph by R. W. Carden, 1910.

Vault, Vaulting (from Lat. *volta*, past participle of *volvere*, to turn). A vault may be either (i) a continuous arch of brick, stone, or concrete, forming a self-supporting structure over a building or a part thereof; or (ii) a vaulted structure, e.g. under a street pavement. The principle of the vault was known in Babylonia and Egypt 6,000 years ago, but was rapidly developed to a much greater degree of efficiency by the Romans, who made remarkable strides in their skilful use of concrete; by the Byzantines of the sixth century A.D.; by the Sassanid rulers of Persia in the sixth and seventh centuries, using brickwork on the grand scale; by the Muslims throughout the Middle Ages; and in western Europe during the Romanesque and Gothic (qq.v.) periods. The Romans used barrel vaults (q.v.) or 'tunnel vaults'; the line of intersection of such vaults is called a groin (q.v.)—*see* Illustration 'A.' Barrel vaults were very heavy. During the Romanesque period they were lightened by means of stone ribs carrying a relatively thin 'web' between them, just as the steel ribs of an umbrella carry the thin silk or cotton cover. The fact that the resulting vault assumed the convex shape ('B') of an umbrella led, however, to various difficulties, especially where the nave of a church was twice the width of the aisles, because the wide semicircular arch of the nave was far taller than the narrow semicircular arches over the aisles. In the early Gothic period the introduction of pointed arches ('C') solved this problem, for they could be made more or less steeply pointed to suit the differing widths of nave and aisles; and thus it became possible to construct

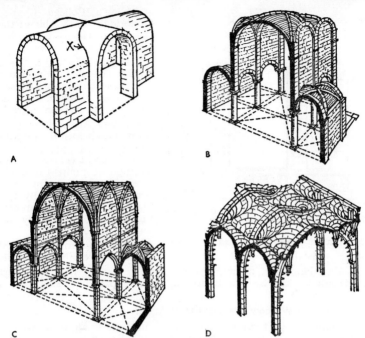

DIAGRAM SHOWING DEVELOPMENT OF ENGLISH VAULTING
(A) *Roman intersecting barrel vaults* (X=*groin*); (B) *Romanesque ribbed vault;*
(C) *Gothic ribbed vault;* (D) *Late Gothic fan vault, from Henry VII's Chapel,*
Westminster

a vaulted roof of which the 'crown' (or top) at the ridge was level,
with a gain in effect as well as in efficiency.   During the later Gothic
period vaulting grew progressively more complicated as intermediate
lierne ribs (q.v.) were added, and the thickness of the stone web
was reduced to 6 inches or so; while the use of massive buttresses
(q.v.) opposite each of the vaulting ribs enabled the walls between
the buttresses to be pierced over much of their surface for great
windows of stained glass (q.v.), which were becoming increasingly
popular.   Thus a late Gothic building became a skeleton of stone
ribs and buttresses, and the actual stone 'web' of the vault was
often less than 6 inches thick, and correspondingly light.   Fan-
vaulting (q.v.), introduced during the last phase of English Gothic,
went even further (*see* 'D'), and elaborate carved stone 'pendants'
(structurally quite superfluous) were hung from the vaulting for
purely ornamental purposes.   The undersides of fan vaults were
conoidal in form, and were carved with tracery which, seen from
below, produced the effect of a fan: hence the name.   The example
illustrated is from Henry VII's Chapel, Westminster; there are others

VENETIAN WINDOW, after Colin Camp-
bell (q.v.), 18th century

at King's College Chapel, Cambridge; Bath Abbey; the cloisters of Gloucester Cathedral, etc.

Velarium (Lat.), a large awning stretched from masts over the seated area of a Roman theatre or amphitheatre, as protection against sun and rain.

Venetian Arch, either (i) a pointed arch with its intrados and extrados (qq.v.) struck from different centres; or (ii) a composite group of windows consisting of one central semi-circular arch flanked by two 'flat' or 'cambered' arches: this type is structurally unsound. *See* ARCH.

Venetian Blind, a window blind composed of narrow horizontal strips or 'slats' of wood, so fixed on tapes as to be easily adjustable.

Venetian Door, a central door (usually having its upper part glazed) flanked by side lights, all forming part of a single wood framework.

Venetian Window, *see* VENETIAN ARCH.

Verandah (a term originally used in India), an open portico attached to a house. *See* PORCH, PORTICO, STOEP.

Verge, on a gable-end, the edge of the roofing tiles, projecting slightly in front of the wall-face. *See* ROOF, PARTS OF A (*illustrated*).

Verge-board, *see* BARGE-BOARD.

Vermiculation (from Lat. *vermiculus*, dim. of *vermis*, a worm), an ornamental imitation, on stone facings, of worm tracks in wood.

Vestibule (from Lat. *vestibulum*), an entrance hall, antechamber, or lobby.

Vestry (probably from Lat *vestiarium*), a robing-room in a church, in which vestments and sacred vessels are also kept. *See* SACRISTY.

Vice, *see* VISE.

Victorian Society, The (offices at 55 Great Ormond Street, London, W.C.1), founded early in 1958 'to study and safeguard Victorian buildings and their contents.'

Vignola, Giacomo Barozzi da (*b.* Vignola, near Modena, 1 Oct.

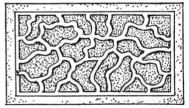

VERMICULATION in masonry

1507; *d.* Rome, 7 July 1573), architect and writer on architecture; commonly called 'Vignola' after his birth-place. He was a leader of the Italian late Renaissance or 'Mannerist' (q.v.) school. After learning painting and perspective at Bologna, he moved to Rome about 1540, studied the ancient monuments there, and worked under Antonio Sangallo the Younger (q.v.). He was next employed by François I in France, 1541–3; then returned to Bologna, and finally, in 1546, to Rome, where he designed the beautiful Villa Giulia, now a museum; also the churches of Il Gesù, S. Andrea sulla Via Flaminia, and S. Anna; and the great castle or pentagonal palace at Caprarola for Cardinal Farnese. He is chiefly known for his two important books—on the Five Orders (1562) and on Perspective (published 1583). These were reprinted and translated many times.

See monograph by G. K. Loukomski, 1927.

Vihára (Sanskrit), a Buddhist monastery, or temple, or hall in a monastery.

Villa (Lat.). (1) In Roman times, a self-contained farmstead serving a country estate, and containing accommodation for the employees as well as the owner. At least 500 villas are represented by ruins to-day in Britain, from several thousands existing in the fifth century A.D. (2) In Italy of the Renaissance, a country house surrounded by formal gardens. (3) In nineteenth-century England, a detached suburban house, smaller than a mansion but larger than a cottage. (4) At the present time, a small or medium-sized detached house of pretentious design and often with meretricious ornament. The current usage of the term is uncomplimentary.

Villard de Honnecourt, *see* HONNECOURT.

Vingbooms, or **Vinckebooms, Joost** or **Justus** (*b.* 1608; *d.* 1675), architect; son of a Dutch painter. He designed the handsome Ridderhuset ('House of the Nobles') at Stockholm in 1656 (completed by Jean de la Vallée, q.v.). His brother Philip (1607–75), also an architect, worked in Amsterdam.

Viollet-le-Duc, Eugène Emmanuel (*b.* Paris, 21 Jan. 1814; *d.* Lausanne, 17 Sept. 1879), architect and writer on architecture; R.I.B.A. Royal Gold Medallist, 1864. After training in Paris and study in Italy, he began, in 1840, the series of drastic restorations of French medieval buildings which have made him famous (and notorious). At the Sainte Chapelle, Paris (1840), and at Notre-Dame, Paris (1842), he was associated with Lassus, but thereafter his chief restorations were carried out alone. They included the *Cité* of Carcassonne (1852 onwards); the châteaux of Pierrefonds (1858) and Coucy (1863); the cathedrals of Amiens (1849 onwards) and Lausanne; the abbeys of Vézelay (1840) and St Denis; the great churches of St Ouen at Rouen (1846–62) and St Sernin at Toulouse (1862). He became professor at the École des Beaux Arts, Paris, in 1863. His prodigious output of books included dictionaries of French architecture (10 vols.) and of furniture (6 vols.).

Visconti, Louis Tullius Joachim (*b.* Rome, 11 Feb. 1791; *d.* Paris, 29 Dec. 1853), architect. He was the son of an archaeologist, who brought him to Paris in 1798. He studied under Percier (q.v.), entered government service in 1822, and became chief architect to Napoleon II in 1850. His most important building was the extension of the Tuileries and Louvre palaces on Paris (begun in 1851), and completed after his death by Lefuel. His other work, all in Paris, included the tomb of Napoleon in the Invalides (1842), and several public fountains and town houses.

Vise, Vice, or **Vys** (all archaic terms), a spiral staircase, usually of stone.

Vitruvius, correctly **Marcus Vitruvius Pollio** (first century B.C.), a Roman architect in government service during the reign of the

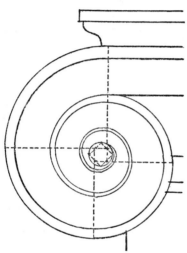

VOLUTE, according to Vignola (q.v.), see also illustration of Capital (B)

Emperor Augustus, to whom he dedicated the remarkable manual of architecture and building construction, *De Re Architectura*, which made him famous. It is still valuable to-day, not only for its accurate information on Roman building materials and methods, but also for its detailed description of older Greek architecture, which he had studied closely. Though popular in its day, the book was forgotten during the 'Dark Ages,' was discovered in a monastic library in the sixteenth century, was printed, translated into many languages, and became, perhaps too completely, 'the architect's Bible.' In Latin and English, it appears in the Loeb Library (1931); also in a good translation by M. H. Morgan (1914).

Volute (from Lat. *voluta*), the spiral scroll which forms the distinctive feature in the capital of the Ionic Order (*see* ORDERS).

Vomitorium (Lat., from *vomitare*, to vomit), or **Vomitory,** one of the passages or exits from a theatre or amphitheatre. The Latin form of the term is usual, but Gibbon writes of the Colosseum at Rome that '64 vomitories . . . poured forth the immense multitude.'

Voronikhin, Andrei Nikiforovic (*b.* Solekamsk, 17 Oct. 1759; *d.* St Petersburg, 21 Feb. 1814), architect; the most prominent figure of the classical revival in Russia. He was trained in Moscow under Bazhenov and Kazakov (qq.v.), and started practice in 1790. He became Professor of Fine Art at St Petersburg in 1800, and there erected his chief buildings: the Kazan Cathedral (1801–11) and the School of Mines (1806)—both in neo-Greek style.

See monograph by G. G. Grimm, 1952.

Voussoir (Fr.), one of the stones forming part of an arch (q.v.). Being wedge-shaped, they make the arch self-supporting. (*Illustrated* ARCH, PARTS OF AN.)

Voysey, Charles Francis Annesley (*b*. Hessle, Yorkshire, 28 May 1857; *d*. Winchester, 12 Feb. 1941), architect and decorative designer, R.I.B.A. Royal Gold Medallist, 1940, was the son of the unorthodox clergyman who founded the Theistic Church. Voysey was a leader of the movement towards simplicity in English domestic architecture, and his work had a great influence in continental Europe about 1900. After being articled to J. P. Seddon, he became assistant to G. Devey (q.v.), and started practice about 1890. He designed a great number of charming houses, but very few other buildings; and none of his houses were large, his own—'The Orchard,' at Chorley Wood, Hertfordshire (1900)—being a typical example. He also made many designs for stained glass, wall-papers, textile fabrics, and furniture. *See also* FICTIONAL ARCHITECTS.

See monograph by J. Brandon-Jones, 1957.

Vriendt, Cornelis de, *see* FLORIS.

Vulliamy, Lewis (*b*. London, 15 Mar. 1791; *d*. there, 4 Jan. 1871), architect, was articled to Sir R. Smirke (q.v.); then travelled in Italy. His most important buildings—all in or near London—were Dorchester House (1848–57, since demolished); the Law Institution, Chancery Lane (1830–2); the façade of the Royal Institution, Albemarle Street (1838); the Lock Hospital (1840–1); and a large number of churches, of which Christ Church, Woburn Square (1831), is typical.

Vys, *see* VISE.

W

Wagner, Otto (*b*. Vienna, 13 July 1841; *d*. there, 11 April 1918), architect, was trained in Vienna and Berlin. He started practice in Vienna about 1864, and began teaching there thirty years later. His work showed a progressive change from Viennese Baroque to the more functional and austere *Modernismus* which he adopted from about 1880 onwards, and which he was largely instrumental in popularizing in Central Europe. His chief buildings, all in and around Vienna, were the Post Office Savings Bank (1905); the Tramways Building; the Länderbank; the University Library (1910); several houses; and a curious church at Steinhof (1905–7).

See monographs by J. A. Lux, 1914, and H. A. Tietze, 1922.

Wagon Roof, or **Waggon Roof**, a timber roof without tie-beams but with curved braces which, when lined internally with boarding, produce the effect of the interior of a covered wagon; found especially in the west of England.

Wainscot. (1) A fine quality of oak imported from central and eastern Europe. (2) Interior wood panelling, whether of oak or not.

Wakalah, or **Okel** (Arabic), a large tenement house or a caravanserai (q.v.).

Wall Board, *see* BUILDING BOARD.

Walsingham, Alan of, *see* ALAN OF WALSINGHAM.

Walter, Thomas Ustick (*b*. Philadelphia, 4 Sept. 1804; *d*. there, 30 Oct. 1887), American architect, was apprenticed to his father, a master-bricklayer. He himself became a master-bricklayer in 1825, but had acquired some architectural knowledge from W. Strickland (q.v.), and in 1830 he started independent practice as an architect and engineer. He became a warm admirer and practitioner of the Greek Revival, his chief venture in that field being Girard College, Philadelphia (1833–47), which has been described as ' the climax and the death-knell' of that singular movement, in America. To prepare himself for this commission, he had made a tour of study in Europe. In 1851 he moved to Washington, and worked there until his retirement in 1865. He added the wings and dome, as one now sees them, to the Capitol, the dome being of cast-iron. His other work in Washington included the completion of the Treasury. Among his buildings elsewhere were many in Philadelphia; the Hibernian Hall at Charleston, South Carolina; court-houses at Reading and West Chester, Pennsylvania; and sundry hospitals, banks, and houses. He took an active part in founding the American Institute of Architects in 1857, and served as its second president from 1876 until his death.

Ware, Isaac (*d*. Hampstead, 6 Jan. 1766), architect and writer on architecture. He is said to have been a chimney-sweep's boy when a passing stranger—the great Lord Burlington (q.v.)—saw him making a sketch of the Banqueting House in Whitehall, 'gave him an excellent education, sent him to Italy to study, and introduced him to his friends as an architect.' This seems to be authentic; and, at any rate, he held a succession of official posts from 1728 onwards, and also designed several notable buildings. Of these, some have been destroyed, including Chesterfield House, Mayfair (1748–9), and Oxford Town Hall and Market (1751–2). Among those surviving are Wrotham Park, Middlesex (1754), and Clifton Hill House, Bristol (1746–50). Of his numerous books, the most important is *A Complete Body of Architecture*, 1756.

Warren, Whitney (*b.* New York, 29 Jan. 1864; *d.* there, 24 Jan. 1943), architect. After studying at the École des Beaux Arts in Paris, he started practice in New York, and founded the firm of Warren & Wetmore. Their work included a number of railway stations, and the Belmont, Biltmore, Commodore, and Vanderbilt hotels in New York City. During and after the First World War Warren took a close interest in Italian claims to Trieste, etc. In 1920 he was chosen to reconstruct the destroyed library of Louvain University. His published works were chiefly concerned with Italian irredentism.

Watching Chamber, in a medieval church, a room or loft from which the custodian could watch the relics or treasures that it contained, to prevent thefts by pilgrims.

Waterhouse, Alfred, R.A. (*b.* Liverpool, 19 July 1830; *d.* Yattendon, Berkshire, 22 Aug. 1905), architect; President R.I.B.A., 1888–91; R.I.B.A. Royal Gold Medallist, 1878. He was articled in Manchester, and started practice in 1853. It was said of him that 'his smile was worth £10,000 a year' to him; but he owed much of his enormous practice to his successes in competitions, beginning with the Manchester Assize Courts (1859); followed in 1868 by Manchester Town Hall. Other buildings were the Natural History Museum, the New University Club, the National Liberal Club, St Paul's School at Hammersmith, the City Guilds College at Kensington, University College Hospital, the Prudential Assurance Company's head offices —all these in London; the Metropole Hotel at Brighton; the university buildings of Manchester, Leeds, and Liverpool; Eaton Hall, near Chester; and collegiate buildings at Oxford and Cambridge. He was followed as President of the R.I.B.A. by his son Paul in 1921–3, and by his grandson Michael in 1948–50. A fourth generation of Waterhouse architects has since appeared. Waterhouse favoured the Romanesque style, and used terra-cotta freely in his public buildings.

Wattle and Daub, a primitive vertical covering formed of interlacing twigs or branches ('wattles') roughly plastered with clay ('daub').

Weather-boarding, *see* CLAPBOARD.

Weathering. (1) The disintegration, hardening, or discoloration of

building materials caused by the action of the elements upon them.
(2) A slope or projection on a wall, buttress, etc., to throw rain-water
off the face of the structure.

Webb, Sir Aston, R.A. (*b.* London, 22 May 1849; *d.* there, 21 Aug.
1930), architect; President R.I.B.A., 1902–4; R.I.B.A. Royal Gold
Medallist, 1905; President Royal Academy, 1919–24. He was
articled in London to Messrs Banks & Barry, and in 1873 started a
practice which became, at the beginning of the twentieth century,
perhaps the largest in England. Most of his work was obtained in
competition. His chief buildings were the Victoria and Albert
Museum (1891); the Imperial College of Science (1900–6); the Victoria
Memorial, including the Admiralty Arch and the re-fronting of
Buckingham Palace (1911–13)—all these in London; Birmingham
Law Courts (1886–91); Birmingham University (1906–9); Christ's
Hospital, Horsham (1894–1904); the Royal Naval College, Dart-
mouth (1899–1904). He also restored St Bartholomew's Church,
Smithfield, London (1886–93).

Webb, John (*b.* London, 1611; *d.* Butleigh, Somerset, 30 Oct.
1672), architect, was trained by Inigo Jones (q.v.), whose niece he
married. He prepared many designs for Jones, including those for a
new palace at Whitehall (never erected). After Jones's death in
1652 Webb's own designs included Lamport Hall, Northamptonshire
(1654–7); Belvoir Castle (since rebuilt); Gunnersbury House, Middlesex (since demolished); the King Charles Block at Greenwich Hospital
(1665–8); and, possibly, Ashburnham House, Westminster (*c.* 1662).

Webb, Philip Speakman (*b.* Oxford, 12 Jan. 1831; *d.* Worth, Sussex,
17 April 1915), architect, was articled in Reading, and in 1852 became
assistant to G. E. Street (q.v.) in Oxford. There he met William
Morris (q.v.), who was Street's pupil for one year only. Webb began
private practice in London in 1856, and was commissioned by Morris
in 1857 to design the famous 'Red House' at Bexley Heath in Kent.
When Morris founded the firm of Morris & Co. in 1861, Webb joined
him, and designed the 'Green Dining Room' at the South Kensington
Museum. His other buildings included several country houses—
Arisaig in Scotland (1863); Joldwynds, Dorking (1873); Rounton
Grange, Yorkshire (1872–6); Clouds, East Knoyle (1881–6), etc.—
and a few town houses. His total output was, however, very small;
and his importance lies in his connection with Morris, and the move-
ments that they jointly led for improved design and craftsmanship.
See monograph by W. R. Lethaby, 1935.

Well, the central open space in a circular or elliptical staircase
(q.v., *illustrated*); or within a tall building.

Welsh Architecture differs very little from English architecture
(q.v.) in its various phases, though there are unusual features at St
David's Cathedral. The outstanding historical buildings of Wales
are medieval castles (*see* CASTLE), e.g. Caernarvon, Caerphilly,
Harlech, Beaumaris, Pembroke. Cardiff contains, in its Civic Centre,
the finest modern buildings in Wales. *See* LANCHESTER and THOMAS,
SIR P.

Wheel Window, a circular window with mullions radiating from its centre, like the spokes of a wheel.

White, Stanford (*b.* New York, 9 Nov. 1853; murdered there, 25 June 1906), architect. After his training under C. D. Gambrill and H. H. Richardson (q.v.), he travelled abroad; then became partner with C. F. McKim and W. R. Mead. For their buildings *see* McKim.

White, Thomas (*b.* Worcester, *c.* 1674; *d.* there, Aug. 1748), architect, sculptor, and master-mason. He may have designed the Guildhall at Worcester, on which he certainly carved some of the external sculpture (1722). Three churches in Worcester are attributed to him: St Nicholas (1730–5), St Swithin (1734–6), and All Saints (1738–42); also Castle Bromwich Church, Warwickshire (rebuilt, 1726–31).

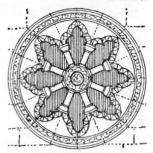

WHEEL WINDOW (*c.* A.D. 1170): *from Barfreston Church, Kent*

Wicket (from Old Fr. *guichet*), a small gate; or, especially, a small door in a large gate, enabling a person to enter without opening the large gate.

Wilkins, William, R.A. (*b.* Norwich, 31 Aug. 1778; *d.* Cambridge, 31 Aug. 1839), architect and writer on architecture. The son of an architect, he graduated at Cambridge as Sixth Wrangler in 1800, travelled in Greece and Italy, and on his return became a leading spirit of the 'Greek Revival' (q.v.). His classical buildings included Downing College, Cambridge (1807–11); Haileybury College (1806); 'London University' (now 'University College, London,' 1826–7); the University Club, Pall Mall East, London (1822–6, since rebuilt); and the National Gallery, London (1832–8). At Cambridge he designed neo-Gothic buildings for Corpus Christi (1823–6), King's (1824–8) and Trinity (1823–5) Colleges. In 1807 he published *Antiquities of Magna Graecia*.

William of Sens (*d.* 1180) was so called because he worked at Sens Cathedral, France, before becoming master-mason or architect of Canterbury Cathedral, 1174–8.

William of Wykeham, *see* WYKEHAM.

William the Englishman (*d.* 1214) became master-mason or architect of Canterbury Cathedral in 1178, in succession to William of Sens (q.v.), who had met with an accident there.

Wilson, Sir William (*b.* Leicester, May 1641; *d.* Sutton Coldfield, 10 June 1710), mason, builder, and architect. He designed the rebuilt church of St Mary, Warwick (1694–1704), in a curious hybrid style—Gothic and Renaissance; also Four Oaks Hall, Warwickshire (1680).

Winders, tapered or wedge-shaped steps, used at the turn of a staircase (q.v., *illustrated*).

Window (from Old Norse *vindauga*, wind-eye), an opening, usually glazed, in an exterior wall or side of a building, to admit light and air. The Greeks and Romans used windows, but during the Middle Ages they were seldom provided except in churches and important buildings, and glazing became common in ordinary dwelling-houses only during Tudor times. A medieval or Tudor window may be divided into 'lights' by vertical mullions, by horizontal transomes, or by tracery. The top of a window is the 'head,' the bottom is the 'sill,' and the sides are the 'jambs.' Each light may be subdivided into 'panes.' Where the glazing is leaded, and in small panes, they are sometimes called 'quarrels'; and they are fixed in narrow strips of lead called 'cames.' Leaded casements are often stiffened by iron 'saddle-bars' (q.v.). Before sash-windows—more accurately 'double hung sashes'—were introduced towards the end of the seventeenth century, windows were wooden or iron casements, usually hung at the side to open outwards or inwards. Modern casements may be of steel, and are sometimes hung at top or bottom. *See* ANCIENT LIGHTS, BAY-WINDOW, BOW-WINDOW, CAME, CASEMENT, DORMER, FANLIGHT, FENESTRATION, HAGIOSCOPE, HOPPER, JESSE WINDOW, LANCET, LATTICE WINDOW, LEADED LIGHTS, LOW-SIDE WINDOW, LUCARNE, MULLION, MUSHRABIYYAH, ORIEL, PANE, QAMARIYYAH, QUARREL, REVEAL, ROSE WINDOW, SASH-WINDOW, SHAMSIYYAH, STAINED GLASS, TRACERY, TRANSOME, VENETIAN WINDOW, WHEEL WINDOW, YORKSHIRE LIGHTS.

Window Tax, a tax levied from 1695 to 1851 upon the number of windows in a house. As an unsightly result, many windows were blocked up to escape taxation.

Withdrawing-room, *see* DRAWING-ROOM.

Wood, John, the Elder (*b*. Bath, 1704; *d*. there, 23 May 1754), architect, commonly called 'Wood of Bath' because of his prominent share in the development and adornment of that city. The son of a local builder, he worked for some years in London and Yorkshire before returning to Bath in 1727. His principal works there were Gay Street (1727 onwards); Queen Square (1729–36); the hospital; North and South Parades; the Circus, which he began in 1754; and the mansion of Prior Park, just outside the city (1735–48). Elsewhere he built the exchange or town hall at Liverpool (1749–54); the exchange and market at Bristol (1741–3); and several country mansions.

See monograph by T. S. Cotterell, 1927.

Wood, John, the Younger (*b*. Bath, 1728; *d*. Batheaston, 18 June 1781), architect; son of John Wood the Elder (q.v.). He completed the Circus, and himself designed the Royal Crescent (1767–75); several small streets; the New Assembly Rooms (1769–71); and the Hot Bath (now the Old Royal Baths, 1773–7)—all these in Bath; also Buckland House, Berkshire (1755–7), and Hardenhuish Church, Wiltshire (1779).

Wornum, (George) Grey (*b*. London, 17 April 1888; *d*. New York, 11 June 1957), architect; R.I.B.A. Royal Gold Medallist, 1952.

Educated at Bradfield, the Slade School, and the Architectural Association School; articled to R. S. Wornum in London, and started practice in 1910. He lost an eye while serving in the First World War. He was little known in his profession until in 1932 he won the hotly contested competition for the new premises of the R.I.B.A. in Portland Place, London—a masterpiece of planning. His other work included several housing schemes in London, the interior decorations of the great liner *Queen Elizabeth* (I), and the British Girls' College at Alexandria, Egypt (1935).

Worthington, Sir (John) Hubert, R.A. (*b.* Alderley Edge, 4 July 1886; *d.* 26 July 1963), architect. He was educated at Sedbergh and at the Manchester University School of Architecture. He served in the First World War. From 1923 to 1928 he was Professor of Architecture at the Royal College of Art. In the Second World War he was consulting architect to the Imperial War Graves Commission for North Africa and Egypt. His large practice has included much work at Oxford: extensions to the New Bodleian Library, and remodelling of the Old Bodleian and the Radcliffe Camera; new buildings for the School of Forestry, the School of Botany, the Special Faculties, and St Catherine's Society; also additions to several colleges. In London he carried out much post-war reconstruction in the Middle Temple. His other buildings include several war memorials; work at Eton College, at Westminster and Rossall Schools, and at the Imperial College of Science; and many commissions in Manchester.

Wotton, Sir Henry, M.P. (*b.* Boughton Malherbe, Kent, 1568; *d.* Eton, Dec. 1639), diplomat. He was the author of a much-quoted little book, *The Elements of Architecture*, 1624.

Wren, Sir Christopher, M.P., F.R.S. (*b.* E. Knoyle, Wiltshire, 20 Oct. 1632; *d.* London, 25 Feb. 1723), architect and scientist. He was the son of a clergyman. After a brilliant career as a scientist and mathematician at Oxford, he became a Professor of Astronomy in 1657, and did not turn to architecture till about 1662, when he designed the chapel of Pembroke College, Cambridge, followed in 1664–9 by the Sheldonian Theatre, Oxford. His rebuilding of St Paul's Cathedral, London, lasted from 1675 to 1710. He also rebuilt fifty-two of the City churches destroyed in the Great Fire of London, 1666. He prepared a remarkable plan for rebuilding the City immediately after the fire, but it was never carried out. In 1669 he became surveyor-general of the king's works, and in that capacity extended, altered, or rebuilt several royal palaces, including Hampton Court, Kensington, Whitehall, Winchester, and St James's; also Windsor Castle. Among other buildings, he designed Chelsea Hospital; part of Greenwich Hospital; Emmanuel College Chapel and Trinity College Library at Cambridge; 'Tom Tower,' extensions to Trinity and Queen's Colleges at Oxford; the Royal Observatory at Greenwich; Winslow Hall, Buckinghamshire; Marlborough House, London; the churches of St Clement Danes, St James, Piccadilly, and St Anne, Soho—all in west London; sundry work in the Middle Temple, London; additions to Christ's Hospital, London; and the library at Lincoln Cathedral. He seems also to have furnished designs for William and Mary College, Williamsburg, Virginia, U.S.A. He restored Westminster Abbey and Chichester Cathedral, and reported upon the restoration of Salisbury Cathedral. Among buildings attributed to him are the Monument, London; Abingdon Town Hall; 'Upper School' at Eton; 'School' at Winchester College; Wolvesey Palace, Winchester; Bromley College, Kent; Morden College, Blackheath; and the College of Matrons, Salisbury.

In 1923 (the bicentenary of his death) the Wren Society, founded in his honour, began the publication of twenty large annual volumes recording his architectural work. His life was written by his son under the title *Parentalia* (1750).

The most recent of many monographs on Wren are by G. Webb, 1937; R. Dutton, 1951; M. S. Briggs, 1953; J. Summerson, 1953; V. Fürst, 1956; E. F. Sekler, 1956.

Wright, Frank Lloyd (*b.* Richland, Wisconsin, U.S.A., 8 June 1869; *d.* Phoenix, Arizona, 9 April 1959), architect; R.I.B.A. Royal Gold Medallist, 1941; the most striking personality in American architecture during the first half of the twentieth century; was trained at the university of Wisconsin. After working in various architects' offices, including that of L. Sullivan (q.v.), he started practice in Chicago in 1893. His travels through Japan in 1906 had a marked effect upon his later designs. Apart from the numerous dwelling-houses which constituted the major part of his practice—among them the remarkable house 'Falling Water,' near Pittsburgh, 1936 —he built the Unity Temple, Oak Park (1905); the Larkin Building, Buffalo (1905); Coonley Kindergarten, Riverside (1908); Midway Gardens Plaisance, Chicago (1913); the Imperial Hotel, Tokio (1916); the Johnson Administration Building, Racine, Wisconsin (1937–9) and its tower (1950); the Guggenheim Museum, New York (1956–9). He described his own work as 'Organic Architecture.' His published writings have had a great influence upon young architects in England and America.

See his own autobiography, 1932; the memoir by his son, entitled *My Father which is on Earth*, 1946; the brief study by B. Zevi, 1947; H. R. Hitchcock, *In the Nature of Materials*, 1942; and G. Manson, *Frank Lloyd Wright to 1910*, 1959.

Wyatt, Benjamin Dean (*b.* London, 1775; *d. c.* 1850), architect; son of James Wyatt (q.v.). He was educated at Westminster School and Oxford, then entered the diplomatic service, but turned to architecture about 1809 and soon created a fashionable practice in London. He also succeeded his father as surveyor to Westminster Abbey. His principal buildings, all in London, were Drury Lane Theatre (1809–12); the Duke of York's Column (1831–4); the Oriental Club, Hanover Square (1826–7); Crockford's Club (1826–7, since demolished); York House, now Lancaster House (1825, previously begun by R. Smirke, q.v.); and the remodelling of Apsley House (1828–9).

Wyatt, James, R.A. (*b.* Burton Constable, Staffordshire, 3 Aug. 1746; *d.* Marlborough, 4 Sept. 1813), architect; President Royal

Academy, 1805-6. He went to Rome as a protégé of Lord Bagot, ambassador to the Vatican. Returning to London in 1764, he became one of the most prosperous architects in England. He is best known to the general public as the drastic restorer of Lichfield, Durham, Hereford, and Salisbury Cathedrals, Westminster Abbey, Windsor Castle, and Magdalen College at Oxford. This work led to his nickname of ' the Destroyer,' and aroused the fury of A. W. N. Pugin (q.v.). He also erected two colossal and amazing neo-Gothic mansions: Fonthill (1786-9, since destroyed) and Ashridge, Hertfordshire (1808-13). His classical buildings are, however, in excellent taste. They include No. 9 Conduit Street, London (1779), the former headquarters of the R.I.B.A.; Heveningham Hall (c. 1788); and Heaton Hall, Manchester (1772).

See monographs by A. Dale, 1936, and R. Turnor, 1950.

Wyatt, Sir Matthew Digby (*b*. Rowde, Wiltshire, 28 July 1820; *d*. Cowbridge, Wales, 21 May 1877), architect; R.I.B.A. Royal Gold Medallist, 1866. He was articled to his brother, T. H. Wyatt (q.v.); then travelled abroad, 1844-6. He became surveyor to the East India Company in 1855, and first Slade Professor of Fine Art at Cambridge in 1869. His chief interest was on the decorative side of architecture, and he was closely concerned with the 1851 Exhibition and the Crystal Palace. His chief buildings were Paddington Station (1854-5); extensions to Addenbrooke's Hospital, Cambridge (1864-5); the Engineering College, Cooper's Hill (1871); and Alford House, Kensington (1872).

See monograph by N. Pevsner, 1950.

Wyatt, Thomas Henry (*b*. Loughlin, Roscommon, Ireland, 9 May 1807; *d*. London, 6 Aug. 1880), architect; President R.I.B.A., 1870-3; R.I.B.A. Royal Gold Medallist, 1873; brother of Sir M. D. Wyatt (q.v.). He started on a mercantile career, but abandoned it, and was articled to P. C. Hardwick (q.v.). In 1832 he began to practise in London, but concurrently acted as district surveyor for Hackney. In partnership with D. Brandon, he built several lunatic asylums and assize courts at Brecon, Cambridge, and Usk. Independently he designed Knightsbridge Barracks, London (1878-1879); the Garrison Chapel, Woolwich (1863); the Fever Hospital, Stockwell; and carried out about 150 church commissions.

Wyatville, Sir Jeffry, R.A. (*b*. Burton-on-Trent, 3 Aug. 1766; *d*. London, 10 Feb. 1840), architect. He was the son of an architect and a nephew of James Wyatt (q.v.) and Samuel Wyatt, both architects. After working first with Samuel and then with James, he started independent practice in 1799, and soon became busy. He built, altered, or extended a number of country mansions, but is best known for his work at Windsor Castle (1824-40), where he remodelled the Upper Ward and heightened the Round Tower. King George IV, in recognition of this work, allowed him to change his name to ' Wyatville ' when knighting him in 1828. His alterations at Windsor made the castle more comfortable, but entailed the destruction of some of the fine rooms decorated in Charles II's time.

Wykeham, William of (*b.* Wickham, Hampshire, 1324; *d.* Winchester, 27 Sept. 1404). He was a great patron of the arts, but not, as was once believed, an architect; though early in his astounding career he held an administrative post in the Office of Works, involving no technical qualifications. The buildings attributed to him are now held to have been designed by William de Wynford (q.v.).

Wynford, William de (fl. 1360–1403), master-mason or architect, is now generally accepted as the designer of most of the buildings previously attributed to William of Wykeham (q.v.). They include alterations to Windsor Castle (1360 onwards); the nave of Winchester Cathedral and Winchester College (both begun 1394), and probably New College, Oxford (begun 1380). He also built the south-west tower of Wells Cathedral (1365–90).

X

Xystus, in classical architecture, an enclosure or colonnade or portico used for athletic exercises and recreation.

Y

Yevele, Henry (*d.* 1400), now regarded as the greatest English medieval architect, was given charge of the royal works at Windsor Castle in 1360. Other buildings credibly attributed to him are Westminster Hall; the nave, west cloister, Abbot's House, and several tombs at Westminster Abbey; the nave of Canterbury Cathedral; the West Gate and city walls of Canterbury; Cowling Castle; and several bridges.

See monograph by J. Harvey, 1944.

Yorke, Francis Reginald Stevens (*b.* Stratford-on-Avon, 3 Dec. 1906), architect; son of an architect; was educated at the Birmingham School of Architecture. He started practice in London in 1930, and since 1944 has worked with partners as 'Yorke, Rosenberg, & Mardell.' Their buildings have included flats and a large school at Stevenage (1947–52); a residential area of Harlow New Town (1953); the Sigmund Factory at Gateshead (1948); the College of Further Education at Merthyr Tydfil (1954); the Educational Centre at Bromsgrove (1955); the North West Hospital at Londonderry (1952); Gatwick Airport Buildings (1956); the Leeds Central Colleges (1953). He was one of the founders of 'the MARS Group' (q.v.), 1933.

Yorkshire Lights, a type of mullioned casement window in which one or more casements slide horizontally behind the fixed lights.

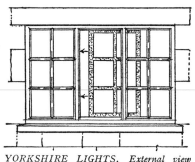

YORKSHIRE LIGHTS. External view showing central sliding sash partially opened

Yugoslav Architecture includes Diocletian's magnificent ruined palace (A.D. 300) at Split, formerly Spalato; numerous medieval churches in Serbia, showing a mixture of Byzantine, Romanesque, and Gothic features; many buildings in Venetian Gothic style along the Dalmatian coast, erected during the Venetian occupation—notably the Rector's Palace (1435 onwards) at Dubrovnik, formerly Ragusa; and several mosques built during the Turkish occupation in the sixteenth–eighteenth centuries, e.g. at Mostar, Sarajevo, and Trebinje.

Z

Zakharov, Adrian Dmitrievich (*b.* St Petersburg 1761; *d.* 1811), architect, was one of the leaders of the Classical Revival in Russia. Trained in the Academy of Fine Arts at St Petersburg, he won a scholarship enabling him to travel in Europe and to study in Paris (1782–6). Returning to Russia, he combined the practice and teaching of architecture. Besides his principal building, the new Admiralty (begun 1806), his work included bridges over the Neva, designs for warehouses and for extensions of the Academy of Sciences in St Petersburg; also the church of St Andrew at Kronstadt; and designs for a monastery at Gatchina.

Zemtsov, Michael (*b.* 1688; *d.* 1743), was the leading Russian architect of Peter the Great's reign. He did not turn to architecture until 1710, when he was apprenticed to Trezzini (q.v.), and after he had succeeded Michetti, another Italian, as chief royal architect, he combined teaching with his practice. His most important work was the completion of the Ekaterinenhof Palace at Reval, begun by Michetti in 1718.

Zenana, or **Zanana** (Persian), the women's quarters in an Indian dwelling-house.

Zevi, Bruno (*b.* Rome, 1918), architect and writer on architecture, graduated at Harvard University, U.S.A., in 1940, and has since spent much of his time teaching in the University Schools of Architecture in Venice and Rome, but has built several blocks of flats in the latter city. His published books, in Italian, include a *History of Modern Architecture*, 1950, and monographs on L. Sullivan, 1947; F. L. Wright, 1947; E. G. Asplund, 1949; and R. Neutra, 1950.

Ziggurat (Assyrian), in Assyrian architecture (q.v.), a temple-tower in the form of a stepped and truncated pyramid. (*Illustrated* p. 372.)

Zigzag, *see* CHEVRON.

Ziyāda (Arabic), the open space between the walls of a mosque (q.v.) and an outer enclosing wall.

Zoning, in modern town-planning, means either (i) the reservation of specific areas for prescribed purposes, e.g. civic, industrial, commercial, or residential; or (ii) restriction of 'density,' i.e. prescribing the maximum number of houses or inhabitants in any given area; or (iii) restriction of the heights of buildings according to the widths of the adjacent streets. This leads to the setting back of upper storeys, with a consequent effect upon architectural design.

Zophorus (Lat., from Gk *zōophoros*), in classical architecture, a frieze (q.v.) decorated with sculptured animal forms.

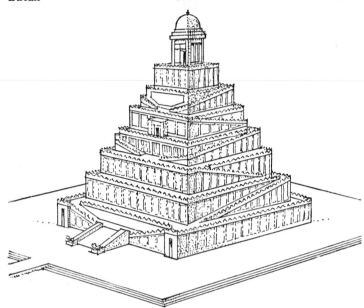

ZIGGURAT. *(Based upon a reconstruction by Charles Chipiez, 1884)*

Zucali or **Zuccalli, Enrico** or **Johann Heinrich** (*b.* Roveredo, Italy, *c.* 1642; *d.* Munich, 1724), architect; became a leader of the Baroque movement in Bavaria. His principal buildings, in or around Munich, were the huge Schleissheim Palace (1684–1704); the neighbouring small Lustheim Palace (1684–8); the façade and western towers of the Theatine Church; additions to the Residenzschloss (1680–5) and to Schloss Nymphenburg; and the Portia Palace (1704). Outside Bavaria, the Electoral Palace at Bonn (1697–1703), afterwards incorporated in the university buildings.